EUROPE IN CRISIS
1598–1648

GEOFFREY PARKER is Reader in Modern History at the University of St Andrews where he has taught since 1972. He graduated from Cambridge University in 1965 and was a Fellow of Christ's College, Cambridge, from 1968 until 1972. His other books include *The Army of Flanders and the Spanish Road, 1567–1659* (1972), *The Dutch Revolt* (1977), *Philip II: a biography* (1978) and *Spain and the Netherlands, 1559–1659* (Fontana: 1979).

FONTANA HISTORY OF EUROPE

General Editor: J. H. Plumb

G. A. Holmes
EUROPE: HIERARCHY AND REVOLT 1320–1450

G. R. Elton
REFORMATION EUROPE 1517–1559

J. H. Elliott
EUROPE DIVIDED 1559–1598

John Stoye
EUROPE UNFOLDING 1648–1688

David Ogg
EUROPE OF THE ANCIEN RÉGIME 1715–1783

George Rudé
REVOLUTIONARY EUROPE 1783–1815

Jacques Droz
EUROPE BETWEEN REVOLUTIONS 1815–1848

J. A. S. Grenville
EUROPE RESHAPED 1848–1878

Elizabeth Wiskemann
EUROPE OF THE DICTATORS 1919–1945

In Preparation

P. D. King
EARLY MEDIEVAL EUROPE 400–1000

R. C. Smail
CRUSADING EUROPE 1000–1250

Ragnhild M. Hatton
EUROPE 1680–1730

Olwen Hufton
EUROPE 1730–1783

Norman Stone
EUROPE 1878–1919

Geoffrey Parker

EUROPE IN CRISIS
1598-1648

FONTANA PAPERBACKS

First published by Fontana Paperbacks 1979

Set in Linotype Plantin

Made and printed in Great Britain by
William Collins Sons & Co. Ltd, Glasgow

A hardback edition of this book is published
by Harvester Press

For my students at
Cambridge and St Andrews
1965-79

CONTENTS

LIST OF FIGURES AND TABLES

Figures

Tables

ACKNOWLEDGEMENTS

No general survey like this can be completed without the writer running up extensive intellectual debts, and recording them is always a pleasure. My thanks go first to my editors, Professor J. H. Plumb and Mr R. L. Ollard, who commissioned me to write this volume and gave me constant support and advice. I am also most grateful to others who read through my typescript and made invaluable suggestions for improvement – Simon Adams, André Carus, James Coonan, Robert Evans, Bruce Lenman, Shelagh Ogilvie and Lesley Smith – and to the many colleagues and friends at home and abroad who gave me the benefit of their detailed knowledge and helped me to see the seventeenth century through European eyes. But perhaps my greatest debt is to the students that I have taught since 1965, both at Cambridge and (since 1972) at St Andrews. Most of the ideas in this book were developed in lectures and tutorials and corrected in the light of the comments and criticisms they provoked, above all from the members of my European Junior Honours Class of 1974–5. I would therefore like to dedicate this volume to all my students in general; and to Colin, Lee, Malcolm, Margaret, Maureen, Paul, both Stephens and both Susans in particular.

St Salvator's College, 10 March 1979
University of St Andrews

NOTE ON CONVENTIONS

CURRENCY

As far as possible, all foreign currencies have been given with a rough conversion into pounds sterling at the exchange rates prevailing at the time, as follows:

4.8	thalers (or rixdollars)	to the £ sterling
4.5	escudos	to the £ sterling
12	livres tournois	to the £ sterling
10	Dutch florins	to the £ sterling
6	Rhine florins	to the £ sterling

DATES

All dates are New Style, even for those countries like England and Muscovy which did not adopt the Gregorian Calendar until later.

NAMES

Where there is a recognized English version of a foreign place-name, I have used it (thus Vienna, Rome, Brussels); otherwise I have preferred the style used today on the place itself (thus Lvov and not Lwów or Lemberg). Likewise, with personal names, where there is an established English usage I have adopted it (John George of Saxony, Gustavus Adolphus and so on); in all other cases the style and title employed by the person concerned have been used, except that accents have been omitted from Slavonic and Scandinavian names (as in other volumes in the Fontana History of Europe).

CONTENT

I have been fortunate in that the preceding and the subsequent volumes in this series are both in print: J. H. Elliott, *Europe Divided 1559–1598* (London, 1968) and J. Stoye, *Europe Unfolding 1648–1688* (London, 1969). I have therefore left out matters dealt with by them (the edict of Nantes in 1598 and the Ukraine revolt in 1648, for example) and indicated in footnotes where the reader may find out about them. Last, in accordance with the convention followed throughout this series, the history of the British Isles has been excluded, except when it impinged upon continental developments.

PRELUDE: PRAGUE SPRING

On the morning of Wednesday, 23 May 1618, the vigil of Ascension Day, four Catholic members of the council of regency for the kingdom of Bohemia went to hear mass as usual in St Vitus Cathedral in Prague. Afterwards, at about 8.30, they came back to the royal palace and climbed the stairs to their chancery, high in a tower overlooking the city. Half an hour later they were surprised by the arrival of a large deputation of Protestants from the estates (or Parliament) of the kingdom, who had been meeting close by. The deputies crowded in, followed by their servants, all of them armed, until almost two hundred men were crammed into the council chamber. They were hot and breathless from the climb, tense and apprehensive in the knowledge of what they had agreed to do. They waited. The leaders asked the councillors if they had been responsible for ordering the estates to be dissolved; they accused the councillors of being enemies to both the religion and the liberty of the kingdom; they threatened to condemn them all to death. Few in the crowd could see what was happening, but the voices rose higher and the room grew hotter. Suddenly, windows were flung open and two of the councillors, screaming with fear, were hurled out into the morning air, sixty feet above the ground. Their secretary, loyal but unwise, protested at this barbarity: he too was thrown out of the window. Miraculously, all three men fell on to the piles of refuse which had been allowed to accumulate in the castle moat: it saved their lives. Scrambling unsteadily to their feet, and aided by their servants, they dodged the bullets fired at them from the council chamber and made their escape.

It is easy to see why the Defenestration of Prague should

have become the best-known single event of seventeenth-century European history: it combined drama with farce, and passion with pity. At the time, it was noted and discussed with close attention in every capital city of Europe, from Stockholm and Moscow to London and Madrid. Everyone identified with one side or the other; everyone could take sides, because the matters at issue were ones of general concern: religion and liberty. 'Religion and liberty stand and fall together' was the view of most contemporaries, and it was generally felt that the fate of religion and liberty in one country would inevitably affect the situation in all the others. If the Bohemians could successfully defy their governors, the political and religious freedom of the subject would be enhanced in every country; if their defiant stance failed, the power of all princes would be exalted. 'Believe me,' wrote a Dutch diplomat to his German colleague in the summer of 1619, 'the Bohemian war will decide the fate of us all.' That is why the pursuit of the chain of antecedents and repercussions connected with the drama of the Defenestration links together almost every corner of Europe.

But can one properly speak of 'Europe' in the seventeenth century? As late as 1876, Bismarck scribbled on the back of a telegram: 'Anyone who speaks of Europe is wrong – it is nothing but a geographical expression.' And yet, in the first half of the seventeenth century at least, the interaction of developments in the different parts of the continent often seemed to produce phenomena which might justly be termed 'European'. Nor was this accidental. Statesmen from Muscovy to Morocco and from Sweden to Sicily deliberately strove to align their cause with that of others elsewhere until, in the words of King Gustavus Adolphus of Sweden: 'All the wars that are afoot in Europe have become one war.' Sometimes alliances were formed in the name of a religion, sometimes in the name of a dynasty, sometimes in the name of a principle; but almost every political development in almost every country in Europe excited interest if not action elsewhere, linking east with west and north with south to an unprecedented extent, reinforcing those economic links which were already drawing the various parts of the continent into an ever-closer contact. The grain of the Baltic, which had fed about one-quarter of the people of the Netherlands since the 1560s, after 1591 also played an important role in sustaining the inhabitants of Spain, Portugal and Italy. The same southern lands began at the same time to buy large quantities of worsted textiles, known as 'new draperies', from England and the Netherlands, because they were both lighter and cheaper than the traditional broadcloths. In return, the Iberian and Italian peninsulas purveyed the spices of Asia, the silver of America and the gold of Africa to the rest of the continent.

And yet, in a sense, Bismarck was right: such was the fragmentation of Europe in the seventeenth century that the experience of any given community often diverged radically from that of its neighbours, making generalization hazardous if not impossible. Even a well-attested and widespread phenomenon such as the economic decline of Spain affected different areas at different times. In coastal Galicia and Valencia the decline lasted from about 1615 to the 1640s; in the Montes de Toledo, although the decline also began in 1615 it lasted until the 1670s; and in Murcia and Segovia provinces, where the decline also ended in the 1670s, it began in 1604 and 1640 respectively. And even within each of these provinces, there was of course further diversity, for a number of reasons. In the first place, patterns of landowning modified the impact of economic hardship in many subtle ways: the presence of a local lord who wished to create rural wealth, and therefore encouraged rural industry and financed agricultural improvement, would save one village while its neighbour declined or rebelled under a lord who preferred to invest his wealth and attention in, say, office rather than in enterprise. Again, if local customs permitted gleaning, common grazing, tree-felling and game-hunting, a village had better chances of surviving a year of dearth. Finally the existence of a local charitable bequest, or proximity to a road or port, could save a community from starvation, even in a region of general misery. And these were only the social and economic influences. Political circumstances also affected a community's fate. If the peasants of the Paris basin, farming some of the richest agricultural land in Europe, grew poorer in the earlier seventeenth century and repeatedly rebelled, while the farmers of the poor sandy soils of Holland prospered and conformed, the explanation lies largely in the different economic, confessional and fiscal policies pursued by the French and Dutch governments.

But which of these two societies was the more typical: the French example of a society in crisis, or the Dutch model of a society in equilibrium? There is, at present, no consensus among historians upon this point. Many eminent scholars have argued that there was no General Crisis – that the term 'crisis' has been used to describe phenomena and events that in other centuries would just be called 'history'. But the turmoil of the half-century between 1618 and 1670, which affected China and India as well as Europe, was both widespread and unusual.[1] It cannot be written off as normal. The acute Voltaire, writing only a century after the events he described, was not wrong when he saw the entire seventeenth century as 'a period of usurpation from one end of the world to the other'. Nor may his explanation, published in the *Essai sur les moeurs et l'esprit des nations* (Paris, 1756), be easily dismissed. The culprits, he believed, were 'The three things that exercise a constant influence over the minds of men: climate, government and religion.' It would be prudent to examine the weight of these 'constant influences' before returning to the more specific causes of our Prague spring in 1618.

CHAPTER I

EUROPEAN SOCIETY AND THE ECONOMY

1. *The Little Ice Age*

'The whole world is shaking', an irate tax-payer warned the Muscovite government in 1648, 'and the people are troubled.' Before long several Russian cities were in full revolt against the Tsar. At the same time, in France, at the height of the Fronde revolt, the historian Robert Mentet de Salmonet declared that he and his fellow Europeans were living in an 'Iron Age' which would become 'famous for the great and strange revolutions that have happen'd in it . . . Revolts have been frequent both in the East and the West.' Five years previously, the appropriately named Jeremiah Whittaker had informed the English House of Commons that 'These are days of shaking . . . and this shaking is universal: the Palatinate, Bohemia, Germania, Catalonia, Portugal, Ireland, England.'[1] Before the decade was out, he might have added Scotland, Holland, Sweden, Italy, the Ukraine, Muscovy and the Ottoman Empire within Europe; to say nothing of the upheavals in Brazil, Morocco, India and (above all) China, in the world outside (see Figure 1). And these were only the major political crises of the mid-seventeenth century: there were also innumerable peasant revolts and urban disorders. In France, which was particularly prone to popular unrest, Provence (an area with some 600,000 inhabitants) witnessed almost 400 revolts in the course of the seventeenth century, 66 of them between 1648 and 1653. In Aquitaine (a province of 1,400,000 people) there were perhaps 500 revolts, more than half of them occurring between 1635 and 1660. This intensity of unrest was by no means confined to France: a similar pattern

Figure 1. The General Crisis of the Seventeenth Century

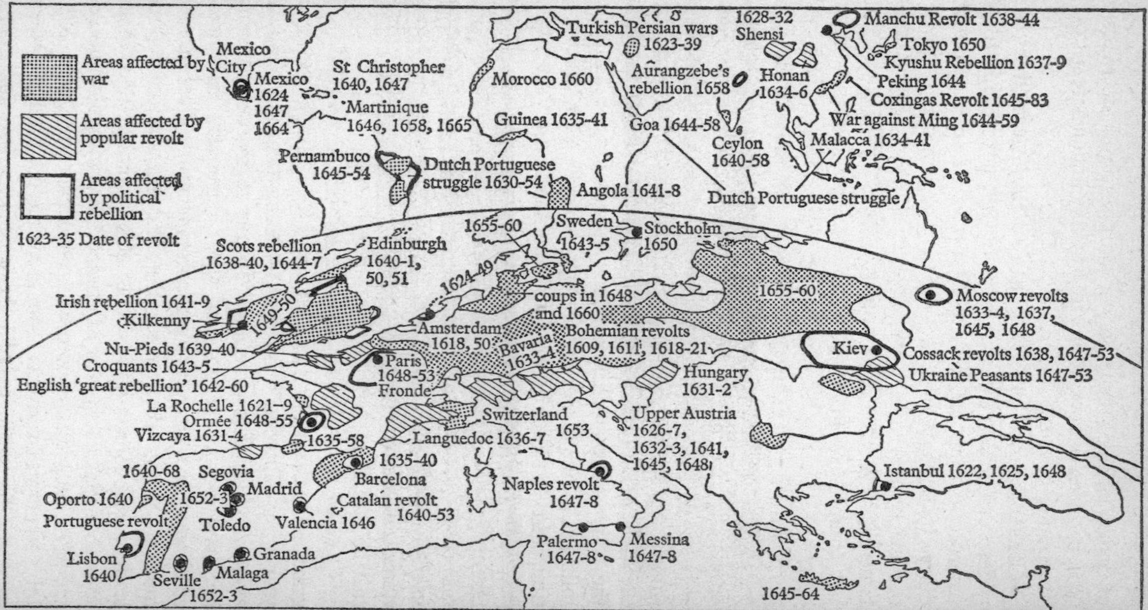

of revolt, reaching something of a crescendo in the 1640s and '50s, has been discovered in almost every area where historians have cared to look.

Contemporaries were, not unnaturally, alarmed by such widespread unrest. The peaceable English vicar Ralph Josselin recorded his perplexity from time to time in a voluminous diary. In January 1653 he noted: 'The world is togither by the eares, overturning one another.' Seven years later he lamented: 'When I looke backe into the world I find nothing but confusions.' As a convinced Puritan, Josselin naturally sought the explanation for this turbulence in God's inscrutable purpose; other men looked elsewhere, mostly to the innate wickedness of men (especially of men from the lower social orders); and some looked beyond mankind. The Italian popular historian Majolino Bisaccioni, who chronicled the simultaneous rebellions in England, Catalonia, Portugal, Italy, the Ukraine, France and the Ottoman Empire, suggested that the wave of revolutions in the 1640s might be due to the influence of the stars – an influence which most people of the time were convinced had an effect on their everyday life. At much the same time the Jesuit Giovanni Battista Riccioli postulated that the variable behaviour of our own star, the sun, might be affecting human conditions through fluctuations in the number of sunspots. The suggestion was ignored at the time, and for many years afterwards; but it can now be shown that he was right.

The constancy of the sun's behaviour has been taken for granted for centuries; and even after the existence of eleven-year sunspot cycles was established in 1843, the sun was assumed to be, if not constant, at least regular. But that was not how it appeared to observers during the seventeenth century, at least after 1610 when the invention of the telescope made proper observation possible. The notebooks of Europe's leading astronomers all reveal an almost total absence of sunspots between about 1645 and about 1715, while noting at the same time that their predecessors had seen them. When John Flamsteed saw a sunspot from his newly built observatory at Greenwich in 1684, he wrote: 'These appearances, however frequent in the days of Scheiner and Galileo, have been so rare of late that this is the only one I have seen in his [the sun's] face since December 1676'; and when G. D. Cassini, founder and first director of the Paris observatory, saw a sunspot in 1671, the *Philosophical Transactions of the Royal Society* at once reported it, adding a description of what sunspots were, for the last one had faded away eleven years before and readers might have forgotten what they looked like.[2] Between 1645 and 1715, fewer sunspots were observed than appear in a single year nowadays.

It was the same with the *aurora borealis* (the Northern Lights caused by particles from the sun entering the earth's atmosphere): after about 1640, even in Scandinavia and Scotland, they were so rare that the few aurorae observed were taken as portents. When Edmund Halley, Flamsteed's successor as Astronomer Royal, saw an aurora in March 1716 he was overjoyed and wrote a paper about it: in sixty years of observation it was the first he had ever seen. And Halley, like all other astronomers between about 1645 and 1715, failed to see the brilliant corona which is visible around the sun during a total eclipse: descriptions of that time mention only a pale ring of dull light, reddish and narrow, around the moon. It was as if the sun's energy was diminished. This deduction is corroborated by an aberration well known to archæologists – the variation in the amount of radioactive carbon (carbon-14) present in the earth's atmosphere in the past. Between 1645 and 1715 there was a significant growth in the carbon-14 deposited in the annual growth-rings laid down by trees of known age, a phenomenon that is normally associated with a reduction in solar energy: a fall in solar energy increases the carbon-14 in the atmosphere, and therefore absorbed by all living organisms, and vice versa.

Because observations of the sun before about 1630 were unsystematic, it is not clear from the solar record whether the sharp reduction in sunspot numbers, aurorae and the rest after 1645 was sudden, or whether it was preceded by a period of solar instability which might also have affected the earth from time to time. Other terrestrial records of climate suggest the latter. Tree-ring analysis sheds light not only on the carbon level but on the climate that prevailed in the year of its formation: a fat ring testifies to a year favourable to the growth of plants (crops and trees alike); a thin ring suggests an unfavourable year. The study of the tree-rings of early modern Europe reveals several bouts of prolonged bad weather and poor growing seasons: the 1590s, the 1620s, the 1640s and 1650s, and the 1690s. This dendrochronological evidence is exactly complemented by variations recorded in the times at which the grapes in French vineyards were judged to be ripe for harvesting: in precisely the same years that the tree-rings were narrow, the grapes ripened late. Finally, the same story is told by human observations of the changing climate. A succession of heavy frosts in south China between 1646 and 1676 ended orange-growing in Kwangsi province; prolonged drought compelled the Mogul emperors to abandon their magnificent new city at Fatipur Sikri, south of Delhi; travellers reported a lower snow-line on the mountains of east Africa and an extension in the deserts of the north-west. In Europe, travellers in seventeenth-century Scotland noted that the main peaks of the Grampians and Cairngorms retained their snow cover all year round; mariners taking sea-temperatures on their summer voyages between Shetland and the Faroes recorded polar water far to the south of its present location; and estate papers of Alpine landlords lamented the disappearance of fields, farmsteads and even villages as the glaciers steadily advanced, extending farther than at any time since the last major glaciation, 15,000 years before. All the evidence, whether gathered by historians, meteorologists or solar physicists, points to a climate of greater extremes of weather, and in particular to cooler and wetter summers in the temperate zone, during the seventeenth century, with a particularly severe period between 1640 and 1660.

It is true that the changes recorded are small – a decrease of no more than one per cent in the total solar radiation; a fall of no more than one degree centigrade in mean summer temperatures – but even changes of this magnitude, if sustained, were of great significance in a world in which between 80 and 95 per cent of the total population was directly dependent on vegetable and cereal crops both for employment and for food and drink. A fall of one degree centigrade in overall summer temperature restricts the growing season for plants by three or four weeks and reduces the maximum altitude at which crops will ripen by about 500 feet. Even today, each day's delay in the ripening of the harvest diminishes the present yield of cereal crops by 63 kilos per hectare, and a drop of 1°C. in average summer temperature reduces the farm growing season in northern Europe by about 30 days. In the seventeenth century, with more primitive agricultural methods and with more marginal land under cultivation, the impact of a fall of 1°C. in average summer temperature would have been proportionally greater still. Indeed, the papers of estate managers and the records of tithe collectors from many areas show a reduction in crop yields during the seventeenth century as a whole, with catastrophic falls during particularly unfavourable periods. Thus in Hungary, tithe yields fell by 72 per cent between 1570 and 1670; in Poland, declining yields began to be registered from 1570, but fell more slowly than in Hungary except during the 1650s when production was halved. In Spain, cereal production slumped in almost all areas between about 161[illegible] and 1670. The people of early modern Europe were powerless to resist the consequences of a cooler climate.

There were more people dependent on the world's food at the beginning of the seventeenth century than ever before. Between 1450 and 1600 the population of the world may have doubled, with Europe feeding about one-quarter of the total. Not all areas of the continent shared in this growth to the same extent – Castile, for example, had 3·5 million inhabitants in 1530 and 5·9 million in 1590, while neighbouring Portugal remained stable at about 1·25 million throughout – but most of the available evidence points to rapid demographic growth in the century before 1570, followed by half a century of either slower growth or stagnation, and then decline or stagnation from 1620 until about 1670 (se

Table 1). The experience of other continents appears to have been the same: few populations increased during the seventeenth century.

The mechanism by which a harsher climate was translated into population decline was relatively simple. If the harvests of cereal crops failed, bread prices soared to a level that was beyond the reach of most poor families (see Figure 2). Since the cultivation of alternative staples, such as rice, maize or potatoes, was in its infancy, there was no other cheap form

Table 1. European Population Data (in millions)

Year	1550	1575	1600	1625	1650	1675	1700
Bohemia			4	3	2·25		
England & Wales	3		4	4·5		5·8	5·8
France		20					19·3
Germany	12		15	14	11		15
Italy	11	13	13	13	12	11·5	12·5
Low Countries	3	3		3·5			4
Poland			8				8
Russia	9		11	8	9·5	13	16
Spain	6·3		7·6		5·2		7
All Europe	85	95	100	100	80	90	100

of nourishment available and people either had to buy bread – whatever the price – or starve. Many starved and died; many mothers, deprived of food, gave birth to still-born babies; other women failed to conceive. And those who survived the famine often succumbed shortly afterwards to disease: epidemics of typhoid, dysentery and plague could wipe out in a few weeks the cumulative population increases of several decades.

Bubonic plague was endemic in Europe from the Black Death of 1347 to the Great Plague of 1665–6. In France alone it has been calculated that at least two million people died of the disease between 1600 and 1670, no less than

Figure 2. Harvest and Price Fluctuations in the Baltic Area, 1598–1620

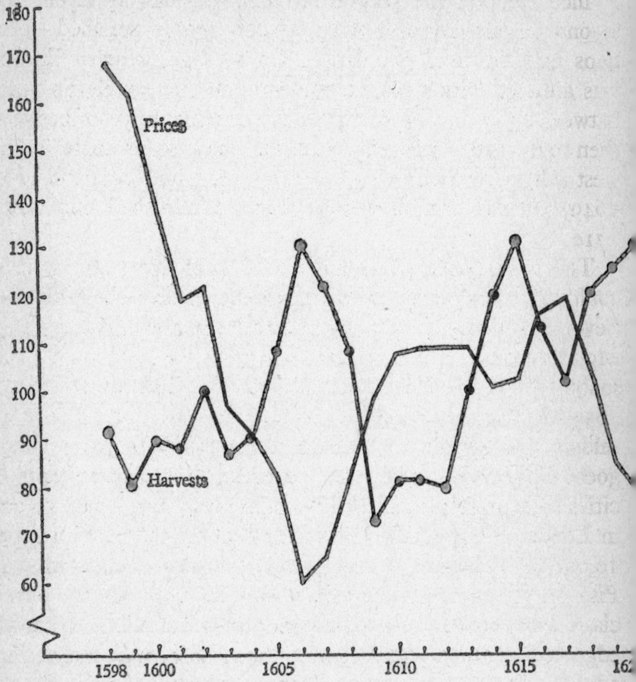

Price of rye at Danzig in grams of silver per last; harvest yields in East Prussia in hundredweights per hectare.

Source: W. Abel, *Massenarmut und Hungerkrisen* (Hamburg, 1974), 131.

750,000 of them (almost five per cent of the kingdom's population) during the acute epidemic of 1628–32. The incidence of this loss was not, of course, uniform: variations were caused by social and geographical circumstances. It has been noted that plague tended to spare populations living in isolated settlements, for instance pastoral farmers, and to concentrate on crowded urban and rural communities. There were also regional differences, not always related to settlement patterns. Thus most of the great cities of northern France escaped the plague of 1628–32, but at Lyon, the second largest city of France, 35,000 people perished – perhaps half the total population. On average, western Europe was afflicted with a plague epidemic once every eleven years between 1347 and 1536, and once every fifteen years between then and 1670. Only after that did the disease abate in the west (although Sicily was free after 1625 and Scotland after 1649). In the east, however, plague diminished only after 1710.

There was little that the medical profession of the time could do to stop the spread of plague or any other disease. Seventeenth-century doctors have always had a bad press – Molière based no less than four of his plays upon their inability to cure their patients, from *The Flying Doctor* of 1659 to *The Imaginary Patient* of 1673 – but there were seldom enough of them to do either much harm or much good. Only 2 doctors existed for every 10,000 inhabitants in cities such as Rouen, Lyon and Paris; less than 1 per 10,000 in London. Only in Italy was the situation better, with 4 per 10,000 in Florence, 5·5 in Pistoia, 7 in Bologna and 9 in Pisa on the eve of the terrible plague of 1630. These physicians were, for the most part, university-trained and knowledgeable (at least in Italy, where they exchanged information, advice, recommendations and even samples of new drugs), but their services were expensive, and so tended to be confined to the wealthier citizens of the towns. Their efforts were therefore supplemented by those of others.

Every community had its *guérisseurs* or 'cunning-folk' who were adept at curing ailments with traditional remedies, often herbal. In Muscovy, some 290 species of plant were used for medicine in the sixteenth century (of which 130 are still used by doctors today). Herbal preparations were sometimes supplemented by the concoctions of a remarkable breed, now largely disappeared, of quacksalvers or mountebanks who advertised their remedies for ailments at fairs and in market places. They were common in the Netherlands and Italy, and Ben Jonson's play *Volpone* shows that they were not unfamiliar to Londoners, too. In Italy, they 'frequently and by swarmes goe from citty to citty and haunt their markett places', addressing the crowds from a stage or scaffold:

> They proclaim their wares upon these scaffolds, and to drawe concourse of people they have a *zani* or foole with a visard on his face, and sometimes a woman, to make comicall sporte. The people cast their handkerchers with mony to them, and they cast them backe with wares tyed in them . . . The wares they sell are commonly distilled waters and divers oyntments for burning aches and stitches and the like, but espetially for the itch and scabbs, more vendible than the rest . . . Many of them have some very good secrets, but generally they are all cheaters.[8]

This commercialization of medicine was, of course, a part of the growth of the European economy, just as the increasingly strict quarantine regulations and organization of permanent health boards were an aspect of the growing power and competence of the state. But neither of these developments was far enough advanced in the seventeenth century to deal with the silent spread of lethal microbes.

Often plague was spread by armies whose movements no one could stop. It is typical that the plague of 1630 entered northern Italy in the wake of an invasion by German troops into Lombardy and by French troops into Piedmont; both armies included plague victims, since both the countries from which they came were in the grip of a major epidemic, and the first plague victim in Milan was a soldier from the German army. Likewise the first victim of the 1645–9 plague in Scotland was a soldier of the Covenanting army, newly returned from England. Figure 3 shows that there was a considerable coincidence between periods of fighting and periods of plague; although the peaks of disease normally followed periods of dearth, military operations could intensify the consequences of food shortage out of all proportion to the degree of debility caused by hunger.

War did not only increase the likelihood of plague. It also

Figure 3. War and Plague in Europe, 1500–1700

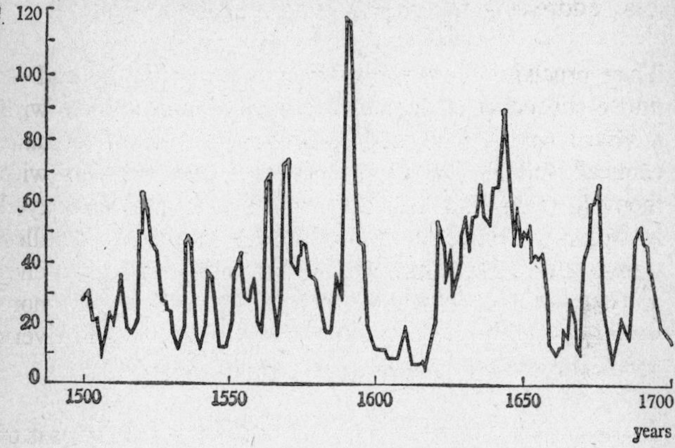

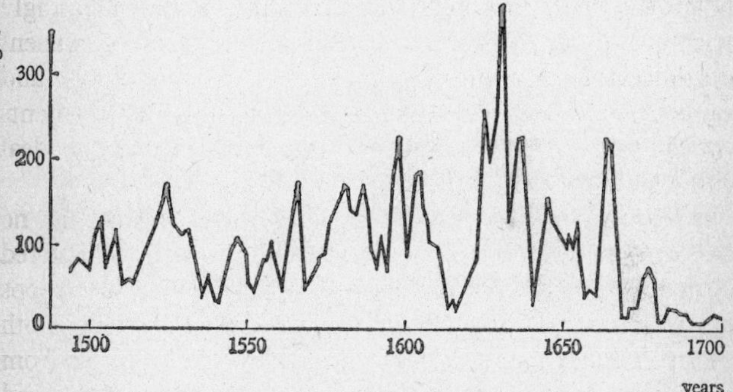

Triennial moving totals of military actions compared with triennial moving totals of places in Europe affected by plague.

Source: J. N. Biraben, *Les hommes et la peste*, I (Paris, 1975), 132.

disrupted trade and reduced the demand for manufactured goods, causing unemployment among artisans and craftsmen. Soldiers could also create acute local food shortages by eating what they needed and burning all the rest. And, eventually, war might even solve these self-imposed problems by eliminating the population as well as destroying its means of subsistence. Sir William Petty, who had carried out a land survey of Ireland, estimated that the population of that country in 1652 stood at 1·1 million people, and that a further 87,000 of the Irish 'perished and were wasted . . . by the sword', 80,000 more had died by 'famine and other hardships', and 297,000 by the plague. Another 40,000 had either been transported or had fled. The impact of war on Poland was almost as catastrophic: in the central province of Mazovia, the Swedish campaigns of 1655–60 destroyed 35 per cent of the towns, 10 per cent of the villages and 40 per cent of the population. When peace was signed, in 1660, 85 per cent of all peasant land was abandoned and commerce was at a standstill. Castile, finally, lost perhaps 288,000 men in her wars between 1618 and 1659.

'From plague, war and famine, good Lord deliver us': the existence of the ordinary inhabitants of seventeenth-century Europe seems to have been in constant danger of disaster. Men lived in constant fear of death or destitution, and if the Christian churches tried to offer consolation and hope in case of the former, they could do little for the latter. The obsessive fear of hunger which runs through the popular literature of the day, especially in picaresque novels such as *Don Quixote*, *Guzmán de Alfarache* or *Simplicissimus*, was merely a reflection of the spectre which haunted all of early modern Europe: poverty.

2. *Rich and Poor*

In the seventeenth century, according to Sancho Panza's grandmother, there were only two families in the world: 'the Haves and the Have-nots.' That was not, however, how all contemporaries saw it: rather, there were degrees of poverty which ranged from occasional need to permanent destitution. There were the 'honest poor': those who lacked property and income of their own and were therefore totally dependent on working for others to earn a living; those who were either too old or not old enough to work; and those who were unable to work by reason of infirmity. Each of these categories deserved some sort of assistance. By their side lurked the army of 'undeserving poor': the beggars and vagabonds who, according to contemporaries, although able-bodied, refused to work. Another type of treatment was reserved for them.

The reason for differentiating the poor, a habit which first became general in the sixteenth century, was simple: there were more of them than ever before. London in 1594 had twelve times as many beggars as in 1517, although the city's total population had barely increased fourfold; in Cremona, Italy, the proportion of registered poor was three times greater in 1600 than in 1550; in Antwerp in the 1590s, and in Lyon, three-quarters of the total population was too poor to pay tax. In the villages of Europe, the poor were still numerous, but less obtrusive: in the communities of the mountains south of Toledo, eighteen per cent of the households were officially registered as poor throughout the seventeenth century, many of them possessing not a stick of furniture; and farther north, one contemporary suggested that 'the fourth part of the inhabitants of the parishes of England are miserable people and (harvest time excepted) without any subsistence'. Such men and their families were wholly dependent on finding work from others in order to eat; often they had to sleep in a barn or an attic in winter, and under a hedgerow in summer. A year of poor harvests, with dear food and little work, led to the death of many of these people, and utter misery for the rest. The groans of the starving poor kept respectable citizens awake at night; people might be observed dying in the fields and in the streets; some even tried to eat their own limbs. The hospitals became so crowded that, for lack of beds, the patients were laid out on (and even in) coffins until, starving and sick, they died and could be carried to the cemetery with a minimum of effort.

The picture of death is seen in the faces of many. Some

> devour the sea ware [sea food]; some eat dogs; some steal fowls. Of nine in a family, seven at once died, the husband and the wife expiring at one time. Many are reduced to that extremity that they are forced to steal and thereafter are executed; and some have desperately run into the sea and drowned themselves.

Suicides certainly rose at times of economic hardship, particularly among young people. A recent calculation of the probable suicide rate in Tudor and Stuart England is surprisingly high – 15 per 100,000 compared with 13 per 100,000 for 1931–41 – and even this is doubtless an underestimate because, as one contemporary noted: 'There are many more self-murderers than the world takes notice of . . . yea, the world is full of them.'[4]

Because harvest failure and high prices led people to spend more of their incomes on food, the demand for manufactured goods was reduced, leading to unemployment among the artisans who made them; there was also more rural unemployment, for a thin harvest required less hands to gather in. Above all, fewer young people were taken into service in difficult years – an important development when in most west European countries perhaps half the adolescent population depended on entering service in order to accumulate enough capital to get married and set up a home of their own. Almost every study of seventeenth-century parish registers reveals a rise in the average age of brides at marriage, an increase due to the greater difficulty experienced in setting up house, and this phenomenon had a crucial influence on population size because it lowered the birth-rate: since child-bearing becomes increasingly difficult (and, without hospital care, hazardous) after a woman passes the age of thirty-six, if she does not marry until she is thirty the number of children she can bear is far smaller than if she married at the age of eighteen or twenty. Many more families now had no children at all.

In some ways, the childless families were the lucky ones. If economic conditions became too hostile, the spouses could always separate and go back into service; or they could take to the road. But children made such solutions far more difficult. Mothers who could not afford to feed their babies had only two avenues of escape: infanticide and the Foundlings' Hospital. The first was frequent: between 1565 and 1640, some 2000 women (of whom one half were unmarried and one-quarter were widows) were convicted of infanticide by the *Parlement* of Paris. Leaving an infant at the Foundlings' Hospital was almost as effective a form of prophylaxy as infanticide: only ten per cent of the inmates at the Paris institution survived their childhood (although some, to be fair, were already ill or diseased when they were left, and many of the healthier ones were reclaimed by their parents when the crisis was over).

It is clear, however, that public authorities in the seventeenth century were far less concerned with the poor who died than with the poor who survived – no doubt because when men die they cease to burden bureaucrats. In particular, governments were worried about the urban poor. There were two reasons for this. First there was the simple force of numbers: if only 20–25 per cent of a village of 600 people were destitute, there were at most 150 persons to cope with; but if 25 per cent of a town like Lyon or Antwerp were starving, there might be 20,000 people on the streets. And within this desperate mass of humanity there might exist a formidable measure of organization, for example among those who belonged to a single trade, craft guild or religious fraternity. In Normandy in 1637 it was the Caen weavers who, fearing that a new tax of sixpence per serge cloth would cause a fall in sales and lead to unemployment, organized a protest demonstration which so impressed the magistrates with its orderly menace that the tax was abolished. In 1639 it was the Avranches salt-workers who, hearing a rumour that the salt they produced was to be taxed (it had previously been free of *gabelle*, unlike the rest of France), elected leaders, composed manifestos and created a para-military organization with which to oppose the central government in the *Nu-pieds* revolt (which took its name from the men who walked barefoot as they carried salt from the pans along the beach to

Avranches). In the same year, in Rouen, it was the tanners and dyers who, their livelihood threatened by new taxes, led their city into the revolt. Their organization was improved by the presence in the ranks of the poor of a number of ex-soldiers, men who found it hard to keep a civilian job after a time in the army, and they drilled and trained the townsmen. In the end the rebel army, numbering only 5000 or so, kept the regular forces of the crown at bay for several hours in a pitched battle outside Rouen in 1640.

The use of military discipline was a new and (to the authorities) frightening development (just as it was in the riots and revolutions which followed 1815, when demobilized soldiers again took a hand in civil demonstrations). The historian Agrippa d'Aubigné, writing of the popular revolts of the 1590s, noted that 'These people were not armed with pitchforks, as in the past; instead almost all of them were musketeers, arquebusiers and pikemen.' They included deserters, militiamen and veterans, and the rebels even tried to persuade regular soldiers to leave the colours and join them; their weapons were either family possessions, prizes picked up after one of the many battles in the religious wars, or else purchased on the open market.

Finally, in the largest towns of Europe – Naples, Seville, Paris and London at least – within the ranks of the poor there existed a professional underworld, possessing its own hierarchy, its own rules, even its own language: argot in French, cant in England, Rotwelsch in German, germanía in Castilian. Much of our information on this criminal underworld comes from literary works – such as Cervantes's *Rinconete y Cortadillo* (about two boys who become part of the Seville Brotherhood of rogues) or Thomas Harman's *A Caveat or Warening for Commen Cursetors Vulgarely Called Vagabones* (an illustrated glossary of terms used by or about rogues) – where the writer's avowed purpose of awakening public awareness of the social menace posed by beggars and vagabonds may have led to exaggeration. However, the records of the city courts, which contain numerous convictions of people with sinister nicknames and appalling criminal records, do not lie. Seville, at least, had a highly sophisticated criminal class, and the journal of the city's prison chaplain, the Jesuit Pedro de León, covering the years 1578–1616, recorded the execution of 309 prisoners, many of them members of well-organized gangs who were clearly a threat to public order. As the author wrote in the preface to his journal: 'All the colleagues who have seen this journal, and they were many . . . agreed that it was full of something which one longs to find in other writings: truth.' It was perhaps for this reason that the volume was never published and was kept on restricted access in the Jesuit college library (where it was only to be read under special licence and even then only for two hours at a time).[5]

However, the authorities could not restrict *public* observation of poverty and crime in this way. Although most towns tried to herd their paupers into ghettos where old houses were sub-divided into minute apartments, and gardens were covered with shacks and sheds, the poor were still too numerous to be ignored, and even the least observant burgers could not avoid the hosts of beggars who clamoured in the street. The traditional reaction of the rich in these circumstances was charity. Between 1601 and 1640, London merchants left no less than 52 per cent of the charitable donations in their wills to the poor. In Venice, major legacies were left to the *Scuole Grandi*, great charitable corporations of pious citizens, whose alms were distributed by the leading patricians of the city. Some of the money went to foundations (such as a hospital for *incurabili* – syphilitics); some was tossed into the crowd at random on festival days; but most went in alms to poor members of the Scuole whose means and characters were known. However, Venetians believed that charity began at home, and that legacies should only be given to the poor after the testator's own family had been left a patrimony which would equip them to withstand any possible future disaster. It was not uncommon for a Scuola to be bombarded with petitions from the relatives of a testator who had left too much money to charity for their liking. They would have sympathized with Francis Bacon's essay *On Riches*: 'Defer not charities till death, for certainly, if a man judge it rightly, he that doth so is rather liberal of another man's, than of his own.'

Fortunately for the poor, not all were so stingy. Many people named a poor man or woman to be godparent to their children; some desired their bodies to be buried in the paupers' grave; others, like Blaise Pascal, lodged the poor in their own houses; others still educated five or six poor children along with their own. St Vincent de Paul led a devoted group of followers, male and female, between 1625 and his death in 1660 on a crusade to bring outdoor relief to the beggars and paupers of France, saving lives as well as souls in the frequent famines which afflicted early Bourbon France. 'Their monastery shall be the houses of the sick; their cell shall be a lodging-house room; their chapel shall be the parish church; their cloister shall be the city streets' was St Vincent's touching, ironic expression when he founded the Daughters of Charity in 1633. Yet private philanthropy, even when organized as thoroughly as the Daughters of Charity (with 100 houses by 1660) or their male counterpart, the Lazarists (with 33 houses by 1660), only scratched the surface of the seventeenth-century poverty problem. The recipients of private largesse were, almost exclusively, the 'respectable poor': those who had fallen on hard times but were still physically clean and possessed moral values acceptable to the rest of society. They were a privileged elite among the poor: sometimes they received charity without even having to ask.

The deserving poor, however, were not the problem. They did not threaten the established social order, or its resources, and their numbers were seldom excessive. The real challenge came from the destitute, the vagrants and the beggars. For them, St Vincent de Paul and his friends in the aristocratic Company of the Holy Sacrament had another remedy: the workhouse. They founded and administered General Hospitals for the destitute in Lyon (1614), Marseilles (1639), Orleans (1642), Paris (1656) and many other places, where hard labour was combined with devotional instruction. The French were not the first in this field. The first Bridewell appeared in England in 1552 (London), in Italy in 1581 (Rome) and in the Low Countries in 1595 (Amsterdam). The Dutch Republic had 11 workhouses by 1621 and 22 by 1682.

The purpose of *renfermement* was, of course, partly social cosmetics – to remove the indigent poor from public view – but there were other reasons. First, the system provided a supply of cheap labour for local industrialists. The cloth-workers of Leiden, for example, employed children from workhouses and foundling homes on a considerable scale in the seventeenth century. From 1630 they even began to import children from the orphanages and poor houses of other towns: between 1638 and 1671 some 8000 child workers were imported to Leiden from Aachen, Jülich, Liège and elsewhere, keeping down local wages and prices, putting adults out of a job, and condemning the children to an early grave. Even where employing the poor did not offer the same opportunities for profit as at Leiden, many argued that vagrants should be made to work simply because it was good for them. In the lapidary phrase of Sir William Petty: '[Better] to burn a thousand men's labour for a time, than let those thousand men, by non-employment, lose their faculty of labouring.'

Such a prodigal attitude was only possible in the towns, however. Few villages, if any, could afford to build a workhouse in the seventeenth century; fewer still could afford a permanent system of social security. And yet neither could they afford to send their poor inhabitants away: the rich farmers needed a reservoir of cheap labour just as much as the rich industrialists of the city. To take a single but typical example, the village of Navalmoral, south of Toledo, had a population of 243 families (perhaps 1000 people) in the 1580s: the top 11 families held one-third of the village's land and one-third of the vines – far more than they could cultivate by themselves; the top 22 families owned half the land between them; and 108 families owned all the land. Of the rest, 28 families owned no land but grazed livestock; 95 families 'lived only from their labour' or 'lived from the work of their hands'; 21 were widows living alone, without any apparent source of income; and 17 were described as paupers, without even a dwelling-place. The Haves and the Have-nots lived in mutual interdependence: the rich needed the labour of the poor in order to maintain their status and style of life just as much as the poor needed the wages of the rich in order to survive. In a year of dearth or high unemployment it was thus to the advantage of the rich to maintain the poor. However, if there were several years of dearth, private resources for rural charity might become scarce; unfortunately, at precisely the same time, the church's resources for alms-giving were also in shortest supply. In the villages of the Montes de Toledo, the church's charitable donations fluctuated in direct relation to the tithe yield: in 1618, a year of good harvest (and therefore of good tithes), 12,000 *maravedís* were distributed in alms; in the 1630s, as harvest yields fell, the sum declined to 2000 *maravedís*; and in 1645, 1647 and 1649 the parish account-book states, 'No charity has been given, since there is nothing to give.'

There was nothing else for the abandoned poor to do in these circumstances but join the mass of people on the roads in search of relief. The flood swept from countryside to towns (and particularly from areas of sparse cultivation such as the Massif Central to fertile plains like Languedoc), and from small towns to the metropolis. A census of the valley of the Haute Tarantaise in Savoy revealed that in the summer of 1608 there was not a single man left: all had gone to work in France. But some migrants went farther afield. Poland was blessed with 30,000 Scots by 1620; there were 40,000 Frenchmen in Catalonia; and so on. Some 400,000 Europeans migrated to America during the course of the seventeenth century, mainly from the countries along the Atlantic seaboard: perhaps 80,000 left England for the colonies between 1620 and 1640, and more still followed in the 1650s. But this movement of peoples did little to reduce the over-population of most of Europe at the time. The rest of the 100 million inhabitants of the continent had to be supported by Europe's own resources.

3. *Supply and Demand*

In the early seventeenth century, the heart of the European economy lay in the countries around the North Sea: the west Netherlands (whether Calvinist or Catholic), the south-eastern counties of England, and the north-western provinces of France. The architectural heritage of these areas testifies still to the sudden wealth that they enjoyed between about 1580 and about 1640: the rebuilding of urban and rural centres in England, from Norwich to Southampton; the growth of Paris, Amiens and the Atlantic ports of France from Boulogne to Brittany; the elegant canal-bank houses of Amsterdam, Delft, Antwerp and Ghent (where 1260 houses – one-eighth of the city – were either rebuilt or refaced in stone between 1600 and 1670). Such investment in bricks and mortar presupposed prosperity and wealth on an extensive scale. So did the canal-building and lake-drainage work which was undertaken in the first half of the seventeenth century. In the North Netherlands 79,825 hectares of lake and marsh were reclaimed between 1590 and 1639, and an important network of canals was constructed. The new inter-city canals, with their tow-paths and horses and crews, provided a regular service of barges to convey passengers and freight quickly and cheaply between the principal cities of Holland. The first of these purpose-built passenger canals was opened in 1632 to link Haarlem and Amsterdam, fifteen miles apart, and before long fastidious Amsterdammers found the carriage charges low enough to send their dirty washing to the cheaper and cleaner laundries of Haarlem.[6] But the canal still made a profit of six to seven per cent annually for its owners, and this encouraged further constructions: by 1648, some 150 miles of passenger canal (*trekvaart*) had become operational, at a cost of 1·5 million Dutch florins. Travel in the Dutch Republic, according to European globetrotters like Fynes Morison or

Peter Mundy, was the cheapest, the most reliable and the quickest in the world. (It was also the safest: Fynes Morison was not the only traveller to breathe a sigh of relief, when entering the Republic, that no more would he need to adopt disguises or hide under the freight of wagons in order to escape bandit attacks.)

This high degree of economic development in the states around the North Sea allowed them, from about 1600 onwards, to dominate the European markets with their goods and services. It was their economic preponderance which generated the surplus capital for rebuilding town-houses, draining lakes and constructing canals. The area bounded by Southampton, Norwich, Amsterdam and Paris was an enclave of advanced techniques and specialized manufacture. It was also – and most importantly, since agriculture still remained the occupation of the majority of the population – an area of unusually sophisticated farming.

There were at least four distinct agricultural zones in Europe. The first and most extensive comprised the regions which produced little more than they needed, where only a very few special goods (such as salt or iron) needed to be either exported or imported. The surplus was small and it was unpredictable: when tithes, taxes and rent or dues had been subtracted, a poor harvest might satisfy nothing beyond the basic needs of the peasant family. It was extremely difficult to change this regime. First, absentee landlords were anxious to prevent overcropping which might deplete the fertility of the soil: they often specified in their leases, therefore, that land should be regularly fallowed and that rotation should be frequent. Second, the division of village land into three or more large fields, in each of which most villagers had a strip or plot (unfenced), made it extremely difficult for any individual cultivator to introduce new farming methods. Even in England, only 744,000 acres (or two per cent of the total area) were enclosed, and thus taken out of the open field system, by the year 1637. Elsewhere the rural population had neither the incentive, nor the time, nor the capital to improve their land. The new crops and the new methods of farming both required a considerable extra input of money and labour, and most tenant-farmers, with much of their produce (however great or small) appropriated in tithes, taxes and seigneurial dues, could see little reason to produce more goods for the benefit of others.

However there were certain areas, forming a second agricultural zone, where either climate or economic geography offered incentives for increased agricultural efficiency, especially in cereal crops where spectacular results could easily be achieved. The most important barometer of improvement was the yield ratio: with an average harvest of four grains for every grain planted, a peasant family produced only a very small surplus, enough perhaps for one extra person; if the yield ratio improved from 4:1 to 8:1, however, the surplus would be enough to feed ten extra persons. That is to say, when the yield doubled, the persons who could be fed tripled and the non-agricultural population which could be supported increased sevenfold. There were a number of areas where this important improvement had taken place by 1600, and others where it was in progress. Some regions regularly produced and exported a surplus of cereal crops: Andalusia and Sicily in the south of Europe (where the climate was so favourable that two crops could be grown in normal years); Poland and east Germany in the north; East Anglia in England. In each case, the areas of surplus production possessed not only fertile soil but also easy access to water transport: the cost of bulk transport by land was prohibitive. After about 1590, the Mediterranean ceased to be a grain exporter, instead requiring periodic consignments of Baltic grain itself, and Polish production expanded yet further to fill the gap. But the surplus, still based upon a relatively low yield ratio, was precarious. The 200,000 tons of grain which annually came down the Vistula for sale at Danzig in the 1600s declined to around 150,000 tons by the mid-century, and in some years it was even less. More was being consumed locally. Even then, not all the grain could be sold: an increasing number of ships bringing western goods to Danzig were leaving empty, because the price of Polish grain was no longer competitive, except in years of abundant harvest. Plague and famine had reduced population pressure in Mediterranean Europe, while improved methods of cultivation had increased yields in England and the Low Countries. In both markets, less Baltic corn was required. Then in 1655–60 the Swedish invasion (known in Polish history as *potop*, the deluge) destroyed crops and cultivators alike and dealt Polish agriculture a blow from which it was very slow to recover.

The third agricultural zone comprised areas remote from the sea or from navigable rivers which tended to concentrate their surplus agricultural effort on raising livestock, either for their skins (as with the wool of Castilian sheep) or for their meat (as with the Danish cattle driven overland to market in Amsterdam, or the Scottish cattle driven to market in London). The scale of this livestock trade was impressive. By 1640, the total production of steers and oxen in Denmark had reached around 275,000 head, of which around one-fifth were exported and the rest eaten locally; the Swiss cantons exported around 18,000 cattle to Italy every year in the earlier seventeenth century and about the same number to the Empire; Hungary also raised large numbers of cattle for export. In Spain, some two million sheep in the early seventeenth century were driven every year from their winter pastures in Andalusia to spend the summer in the uplands of Old Castile, their movements and the marketing of the wool controlled by the *Mesta* (an association of sheep-owners). There were probably as many sheep again, in Castile, grazed locally in the villages and towns.

The fourth and final agricultural zone comprised the enclaves of intensive cultivation that surrounded most large towns. In 1500 there were 26 towns in Europe with a population larger than 40,000; in 1600 there were 42; in 1700 there were 52. Almost all of them were situated west of a line stretching from Copenhagen to Venice, with concentrations of several cities in Italy (11 in 1600) and the Netherlands (7 in 1600, with Cologne, London, Paris and Rouen nearby). In an expanding fringe around each large urban agglomeration, intensive husbandry was practised, often on estates bought by members of the urban bourgeoisie, to produce both the surplus food and the industrial crops (dyestuffs, hops and so on) required by the towns. The sustained and increased urban demand in these areas produced a revolution in agrarian techniques from about 1550 onwards, with larger farm animals, new crops (especially maize, buckwheat and potatoes) and better yields. These developments were most pronounced in the west Netherlands (where population density and urban density alike were highest): in 1622, 59 per cent of Holland's population lived in towns of over 3000 inhabitants. But progress was also becoming noticeable in south-west England by 1650 and in north-west France by 1700, with yield-ratios rising to 7:1 and even 8:1 and providing the crucial support for greater economic diversity. The areas directly involved in the market economy of Europe multiplied; the number of households that produced only for themselves declined.

Improvement on this scale was not common, however. In most respects, the economy of early modern Europe was extremely inflexible. First, there was resistance to change of any sort, whether new tools or new crops. Maize, for example, was introduced into Spain in the 1520s and it was soon noted that the crop could be substituted for fallowing and was more resistant to freak weather which damaged corn; but farmers refused to cultivate it until after 1600, and thereafter used it mainly for sheep fodder. Artisans were equally conservative, both in their choice of raw materials and in their methods of work: manufacture of the 'new draperies' (made with lighter wools) was bitterly resisted by the weavers' guilds and introduction of machines was bitterly resisted by everyone. Second, it was often impossible to react to fluctuations in demand. A fall in demand led not to a search for new markets or new processes, but to lay-offs and stock-piling; an increase in demand, especially for perishable goods, led to waste because there were neither wagons nor containers enough to distribute the surplus goods. A bumper wine harvest or herring catch was often wasted because there were not enough barrels to store it in.

Improved economic performance and diversification were therefore confined to regions where the agricultural surplus was based on significantly higher yield-ratios and where capital was abundant. And in those areas, other advances were also noted. There was, for example, something approaching a revolution in the use of fuel. In England and Scotland, coal was mined on an unprecedented scale: it is estimated that annual output rose from 210,000 tons in the 1550s to 2,982,000 tons in the 1680s, a fourteenfold increase. Even by 1640 London had become so dependent on coal for domestic and industrial purposes that the Scots' capture of Newcastle, London's principal source of supply, contributed to the fall of the government. In the North Netherlands there was a parallel growth in the digging of peat for industrial use: hundreds of thousands of tons were used every year for brewing, bleaching, sugar-refining, brick-making, spirit-distilling, soap-boiling and salt-panning – all of them fuel-intensive activities. (Peat is only one-sixth as efficient as coal, but it was cheaper and more plentiful locally.) Water and wind were also harnessed to turn industrial mills: for rolling metals, for fulling cloth, for printing ribbons, for grinding corn, even (from 1594) for powering saws. In the Dutch Republic alone there were perhaps 3000 windmills at work in the seventeenth century, each of them producing the same energy as 100 men or 40 horses. It was a great saving in labour and costs.

There were many other industrial innovations in the earlier seventeenth century. Knitting-frames were introduced in England in 1598; the ribbon-frame or Dutch Loom was used in the Netherlands after 1604; the silk throwing-mill was developed in several areas following its description in Vittorio Zonca's *New Theatre of Machines and Buildings* (Padua, 1607). This was one of several illustrated books composed at the turn of the century which drew new inventions to the attention of the educated public: Olivier de Serres's *Theatre of Agriculture* (Paris, 1600), of which the French government presented a free copy to every parish in the hope that farmers would mend their ways; Jacques Besson's *Theatre of Mathematical and Mechanical Instru-*

ments (Lyon, 1578), which showed, *inter alia*, how to drive bridge-piles into deep river beds (a method faithfully copied in the construction of Parma's siege bridge over the Scheldt at Antwerp in 1584–5); and Simon Stevin's *New Method of Fortification* (Leiden, 1594), which stressed the cheapness as well as the effectiveness of Dutch bastion defences. One of the reasons, finally, why Galileo, Hariot, Fabricius and Scheiner all discovered sunspots almost simultaneously in 1611 was Galileo's description of how to make an astronomical telescope, which he included in his *Starry Messenger* published the previous year (and that instrument was itself designed on the basis of reports received of a field-glass used by the Dutch army in 1608–9).[7]

This openness about new methods in some fields forms an interesting contrast with the extreme secrecy which surrounded others. The textile industry, which was practised in almost every country, was particularly full of jealously guarded techniques. In Piedmont, anyone who revealed or attempted to reveal information concerning the manufacture of textile machinery was sentenced to death; in Florence, the government in 1575 offered a reward of 200 scudi (about £40 sterling) for every Florentine brocade worker who had gone to work abroad and could be brought back dead or alive. All were authorized to 'kill with impunity any of the abovementioned expatriates'.

In the end, production in early modern Europe depended on human energy and ingenuity – on serf-power or peasant-power in agriculture; on serf-power in mining; on artisans in manufacture. The increased use of peat, windmills and canals was the ultimate refinement of a centuries-old technical tradition rather than a stepping-stone to the technology of the Industrial Revolution. Technological progress often amounted to no more than the substitution of materials and fuels of fossil origin for vegetable raw materials and fuels – especially for wood, which was still in 1600 the most important of all natural resources, used extensively for building, transport (both on land and water), fuel and manufacture (both for tools and as a raw material). Moreover, timber could be recycled, with the same piece used over and over again in buildings, ships and artefacts. Manufactured goods were highly prized (as a glance at any inventory of the time will show: tools, roof-beams, even horseshoes and nails were scrupulously listed as valuable assets) and recycling saved money and resources. The re-use of materials remained an attractive proposition for as long as the basic economic activities of man – weaving, farming, fishing and so on – were carried on in the traditional way, so that tools and materials could be handed on from one generation to the next. This conservative system suited early modern capitalists too. Except in ship-building, where both Dutch and Venetian yards introduced production-lines in which pre-cut numbered timbers were assembled in sequence to produce ships, all European industries were labour-intensive and not capital-intensive. Increases in demand were met, if at all, by engaging more workers and supplying them with raw material and credit until they could manufacture the goods in their spare time. This putting-out system worked well, because it offered an income to rural families at times of slack agricultural employment, yet it cost the entrepreneur little.

It would be wrong to infer from the above that there was little or no increase in the economic production of early modern Europe. Although the response was sluggish, increased demand did eventually result in expanded output. The new demand stemmed from two developments. First, there were considerable new markets overseas. The discovery, colonization and economic subjugation of America by Spain, Portugal, Holland, France and England created a large new market for European goods. The various East India companies also exported western manufactures to India and south-east Asia, while the Levant and Russian companies of the western states supplied textiles and metal goods to the Mediterranean and Baltic lands. However, the principal export of the west to all these markets save America was silver bullion. It has been estimated that about 80,000 kilograms of silver were exported annually to the east from Europe around 1600, which was used to purchase the Baltic furs, timber and grain and the Oriental luxuries that western consumers desired (thus dissipating almost half the treasure imported from America).

There was, however, a significant increase in the demand for European goods within the continent itself. The doubling of the population was a powerful stimulus to growth, for twice as many people required twice as much food, twice as many clothes and twice as much accommodation – at least in theory; and even though, individually, the poor had to make do with less, collectively they still increased aggregate demand. Nevertheless the sectors of most spectacular growth in the European economy were not connected with the staple goods. Although the total productive area had been increased, with some marginal lands coming into cultivation for the first and only time since the thirteenth century, a greater proportion than before was taken up with the growing of non-essential items: wine, olive oil, dye-stuffs, cork, mulberries (for silk). The burgeoning demand for these goods came not from the poor but from the rapidly increasing number of middle- and upper-class households, whose size was swollen by the rural and domestic servants who lived in. No less than 28 per cent of all known households in seventeenth-century England had one or more of them living in; and servants, fed and clothed by their masters, sometimes given a small wage as well, made up around 10 per cent of the population of western Europe. Their futures were uncertain – many changed their masters once a year at the annual feeing-fairs; some ran away before their time had been served; others were dismissed at times of dearth in order to save money – but on the whole, domestic service raised the standard of living not only of those so employed, but of their families at home which had one less mouth to feed.

However, not all areas profited equally from this overall expansion of demand. As the European economy diversified, so it began to polarize. In the Middle Ages, Europe had not been divided into developed and underdeveloped countries, for each state was both at once. Nor did this situation change overnight: even in 1650 there were still backward areas in the Dutch Republic (Drenthe and Overijssel for instance) and still advanced areas in Poland (above all around Danzig). But there was a growing tendency for some parts of the continent to concentrate on producing raw materials and labour-intensive, low-grade manufacture, while others sought to monopolize the more advanced, more capital-intensive (and usually more profitable) industrial processes. The former included the areas with a high urban density: England, France, Italy and the Netherlands manufactured more than their fair share of luxury goods and essential artefacts, securing in exchange a disproportionate share of the surplus product (and therefore the wealth) of the European economy. However, the countries of the north European plain, where towns were few and far between, produced and exported a surplus of cheap raw materials and unfinished manufactures, receiving in return the overpriced yet sophisticated goods of their urbanized neighbours.

Once this polarization had advanced beyond a certain stage, the economic imbalance thus created stood in need of protection by the groups that it favoured. The Fuggers of Augsburg of the sixteenth century or the Hanseatic merchants of the later Middle Ages had prospered without an army or navy to protect them, because their competitors were too weak; but their commercial successors after 1600 could not. In the seventeenth century, there was no profit without power and no security without strength, so that economic absolutism by governments was essential to the prosperity of merchants and manufacturers. The rise of the Dutch Republic to economic pre-eminence, for example, would have been impossible without the victories at sea won by Heyn, Tromp and de Ruyter against the Republic's Spanish, English and French competitors. Of course there was more to the Dutch success in world markets than sea-power. Throughout the seventeenth century Dutch entrepreneurs were able to produce goods at lower prices than anyone else, and to market them more efficiently; from their strong agricultural and industrial base they successively acquired preponderance in the supply of commercial services (transport, insurance and so on) and financial services (both banking and investment). Dutch farming, with its emphasis on capital-intensive, high-profit crops, was the envy of Europe; its textile and ship-building industries were far ahead of all competitors; its commercial fleet by 1670 was larger than those of England, France, Spain, Portugal and the Empire combined; and its Amsterdam Bank and Exchange formed the financial capital of Europe. However, this dazzling economic achievement needed to be protected. The Republic's navy had to be sent into action repeatedly to ensure that there should be free trade in Europe, where the Dutch could compete with advantage, but simultaneously to impose severe protectionism in the wider world, where the supply of expensive luxury goods to Europe and of European goods to Asia and Africa had to be carefully controlled in order to avoid glutting the relatively small market which existed. As a shrewd English envoy in Holland acidly remarked: 'It is *mare liberum* in the British seas but *mare clausum* on the coast of Africa and in the East Indies.' When the Dutch fleet could no longer enforce these harsh commercial conditions, the Republic's prosperity began to decline.

One reason for the determined protectionism followed by early modern governments was the mistaken belief that the total market available for goods was static, so that the production of one country could only expand if it broke into the markets previously supplied by somebody else. In the concise phrase of Francis Bacon: 'The increase of any estate must be upon the foreigner (for whatsoever is somewhere gotten is somewhere lost).' Foreign trade was normally viewed as a form of warfare, and protectionist policies were intended to safeguard local production from foreign competition while opening foreign markets to one's own goods. This was particularly true between 1620 and 1670. Exporting nations such as England and the Dutch Republic found few new markets for their goods, whether local manufactures or colonial re-exports; existing markets in Poland, Germany and Spain contracted; and elsewhere demand rose only slightly where before 1620 it had risen rapidly. During a recession of this magnitude, protectionist policies were essential if local exporters were not to go to the wall. But there was more to the matter than this. Governments often pursued active economic policies because of the direct profits they yielded: the enrichment of subjects, if any, was incidental. Christian IV of Denmark (1596–1648), for example, defended his economic policies – which included land speculation in North Germany, lending money at interest to entrepreneurs, and the economic exploitation of Lappland – on the grounds that 'they bring honour to us and no injury, God willing, to the merchants'. Christian and his fellow-monarchs lived at a time of acute tension between governments and their subjects. The economic climate made tax-payers unusually reluctant to accept new tax burdens and uniquely anxious to administer any funds which they provided. It was therefore considered essential for monarchs to increase those sources of income from their domains or from speculative investments that were free of any checks or controls by their subjects. In the seventeenth century, economic absolutism was seen as no less important to the strength of a state than confessional or political absolutism.

CHAPTER II

European Society and the State

1. *Confessional Absolutism*

Almost every major political crisis in Christian Europe during early modern times involved religious disagreement. It was no accident that the crowd of revolutionaries in Prague who threw ministers of their king out of the window in May 1618 were Protestants, whereas both the monarch and his ministers were Catholics, for the troubles had started with official moves that appeared to threaten freedom of worship for non-Catholics. Nor were such confrontations at all uncommon, for by 1618 almost every European government endorsed the principle formulated in 1555 at the religious peace of Augsburg: *cuius regio, eius religio* – the faith of the subjects should be the same as that of their ruler. In the unified states of western Europe, such as Castile, Sweden or Scotland, this meant the imposition of a single orthodoxy on all subjects, with an inquisitorial machinery (whether Catholic, Lutheran or Calvinist) to punish those who failed to conform.

In Venice, a state with two million subjects, a special inquisition held regular sessions to interrogate and punish any persons found guilty of heterodox religious views. During the seventeenth century, at least 1494 cases were heard, 20 or more of them ending in the death sentence. In the Spanish Empire, the 'Holy Office' consisted of 22 tribunals stretching from Sicily and Sardinia to Mexico and Peru, controlled by a central council (the *suprema*) which met in the royal palace in Madrid. It has been estimated that between 1550 and 1700 these tribunals handled 150,000 cases, most of them originating in information supplied either by neighbours or by one of the army of Familiars maintained by the Inquisition in all areas. An analysis of 42,000 surviving cases reveals that 75 per cent concerned religious deviance (witchcraft, Protestantism, Jewish practices) and the rest morals (bigamy, sodomy, adultery and the like). Of these, 687 of the accused were executed, and a further 619 were burnt in effigy (because they had either escaped or died before sentence could be passed). Despite these modest figures – modest in relation to the millions of inhabitants who lived within the jurisdiction of the Holy Office over the century and a half covered – the Inquisition created great unease among a large number of people. Arrest was arbitrary, usually the consequence of an anonymous denunciation; trial was secret, protracted and often accompanied by torture; imprisonment (at the expense of the accused) during investigation and trial usually proved unpleasant, and sometimes fatal; and any discovery of guilt was punished by confiscation of goods, public humiliation and perpetual infamy (even after the death of the condemned and reconciled person, his penitent's gown was displayed in the local church – and if it disintegrated or faded, it was replaced).

These instruments of confessional absolutism played a major part in redrawing the religious map of Europe. The Reformation had passed its zenith by 1590 when Protestantism was, in one form or another, the official religion in almost half the European continent. By 1650, the Protestant share of Europe had shrunk to about one-fifth; the rest had reverted to Catholicism. In the Habsburg lands and in Bavaria, militantly Catholic rulers persecuted their Protestant subjects until by 1628 few were left (except in Hungary). In Poland of the 560 or so Protestant churches existing in 1572, only 240 were left in 1650 (and only 80, mostly small, by 1780). In France, the Huguenots were forbidden to look for new converts after 1598; they lost all their political privileges in 1629; and they were expelled from the country altogether in 1685. There were, it is true, some gains by the Calvinist church after 1590 – Hesse-Cassel in 1604; Holstein-Gottorp in 1610 – but these were victories over Lutherans, not

Catholics, and they scarcely compared with the enormous gains made by the Roman church.

There were many reasons for the resurgence of Roman Catholicism. Perhaps the most important was its ability to present, under papal direction, a united front to the secular world. Although there were certainly divisions – most notably the feud between the Jansenists and the Jesuits – at least until the 1640s the disputes were kept within bounds and tended to involve only theologians.[1] The Protestants, by contrast, disagreed savagely among themselves and did their best to mobilize lay support. During the first decades of the Reformation there had been considerable co-operation among the various Protestant creeds: in Germany, many pastors could provide both Lutheran and Calvinist services as required by the local regime; in Poland, the Lutherans and Calvinists of Danzig used the upper and lower floor of the same building, and shared the same choir and acolytes by holding their services at different times of day. This easy-going attitude did not survive the sixteenth century. Attempts to unite the Calvinists, Lutherans, Bohemian Brethren and Hussites of the crown of Bohemia (the *Confessio Bohemica* of 1575, renewed in 1608) achieved only limited success; the Union of Torun (1595) between the Lutherans, Calvinists and Brethren in Poland proved abortive. Matters were no better farther west. Although the Synod of Dort (Dordrecht) in 1619 was attended by Calvinists from Germany, Geneva, the Dutch Republic, Scotland and England, the assembly went out of its way to censure Lutheran opinions, and expelled 300 of its own ministers for holding views which were deemed favourable to Catholicism. In 1631 the Lutheran elector of Saxony, even though the total extirpation of the Protestant cause in Germany was in sight, still showed the utmost reluctance to allow his clergy to explore the grounds for a reconciliation with those whom he termed 'the Calvinist heretics'.

The ceaseless and intemperate bickering and feuding between, and within, the various Protestant creeds gradually eroded the support of important lay patrons. Their return to the Catholic faith of their grandfathers was a second major reason for the recovery of the Catholic church in the seventeenth century. During the formative years of the Reformation, the favour of magistrates and landowners had permitted the foundation of the churches, schools, seminaries and printing-presses without which no creed could establish or maintain a popular appeal. After the 1570s, this vital support was gradually withdrawn. In Poland, there were 59 non-Catholic lay senators (members of the upper house in the Diet) in 1572, but only 41 in 1586 and only 6 in 1632. The trend was similar in both France and the Habsburg lands: many of the leading nobles abandoned their Protestant beliefs in favour of Catholicism, including some political figures of the highest importance – Condé and Turenne in France, Eggenberg and Trautmansdorff in the Empire all began life as Protestants and then turned against their former co-religionists. It is true that many of the conversions were occasioned by the bribes and pensions offered by the government, by 'honours and the belly' as an English observer noted in 1619; but the factionalism of the Protestants also played its part.

So did the efforts made by the Catholic establishment to make its teaching attractive to the nobility of Europe. In France, Pierre de Bérulle (1575–1629), who once described himself as 'the confessor of the well-to-do', introduced new religious orders for pious noblemen (the Oratorians, from 1611) and for devout noblewomen (the Carmelites, from 1604). In Poland, where aristocratic power had become supreme, even the Christian message was 'ennobled': peers were encouraged to believe that Polish was spoken in Paradise; that even in Hell the superior status of the nobles would be respected so that their punishments (if any) would be administered in secluded areas of the underworld; and that God was a constitutional monarch who took the advice of his celestial Diet before making decisions. The clergy was well aware that its future lay in the hands of the nobles, not with the crown or the peasants: one-third of all the books printed in the kingdom during the seventeenth century were panegyrics of the aristocracy, and 80 per cent of them were written by clerics. The church even established a special censor's office to expurgate any work written by a priest which might offend the magnates. Not surprisingly, the nobles streamed back into the Catholic fold, banishing the pastors and closing the schools of other religions on their estates, and supporting legislation in the Diet directed against small Reformed groups such as the Unitarians (whose school and Academy at Rakow were closed down by law in 1638 and whose adherents were expelled in 1658).

The Catholic church had learnt many lessons from its rivals, however. Like the Reformers, the Popes saw the value of concentrating attention on princes. Legates and eloquent members of the new religious orders (like the Society of Jesus) were sent out to strategically placed courts, such as Brussels, Munich, Paris and Vienna, where they directed the foundation of schools for the aristocracy, seminaries for the clergy, and spiritual missions for the laity. Within a generation, their efforts had produced a group of devout rulers whose principal desire was to further the work of the church: Sigismund III of Poland (1587–1632), Louis XIII of France (1610–43), and above all Ferdinand II of Styria and Maximilian of Bavaria. Born in 1578, educated at the Jesuit university of Ingolstadt and able to speak five languages, Ferdinand brought a considerable intellect to the government of Inner Austria when he reached the age of majority in 1595. From the first, he laboured to end the religious independence of the Protestants and the political independence of the estates in his dominions; and before long he had got rid of both. Ferdinand saw politics as a weapon to be used in the great religious struggle of his day between Catholic and Protestant and, whether as archduke or (after 1619) as Emperor, he placed all his authority behind the Roman church. Duke Maximilian of Bavaria, who had attended Ingolstadt with Ferdinand, shared this vision. Inspired by the archduke's adviser, Caspar Scoppius, both statesmen began to dream of re-Catholicizing all of central Germany, realizing the vision of a priest-state set out by Tomas Campanella in his *City of the Sun* (written in 1602). They gathered around them the ablest Catholic writers and preachers to be found, and lost no opportunity of increasing the power of the church of Rome both inside their states and beyond, employing to that end all the means which the growth in governmental power during the sixteenth century had provided.

2. *Political Absolutism*

The early modern period was a time of revolution in government in Europe, at least as far as numbers were concerned. The salaried employees of the French crown increased from 12,000 in 1505 to 80,000 in 1664 (excluding the armed forces in both cases) and there were about the same number of officials administering the estates and law-courts of the various separate lordships into which much of France was divided until the Revolution. The amount of paperwork handled by some of these bureaucrats was astonishing: copies and minutes of some 18,000 letters have survived from the office of the French secretary for war alone between 1636 and 1642. 'I sometimes wrote to Monsieur de Bullion [the finance minister] as often as six times a day,' the secretary later reminisced wistfully. The situation was much the same in Castile, where fourteen central councils generated mountains of paper for the king to deal with. The council of war, to take but one example, which had produced only two or three bundles of papers a year in the 1560s, was turning out over 30 bundles a year in the 1590s – the equivalent of 2000 letters annually.

The pressure on the ruler at the centre of this administrative jungle was fast becoming intolerable. Philip II (1556–98), who on occasion had to sit and sign up to 400 letters in a single day, belonged to a dying generation of monarchs who still made the effort to exercise a personal control over their governmental machine, either by looking through state papers at random intervals or by intervening directly in the daily transaction of business. Henry IV of France (1589–1610) still belonged to this tradition, frequently adding postscripts in his awkward italic hand to his secretaries' letters, and personally checking the public accounts prepared by his financial advisers. Duke Maximilian of Bavaria (1595–1651) was equally conscientious, and was proud of it. In a letter of 1611 to his cousin, the queen of Spain, he boasted that, 'I see to my affairs myself and check my accounts myself . . . Reputation and greatness depend not on spending, but on spending well and on saving, so that a little will make a lot, and from a few hundred will come a few thousand and from the thousands will come millions.'[2] But the advice fell on deaf ears: neither the queen nor her husband, Philip III (1598–1621), took heed. It has been calculated that between 1609 and 1612 the king of Spain returned 46 per cent of the reports (known as *consultas*) sent to him by the council of state (the body responsible for foreign affairs) endorsed with a mere *así* (yes), while a further 45 per cent were returned with 'yes' and a minor detail to be amended. It was not an impressive record, yet even these perfunctory comments could take a week to secure, and consultas might take anything between six days and six weeks to be returned to the relevant council. The average seems to have been three weeks.

Not all rulers came up even to this standard. Elector John George of Saxony (1611–56) was seldom disposed to transact business; his sometime master, the Holy Roman Emperor Rudolf II (1576–1612), rarely wrote anything – hardly any holograph letters from him have survived. In 1600 Rudolph seems to have made an attempt on his own life, and he certainly considered suicide at other times too. From 1600 until his death he spent long periods in solitary seclusion in his palace at Prague and refused to do anything at all; the imperial government had to manage without him as best it could. Frederick William I of Brandenburg (the 'Great Elector', 1640–88), was educationally subnormal (at the age of nine he still could not count to ten or recite the alphabet) and was always subject to psychopathic fits of rage. One could compile a long list of seventeenth-century rulers who were either wicked or slow-witted, or both; but to no purpose. Even for princes without the mental stresses of Rudolf II or Frederick William I, the demands of public office had become excessive. The growing bureaucratization of government created intolerable strains on rulers reared on manuals of courtly behaviour by Castiglione or Gracián, and taught fencing and dancing instead of accountancy and mathematics. Over one-third of James VI and I's *Basilicon Doron*, a book of advice for his son and heir published in 1597, was taken up with 'the king's duty in behaviour' – how he should eat, dress and comport himself. It said nothing about how to manage parliaments or raise loans.

Behaviour, however, was conceived to be a matter of the highest importance to seventeenth-century monarchies. Kings were still expected to be, first and foremost, gentlemen: rulers like Philip II or Maximilian of Bavaria who spent too much time at their desks were criticized as 'unkingly'. The early modern revolution in government had been accompanied by a change in the life-style of court society. Manners and ceremonials were codified and embellished; access to the royal person and household were controlled – only the educated and well mannered were admitted, so that cultural and behavioural conformity was achieved. This hothouse atmosphere naturally produced some monstrous fruit. In the interests of royal magnificence even the most basic functions were ritualized, and thereby prolonged, to an absurd degree. An increasing amount of time was taken up with apparently simple activities such as eating or dressing: nothing in a king's life could be done in a hurry. Small wonder that many monarchs sought a temporary escape from the prison of court ceremonial. Philip IV of Spain, at least in the 1630s, retired after lunch for two hours every day in order to read, to write poems and music, and to study the languages of his non-Castilian subjects. He also regularly attended the theatre, sometimes incognito (and occasionally having affaires with actresses). Louis XIII of France composed and performed ballet and lute music; Sigismund III of Poland was a painter of talent;

James VI and I wrote and published a dozen books.

Books, music and pictures could only influence, however; they could not command. The main problem facing the monarchs of the earlier seventeenth century was ensuring obedience from their subjects and particularly from their servants. In England, the justices of the peace and even the judges (such as Sir Edward Coke) could disregard and sometimes disobey the orders issued by the crown; in France, the provincial law-courts (*Parlements*) had extensive powers to revise and even to reverse the laws promulgated by the king and his council. How could a king insist that his officials should break their institutional loyalty in the national interest (as he saw it)? How could a king ensure that his orders were being carried out?

After 1600, the preferred solution to these problems in most European states was to delegate detailed control over the administration to a chief minister or 'favourite': Buckingham in England (1618–28), Khlesl in the Empire (1612–18), Richelieu (1624–42) and Mazarin (1643–61) in France, Lerma (1598–1618) and Olivares (1622–42) in Spain were but the most famous. Even rulers who had received the sort of education that would have enabled them to understand all governmental tasks themselves preferred to entrust policy supervision to a vice-regent: Gustavus Adolphus of Sweden, fluent in seven languages and a writer of history books, delegated full powers to Axel Oxenstierna; the Emperor Ferdinand II, a university graduate, entrusted his government to the supervision of Prince Eggenberg. To Philip IV of Spain, the need for a ministerial supervisor seemed self-evident: 'The task could scarcely be performed by the king in person, since it would be incompatible with his dignity to go from house to house to see if his ministers and secretaries were carrying out their orders promptly.'[3] In this task, moreover, the chief minister or favourite so appointed enjoyed a decisive advantage over his master, because he could command the allegiance of an extensive network of clients whom he could introduce into the administration to circumvent any points of independence or opposition. Richelieu, who was typical in this respect, governed France between 1624 and 1642 through a small army of *créatures* (sc. people he had 'created'). Many came from his native Poitou (such as the famous Father Joseph); some were his relatives (his nephew became general of the galleys); others were family friends (like the finance minister Bouthillier); others still were his personal discoveries who owed their every advancement to the cardinal's favour (like Mazarin himself, who developed the system further, until by 1661 he had 114 'creatures' in the ministry of finance alone). The creatures worked as a team. They did each other favours and they exchanged information. They took every opportunity to praise Richelieu to the king and they made sure that their advice and proposals coincided with his, since they knew that their political survival depended on the cardinal retaining the confidence of the king. Their devotion was total: when one creature was offered the hand of a relative of Richelieu, he first expressed his gratitude and then assured his patron that it did not matter precisely which relative he got 'Because in fact it is Your Eminence that I am marrying.'

The dangers to royal authority presented by such a tightly knit administrative network dependent on a single minister were obvious to all, and it did not long survive. There were few favourites exercising supreme power before 1600, and few after 1670: Louis XIV abandoned the practice on the death of Mazarin in 1661; Emperor Leopold I on the death of Prince Portia in 1665; Charles II of England after the fall of Clarendon in 1667. What was really needed, and what developed later in the century, was a ministerial system with departmental heads taking major decisions collectively, as a cabinet, subject to royal approval. But such a solution was unacceptable in the early seventeenth century: society in western Europe was still dominated by the concepts of patriarchal power, hierarchy and lineage. The sovereign had to maintain the fiction that he ruled his people directly, and that he was aided in this task – as kings always had been – by his nobles. The favourite, whether in Lutheran constitutional Sweden or in Catholic absolutist Castile, had to be an aristocrat, a grandee of established family. Those who were not, such as Buckingham or Khlesl, lived under constant threat of removal by noble pressure.

Another source of instability in the favourite-system was the policies they were called upon to implement, most of which involved securing a greater measure of centralization. In Spain, Olivares claimed to be working towards 'union and equality in the law, customs and form of government'; while James I of England declared that 'his wish above all things was, at his death, to leave one worship to God, one kingdom entirely governed, one uniformity of laws'. Ministers were expected to work towards this end. The heavy emphasis on law was not accidental. It was a maxim of medieval kingship that *rex est animata lex* ('the king is the incarnation of the law') and many people, including influential political theorists like Jean Bodin, believed that the ability 'to make laws binding on all in general and each in particular' was the most important attribute of a sovereign. A considerable proportion of the energies of every early modern state was devoted to issuing laws and creating courts to enforce those laws. The medieval concept of law, which was founded in an Aristotelian vision of society and presupposed an eternal and universal Reason without an individual legislator, was giving way to a Mosaic vision in which law was the work of God's will.

The new attitude towards the law was seen in a number of ways. First, there was the increasing resort to Roman Law with its insistence on criminal prosecution by a salaried official (the state prosecutor), conducted in writing and in secrecy instead of by the parties themselves in open court. The inquisitorial procedure began to replace the traditional accusatorial one. Next came the urge to homologize and rationalize the different legal systems and court procedures in use in individual states: the province of Luxemburg alone had 101 separate customary laws until in 1623 they were homologized into a single code for use everywhere in the province. Finally, there was a move to print the law, so that everyone could know where they stood. Indeed, printing was introduced into some countries expressly so that the laws could be published, and some of the largest print-runs recorded for secular works concerned definitive legal compilations like the complete laws of Lombardy (*Constitutiones* in 1541, *Ordines ac decreta* of the supreme court in 1587, *Compendio* of all proclamations in 1609) or of Castile (the *Nueva Recopilación* in 1567). Often the only book noted in household inventories was a copy of the local law-code: they were more common than Bibles. But in relatively few cases was the code a national one: the Common Law of England was unusual in this respect. Most other states had several separate legal systems: France had 700 or so, even in 1600, some of them of considerable complexity; the Low Countries had roughly the same number.

This untidy situation arose from the nature of the early modern state itself. Almost all of them were federative aggregations of smaller units. Some were new states, such as the Dutch Republic, created by the Union of Utrecht signed in 1579 by the representatives of seven North Netherlands provinces and certain others; others were old states to which new parts were annexed, such as France, where the independent possessions of the Bourbon family – Béarn, Navarre Armagnac, Vendôme, Rodez and so on – only became part of the royal patrimony at the accession of their lord, Henry IV, in 1589. Such new provinces were seldom fully integrated: most princes preferred to allow each annexed province to retain its local institutions (its supreme court, its parliament, its fiscal offices), its own legal system and law code, its own charter of liberties (often reiterated in the treaty of annexation) and its own language (where this was different from that of other territories). The classic illustration of the composite state characteristic of early modern times was the Spanish monarchy, where Philip III and IV ruled over a very large number of distinct territories (laboriously listed in the preamble to their letters patent). Some of them were separated by sea or land (Italy, the South Netherlands, the New World), others were contiguous (Aragon, Navarre, Castile, Portugal); some of them were originally acquired by inheritance (Sicily and Portugal), others by conquest (Lombardy and the New World).

And yet there was much that even a powerful monarch like the king of Spain could not do. In the much-quoted phrase of a Madrid lawyer in 1647: 'The kingdoms must be ruled and governed as if the king who holds them all together were king only of each one of them.'[4] The monarch could only rule in these annexed or united territories by working through the traditional structures and the traditional local elites, and attempts to change the balance which had been struck at the time of union met with tenacious resistance: the decision of Philip IV and Olivares to impose new taxes in the teeth of opposition from local elites provoked rebellions first in the Basque provinces (1631–4), then in Portugal (1628, 1629, 1637, 1640) and finally in Catalonia (also 1640). It was the same in other states. In 1628–32, the attempt of Louis XIII and Richelieu to abolish the fiscal independence of the provincial estates produced revolts in Languedoc, Burgundy and Provence led by members of the local elites. Also in the 1630s, the efforts of Charles I, Laud and Strafford to impose new policies on Scotland and Ireland without the consent of the local leaders provoked rebellions which brought down the entire Stuart monarchy.

It is noticeable that each of these revolts took place in provinces far from the seat of government, often relatively recently united with the central state. Many of the areas concerned were in difficult terrain, or were separated from the capital by sea or mountains. 'Distance', it has been observed for the early modern period, 'was public enemy number one.' Governments feared that a decision taken in the capital would be overtaken by events before it could be put into effect in the provinces. It took a minimum of two weeks for a letter from Madrid to reach Milan or Brussels, and three weeks to reach London or Vienna; it took a minimum of two months for a letter from Madrid to reach Mexico; and it took a minimum of a year for a letter from Madrid to reach Manila in the Philippines.[5] These were the fastest times; there was no average. No one could predict with certainty, as he sent his letter, the day or even the week of its arrival, for floods, storms, brigands or snows could cause indefinite delay. The postal couriers of Europe were both diligent and resourceful, adopting disguises or fitting crampons to their snow-boots whenever necessary; but they could not overcome the physical problems posed by distance. The state of the posts was as much a talking-point among early modern correspondents as it is today.

Some areas seemed even more remote because their inhabitants spoke a different language: Basque and Catalan in Spain, Occitan and Breton in France. They understood the language of the government with difficulty, if at all. Only the Habsburg governments in Madrid, Brussels and Vienna were prepared to use more than one language as a regular means of communicating with their subjects (and the dynasty itself actually led the way, Maximilian II learning to read and speak Czech as well as German, Philip III mastering French as well as Castilian).

The combination of remoteness, inaccessibility, local autonomy and linguistic diversity could produce regions which were virtually ungovernable 'dark corners of the land'. Even small and apparently unified states like England had them: 'We have Indians at home – Indians in Cornwall, Indians in Wales, Indians in Ireland,' a London-based pamphleteer lamented in 1652. Larger countries had correspondingly larger problems. Whole areas of the kingdom of Poland-Lithuania were still pagan, and in 1579 King Stephen Báthory consoled his Jesuit advisers: 'Do not be envious of the foreign lands in Asia and America that your Spanish and Portuguese brethren have won for God. Just near here, in Lithuania, you have Indians and Japanese.' The Polish Jesuits took heart: 'We do not need the East and West Indies,' they boasted 'Lithuania and the North are the real Indies.'[6]

Few governments, however, regarded any of these problems as paramount. They did not really recognize them as 'problems' at all: geography and language, at least, were regarded as immutable; and the traditional reaction to regional autonomy was to leave it alone. Most rulers were far more worried about their aristocracies.

There were three distinct aristocratic regions in Europe. First came the countries where the nobles and their families made up eight per cent or more of the total population – Hungary, Spain and Poland; next came the areas with around five per cent of aristocrats – France and the Empire; and last came the states with less than three per cent – the British Isles, Italy, the Dutch Republic and Scandinavia. Each aristocracy was not, of course, a homogeneous body. The traditional families had been augmented on a grand scale by the prodigal creation of new titles (a process known to historians as the inflation of honours). In the kingdom of Naples, there were 118 titled nobles in 1590 and 161 in 1613, but there were 271 in 1631 and 341 in 1640. In Castile, Philip III (1598–1621) created 5 new dukedoms, 42 marquisates and 63 earldoms, where before there had only been 21, 42 and 56 respectively. In England, the Stuart kings more than doubled the size of the English peerage between 1603 and 1628, from 56 to 126. Many of the new nobles of the seventeenth century were financiers who desired some of their rewards for lending money to the crown in the shape of honours: the aptly named count of Montrésor and his aristocratic colleagues (whether recently created or not) made up no less than 71 per cent of the financiers condemned in 1661–5 by the French *chambre de justice* which examined all public accounts for the 1640s and '50s. Moreover, of the 73 individuals who had advanced the largest loans to the crown (124,000,000 livres in all), 66 were noblemen. The peerage, at least in its upper échelons, was thus extremely rich.

Few were rich enough, however, to perform the traditional role of the aristocracy: going to war. The cost of fortifications put them out of noble reach; yet without them, no siege could be withstood for long – as the Protestant duke of Bouillon found when Henry IV of France advanced on Sedan in 1606. At the same time, the increase in army size during the sixteenth century made it impossible for the feudal aristocracy to raise an army which could take to the field against all-comers; and the new nobles, who alone could afford to mobilize large forces, lacked the traditional territorial base and allegiances from which to recruit.

So among the aristocracy of every state there existed a group whose wealth, at least in relative terms, was declining, whose social role was being eclipsed, and whose political influence was waning. They tended to protest vehemently when the combination of war spending and falling economic productivity led governments to impose new taxes (or to revive old ones) payable by noblemen. They argued that they were already serving the king with their persons and with their swords, so that it was unjust to ask them to pay taxes in addition; but they could not protest for too long or too loud. Many of them were deep in debt – cases are known where half an estate's income was mortgaged – and their economic survival depended upon royal favour: the grant of a lucrative royal office, or the king's permission to declare a moratorium on debt-repayments, or a government order reducing interest rates on their loans, were all essential to noble solvency. The aristocracies of Europe had invested so heavily in office and the court that their freedom of political action was severely restricted: risking the loss of royal favour was too terrible to contemplate.

Other political groups were equally reluctant to take up a radical stand against royal power, at least on a theoretical level. The arguments advanced in the earlier seventeenth century to justify disobedience or resistance to those in authority were usually unconvincing when set against the manifold passages in the Bible enjoining obedience to 'the powers that be'. The arguments in favour of papal supremacy over kings put forward by the Italian Robert Bellarmine, and the idea of justifiable tyrannicide developed by the Spaniard Juan de Mariana, were too extreme to command much support; and the contractarian theories of some Calvinist radicals were overborne by the works of their more conservative colleagues which exalted the power of rulers who were answerable only to God. Of over 1·25 million words of political theory published in the seventeenth century by the Calvinist professors at the Academies of Saumur and Sedan, scarcely one dealt with the limits to obedience: the omnipotence of sovereignty was taken for granted. The discussion was no longer about whether absolute power should exist, but about who should exercise it. 'We do but flatter ourselves,' wrote the English royalist Sir Robert Filmer in 1648, 'if we hope ever to be governed without an arbitrary [sc. absolute] power. No, we mistake. The question is not whether there shall be an arbitrary power, but the only point is, who shall have that arbitrary power, whether one or many.'[7]

The most effective defence of liberty against tyrants, whether one or many, in the seventeenth century was not radicalism but conservatism. Even statesmen like Olivares expressed approval for the conservative, neo-stoic doctrines set out by philosophers like Justus Lipsius (1547–1606), with their insistence on the need for individual resilience in politics and their rehearsal of classical maxims concerning the conservation of states. Governments embarked on innovatory policies only with extreme reluctance. They had to recognize that most members of the political nation were invincibly opposed to change, wishing rather to preserve government and society in the form in which their forefathers had enjoyed them, and expecting the state to preserve the *status quo*, no more. Governments were not expected to make new laws. It was indeed argued that the new legislation merely rediscovered old laws which had previously lain hidden: in the Holy Roman Empire, the German word used for 'judgement' was often *Rechtsfindung* (discovery of the law). Nor were governments expected to initiate new social or economic policies (except to cope with new problems such as increased vagrancy), or to impose new taxes. It was as if the revolution in government of the sixteenth century had never been. But the absolutist state could only respect these preferences of the governed in peacetime. If the wars of the twentieth century made a degree of war socialism necessary, those of the seventeenth ushered in a period of war absolutism, which was copied even by other states not directly involved in hostilities. War, which in the seventeenth century was almost as much the normal state as peace, was a major catalyst of European life and one of the hinges on which the history of the continent turned.

3. The State and War

Part of the charm of Renaissance writers is their firm conviction that they were living in a Golden Age. Their world was bigger and better than anything in the past and, they sometimes reflected, the heroes of antiquity would have been miserable failures as Renaissance men, particularly as Renaissance soldiers. 'We must confesse,' wrote Sir Roger Williams, an English general, in 1590, 'Alexander, Caesar, Scipio, and Haniball, to be the worthiest and famoust warriers that euer were; notwithstanding, assure your selfe, . . . they would neuer haue . . . conquered Countries so easilie, had they been fortified as Germanie, France, and the Low Countries . . . haue been since their daies.'[8] We may smile at this characteristic Renaissance hyperbole, but in the field of warfare at least it was fully justified: the military realities of the sixteenth century were indeed far more complex and far more daunting than those of Classical times.

European warfare had been transformed between 1450 and 1530 by four basic changes. First came the improved fortifications of which Sir Roger Williams wrote, paralleled by the introduction of powerful new firearms. The development of large siege cannon – made of cast iron from the 1380s and of bronze from the 1420s – rendered the high, thin walls of the Middle Ages quite indefensible. A brief cannonade brought them crashing down. The reason why the kingdom of Granada fell to the Christians so easily in the 1480s, when it had resisted them successfully for seven centuries, lay in the fact that Ferdinand and Isabella were able to bring a train of almost 180 siege guns against the Moorish strongholds. The English possessions in France were likewise reconquered in the 1430s and 1440s largely by Charles VII's artillery; at Castillon, in 1453, the big guns even won a battle. Not surprisingly, by 1500 every major European state possessed a powerful artillery park for use against its neighbours or against its dissident subjects. Military architects in Italy, where siege-warfare was most common, experimented with new techniques of fortification which might withstand the more intense battery, and a combination of low, thick walls protected by arrow-shaped bastions was perfected between about 1450 and 1525. It revolutionized the entire pattern of European warfare because it soon became clear that a town protected by the new defences could not be captured by bombardment, however many of the new siege-guns were used. Instead it had to be laboriously encircled, usually with elaborate siege-works, and starved into surrender. The French military writer Fourquevaux declared in 1548 that towns whose fortifications were more than thirty years old (that is, built before the age of bastions) hardly deserved to be called fortified at all. There was therefore a scramble among the great powers to build the new-style defences wherever a risk of attack existed: in Lombardy, Hungary and the Low Countries in the sixteenth century, and in Poland, France and the Empire in the seventeenth. The fortified towns were most effective when they were set in the middle of plains or plateaux, so that they dominated the surrounding countryside and forced all enemies to concentrate their energies on reducing them. Sieges therefore came to dominate land warfare wherever bastions were built; battles became irrelevant unless they helped to determine the outcome of a siege (for example by defeating a relief column).

In naval warfare, too, the improvement in the manufacture of cannon also exercised a crucial influence. The new heavy bronze guns could deliver a broadside which would smash through the decks, rigging and crew of any enemy ship. In the states of Europe that bordered on the Atlantic, specialized warships were built which were designed to include the maximum number of guns. By the 1540s ships were carrying guns as heavy and as powerful as any they would carry until the age of steam. The 130 ships of the Spanish Armada carried 2421 cannon of all sizes, an average of 19 each; but in 1665 the Dutch navy, with 51 warships, carried 3169 guns, an average of 62 each. In the Mediterranean, too, fighting ships were equipped with increasing quantities of ordnance. Whereas the Christian galleys of the fifteenth century carried but a single 'bombard', those at the battle of Lepanto (1571) each carried one 50-pounder, two 12-pounder, two 6-pounder and six lighter cannon. But as artillery bombardment replaced ramming and boarding as the standard tactic in European naval warfare, the galley was outmanœuvred, since her guns could only be mounted in the bow and the stern and (until the invention of the gun-turret in the nineteenth century) there was no way of traversing them.

Other sorts of fire-arms also became important in Europe during the Renaissance. Very slowly, hand-guns which fired a smaller shot were developed. The Hussites had used a primitive form of arquebus in the 1420s, but this innovation was not adopted by other armies until the end of the century. From the 1550s a much larger hand-gun, the musket, was introduced; fired from a forked rest, it could kill a man at 300 paces. Such killing power was a great improvement – as the arquebus had not been – on the bow and arrow. The archer could still achieve a more rapid rate of fire than the musketeer, but his effective range was less. More important, a good archer required a lifetime of training to produce the necessary stamina and accuracy, whereas a musketeer could be trained in a week. There was therefore no limit except the availability of weapons upon the number of musketeers which might be recruited at short notice and sent into action. The same was true of the other common infantryman of early modern armies – the pikeman – and this easy availability of footsoldiers led to a third important change in the pattern of European warfare: the shift from cavalry- to infantry-based armies.

For most of the Middle Ages, the principal arm in any

military force was the heavy cavalry, made up of fully armed knights on horseback, three hundredweight of mounted metal apiece, moving at speed. The knights were clumsy, expensive and scarce, but they were still capable of winning great victories: Antioch (1098), Bouvines (1214) and Roosbeke (1382), for example. There were also, however, disastrous defeats, especially in the fourteenth and fifteen centuries, when it was discovered that a heavy cavalry charge could regularly be stopped either by volleys of arrows or by a forest of pikes. Later it was found that pikemen could be used offensively to charge other groups of pikemen, once the mounted knights had been impaled and disposed of. The victories of the Swiss infantry against Charles the Rash of Burgundy in the 1470s wrote the lesson large, and in the Italian wars the infantry component in every army became steadily more numerous and more decisive. Charles VIII invaded Italy in 1498 with about 18,000 men, half of them cavalry; Francis I invaded in 1525 with some 30,000 men, one-fifth of them cavalry. The number of horsemen had thus decreased both absolutely and relatively. This shift in emphasis from horse to foot was crucial for army size. Whereas there was a limit to the number of knights who could manage to equip themselves and their horses ready for a charge, there was virtually none to the number of ordinary men who could be enlisted and issued with a pike, sword and helmet. A pikeman's basic equipment cost little more than his wages for a week, and in some cases even this paltry sum could be deducted from the soldier's pay.

These three structural changes in warfare therefore permitted a fourth: a persistent and substantial increase in army size. The predominance of siege warfare made it essential to encircle towns with enormous armies of infantrymen, and the forces fielded by every European state therefore increased prodigiously, as Table 2 illustrates. What does not appear so clearly, however, is that the number of troops permanently retained by the various governments in peacetime also grew significantly. Professional standing armies – regularly mustered, organized into small units of standard size with uniform

Table 2. Increases in Military Manpower, 1470–1710

Date	*Spanish Monarchy*	*Dutch Republic*	*France*	*England*	*Sweden*	*Russia*
1470s	20,000	—	40,000	25,000	—	—
1550s	150,000	—	50,000	20,000	—	—
1590s	200,000	20,000	80,000	30,000	15,000	—
1630s	300,000	50,000	150,000	—	45,000	35,000
1650s	100,000	—	100,000	70,000	70,000	—
1670s	70,000	110,000	120,000	—	63,000	130,000
1700s	50,000	100,000	400,000	87,000	100,000	170,000

Source: G. Parker, *Spain and the Netherlands, 1559–1659* (London, 1979), 96

armament, quartered sometimes in specially constructed barracks – were maintained by many Italian states in the fifteenth century. Other states were not slow to follow. The kings of Spain kept 10,000 trained men as a permanent garrison in their Italian dominions from 1535 onwards, using them to form the core of every military undertaking from the campaigns against the Turks in the Mediterranean to the duke of Alva's march to the Netherlands in 1567 and the intervention in the Bohemian revolt in 1619–20. In the 1570s the Austrian Habsburgs introduced a similar permanent organization for their armies along the Hungarian and Croatian border with the Ottoman empire. In the 1660s even England began to support a standing army (of about 6000 men, with a further 3000 men in Scotland and 7000 in Ireland) to guarantee national defence and internal order. Each of these permanent armies required a separate network of military institutions and ancillary services: military treasuries, judicial courts, medical care (sometimes involving special teaching hospitals and permanent mobile field-surgery units) and a chaplaincy service besides the more obvious secretariat, quartermaster and victualling arrangements. The demand for military administration was a powerful stimulus to bureaucratic growth in Europe.

At length, the need for military education was also recognized. In 1606 the duke of Bouillon, a semi-independent French prince, established a military academy for Calvinist nobles at his capital, Sedan; in 1617 Count John of Nassau, also a Calvinist, opened another at his capital, Siegen; and in 1618 Landgrave Maurice of Hesse, a Lutheran, opened a third at Cassel. Ironically, the Thirty Years' War forced all these schools for soldiers to close, but a second innovation by John of Nassau survived: the drill-book. The count found that the best way to train men to use their weapons properly was to draw a series of clear pictures depicting each separate position for loading a musket (42 positions) and handling a pike (32 of them). At his direction, Jacob de Gheyn published his *Exercise of Arms* in six languages in 1607.

It is surprising that such a bellicose century did not produce more in the way of military education. Elsewhere in Europe, certain schools for the elite might provide tuition in mathematics and architecture, in view of their military usefulness; but requests for 'an academy and college to train the aristocracy in war', such as the one put forward to the French crown by the nobles of Languedoc in 1614, were refused. The only way for a potential officer to learn the art of war was to find one and to fight in it, however briefly. John Evelyn, the English diarist, was by no means unusual in spending a few days as a pikeman in the Dutch army besieging Gennep in August 1641, while on his way to a Grand Tour of France and Italy.

The reason why no further military academies were built until the eighteenth century was simple: they cost money. There came a point at which early modern governments could not afford to spend any more on war. Most of them already spent 25 per cent of their income on defence in peacetime, and this figure increased above 50 per cent, even to 80 per cent, during a war. The state had become, in effect, a military institution in its own right. And war was expensive for others besides governments. The town of Danzig, for example, spent

Figure 4. War and Peace in Europe, 1598–1650

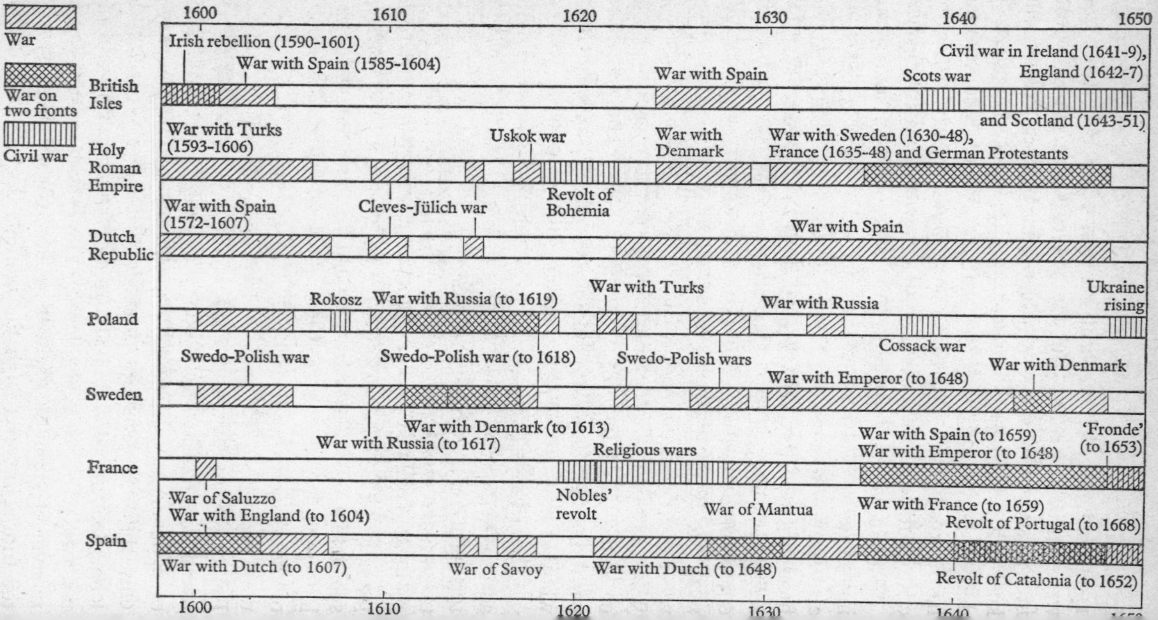

War
War on two fronts
Civil war

1600 1610 1620 1630 1640 1650

British Isles
Irish rebellion (1590-1601)
War with Spain (1585-1604)
War with Spain
Scots war
Civil war in Ireland (1641-9), England (1642-7) and Scotland (1643-51)

Holy Roman Empire
War with Turks (1593-1606)
Cleves-Jülich war
Uskok war
Revolt of Bohemia
War with Denmark
War with Sweden (1630-48), France (1635-48) and German Protestants

Dutch Republic
War with Spain (1572-1607)
Cleves-Jülich war
War with Spain

Poland
Rokosz
War with Russia (to 1619)
War with Turks
War with Russia
Cossack war
Ukraine rising

Sweden
Swedo-Polish war
Swedo-Polish war (to 1618)
Swedo-Polish wars
War with Emperor (to 1648)
War with Denmark
War with Denmark (to 1613)
War with Russia (to 1617)

France
Religious wars
War with Spain (to 1659)
War with Emperor (to 1648)
'Fronde' (to 1653)

Spain
War of Saluzzo
War with England (to 1604)
Nobles' revolt
War of Mantua
War with France (to 1659)
Revolt of Portugal (to 1668)
War with Dutch (to 1607)
War of Savoy
War with Dutch (to 1648)
Revolt of Catalonia (to 1652)

1600 1610 1620 1630 1640 1650

fourteen per cent of its income on defence between 1593 and 1598, and nineteen per cent between 1611 and 1616; both were periods of peace. But there were fewer years of peace in the seventeenth century than ever before: Poland only knew 32, France 47, England 59. Spain, if the efforts to defend her overseas pirates and interlopers are counted, hardly knew peace at all (see Figure 4). In the first half of the century there was not one complete calendar year of peace.

This increased belligerence naturally forced up state spending on defence, but the cost of fighting even short wars was also steadily rising. The general inflation of the period, with food prices rising fivefold and industrial prices threefold between 1500 and 1630, increased the expense of feeding and equipping every soldier; and the growth in army size multiplied the effect of this increase. The cost of fighting a war was fast becoming a burden that no state could bear for long. War had become, in the words of a Spanish general, 'a sort of traffic or commerce, in which he who has most money wins', in which (according to another general) 'victory goes to whoever is left with the last escudo.'

'The matter of greatest difficulty' in war, wrote an English adviser to the Dutch Republican government, 'is in proportioning the charge of the warres and the nomber of souldiers to be maynteyned with the contribucions and meanes of the countreys.' Although some aid might be received from sympathetic foreign powers (the Dutch, for example, received substantial subsidies from both France and England over a long period), most governments sought credit on the security of the yield of future taxes. Borrowing might be delayed if the Treasury was already full when war began (Henry IV of France was in this happy position in 1610) but if operations lasted for more than a few months, loans were essential. However, deficit finance was only an interim solution: there were only sufficient securities provided the war did not last too long. Bankers were only prepared to advance the yield of a tax two or three years ahead; they would seldom accept repayment from the yield of a tax four or more years in the future, however high the interest. There would come a point in a prolonged war, therefore, when the bankers were entitled to appropriate all current revenues in repayment of loans made in the past, but refused to offer any further loans for the future. Two solutions suggested themselves: to create new taxes which could be immediately offered as security for more loans, or to declare a state bankruptcy, confiscating the capital of all loans already advanced and ending all repayments from current revenue to the lenders. Both responses to penury were fraught with danger, however. In the case of a new tax, the group who became liable to pay it might launch violent protests against the new imposition, as the Paris mobs did in 1648 when the government attempted to levy a roof-tax. In the case of a state bankruptcy, the government deprived itself of the services of the financiers whose loans alone could sustain the war. There had therefore to be a reconciliation between the crown and its creditors, with the latter receiving government annuities at five, six and seven per cent in return for a promise to provide new cash loans. This technique was a particular favourite of the Spanish treasury, which declared a 'decree of bankruptcy' during our period in 1607, 1627 and 1647; but it was also used by the French government in 1599 and 1648.

Not surprisingly, with financial chaos on this scale behind them, the armies of early modern Europe were often left to fend for themselves. Indeed, they were expected to: troops were encouraged to levy contributions on their own authority from the local populations in their path; and in longer conflicts a regular contributions system was established, often administered jointly by civilian and military officials. In the principality of Lippe, in north-west Germany, the local government officers during the Thirty Years' War organized the collection of contributions to both sides: for the Swedes garrisoned at Minden and for the Imperialists based on Lemgo. Even in Franconia, where the war was more volatile and the governments less stable, local officials regularly exchanged news about troop movements and regional developments. Contemporary newsletters, carried by special messengers, contained detailed reports and informed guesses about military developments which enabled areas to accumulate money and provisions before an army arrived, and thus purchase protection.

At this level of sophistication, however, the need to raise money to finance the war began to conflict with the need to win it. Contributions and protection systems flourished, on the whole, only where armies were relatively stationary – perhaps engaged in siege warfare, perhaps encamped while they awaited the outcome of negotiations – and therefore in need of long-term material support from the same area. On the move, most commanders in the seventeenth century preferred destruction to exploitation. Gustavus Adolphus, Montrose and Turenne, whenever they were in enemy territory, destroyed everything and killed everyone that they could find. No exemptions were allowed. Even in the 'gentlemanly' English Civil War, so often contrasted with the barbarous Thirty Years' War, there were several massacres, while local attempts to negotiate a truce (as in Lancashire, 1642) or to achieve neutrality (as in Cheshire at the same time) were overruled.

Armies had become states within states, societies with their own rhythms of birth, marriage and death, organisms with their own identity and motivation. The self-sufficient military world portrayed in the novels of Hans Jakob Christoffel von Grimmelshausen, in which civilians appear almost as visitors from outer space, was created by the imperfect development of the early modern state: strong enough to create a mighty army, it was still too poor to finance it and too weak to control it. The prototypes of Mother Courage and Simplicissimus were created not by novelists but by politicians.

CHAPTER III

The Time of Troubles in the East, 1593–1618

1. The Austrian Habsburgs and the Turks

Although the year 1598 makes a good dividing line in the history of western Europe – with the death of Philip II, the peace of Vervins, the edict of Nantes and the creation of the archdukes' state (see pages 131–9) – it makes little sense farther east. A far more important date was 1593, with the outbreak of the long Turkish war in Hungary between the Turks and the Habsburgs.

Neither side was anxious to fight. The Holy Roman Emperor, Rudolf II, was more concerned to pursue his study of alchemy and magic than to direct a war, and the forces of his Spanish uncle, Philip II, were fully committed in the struggle against England, the Dutch and the French. In November 1590 both Emperor and Sultan had been glad to renew the treaty of 1547 which preserved peace in Hungary and provided for a regular annual subsidy to the Ottoman treasury. Rudolf even increased the tribute by adding personal pensions for the Sultan's leading advisers – perhaps because he feared Ottoman imperialism would recommence in the west now that the Sultan had defeated Persia and secured (by a peace signed on 21 March 1590) booty, prestige, and possession of the rich Caucasian provinces lying between the Caspian and Black Seas.

The border between the two Empires ran from the Adriatic south of Trieste to the Tatra mountains south of Krakow, crossing the Great Hungarian Plain and all the major rivers which flow through it: Sava, Drava and Danube. At the southern end of the frontier were the Dalmatian possessions of the republic of Venice and the republic of Ragusa; at the northern end lay the large principality of Transylvania (since 1541 under nominal Ottoman suzerainty); in between lay the ancient kingdom of Hungary, divided between the two empires. It was the absence of any natural frontier similar to the great rivers which flowed through the Netherlands, or the Pyrenees which separated France and Spain, that made the border between the Habsburg and Ottoman Empires so easy to breach. The frontier floated around a series of heavily fortified towns and strongholds garrisoned both by regular troops paid by the government and by refugees from the other side fighting for booty. This defensive network, which was not unlike that of the later Roman Empire in the same area over a millenium before, provided both a buffer zone against small attacks and an early-warning system against large ones. It also provided a living for bandits, refugees and freebooters, known as *uskoks* (meaning 'refugee') on the Habsburg and *akinci* (meaning 'raider') on the Ottoman sides. It was they who began the Balkan war.

In 1591, following a series of successful raids by the uskoks, operating by land and in the Adriatic, the Turkish governor of Bosnia sent into Croatia an expedition which captured a number of Christian outposts; in 1592 a larger force returned, captured the important town of Bihać and defeated an imperial relief army. In 1593 a still larger Turkish army invaded, but this time the Habsburg relief force surprised them and thousands of Turks were drowned in the River Kulpa as they fled. Both sides now prepared for war in earnest, the Emperor seeking allies as well as raising troops. In the west he persuaded the Pope to mobilize and pay for an army of 11,000 men, with the aid of which (and a little money from Philip II) the Christians captured the fortress of Gran on the Danube, the key to the Ottoman defensive system in central Hungary. In the east, envoys from the Emperor and the Pope persuaded the three semi-autonomous princes of the Balkans normally under Turkish control – Aron of Moldavia, Michael the Brave of Wallachia, and Sigismund Báthory of Transylvania – to join them. In October 1595

Figure 5. South-eastern Europe, *circa* 1600

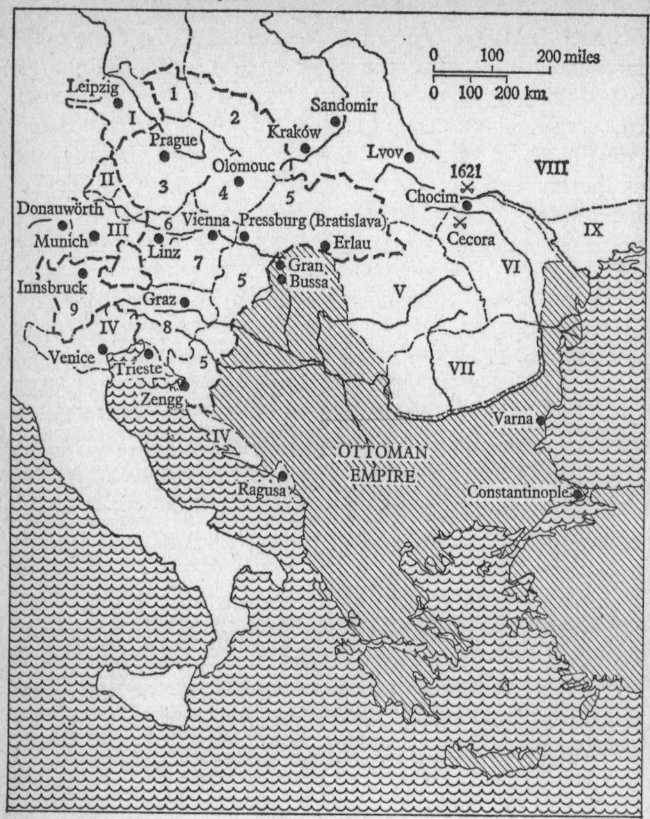

---- Habsburg lands

Ottoman direct rule

Non-Habsburg lands

I Saxony
II Upper Palatinate
III Bavaria
IV Venetian Republic
V Transylvania
VI Moldavia
VII Wallachia
VIII Poland
IX Tatars

Habsburg lands

1 Lusatia
2 Silesia
3 Bohemia
4 Moravia
5 Hungary
6 Upper Austria
7 Lower Austria
8 Inner Austria
9 Tyrol

Michael the Brave, who ruled the richest of the three provinces and was the most open in his support for the Habsburgs, routed an Ottoman army sent against him and thereby encouraged other Balkan groups to defy their Turkish masters (see Figure 5). Michael, who spoke and wrote Greek, posed as the champion of Greek Orthodoxy as well as of Balkan independence in order to win support, and his rebellion presented the first serious threat to Ottoman control of the Balkans for almost two centuries.

These reverses were an inauspicious beginning to the reign of Sultan Mohammed III (1595–1603), one of the 130 sons of Murat III (who also sired uncounted daughters by his 40 concubines). Nevertheless, Mohammed acted with decision: at his accession, he had all his nineteen surviving brothers and over twenty of his sisters strangled (an engaging family custom of the Ottoman dynasty), and he prepared to lead an army into Hungary in person. The magnitude of this undertaking must not be forgotten: it took 30 days for a courier to travel the 500 miles from Istanbul to Belgrade, gateway to Hungary; an army of 100,000 men took twice as long. That, however, was the easiest part of the journey: the route was kept in good repair and was defended by a chain of small forts. Beyond Belgrade, where the troops from the Balkan provinces of the Empire would join the levies from Anatolia and the Arab lands, the route had to be laid out specially (marked by wooden stakes or stone cairns) and pontoon bridges had to be assembled (sometimes from prefabricated sections). The army was accompanied by great herds of sheep and cattle for meat, and oxen, buffalo, camels, mules and draught-horses were used to pull guns, supplies and baggage-wagons. (Some of the animals were specially bred for military use under government supervision; similarly the cultivation of rice in the Balkans, for instance along the Rivers Maritsa and Vardar, was given official encouragement because beef or lamb pilaff formed the staple diet of the Ottoman soldier.)

It was the capacity for detailed forward planning which enabled Mohammed III, in 1596, to assemble in Hungary an army of 100,000 men, which first captured the important stronghold of Erlau, cutting communications between Austria and Transylvania, and then defeated the main Habsburg army, in spite of Italian and Spanish support, at a great battle near Erlau, at Mezo Keresztes (26 October). Although some western observers had criticized the traditional Ottoman tactics, with the Sultan and his janissaries in a fortified laager at the centre and the heavy cavalry on the wings, overwhelming numerical superiority coupled with courage and training were quite enough to overcome Christian opposition.

After the campaign, the victorious Sultan returned home to his harem, but kept a watchful eye on the Balkans, where the rebellion of the princes was beginning to disrupt the supply of Rumanian grain to Istanbul. Luckily for the Turks, Michael the Brave and his allies soon fell out. Early in 1599 Andreas Báthory, raised in Poland, succeeded his cousin Sigismund as prince of Transylvania. Immediately he took steps to reverse the foreign policy of his country: the Emperor and the Balkan princes were cast aside, and an alliance was sought with Poland (the two countries had been united under Sigismund's uncle Stephen Báthory, from 1576 until 1586). Frustrated, Rudolf II authorized Michael the Brave to invade Transylvania and depose Andreas, which he did on 1 November 1599; but Michael exceeded his instructions and overran Moldavia too, in 1600, proclaiming himself ruler of all three states and attempting to unite them into a single, independent realm. None of his neighbours wanted this: Poland, cheated of her alliance, invaded Transylvania while the Turks attacked Wallachia. In desperation, Michael offered his submission to the emperor, and helped the imperial army to drive the Poles out of Transylvania (battle of Guruslau, 3 August 1601); but a week later the imperial commander, fearing Michael's ambitions for a separate state, had him murdered. These events, although confusing, were of critical importance for south-eastern Europe, for they delivered the Balkans into Turkish hands until the nineteenth century. The three principalities all returned to Ottoman obedience, and rulers favourable to Istanbul were installed in the course of 1601 and 1602.

The long Turkish war dragged on until November 1606, but neither of the belligerents had much stomach for the fight. The Turkish captures of Pest (1604) and Gran (1605) were not followed up, for the cost of the Sultan's armies, now made up largely of salaried infantrymen (the janissaries), was a serious drain on his resources. In addition, under the leadership of Shah Abbas the Great (1587–1629), the Persians in 1603–5 reconquered the Caucasus region and drove the Ottoman frontier back into Anatolia, making a war on the Persian front unavoidable (the Turks lost: by 1612, when peace was made, most of Mesopotamia was in Persian hands). Finally, the strain of unsuccessful war produced a wave of revolts, known as the Celali uprisings, among an important part of the traditional ruling elite – the *ulama* – who felt that the Sultan's harem had deprived them of political and religious influence. From 1596 they secured the support of many mutinous troops and penurious religious students (both army and universities were starved of public funds), and for a time in 1603 the rebels gained control of the capital. They remained a force to be reckoned with until at least 1608.

The Emperor Rudolf also had his problems. The 'Holy Roman Empire of the German Nation' was made up of about 1000 separate territories, of which about 300 were important. By 1600, some of these states were very large (the Protestant electorates of Saxony and Brandenburg and the Catholic duchy of Bavaria all had one million or more inhabitants – equal to the populations of Scotland and Sweden); others were of moderate size (including Württemberg, Hesse, the Rhine Palatinate and the clerical electorate of Trier, all with around 400,000 people); but the majority were small (especially the Imperial Free Cities, only five of which had more than 30,000 inhabitants). There was some fluidity in this congeries of states. On the one hand there was fragmentation (Hesse, Saxony and many other areas being divided); on the other there was amalgamation (Brandenburg and

Prussia were linked in 1618, Cleves and Mark were added in 1614, eastern Pomerania in 1648). Furthermore, two families dominated, between them, almost half the Empire: the Habsburgs with the compact bloc of territories in the south-east and a string of lands in Swabia and Alsace; and the Wittelsbachs with Bavaria, the Upper and Lower Palatinates, and the ecclesiastical lands of Cologne and Münster (although the branches of the family did not usually see eye to eye).

Beneath the complex political structure of Germany lived some fifteen million people (excluding the population of the Habsburg provinces), and the number was rising fast. The political arithmeticians of the day, led by Hermann Conring of Helmstedt (1606–83, political adviser to Sweden, Wolfenbüttel and Denmark), pointed to the rapid reclamation of land and the recolonization of deserted villages and crofts in most areas of Germany in the years before 1618, while a host of textbooks appeared on land improvement and better husbandry. Some of these were merely translations of earlier Classical, French or Italian treatises, but in 1593 the first of 200 or so native German books of husbandry was published. These works reflected not only improvements in agriculture, but also the desire to make improvement regular and more general. Economic growth was registered in other sectors. Trade by land and water increased; production of minerals, textiles (especially linen), metals and other goods grew; new banks were founded (including the public banks of Hamburg in 1619 and Nuremberg in 1621). There were of course some areas where prosperity was not so evident in 1600 as it once had been – for instance in the Rhineland – but in an area as vast as the Empire it was inevitable that some areas should not have been burgeoning at any one time. The overall impression of German economic life in the early seventeenth century, however, is one of prosperity and expansion.

Although there was thus nothing ineluctable about the general economic collapse of Germany after 1618, a political and religious confrontation was far more predictable. The long Turkish war had led to a crisis of authority between the Emperor and his subjects on several levels. To take the religious issue first, the Protestants had used the threat of Turkish attack to extract religious concessions from the Emperor. This was an almost standard procedure: since the 1520s, every Ottoman thrust up the Danube valley had allowed the Protestants to sell their military and financial support for a campaign against the Turks in return for guarantees of religious toleration. As Leopold von Ranke pointed out long ago: without the Turkish threat, German Protestantism would scarcely have survived.[1] The requests for military aid during the war of 1593–1606 were no different in this respect. Both Calvinist and Lutheran princes used the Emperor's need in order to consolidate their religious position. The Calvinists failed, however, to secure political recognition for their creed, which had not been guaranteed by the peace of Augsburg of 1555 (since at that time there were no Calvinist princes of consequence in the Imperial Diet).[2] This failure was of some importance, since the Catholic princes had become more self-confident. Their attempt to have Calvinism outlawed at the imperial Diet of 1566 had proved a miserable failure, but in defeat they found unity and at later Diets they began to act as a party with a programme: they sought to halt the secularization of church lands by Protestant lords, and generally to reduce Protestant influence in the Empire. Since the Catholics commanded a numerical majority in the two most important imperial institutions – the Diet (*Reichstag*) and supreme court (*Reichskammergericht*) – once they acted in concert there was no constitutional way in which the Protestants could defend their interests. In 1601 they therefore ceased to accept the decisions of the supreme court in ecclesiastical disputes. In 1603, the Protestants demanded equal representation with the Catholics in both the Diet and the supreme court; and when this demand was refused a second time, in 1608, the Calvinists walked out of the Diet, followed by some Lutheran supporters.

The Protestants were alarmed not only by their lack of constitutional protection, but also by a clear indication that guarantees were more necessary than ever. In 1607 the

Catholic inhabitants of the imperial free city of Donauwörth complained to the Emperor that they were being harassed in the exercise of their religion by the Protestant majority. The Emperor, after some delay, charged the neighbouring Catholic duke of Bavaria to protect the oppressed Catholic minority, which he did in December 1607 by occupying the city with an army (later the Protestants were expelled and the city was annexed to Bavaria). Duke Maximilian I was one of the ablest rulers of his day. He dedicated his life to the aggrandizement of his state and his religion and he pursued these goals with skill and determination. He never seems to have relaxed, even in his devotions (which took up three hours of every day); the rest of his time was divided between sleeping, eating and working. His duchy was quite large (11,000 square miles and one million subjects) and Maximilian supervised the administration personally in order to derive the greatest profit from it. 'Finance is a delicate matter', he wrote in his political testament of 1651, 'and the prince alone must know its secrets.' Between 1598 and 1618, Maximilian was able, by frugality and firmness, to accumulate a personal fortune of perhaps 5 million florins (or about £830,000 sterling). It was this combination of liquid assets and strength of purpose that made Maximilian such a formidable figure in European politics. Unlike most of his fellow-rulers, he had money to put where his mouth was.

The occupation of Donauwörth led to a hardening of the religious divisions of Europe. Bavaria's action clearly violated the constitution of the Empire, yet the emperor appeared to tolerate it and the Catholics openly celebrated it. The German supporters of the Roman church looked increasingly to Munich for leadership and inspiration, and the court of Maximilian became a haven for Catholic intellectuals, like the polemical writer Adam Contzen, SJ (1571–1635) who in 1624 became the duke's confessor and kept his superiors in weekly touch with the state of the devout duke's conscience.

More immediately, the events at Donauwörth provoked the formation of two rival confessional alliances in the Empire. After the Diet of 1608, at which the imperial commissioner had been the ultra-Catholic Archduke Ferdinand, the Calvinist princes (concerned about their anomalous position in Germany) reached an agreement with the Lutheran cities of South Germany (fearful of another attack by their Bavarian neighbour): the Evangelical Union was signed on 16 May 1608. It soon included nine princes and seventeen imperial cities; but effective control lay in the hands of its director, the Elector Palatine Frederick IV, and its military commander Christian of Anhalt (an important adviser of the elector and his lieutenant in the Upper Palatinate). The formation of a Protestant alliance provoked the Catholics of the Empire to follow suit. The Catholic League of Landsberg, formed in 1556, had been dissolved in 1599 largely because Maximilian found that Bavaria was financing the association almost single-handed. Talks with other Catholic princes at the Diets of 1603 and 1608 about reviving the league always broke down over the financial issue, but in 1609 Maximilian exploited the Protestants' Union to reach an agreement with the leading prelates of southern Germany over the formation of a new league with an army of 25,000 men, to be paid for by all members. The act forming the Catholic League was signed at Munich on 10 July 1609, with Maximilian as director, and Jean t'Serclaes, baron Tilly, as military commander. At first the Rhineland prelates stood aloof, but the Cleve-Jülich crisis (pages 125–7 below) soon persuaded them to join: the three electors (Cologne, Mainz and Trier) signed on 30 July 1610 and before long, Maximilian could count on the support of twenty territorial rulers, while Philip III of Spain accepted the position of Protector to the League, and began to send subsidies.

The Protestant Union also sought foreign support. The deaths of Henry IV of France and Frederick IV, in May and September 1610, cleared the way for an agreement between the new elector, Frederick V, and James I of England. In the summer of 1610 negotiations began both for an alliance between England and the Union, and for a marriage between Frederick V and James's daughter Elizabeth: the first was achieved in April 1612, the second in February 1613.[8] These moves were popular with many political groups in Europe, since they were 'knitting knots' (in the phrase of Sir Henry Wotton) between the various enemies of the Habsburgs. Wotton himself stayed at Heidelberg, capital of the Palatinate, on his way to a second embassy in Venice for James I, and he encouraged contacts between the Venetian opponents of Habsburg imperialism and Frederick's adviser Christian of Anhalt. The Dutch Republic, increasingly dominated by Frederick's uncle Maurice of Nassau, signed a treaty of alliance with the Union in May 1613. There were also cultural contacts between the Hague, Heidelberg and London. The Dutch scholar Janus Gruter became the Palatine librarian; works by English alchemists such as Robert Fludd were printed in the Palatinate; and it has been suggested that a sort of alternative culture, based on the notions of the Rosicrucians (a group of scholars who believed that alchemy would yield the key to nature's power), bound scholars in the three capitals together. But it needed more than a 'Rosicrucian Enlightenment' to make the Evangelical Union into a significant force in European politics. If it were to force the Emperor to make concessions, the Union needed to threaten the Habsburgs' control over their patrimonial provinces, for it was upon them, and their resources, that the imperial position truly rested.

The Habsburg lands were made up of many separate territories, most of which had retained their own institutions and, until 1619, their own ruler. In 1598 there were four different Habsburg courts in the family's provinces: Lower Austria (capital Vienna) and Upper Austria (capital Linz), ruled by Archduke Matthias; 'Inner Austria' (Styria, Carinthia and Carniola, capital Graz), ruled by Archduke Ferdinand; Tyrol and its Swabian appendages (capital Innsbruck), ruled after 1602 by Archduke Maximilian; and Bohemia and its allied lands of Moravia, Silesia and Lusatia (ruled from Prague) with north-western Hungary (ruled from Bratislava), under the direct government of the Emperor Rudolf. Relations between the four courts were strained. Although on the surface the seniority of Rudolf was recognized – 'I humbly and completely bow myself before Your Majesty's gracious and sovereign will, to deal with me as may be pleasing,' grovelled the Archduke Maximilian on one occasion[4] – in practice they frequently disregarded or disobeyed his wishes, especially after 1600 when the Emperor spent more and more time in seclusion. The Spanish ambassador did not manage to set eyes on Rudolf at all for two years (1607–8) and rumours that the Emperor was dead, although exaggerated, proved hard to combat. There were periods of diligence (the journals of his Bohemian chief minister, Lobkovic, record frequent audiences with Rudolf) but they were rendered worthless by the Emperor's inability either to decide or to delegate. In particular he refused to delegate to his closest male relative (and probable successor), his brother Matthias (see Table 3).

Relations between the brothers had never been good. They did not grow up together (Rudolf spent the years 1564–71 in Spain) and no sooner had Rudolf mounted the throne in 1576 than Matthias defied his brother's command and went to the Netherlands to become the nominal leader of the rebellion against Philip II.[5] When he escaped from the 'Netherlands labyrinth' (as he called it) in 1581, he retained some of his Protestant advisers to assist him in the government of Upper Austria, to which Rudolf appointed him, and he refused imperial requests to dismiss them. In 1586–7 he again ignored the Emperor's express command when he embarked on a tour of Protestant Europe, visiting Nuremberg, Hamburg, Copenhagen and parts of Poland. This flirtation with international Protestantism contrasted sharply with the behaviour of some other members of the House of Habsburg. In Inner Austria, the Archduke Ferdinand decreed the expulsion of all non-noble Protestants in his lands (about 10,000 were forced to leave) and the public burning of their books. At the same time (August 1599), in a rare burst of political activity, Rudolf dismissed a number of his senior advisers and replaced them with a group of younger men, most of whom favoured absolutism in politics and Counter-Reformation Catholicism in religion. The group, led by Zdenek Lobkovic (promoted Grand Chancellor of Bohemia) and Franz von

Table 3. The House of Habsburg, 1550–1650

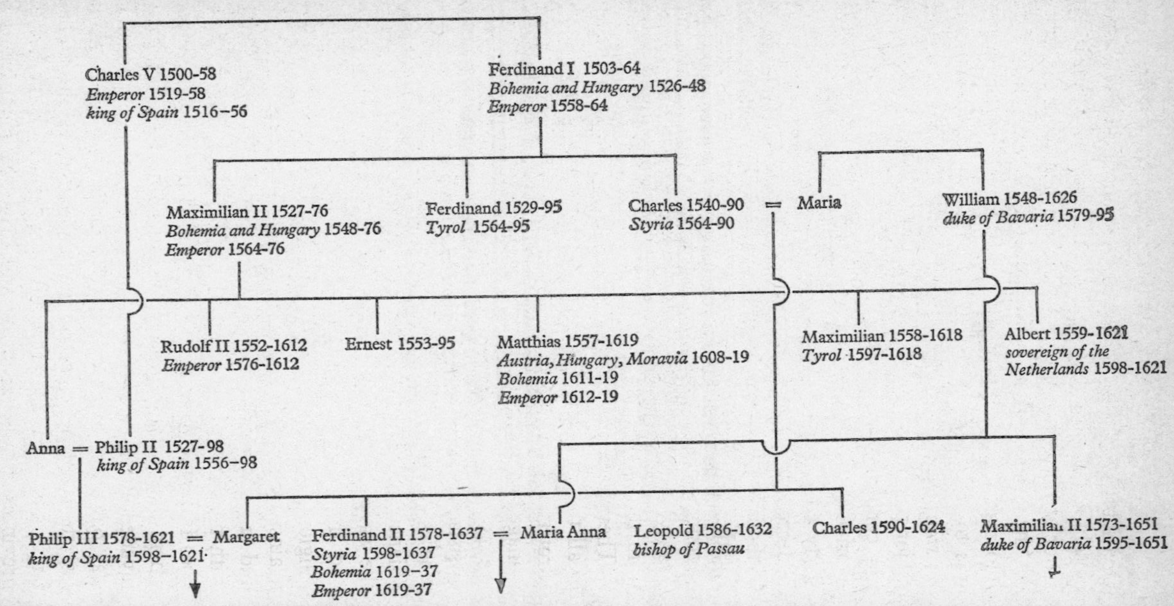

Dietrichstein (elected bishop of Olomouc in Moravia), became closely allied with the papal nuncio and the Spanish ambassador at the imperial court, which earned them the sobriquet of 'the Spanish party'. For about four years they directed imperial policy. One of their first moves, in October 1599, was to set in action the special tribunal (*Reformationskommission*) established in Upper Austria in the wake of the major peasant revolt of 1595–7. But instead of merely effecting compromises between lords and peasants, it began to deprive Protestants of lands and offices. In 1602, the Spanish Party continued its assault on the Reformed churches with a decree which outlawed all worship in Bohemia except Catholicism and Utraquism (as the Hussite faith was known). At the same time, following its victory over the Polish opponents of Michael the Brave, the Habsburg army invaded Transylvania and began to confiscate property and churches from the Protestants and to indict many nobles for treason.

These were indeed rash moves in wartime, for the estates of all the Habsburg provinces were controlled by Protestants (Protestants and Hussites in Bohemia) and most of them had managed to extort formal charters from their rulers during the 1570s containing guarantees of full religious toleration. Resistance was therefore immediate and almost universal. The estates of Upper and Lower Austria formed a defensive alliance; the estates of Moravia refused to vote any taxes for the war until the unpopular religious measures were repealed; and the estates of Hungary called for help from their co-religionists in Transylvania (which was already in full revolt against Habsburg occupation) led by the former chief adviser and uncle of the Báthory princes, Stephen Bocskay. In 1605, with the Sultan's blessing and the aid of an army of desperadoes from the mountains commanded by Bethlen Gabor (of whom more later), Bocskay liberated Habsburg Hungary and invaded Bohemia. This was a threat that the Spanish Party was powerless to parry: their Catholic supporters made up less than ten per cent of the population of the Bohemian lands, and it was therefore left to the estates of the hereditary provinces to raise an army and drive the Hungarians back, while the Emperor shut himself away in his palace and refused to see anyone.

This breakdown in authority alarmed the Archdukes, who feared that the entire house of Habsburg might lose its position through Rudolf's incapacity. So in April 1605 they held a secret meeting at Linz and resolved to force the Emperor to authorize Matthias to conclude a settlement with the Hungarians and Bocskay and with the Turks, and then to recognize Matthias as his heir. Matthias acquitted himself with some distinction: although in 1605 the Turkish Grand Vizier recaptured Gran and joined forces with Bocskay, by the treaty of Vienna (23 June 1606) the Hungarians were granted complete freedom of toleration; and by the treaty of Zsitva Torok (11 November 1606), an honourable peace was made with the Turks. Bocskay was reluctantly recognized as prince of Transylvania, but his death the following month seemed to remove the only person capable of causing further disruption in the Habsburg lands.

Yet these settlements created as many problems as they solved. The toleration granted to the Protestants of Hungary excited the envy of their co-religionists in the Austrian and Bohemian lands, and they began, through the estates, to put pressure on the Emperor to grant similar concessions to them. Rudolf refused, and he also refused to make Matthias his heir. Inevitably, the two disgruntled parties were drawn together, and negotiations began between Matthias and the estates of the patrimonial provinces. In January 1608 Matthias was accepted by the Hungarian estates as their king and in April, by the treaty of Pressburg (now Bratislava), Matthias and the estates of Austria, Hungary and Moravia agreed to raise an army with which to force Rudolf to abdicate in favour of his brother. In June he did: by the treaty of Lieben, Matthias became ruler of the three provinces. But at first the Archduke showed reluctance to fulfil his side of the bargain and give fresh religious guarantees to his new Austrian subjects. He should have known better: in 1578 the estates of Upper Austria had raised a small army and refused to recognize Rudolf II until he had confirmed toleration for the Protestants; while throughout his long residence at Linz and Vienna, Matthias had witnessed the skilful management of the estates by the Protestant nobles, led latterly by George Erasmus Tschernembl (1567–1626). Now, in August 1608, the estates of Upper Austria formed a Confederation to preserve their religious freedom; in September they formed a provisional government; and in October they allied with the estates of Lower Austria and with Christian of Anhalt, the Calvinist administrator of the Upper Palatinate, who promised to send military assistance if the Confederates were attacked. This proved too much for Matthias: on 19 March 1609 he reluctantly confirmed all the religious and political liberties of his subjects.

These developments left only Bohemia, Silesia and Lusatia under the direct government of Rudolf. Their estates had stood aloof from the Pressburg Confederation, nor were they parties to the treaty of Lieben. But they too used the good offices of Christian of Anhalt, and the threat of force, to secure wide-ranging guarantees of political and religious freedom from the reluctant emperor: a 'Letter of Majesty' was signed on 9 July 1609, granting the same religious toleration to the Bohemian lands as the other hereditary provinces enjoyed under Matthias, and creating a standing committee of the estates, known as the 'Defensors', to ensure that the religious concessions were properly carried out. Perhaps it was a natural repugnance to this serious limitation on his sovereign power which led Rudolf to allow his cousin Leopold, bishop of Passau, to invade Bohemia in January 1611 with 7000 imperial troops, veterans of the Cleves-Jülich episode of the previous year. But they did not get far. As the Passauer troops occupied the suburbs of Prague, the Defensors began to raise troops themselves and called on Matthias for help. When he arrived in March, it was agreed that Rudolf should be declared incapable of governing Bohemia, deposed, and replaced by Matthias. The Archduke's troops quickly restored order to the kingdom and in May he was crowned, his coronation charter specifically confirming the 'Letter of Majesty'. Rudolf, hidden deep in his palace to avoid hearing the sounds of his brother's triumph, passed irrevocably into insanity: he died on 20 January 1612. Six months later Matthias, now 55 years old, achieved his lifelong ambition and was crowned Holy Roman Emperor.

The new Emperor was no more active or decisive than his brother, but he did delegate responsibility for the decisions that he could not be bothered to take himself. He gave wide powers to the old imperial privy council, now headed by his personal adviser, Melchior Khlesl, bishop of Vienna. But it needed more than the revitalization of the Privy Council to solve the problems facing the Empire in 1612. Matthias, like all his brothers, had no legitimate children; the Protestants still refused to bring their disputes to the imperial tribunals; and the existence of two armed religious leagues in the Empire posed a permanent threat to peace. Only the first issue – the succession problem – was settled before Matthias died in 1619. The surviving Archdukes agreed that the only possible candidates were Ferdinand of Styria and Philip III of Spain, but there was no agreement on which. From 1612 onwards, negotiations took place between the two principal parties until on 29 July 1617 the treaty of Graz was signed at Ferdinand's capital. In return for Spanish support for his claim to succeed Matthias, Ferdinand promised to cede to Spain the Habsburg lands in Alsace and the imperial fiefs of Piombino and Finale Liguria in Italy; he also recognized that a male heir of Philip III should be preferred in the Austrian succession to any female issue of his own; and he promised to send military aid to the Spaniards in Lombardy whenever asked to do so.[6]

The choice of Ferdinand was important, for the Archduke had already shown himself to be a man of determination and decision when it came to ensuring respect for the Catholic church and his own authority. Although he seems to have followed no political philosophy of absolutism, he was a fierce defender of his absolute power in both religious and secular matters: he would neither share his authority with his subjects nor abdicate his responsibilities to them. 'The prince must be subject to no one,' his spokesman informed the estates of Styria in 1600, and his views did not moderate with time. All this was known to the states of the crown of Bohemia and yet, incredibly, in July 1617 they meekly and unanimously accepted Ferdinand as their king-designate; and in December, while Matthias returned to Vienna, Ferdinand went on to Hungary to be recognized as king-designate there too.

Matthias's efforts to secure a religious peace were less successful than his dynastic achievement. In the Empire, he convoked a Diet in 1613 (the last until 1640) in the hope of restoring the authority of the imperial institutions and of persuading the Union and the League to dissolve. But neither the Protestants nor the Catholics would play. On the contrary, both alliances were strengthened. The Union, it is true, suffered some loss of prestige with the defection of the count of Neuburg (one of the claimants to Cleves-Jülich) in 1614, followed by that of the elector of Brandenburg three years later; but the able diplomats of the Palatinate (Christian of Anhalt and, to an increasing extent, Ludwig Camerarius) established ever-closer contacts with England and the Netherlands in the west and with the Habsburg provinces in the east. Of all the foreign students who came to study at Heidelberg university between 1608 and 1618, 35 per cent came from Bohemia, Hungary or Poland.

In the hereditary provinces themselves, however, the Catholics began to tighten their grip. Despite the efforts of the Protestant leaders, the Diet of all the provinces held at Prague in 1615 voted the Emperor valuable new taxes and agreed to take over the repayment of considerable public debts. The leaders of the 'Spanish party' were encouraged. They recommenced the harassment of the Protestants wherever possible (for example in Dietrichstein's diocese of Olomouc) and they increased their control over the provincial governments (of the ten governors left by Matthias to administer Bohemia during the winter of 1617–18, seven were committed Catholics). This tougher policy received strong support from an important quarter: the court of Spain, where the former Spanish ambassador to the imperial court, Don Baltasar de Zúñiga, was fast becoming the dominant figure in foreign policy. He assured the Emperor on several occasions that Spain would provide full military and financial support if it should be needed to preserve Habsburg authority. Matthias had only to ask.

2. The Vasas and their Enemies

If the Habsburgs were the dominant dynasty in western and central Europe in the late sixteenth century, then the Vasa family held an analogous position in the north and east. In 1587 Sigismund Vasa, only son of King John III of Sweden, was elected king of Poland; in 1592 he succeeded to the Swedish crown on the death of his father. The young Sigismund was heir to an extensive empire: Poland–Lithuania, merged formally in 1569 after almost two centuries of dynastic union, was the largest state in Europe except for Muscovy, covering almost one million square kilometres; Sweden, which ruled Finland and Estonia even if the southern provinces of Halland, Bleckinge and Skane remained Danish, was also of enormous size. Taken together, they stretched from the Arctic Ocean, where Swedish colonization was increasing from 1550, across both sides of the Baltic to the shores of the Black Sea, where the Don cossacks wrestled with the forces of the Crimean Tatars for control of the steppe-lands. Certainly this vast corridor of territory lacked easy access to the west – for the Danes controlled both sides of the Sound (which alone gave maritime access to Poland, Finland and most of Sweden) – but there were alternatives. A lively land trade existed between Poland and the west via Bohemia and south Germany; there was the chance of creating a viable sea route via the North Cape (the foundation of Archangel in 1584 and its growing trade showed what could be done); and there was Sweden's one North Sea port, Alvsborg, which might be developed as an entrepôt independent of Danish control. But these strengths of the Vasa Empire were overwhelmed by other considerations. In the first place, geography was against it. The distance between the White and the Black Seas was 1300 miles, which rivalled the length of imperial Spain's communication lines (and military operations were required on both fronts at times); the population of both kingdoms was sparsely spread across most of the land; and the steppe, the forests and the lakes made the exercise of power extremely difficult, even for an efficient government – and neither kingdom possessed that. Sweden had rebelled against Denmark and begun its independent existence in 1523 with no civil service or administrative structure of its own: her first king, Gustavus Vasa, had been forced in the 1530s to kidnap foreign diplomats, to advertise abroad for secretaries, and (when that failed) to write business letters himself. Admittedly matters improved after this: a council, Diet and a regular administration headed by eighteen royal secretaries had emerged by the 1590s. But the government remained very much based on the household until the reforms of 1634: its revenues were mostly collected in kind and its officials were therefore often remunerated with lands, titles and gifts – even warships in the 1580s – rather than with money. The Polish administration was somewhat better, with a longer tradition behind it, but there was still no bureaucratic organization comparable to that of France, Castile or England.

However, the greatest problem facing young Sigismund Vasa in 1592 was neither the underdeveloped economy of his dominions nor the lack of a bureaucracy: it was aristocratic constitutionalism. In both his kingdoms, the nobles claimed a prescriptive right to control and censure the executive power of the crown. In Poland, the death of the last king of the Jagiellonian dynasty in 1572 allowed the nobles to bargain with the various candidates for the succession, winning widespread constitutional and religious concessions, which were confirmed and extended by the candidates for election in 1574 and 1586–7. No taxes could be levied without the consent of the aristocratic Diet, nor could war be declared; the Diet had the constitutional right to oppose the king under certain circumstances; and, after 1589, all decisions had to be unanimous in order to be binding. The Diet, composed of 140 senators drawn from the magnates and 170 deputies drawn from the gentry, formed a closed oligarchy of about 300 families which, in effect, ran the country. Their leaders were entrusted for life with the highest offices of state, the chief of which were the hetman (or commander-in-chief) and the chancellor. The holders of these two offices were almost independent. Stanislaw Zolkiewski, hetman 1588–1620, conducted his own foreign policy during the war in Russia; Jan Zamoyski, chancellor 1578–1605, founded a vast domain centred on his beautiful new town of Zamosc, and stage-managed Sigismund's election in 1587 even to the point of defeating in battle and capturing the chief rival claimant, Archduke Maximilian of Austria.

The power of the nobles in Sweden was almost as great in the later sixteenth century. Although Gustavus Vasa had ruled until his death in 1560 with absolute authority, his son Eric XIV had been deposed in 1568 and murdered in prison in 1577; and his second son, John III, had been successfully opposed throughout the 1580s by a group of his nobles acting through the council of state. The religious position was more satisfactory. Although the doctrinal views of John III were not consistent, at least he was staunchly Protestant, and by the end of the century there were less than 250 Roman Catholics in Sweden, of whom many (like the queen, Catherine of Poland) were foreigners. The fact that his son and heir, Sigismund, had been brought up a Catholic does not seem to have worried John overmuch. His main dynastic problem was his brother Charles, who ruled a vast duchy in central Sweden where neither the secular nor the religious policies of the crown were enforced unless the duke so decreed. Tension between the king and the duke only ceased in 1590 when Charles helped his brother to overcome the councillors who had opposed him. In return the duke became the unquestioned master of Sweden until his brother died in November 1592.

The vast Vasa inheritance therefore called for a monarch of

rare gifts if it was to be held together. Alas, the twenty-six-year-old Sigismund was not such a man. His Jesuit mentors had not taught him the limits of the possible in either politics or religion. Instead, even friends noted that he was content to entrust his cause to God, since that avoided the need either to make a decision or to feel remorse for failure. His Polish subjects jested that 'Three Ts make up our king: taciturnity, tardiness and tenacity'; and indeed Sigismund was morose and often silent, given to delay in making decisions, but obstinate once he knew what he wanted. He had an artistic temperament – manifested in his painting and goldsmith work, in his 'culture tower' built at the Wawel castle in Krakow to contain his collection of Dutch and Italian art, and in his buildings (his extensions to the Warsaw palace in the style of the Escorial, his country house at Ujazdow, and his hunting lodge at Nieporet linked to the Vistula by a special canal for greater ease of access). But none of this impressed either nation of his subjects. And it certainly did not impress Duke Charles, who wished to prolong the dominant position in Sweden he had enjoyed in John III's last years. He did not yet aspire to the throne, for he respected his nephew Sigismund's legal right to rule; but he wished to be installed as regent with full powers and he was prepared to browbeat and eventually to destroy anyone who stood in his way. In the manner of Gustavus Vasa, Charles punched loyal opponents of his policies on the nose, even in full council; the disloyal ones were executed. In 1597, with the aid of the third estate in the Diet, Charles outlawed the council of regency installed by his nephew to protect his interests. An invasion led by Sigismund, for once with generous support from his Polish subjects, was defeated in 1598 and the king was declared deposed by the Swedish estates (March 1600). Charles was elected 'leader' of the kingdom (but refused to take the royal title) and set about removing all his rival's supporters from Sweden, Finland and Estonia. Only when this process was completed, in 1604, did Charles accept the crown.

The effects of the disruption within the Vasa family began

to show themselves immediately. In August 1600 Charles sent an army of 17,000 men to invade the Baltic lands of the Teutonic Order, hotly contested for over 40 years by Poland, Russia and Sweden. The Swedes had captured Estonia, with its ports of Reval and Narva, in the 1560s; Poland had secured the more southerly province of Livonia, with its port of Riga, and this Charles's forces now overran. It proved to be a serious mistake. Although the Poles would not fight to save Sweden for Sigismund, they had interests of their own in Livonia. An elite army was raised which reconquered Livonia in 1602–3, and routed Charles's army at Weissenstein in 1604 and Kirkholm in 1605 (where 7600 of the 11,000 men under Charles's personal command were slain by a mere 3400 Poles). Then, suddenly, the fighting stopped. It was not until the 1620s that the Livonian question was settled in Sweden's favour.

There were three reasons for this hiatus. First, Poland was shaken by a major rebellion; second, Sweden became involved in a costly war with Denmark; and third, both Sweden and Poland became deeply involved in the affairs of Muscovy. The Polish rebellion which began in 1606 and lasted three years, known as the *Rokosz*, constituted the immediate reason why the victory at Kirkholm was not followed up. Sigismund had made many enemies in his southern kingdom: his failure in Sweden had been expensive, as were his operations in Russia and Livonia, and the dying Chancellor Zamoyski delivered a bitter criticism of Sigismund's military and financial shortcomings in the Diet of 1605; the king's refusal to prevent Catholic attacks on Protestant churches and property in royal towns (most notably in Krakow, the capital, where riots in 1591 led to a ban on Protestant worship in the city) alarmed the Reformed communities and led in 1599 to a rapprochement between Protestant and Orthodox leaders. Finally, the king gave offence in more personal matters: his choice of foreign advisers after the death of Zamoyski, his addiction to painting and ball games, his alliance with the Habsburgs (consolidated in 1605 by his marriage to the sister of his deceased wife Constance of Styria, which many considered to be incestuous – see Table 4) were all unpopular. The Rokosz gathered strength from all these tensions. In March 1606 representatives of the Protestant and Orthodox gentry in the lower house of the Diet proposed legislation which would permit a greater degree of toleration and thus end the religious riots. These measures were accepted by the Catholic deputies, but were rejected by the king, the Catholic clergy and a group of influential Catholic magnates who called for a reduction in the power of the gentry in the Diet. The gentry responded to this challenge by calling a meeting of their own at Sandomierz, a town between Warsaw and Krakow, where they drew up a list of grievances that Sigismund was called upon to redress. The dissidents were led by a prominent Catholic, Mikolaj Zebrzydowski, military governor of Krakow, who had been personally insulted by the king and his second wife: the governor's apartments in the royal palace had been summarily requisitioned for the use of the queen's ladies-in-waiting (all of them Germans, which made matters worse), and Zebrzydowski's personal possessions had been thrown out into the street. It was behaviour like this by the king that gave strength to the rebels' cause and provoked them to demand more radical concessions (including the appointment of the principal civil servants by the Diet and the subordination of the General Diet to the provincial diets, as in the Dutch Republic).

At first Sigismund indicated a willingness to accept these demands, because support for the rebels was so strong; but he made concessions only to his Orthodox subjects, who therefore abandoned their opposition. The Protestants were offered nothing and, exasperated, early in 1607 they declared Sigismund deposed. This move, as the king had hoped, completely split the Rokosz, and in July a royal army aided by troops provided by the magnates routed the rebels. The magnates' intervention was decisive: on the one hand it ensured that the rebels were treated leniently when they surrendered, in the course of 1608 and 1609; on the other it allowed the great nobles to dominate both the crown and the Diet. The magnates and not the gentry now controlled the formation of

Table 4. The Vasa Connection, 1560–1660

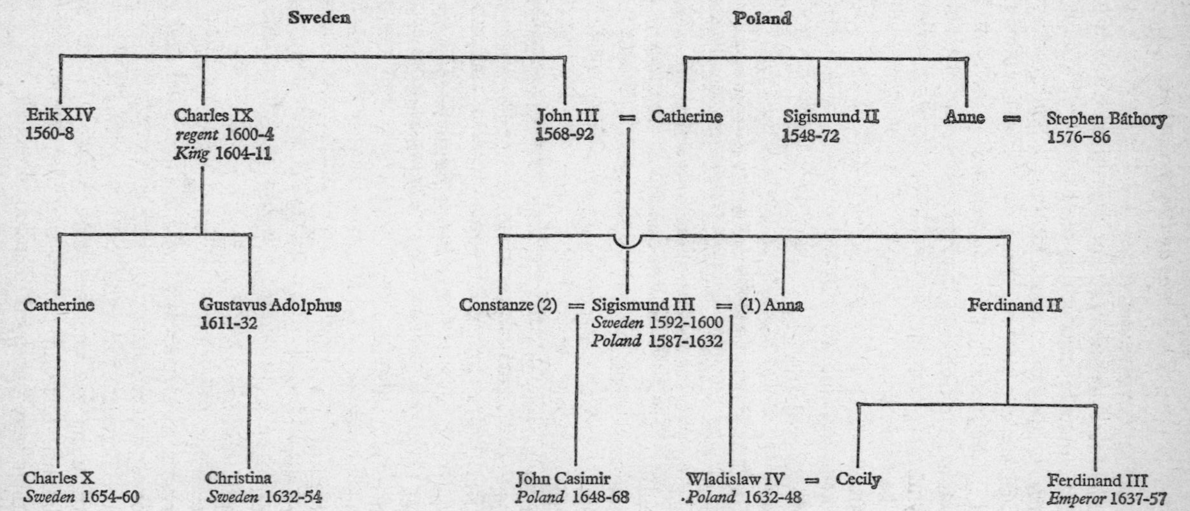

policy in all matters of state.

The Polish rebellion might have given Sweden a welcome breathing space in which to reorganize her finances, strained to the limit by the civil war and the Livonian campaign, and to remedy the military deficiencies exploited by the Poles. But a brief visit in 1601–2 by Count John II of Nassau, a noted military reformer, had not proved long enough to effect any improvements in the Swedish army. But Charles IX chose to keep his forces in a state of permanent readiness; the anarchy in Russia following the death of Tsar Boris Godunov in 1605 encouraged him to maintain an army in Estonia and, in 1609, to send an expeditionary force into Muscovy. But, just at this moment, he became involved in another major war in the west, with Denmark.

Relations between Denmark and Sweden had been bad from the uprising of 1523, led by Gustavus Vasa against Danish overlordship, until the treaty of Stettin in 1570.[7] There was a generation of peace after this, with any minor disputes settled by joint frontier meetings of Swedish and Danish negotiators. Around 1600, there were still only two main disagreements. The first was caused by Sweden's campaigns in Livonia, which involved the blockade of the port of Riga. This caused trouble because the Danish crown, by virtue of its control of the Sound and its exaction of heavy dues from all ships passing through, was anxious to check all piracy and interference with free trade in the Baltic, lest it frighten foreign shippers away; and also because Denmark owned the island of Osel, just off the gulf of Riga, so that foreign ships on their way to and from Riga often took refuge there from Swedish attack, leading to frequent violations of Danish territorial waters. The other area of conflict lay along the Arctic fringe of Scandinavia, where colonists and civil servants from Denmark (which since 1380 had also ruled Norway) were competing with an increasing Swedish presence. Between 1606 and 1609 in particular, new Swedish settlements and churches were founded in the Far North, administrators and pastors were dispatched, and communications were improved. Tension mounted.

Yet the existing machinery of arbitration should have been able to resolve these problems easily. That it did not was due to the personality of the two kings: Charles IX and Christian IV. The aristocracy of Denmark enjoyed precisely that position of power to which their Swedish counterparts had unsuccessfully aspired in the 1580s: they had made their monarchy elective and had imposed severe restraints upon the sovereign's freedom of action. The rapid growth in the country's prosperity, especially through the burgeoning export of cattle (up to 40,000 head were exported annually by land between 1596 and 1625), gave the leading nobles enormous financial power. The country's 500 or so aristocratic families owned almost half the land of Denmark. More than four-fifths of them were able to live comfortably on their landed income, and from this position of economic resilience the great families were able to keep their king under control. But ever since his accession in 1596 Christian had striven to improve his subordinate role. He pursued an active foreign policy, buying up lands in North Germany, subsidizing his neighbours there, and maintaining close contacts with his brother-in-law James I (whom he visited in 1606). Christian actively participated in economic ventures, often providing the necessary capital (and building up a large personal fortune therefrom), and he took a personal interest in every aspect of government, especially when it afforded opportunities for profit, such as the exploitation of the Arctic lands of his crown. He made a voyage to the North Cape himself in 1599, and observed that it might be possible for large convoys of foreign merchant ships to sail to the White Sea and thus avoid paying the Sound tolls which, as the personal prerogative revenue of the monarch, constituted the best guarantee of his political independence. (In fact Christian's fears were misplaced: in each of the early years of the seventeenth century, over 2000 ships entered the Baltic but only about 20 ships reached Archangel.)

Sweden's policies in the Baltic and in Lappland therefore threatened Christian personally: he could not afford to ignore them. In 1603, in 1604 and in 1610 he tried unsuccessfully to persuade his council to regard Swedish aggression as a *casus belli*, but in the last year the council did agree to appeal to the Swedish estates to repudiate the aggressive policies of their sovereign. Although in December Charles's own council reminded him that, on top of hostilities in Russia, a war with Denmark would be 'intolerable, indeed impossible to endure', the old king paid no heed. Despite suffering a severe stroke in August 1609, he clung grimly on to power, threatening to abdicate unless the council and estates endorsed his foreign policy. Until the very outbreak of war he believed that the Danish council, international opinion or Protestant solidarity would restrain Christian, and allow Sweden to get away with her provocative policies. He was wrong.

On 4 April 1611 Denmark declared war and began immediate hostilities. Within a few weeks Kalmar, the most important stronghold in Sweden, had fallen to Christian, and in October Charles, a broken old man of sixty-three, died. He left to his elder son, Gustavus Adolphus, a kingdom assailed from without and disintegrating from within. Charles had managed to alienate all his former supporters with his unsuccessful yet expensive policies and his arbitrary yet capricious ways. He had scarcely consulted his council during the last two years of his reign, ruling instead through his household officers. But in 1609 a young nobleman, Axel Oxenstierna (1583–1654), entered the council and, through his own efforts and those of his relatives already there, he began to formulate a policy to follow when King Charles should die. The council, supported by the estates, were fortunate that Gustavus was only seventeen, because the Swedish constitution declared that he might not take full control until the age of twenty-four. Explicit guarantees could therefore be imposed on the new king in return for admitting him to his kingdom: the clergy obtained an assurance that Lutheranism would be Sweden's only religion (which Charles, with his Calvinist leanings, had questioned) and a promise that they could be self-governing; the nobles were granted widespread social privileges and a dominant position in the government; subjects at large were guaranteed sound justice. All these points were included in the accession charter of Gustavus Adolphus, sworn on 31 December 1611, and the new council, guided by Oxenstierna, began to direct a spirited defence against the Danish invasion. It was too late to expect success, unless preventing further Danish advance could be deemed a success; and in the autumn of 1612 Sweden was glad to accept an offer from the Dutch Republic to arrange negotiations. She offered to renounce all her pretensions in the Baltic and the Arctic and promised to pay a large war indemnity. These terms were accepted by Denmark in January 1613 at the peace of Knared, and until the indemnity was paid, the city of Alvsborg, Sweden's only North Sea port, was surrendered. It was only returned in January 1619 upon payment of 1,000,000 rixdollars (£200,000 sterling) to Christian personally.

Raising the taxes and loans for the Alvsborg ransom provoked unrest in Sweden: there were popular revolts in the provinces of Dalarna (1613) and Vastbo (1617) and there was resistance to the new taxes by many towns and nobles (even the queen mother refused to pay). A handful of domestic reforms – a Judicial Ordinance in 1614 improved the legal system; the procedure of the Diet was streamlined by another ordinance in 1617 – did little to appease the discontented, for Sweden's commitment in Russia continued to necessitate expensive military campaigns until 1617. Gustavus also had to face the constant threat of a new attempt by Sigismund to recover his inheritance. Over 400 Swedish exiles still resided in Poland, hoping for the restoration of a Catholic king: Gustavus could never afford to neglect the threat of a new invasion or a *coup*, and he anxiously made alliances with the Dutch Republic (1614), with the German Protestant Union (1615) and even with Denmark (1619). But none of these diplomatic successes would have been adequate if Sigismund had actually invaded again, as he had in 1598: few would have fought to the death for the young Gustavus or the memory of his choleric, autocratic father. The junior branch of the house of Vasa was saved not by its own efforts, but by Poland's involvement in Russia.

3. *The Rape of Russia*

The peculiar policies of Ivan the Terrible, Tsar of Muscovy from 1533 to 1584, according to an English observer in Moscow, Jerome Horsey, had bred 'a generall hatred, distreccion, fear and discontentement throw his kyngdom . . . God has a great plague in store for this people.' Ivan had destroyed many of the ancient aristocratic (*boyar*) families of Muscovy and he had deliberately purged the northern and central areas of his opponents, banishing them to the borders and creating a separate state (*oprichnina*) at the centre. But he had then forced further flight from this central core by the taxes and conscription imposed upon it for the war in Livonia after 1561: whole villages were depopulated, great estates were ruined. Perhaps half the land in central Muscovy was totally abandoned, and a further 40 per cent was too sparsely populated to merit a tax assessment by the 1590s. The tax paid by the average gentleman's estate rose from 8 roubles in the early sixteenth century to 42 in the middle and 151 by the end. Small wonder that so many nobles and peasants preferred to try their fortunes in the 'new lands' to the south and east. And of the dogged survivors, Giles Fletcher wrote prophetically in 1591: the Tsar's 'tyrannous practice . . . hath so troubled that countrey, and filled it so full of grudge and mortall hatred ever since, that it wil not be quenched (as it seemeth now) till it burne again into a civill flame . . . The desperate state of things at home, maketh the people for the most part to wishe for some forreine invasion which they suppose to bee the onely meanes to rid them of the heavy yoke of this tyrannous government.'[8] Such defeatism can only have been strengthened by the disastrous crop failures from 1601 to 1604, when the price of grain rose fifteenfold, the capital starved and peasants drowned themselves in the swamps. Even more refugees fled to the borderlands of the Muscovite state to join the boyars and other exiles who nursed potent grievances against the central government.

That the Muscovite state survived intact for two decades after Ivan's death was due largely to the ability of his son-in-law Boris Godunov. From 1585 he was the leading member of the regency council of Ivan's simple-minded son and successor, Fedor; in 1591 he was made chief adviser, with the right to correspond directly with foreign governments; and when Fedor died in 1598, he was elected Tsar himself. Boris followed a policy of disengagement from the Baltic, securing a peace with Poland in 1587 and with Sweden in 1595, and he took steps to secure the southern and eastern frontiers of Muscovy. After defeating an attack on Moscow by the Crimean Tatars in 1591, the government began to build a network of fortified towns along the middle Volga (Samara 1585, Tsaritsyn 1588, Saratov 1590) and the Don (Voronezh 1586, Elets 1592). In 1598 Boris led in person a campaign against the Tatars. These were sound measures, although they did not offer total security to the inhabitants of southern Russia (in the first half of the seventeenth century at least 200,000 Russians were captured in Tatar raids and most were sold at Kaffa as slaves to Ottoman merchants or galley-captains). Farther east, the Stroganov family had begun in the 1560s to send expeditions from their mining base at Perm to explore the lands beyond the Urals for iron ores and salt. At first they merely traded for the abundant furs accumulated by the local inhabitants of Siberia, but in the 1580s the Stroganov adventurers began to go fur-trapping themselves, establishing fortified towns, which the government supplied with a garrison and colonists (some of them deported criminals). By 1610, about 200,000 sable furs a year were reaching Muscovy from Siberia, and this prosperity encouraged the Moscow government to send adequate resources to suppress a serious Tatar rebellion in 1606–8 and to defeat sundry invasions of Siberia by Kalmuk tribesmen from the steppe. By 1622 there were some 23,000 Russian colonists east of the Urals.

The continuity of the fur rush in Siberia throughout the early decades of the seventeenth century is most remarkable, since the Muscovite state on whom the colonists depended for defence all but collapsed. The 'great trouble' (*Smuta*) in Muscovy began in the first famine-year, 1601, with the discovery of a conspiracy against Boris by the Romanov family whose leader, Fedor, was the cousin of Tsar Fedor and had been a popular candidate for election as Tsar in 1598. After the plot, Fedor was forced to take monastic vows (to prevent him from ever becoming Tsar: his monastic name was Filaret); the other Romanovs were deported and their lands confiscated. As the harvest failures continued, in September 1603 there was an important popular revolt by peasants and serfs from the south. It was defeated in a pitched battle near the capital, but the survivors retired to the south and soon joined another popular leader, the False Dimitri.

At least twenty persons claimed to be Dimitri, the lost brother of Tsar Fedor (who actually died in 1591) in the decade following 1604, and all of them managed to convince some people of the truth of their claim. Muscovy had been ruled by the direct descendants of Rurik for more than seven centuries and the members of that house were popularly thought to possess supernatural powers and an authority that merely elected Tsars could not match. The natural disasters of 1601–3 were seen by some as proof that Boris did not have the mandate of heaven to rule and that only the restoration of a male *Rurik* would bring peace and prosperity back to Russia. Any False Dimitri thus held certain natural advantages, and the existence of the discontented boyars, cossacks and other refugees in the south-west offered a task-force with which to translate sympathy into action. In addition, the first False Dimitri enjoyed the support of many of the magnates of Lithuania (where he had lived at least since 1601). They provided him with an army of 3500 men in October 1604 when the Pretender entered Muscovy. At first he met with success, defeating a royal army at Novgorod, but in January 1605 his forces were crushed by a second army under Prince Basil Shuisky. Dimitri fled to Putivl on the Oka. His Polish supporters began to drift homewards and the Polish Diet called on the king to repudiate Dimitri: 'What is all this: a scene from a comedy of Plautus or Terence?' thundered Chancellor Zamoyski. But Dimitri was saved by the sudden death of Boris Godunov in April. Although Moscow at first recognized Boris's son Fedor as Tsar, the army declared for Dimitri and Fedor Godunov was tortured to death, his relatives deported. In June Dimitri entered Moscow and was crowned.

The boyars, led by Shuisky, had expected the inexperienced Dimitri to prove a pliant puppet. He was not. Although his origins remain unknown (the story that he was a renegade monk, propagated by Boris and popularized in Mussorgsky's opera, is almost certainly false), Dimitri had been brought up to believe that he really was the Tsarevich and he began to implement new policies of his own. He reinforced the authority of the lords over their serfs, but allowed serfs who had fled to the south before 1601 to be free; he planned to send young Russians to study abroad; and he continued to support Siberian expansion. But these policies did nothing to gain him support, while Dimitri had weaknesses which the boyars could exploit in order to discredit him. First, he retained the services of the German and Polish foreigners who had helped him to power and he gave them lavish rewards; second, and more important, he neglected the Orthodox church and instead installed a Jesuit chapel in Moscow; third, and crucial, on 18 May 1606 he married a Polish princess and had her crowned Tsaritsa. One week later, Shuisky engineered a popular rising in Moscow against the Poles who had arrived in their hundreds to attend the wedding, and while the city was in turmoil he and his fellow-boyars entered the Kremlin and murdered Dimitri. The next day Shuisky was proclaimed Tsar by the boyars. But there was no attempt to seek approval from either the church or the estates, and it was not long before unrest began anew. This time it was the gentry who led the opposition, and they too secured the services of a False Dimitri (this one was a former supporter of Dimitri I, and actually claimed to be the late Tsar, having escaped from the Kremlin massacre). The new Dimitri – whom we might call Dimitri II – was in Poland, trying to drum up support. He now appointed as his field commander a cossack who had just returned from captivity aboard a Turkish galley: Ivan Bolotnikov. The new commander went to Putivl, 350 miles south-west of Moscow, where the provincial commander had declared for Dimitri II (a personal friend of his). Bolotnikov took charge of the regular troops there, rallied the fugitives and the remnants of the earlier rebel armies of 1603 and 1605, and marched on Moscow. In 50 or more cities the populace turned against their local nobles, stirred up by the anti-boyar propaganda produced by Bolotnikov. Even the gentry in Shuisky's army refused to fight for the 'boyars' tsar': they had risen to land and riches, under Ivan IV and Boris, by virtue of their service to the crown and they feared that Shuisky would neglect them in favour of the traditional aristocracy. Although it was the division of interest between the service gentry, who wished to preserve their position, and the peasants and refugees who wished to change theirs, that eventually undermined the movement, Bolotnikov nevertheless came within an ace of success. In mid-October, his army laid siege to Moscow, where Shuisky's supporters received letters in the name of Dimitri to 'seize Moscow, destroy the houses of the magnates, the powerful and the well-born, and take their wives and daughters for yourselves'. Shuisky countered by organizing the Orthodox clergy to preach energetically on his behalf. Just as it seemed that the Moscow poor would rise in favour of Dimitri and let the besiegers in, an important group of gentry defected from Bolotnikov's army (November 1606). Moscow was saved and Shuisky gradually gathered enough support to force the rebels' surrender (October 1607).

Unfortunately for Shuisky (and Muscovy), at the same moment, the parallel revolt in Poland was also suppressed and Dimitri II was at last able to invade Muscovy in person at the head of a large army. By May 1608, some 5000 Poles were marching on Moscow and, while the capital was under siege, Dimitri's Polish and cossack forces occupied most of south Russia. In this desperate situation, Shuisky decided to call in foreign aid. This could only come from the north, since he was cut off in all other directions: ironically, only Ivan IV's *oprichnina* areas in the north and centre, purged of boyars like Shuisky, remained loyal to the boyars' Tsar. So in August 1608 Tsar Basil sent an appeal for military aid to Charles IX of Sweden, offering in return to cede the Baltic province of Kexholm. This appeared to be a good bargain for Charles, and a treaty was signed at Viborg on 8 March 1609. An expeditionary force of 5000 Swedes raised Dimitri's second siege of Moscow in March 1610 and the Pretender withdrew.

Already, however, a far greater menace to Shuisky than Dimitri had appeared. On 21 September 1609, using the Swedish intervention as an excuse, Poland launched her own invasion of 20,000 men into Russia. As his forces besieged Smolensk, a town still loyal to Shuisky and protected by new stone fortifications (built by Godunov in 1597–1600), Sigismund systematically set about withdrawing all the Poles from the camp of Dimitri. Many were reluctant to come, reckoning that they stood a better chance of riches with the Russian Pretender than with the Polish king, but eventually Dimitri and his supporters submitted to Sigismund and agreed to accept his son Wladislaw as the next Tsar (10 February 1610). The new alliance met with rapid success: the army of Shuisky and his Swedish colleagues was routed by the Poles at Klushino on 4 July and a riot in Moscow on the 27th at last forced Shuisky to abdicate. A month later the boyars' council, which controlled the capital, agreed to recognize Wladislaw as their Tsar and a Polish garrison was installed.

Had Sigismund accepted the offer of the boyars, all would have been well. But for various reasons he procrastinated. First, his army still lay about Smolensk and the continued support of the Polish Diet depended on its capture and annexation to the Commonwealth (it had only been Russian since 1514). Second, he desired the union of the Commonwealth and Muscovy to be in his own person: he did not wish Wladislaw (who was now fifteen years old) to become Tsar and, perhaps, pursue an independent policy. Finally, there was a bitter dispute over the religion of the Tsar-elect. The boyars insisted that Wladislaw should become Orthodox but Sigismund would not hear of it, and neither would his Catholic supporters who had long advocated a crusade to the east to convert the Orthodox 'schismatics' back to the Roman faith. Much jingoistic literature had been devoted to this theme, under royal patronage (for instance Peter Grabowski's *Poland of the Plains* of 1596, and Paul Palczowski's *Moscow Canticle* of 1609) and the Pope had declared the invasion of Muscovy to be a 'crusade': Sigismund could not suddenly turn his back on all this. But time was slipping away. While the Poles made difficulties and the Swedes licked their wounds, the Orthodox bishops and some of the boyars began to circulate letters warning their compatriots of the danger to their religion posed by a Polish candidate and describing the brutal behaviour of the Polish troops about Smolensk. Gradually there gathered a party known as the 'national movement', consisting of ex-supporters of Dimitri II (murdered in December 1610), Don cossacks, with townsmen and service gentry from the old *oprichnina* areas which had supported Shuisky. In the resulting anarchy, Swedish forces again intervened and, by agreement with part of the national movement, occupied Novgorod and all the Baltic provinces. Charles IX offered his second son, Charles Philip, as a candidate to be Tsar. At the same time, in June 1611, Smolensk fell to Sigismund and the Polish Diet immediately decided to end all further taxes for the war: they were happy with their gains and saw no advantage in further expenditure. This left the Polish garrisons in Muscovy in a most awkward position, since the forces of the national movement had them under siege. First they ate grass and offal, then they ate each other, and the survivors finally surrendered. The Moscow Kremlin fell on 6 November 1612.

Next, the leaders of the national movement who were in

Moscow – a bizarre mixture of cossacks, townsmen, gentry and a few boyars untainted by the Shuisky regime – formed themselves into a 'national assembly' (*Zemsky Sobor*) to choose a new Tsar. Some members favoured Charles Philip of Sweden, but his cause was ruined when he failed to come to Moscow; the cossacks, by contrast, wished to choose the only surviving relative of Ivan IV, Michael Romanov, son of Fedor, the unsuccessful candidate of 1598. On 3 March 1613 he was elected.

The new Tsar, who was only sixteen, was intended to be in a certain sense a constitutional monarch. Like Shuisky, Wladislaw and Charles Philip, he was made to give certain guarantees to his subjects before his coronation. Since these undertakings were not written down, their exact nature remains unknown, but Michael seems to have promised to govern only with the advice of the estates, which remained in almost constant session during his reign) and to give the boyars a share in government. With their aid, the new Tsar began to restore order. The first success was scored in 1614 when all the cossacks accepted Michael's authority (even though some of them still believed Dimitri II to be alive). This settled, to some extent, the problem of order in the south. The restoration of peace in the north and west, where bandit gangs operated right up to the gates of Moscow with impunity, was more difficult since it depended on reaching a settlement with Sweden and Poland, and neither antagonist seemed ready to give in gracefully. In 1615, indeed, a Swedish army invaded Muscovy again and laid siege to Pskov. Only when it failed to capture the town were talks begun. Eventually, by the peace of Stolbova (5 March 1617), Sweden recognized Michael as Tsar and returned Novgorod in exchange for a cash indemnity and full sovereignty over Kexholm and Ingria, which linked together her existing provinces of Estonia and Finland. Russia was now completely cut off from the Baltic: Archangel on the White Sea was her only port.

No sooner was the Swedish question solved than Poland launched another invasion. The disintegration of her army in

Russia into confederations of mutinous troops after 1612 had caused great devastation in Poland itself, and the Diets of 1613–16 agreed to increase the basic tax-rates in the kingdom to allow Sigismund to pay and demobilize the mutineers. The new taxes were permanent, however, and when the veterans had been dealt with, Sigismund decided to use his increased revenues to invade Moscow once more. His forces, commanded by Prince Wladislaw, advanced slowly but inexorably towards Moscow, which they stormed in October 1618. The assault failed, however, and at Deulino (just outside the city) a peace was signed on 3 January 1619. The terms were harsh: Smolensk remained Polish and there was no recognition of Michael's title – Wladislaw still claimed to be Tsar. Muscovy's only gain, apart from the end of hostilities, was that by the exchange of prisoners of war agreed in the treaty, Michael's able father, Fedor Romanov, now known by his monastic name of Filaret, returned to Moscow in July 1619 and was almost immediately appointed patriarch.

At last the Tsar had defeated his enemies and forced recognition of his title from most foreign powers. In 1617 even the Emperor acquiesced, leaving only Poland insisting that the Romanovs were usurpers; and, under the direction of Filaret, the new regime in Moscow began to enforce obedience throughout Russia. The bureaucracy was reorganized and the bandits were defeated. New policies were initiated, of which one of the most striking was a land survey: from 1627 onwards, teams of officers armed with measuring ropes and abacus boards began to produce maps of Muscovy – the earliest known Russian cartographic work. What they did not show, however, were the large areas of wasteland which still remained in most areas: the time of troubles had reduced the Russian population by perhaps one-quarter and blighted its development as a European great power by about a century.

By 1619, therefore, the Baltic states were all at peace for the first time in two decades. Russia and Sweden had both survived serious threats to their existence; Poland and Denmark had suffered little from the failure of their expansionist designs. The Dutch, whose interest in the Baltic grew with the number of their ships sailing through the Sound, had shown by their mediation in the peace of Knared in 1613 that they wished to preserve the *status quo*, and had the strength to do so. Yet the peace of the Baltic was to be shattered in the 1620s by events farther south which neither the Dutch nor any other single state could control.

CHAPTER IV

Armed Neutrality in the West, 1598–1618

1. *The Recovery of France*

'The only good history books', Michel de Montaigne argued in one of his essays written during the 1580s, 'are those written by the people who shaped the events themselves, or who were involved in shaping them; or who at least had the luck to shape other similar ones.' No doubt Montaigne would therefore have esteemed highly the account of the reign of Henry IV (1589–1610) written by his principal minister, Maximilian de Béthune, baron de Rosny and (from 1606) duke of Sully. But Sully's *Royal Economies*, written after his fall from power in 1611, was not dispassionate history. Even though some 40 per cent of the work was composed of official documents, subsequent research has shown that many of them were either altered or forged by Sully to magnify the achievement of Henry IV and Sully's part in it. In the absence of any other comparable work on the subject, the main historical problem in assessing the achievement of the first Bourbon king consists of disengaging the real Henry from the wishful thinking of Sully's memoirs.

Henry IV was not born to be king of France. Although second cousin and brother-in-law to his predecessor on the throne, Henry's title to succeed was his direct male descent from Louis IX (d. 1270), and depended on all closer male relatives of the Valois family dying without male offspring. Remarkably, they all did. By the time of his accession in 1589, Henry was already a mature and experienced leader of men. Thirty-six years old, he had been brought up at the small court of his father the king of Navarre in Pau, at the foot of the Pyrenees. He received a Calvinist education, although joining the Catholic church between 1572 and 1576. Thereafter he became the undisputed leader of the French Huguenot party. He conducted his own foreign policy, entering into alliance with (and receiving subsidies from) England, the Dutch and the Elector Palatine. He also led his troops into battle in person – 'Follow my white plume,' he once told his officers: 'you will find it wherever there is danger' – and although out-generalled by the duke of Parma at Paris in 1590 and at Rouen in 1592, Henry was able to win convincing victories over all his other adversaries. The king took his masterful ways with him from the battlefield into the council chamber. He suppressed the estates of Périgord in 1606 as a punishment for their support of the peasant rebellions in the province during the 1590s; 'I wish to be obeyed,' was his uncompromising retort to those who presumed to question his decisions; and even his children were required to conform – the king would sometimes flog them himself when they irritated him. But Henry IV also won respect, in an age which revered *machismo*, by the great physical stamina which he displayed in battle, in hunting, in prolonged tennis matches, and between the sheets with one of his many voluptuous mistresses. Witty, wise and warm-hearted, Henry's personal qualities played an important part in the restoration of French royal authority after almost forty years of impotence and humiliation.

On any assessment, the contrast between France under Henry IV and under his immediate predecessor was remarkable. When Henry III was assassinated in 1589, royal commands were only obeyed in the Loire valley, the treasury was empty, and the majority of the political nation belonged to organizations paid by foreign powers to oppose their king. When Henry IV was himself assassinated in 1610, after nineteen unsuccessful attempts, the tables were turned: he was obeyed by all, the treasury had a surplus, and France sent regular subsidies to those foreign powers whose continuing independence France wished to guarantee. In addition, the civil wars which had recommenced in 1588 (and had been paralysing France at regular intervals since 1562) were successfully terminated. Foreign interference was ended by the peace of Vervins (2 May 1598), which more or less restored the *status quo ante bellum*; the Catholic leaders were persuaded to stop fighting by massive cash bribes totalling 7 million écus (£1·75 million sterling, well over an entire year's crown revenues); and the Huguenot (Calvinist) leaders were pacified by the set of guarantees for their political, military and religious integrity known as the Edict of Nantes. There were four separate documents. First, 95 public articles (signed on 13 April) and 57 secret articles (signed on 2 May) laid down in detail the religious toleration accorded to the Huguenots: the exact places where Huguenot worship might and might not take place were listed; three Protestant universities (Montauban, La Rochelle and Nîmes) were recognized; periodical national synods of the Reformed church were allowed. In addition, the king issued two personal undertakings (*brevets*, signed on 3 and 30 April) which recognized the autonomy of a Protestant clerical establishment, with its own Assembly, and promised that the Protestant garrisons which occupied one hundred named towns, known as the *places de sûreté*, would continue to serve there, paid from public funds. The status of the two varieties of document was as different as their content: the edict, which dealt with toleration, had the force of law; but the brevets, which created a Huguenot state within a state, were acts of grace, dependent on the continuing goodwill of the crown.[1]

This settlement at first pleased no one. The Huguenots feared that their guarantees offered inadequate protection and resented a clause which forbade them to proselytize. The Catholics, for their part, were appalled by the military independence and political autonomy conferred on the Protestants, and the Pope condemned the edict out of hand (mainly because it recognized the principle of religious toleration), followed by most of the French Catholic clergy. The *Parlement* of Paris agreed to register the edict in February 1599 only after repeated threats of sanctions by the king (and even then permission to print it was delayed for a further two months to allow tempers to cool), while the *Parlement* of Rouen managed to avoid registering the edict at all until 1609 (although it did observe the terms). Only as time passed were fears calmed and doubts abated. The brevets were renewed in 1608, 1611 and 1615, which reassured the Protestants; and the king satisfied the Catholics by demonstrating that his conversion to their faith in 1593 was genuine. He recalled the Jesuits to France in 1603 (they had been expelled in 1594 after the Jesuit-trained Jacques Chastel had almost assassinated Henry IV) and he encouraged the formation of new religious orders and the reform of old ones (the most important being the purification of the Cistercian nunnery of Port-Royal near Paris in 1609: it became, under its eighteen-year-old abbess, Angélique Arnauld, the chief stronghold of Jansenism). The French Catholic church was also regenerated by the Christian humanism associated with Bishop François de Sales, the strict Augustinianism of Cardinal Pierre de Bérulle, and the Spanish-inspired mysticism of the Carmelite, Capuchin and Charterhouse Orders. The total number of religious establishments in France doubled between 1600 and 1650.

Re-edified and renewed from within, the Catholic authorities in France abandoned their attempts to extirpate Protestantism by overt force. Instead, a more subtle approach was adopted. Although Huguenots were banned from holding all judicial and administrative offices not mentioned in the brevets, pensions and bribes were paid to the leading Protestant nobles to keep them loyal. At the same time, some of the best Catholic priests were sent into Huguenot areas in an effort to convert the Protestants by example. These endeavours were remarkably successful: the size of the Huguenot church declined from 1,250,000 members in 1600 to 500,000 or less in 1680. Only then was it possible to act unilaterally against them by revoking the Edict of Nantes (1685). Those who criticize Henry IV for shelving the Huguenot problem, not solving it, are apt to forget that his hands were tied. Many of his leading Catholic subjects had fought against him for over a decade; at least the Huguenots were personally above suspicion. And in any case, the 741 churches of the Reformed religion were attended by over seven per cent of the French population and were defended by the best troops in the kingdom. Even had he desired to crush his former supporters, Henry lacked the means: he began his peacetime reign with a derelict economy, an empty treasury and a state that was too large to govern effectively.

The kingdom of France covered roughly 480,000 square kilometres in 1600, with a population of between sixteen and twenty million people. She was thus almost exactly the same size as her great rival, Spain, with 490,000 square kilometres (but her population was more than twice as large: Spain's was eight million). Another similarity between the two states lay in their federative political structure: both had become great through a process of territorial unification during the late fifteenth and early sixteenth centuries. France contained a core of territories governed directly from Paris (and known as the *pays d'élections* after the tax officials, the *élus*, who apportioned tax quotas between the parishes), and a periphery of provinces, known as the *pays d'états* (provinces with estates) where local institutions seriously impeded the exercise of royal authority. The principal *pays d'états* – Brittany, Burgundy, Dauphiné, Guyenne, Languedoc and Provence in 1600 – covered almost one-third of France. The position in Spain was curiously similar: Castile formed the core and took up two-thirds of the area; the rest was occupied by Navarre, the Basque provinces, Valencia, Aragon and Catalonia. Where France and Spain differed was in natural resources. Early modern France was a country of vast economic diversity, and this meant that she could be largely self-sufficient. Her fields produced all the staples of life and many luxuries; new crops such as maize, buckwheat, beans, tomatoes and potatoes all made their appearance. Except in years of wholesale famine (and there were none between 1598 and 1617), France was rarely obliged to import any food from abroad. On the contrary, she normally exported the produce of her fields: between 1635 and 1645, French exports to the Dutch Republic averaged 16 million livres annually, of which almost 40 per cent were wine and brandy and about 22 per cent were cereals. (This may seem a surprising figure in view of the frequency of bread riots in France at this time; but while some areas produced a considerable surplus, others produced barely enough.) Among France's other exports to the United Provinces were salt, olive oil and Mediterranean fruit (20 per cent), and linen (10 per cent); in return she imported from Holland goods worth 21 million livres every year, including textiles (32 per cent) and Oriental products (41 per cent).

The government of Henry IV had done its best to stop this importation of manufactured and luxury goods, which led to an outflow of bullion. On the one hand, sumptuary laws were passed limiting the use of cloth of gold and silver; on the other, special royal factories were established to produce the luxury goods sought by the aristocracy – crystal glass, silks, satins and tapestries (at the famous Gobelins and Savonnerie de Chaillot workshops). The king set up a Commission for commerce in 1602 under Bartélemy de Laffemas which also restored silk weaving in Tours and Lyon, encouraged linen production in Picardy and Brittany, and increased the total woollen output of France in the early seventeenth century to about 670,000 pieces of cloth annually (manufactured by some 34,000 enterprises and valued at about 20 million livres). In agriculture the government resorted to propaganda, distributing 16,000 free copies of *The Theatre of Agriculture* by Olivier de Serres (1600), which explained how to drain and polder new land, how to improve yields, and how to introduce new crops. Thanks to the beneficent climate in the first two decades of the century, harvests were plentiful, food was cheap and population grew. As Sully wrote in his memoirs, 'tillage and pasturage' became the 'two breasts of France' whose milk nourished and increased the well-being of all her inhabitants. And Sully himself made an important contribution towards improving this milk-supply: he lowered direct taxes and he supervised the construction of bridges, roads and canals, spending 5·5 million livres on communications between 1605 and 1610 – a figure which was not repeated before 1680. The effect on a previously isolated region of opening a new road, or of improving a road so that it could take wheeled traffic, is hard to imagine: the trade in bulk agricultural produce was particularly stimulated, since a four-wheel wagon pulled by a team of ten or twelve horses could carry a load of seven tons; several such wagons could move a harvest.

The revenues which financed these and other improvements were raised amid a general climate of financial reform and retrenchment. In 1599, the year after the end of the war, Sully halved the state debt, which stood at 296 million livres (£24 million sterling), partly by repudiation of foreign debts and partly by offering immediate repayment to creditors in return for a reduction in their claim. In 1601 the government brought the interest rate on its outstanding debts down to 6¼ per cent. By this time, the state budget was balanced and a small surplus began to accumulate, thanks to the introduction of a number of new taxes, the most famous of which was known as the *paulette* or *droit annuel*. This was a voluntary tax paid by office-holders every year to the government in return for a guarantee that their offices could be sold at any time to a person chosen by them. Fixed in 1604 at one-sixtieth of the annual value of the office, the *paulette* was an excellent investment for office-holders anxious to provide for their children. But it had important, perhaps unforeseen, social consequences: it created a new elite, known as the 'robe nobility' (as opposed to the 'sword nobility'), which sold or bequeathed offices of the crown at its own pleasure. Judges, tax-inspectors and most other civil servants now came to be drawn exclusively from the ranks of the robe aristocracy much as they had been in the days of the feudal monarchy, except that the new elite quickly formed trade unions (the *syndicats d'officiers*) which jealously guarded their salaries, their career prospects, and the autonomy of their provincial institutions (see pages 272–4 below). For Sully, however, the importance of the *paulette* lay in its yield – 2 million livres a year: about ten per cent of total revenue – which enabled him to reduce direct taxes like the *taille* which weighed so oppressively on the population at large.

Even after the peace of Vervins in 1598, about half of

Henry IV's revenues were expended on the army, the navy and the artillery, or on fortifications and subsidies to France's foreign allies. Particular attention was paid to the northern and eastern frontiers, and Henry had the fortifications of 47 different towns either rebuilt or improved, while the frontier provinces themselves were meticulously surveyed and mapped (see Figure 6). He could not ignore Spain's permanent military establishment of 10,000 men in Italy and 50,000 men in the South Netherlands, linked by a network of military corridors, known to contemporaries as 'the Spanish Road', along which men, money and munitions could be moved from Milan to Brussels, and back, with considerable speed. In the event of a new war with the Habsburgs, the safety of France would depend on breaking this chain of communication as it ran through the territories of Spain's allies, Savoy and Lorraine.

The first opportunity of attacking the Spanish Road came very soon after Vervins, in a dispute over the ownership of the tiny marquisate of Saluzzo, an enclave in the western Alps surrounded by the lands of the duke of Savoy. The last marquis had left Saluzzo to the French crown at his death in 1548 (at a time when France was occupying all Savoy) but, in the absence of strong crown control during the religious wars, the marquisate became a hotbed of Calvinism. When in 1588 the Huguenots captured Château-Dauphin, capital of Saluzzo, the Catholic duke of Savoy invaded and annexed the enclave. At the peace of Vervins, ten years later, the Saluzzo question was referred to papal arbitration since, although France's claim to the territory was clear, the duke of Savoy was most reluctant to permit a powerful French garrison to base itself in the heart of his lands. He therefore offered, in 1600, to cede to France the territory of Bresse on his western frontier if, in return, he could retain Saluzzo. Henry IV was agreeable, but suddenly Spain intervened to point out that the surrender of Bresse would block her vital supply-route to the Netherlands. The duke of Savoy was promised full Spanish military support if he rejected the agreement with France, which he did on 7 August. It was

Figure 6. France's Eastern Frontier, 1598–1648

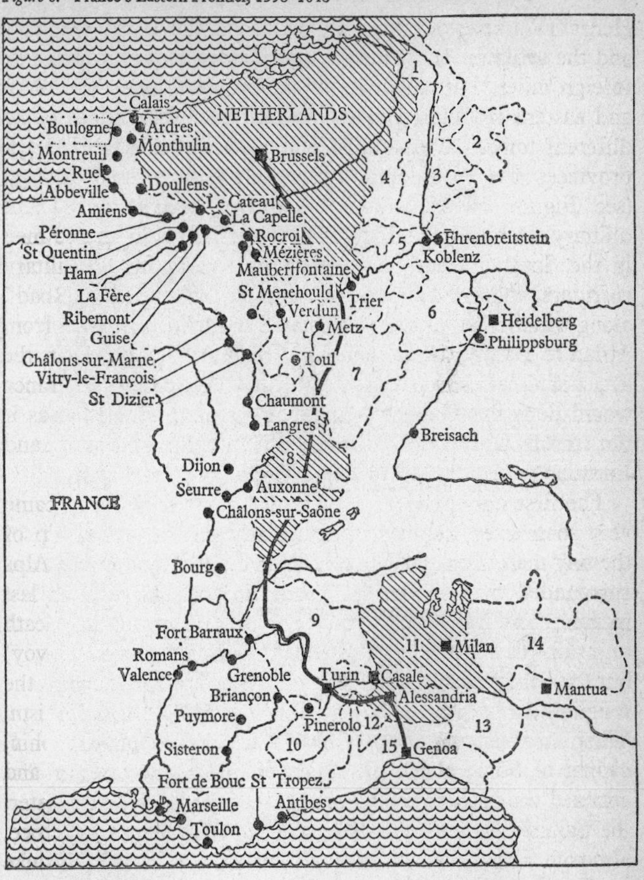

Spanish Road

Spanish Habsburg dominions

French fortified towns

Other towns

1 Cleves
2 Mark
3 Berg
4 Jülich
5 Trier (and Speyer)
6 Rhine Palatinate
7 Lorraine
8 Franche-Comté
9 Savoy
10 Saluzzo
11 Lombardy
12 Mantua-Monferrat
13 Parma
14 Venice
15 Genoa

a foolish move. Henry IV was already at Lyon and had mobilized an army; four days later he declared war on Savoy and launched an invasion of 50,000 men into the duchy; within a week, almost every area west of the Alpine passes was in French hands and not a single Spanish soldier had arrived to help the duke. But as the months passed, Spanish support for Savoy built up, and in January 1601 Henry accepted a renewed offer of papal mediation in the dispute. France gained from Savoy not only Bresse, but Bugey and Gex as well, and Savoy retained a narrow corridor of territory, the Val de Chézery, which allowed Spanish troops and treasure to cross from Lombardy to Franche Comté without touching French soil. But only just: the Spanish Road was confined at this point to a single bridge across the Rhône, the bridge of Grésin, which the French could and did break whenever they desired to prevent reinforcements from reaching the Low Countries.

The war of Saluzzo, spectacularly successful as it was, proved to be Henry IV's last major military operation. From 1601 until just before his death in 1610 he was able to achieve his diplomatic objectives by peaceful means, especially by subsidies judiciously provided to Spain's enemies. The Dutch in particular were generously assisted, receiving over 12 million livres (about £1 million sterling) between 1598 and 1610. Between 1605 and 1607, when the Dutch faced the might of Spain alone, the subsidies rose to almost 2 million livres a year, which represented ten per cent of France's total budget. Subsidies were also sent to Geneva (about 70,000 livres a year after the duke of Savoy's unsuccessful attempt to capture the city in 1602: the *Escalade*), and to several German Protestant princes. But otherwise France under Henry IV followed a policy that aimed to prevent the outbreak of confessional strife in Europe which might start a new religious war in France. In this the king followed the advice not of Sully, who often argued in favour of aggression against Spain, but of four older men who had only entered his service after counselling his predecessor Henry III, and in some cases his rivals in the Catholic League: Pomponne de Bellièvre (1529–1607), Pierre Jeannin (1540–1622), Nicholas de Neufville, seigneur de Villeroy (1542–1617) and Nicholas Brûlart de Sillery (1544–1624, who succeeded Bellièvre as chancellor in 1607). These four elder statesmen, who came to be known as 'the dotards' (*barbons*), had played an important part in negotiating the compromises between Protestants and Catholics which brought the religious wars to an end. After the war of Saluzzo they intervened to negotiate a reconciliation in the disputes between James I of Great Britain and the Papacy in 1606–9, between Venice and the Papacy in 1606–7 and between Spain and the Dutch in 1607–9. The results of this mediation were always creditable, if not uniformly successful. Although the truce of Antwerp in 1609 was more or less dictated by the French representative, Jeannin, the other conflicts continued with undiminished animus (although France gained some credit for her abortive peace initiatives: 'At least', one ambassador observed in 1609 as England's controversy with the Papacy dragged on, 'no one can say we did not warn them').

The only apparent aberration amid this continuity in France's peace policy occurred in 1609–10 during the first Cleves-Jülich crisis. On 25 March 1609 the duke of Cleves, Jülich, Mark and Berg died, leaving no issue. The Emperor Rudolf II summoned the various claimants to appear before him and in the meantime sent in an imperial administrator, his cousin Leopold (bishop of Passau and a cousin of the late duke), with some troops. In July, when the claimants refused to accept his adjudication, the Emperor declared the duchies sequestered, and in December hostilities commenced between Leopold and the two leading claimants, the son of the count of Neuburg and the elector of Brandenburg, both Lutherans and both descended from sisters of the late duke. It was because of the exalted connections of these claimants (and of some others – see Table 5) that the high-handed policy of the Emperor failed. Imperial electors could not be treated in this way, and in January 1610 the Union of the German Protestant princes agreed to attack the Habsburg forces in Jülich. At the same time, Henry IV began to mobilize. His

Table 5. The Cleves-Jülich Succession

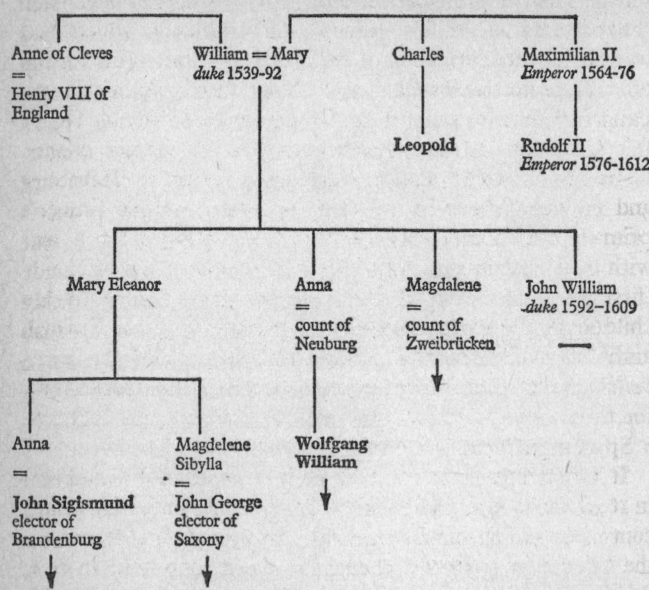

exact intentions, however, must remain a secret for, on 14 May 1610, as he rode out of Paris to join his troops on the north-east frontier, a Catholic fanatic, François Ravaillac, stabbed the king to death.

The apparently authentic account of the king's 'Grand Design' in Sully's *Economies Royales*, printed under his direction in 1638 and again with additions in 1662, must be discounted; for it only appears in the 1662 version and is missing both from Sully's own manuscript and from the 1638 edition. The material appears to have been added in order to convince Louis XIV's contemporaries that their sovereign's bellicose intentions were merely a continuation of his grandfather's. The available evidence suggests that French involvement in Cleves-Jülich was modelled on the successful Saluzzo war a decade earlier. The scale of the operation was similar: 50,000 men and 57 guns to Savoy in 1600; 50,000 men and 33 guns to Cleves in 1610 (albeit some were provided by the German Protestants and their allies). But the aim was slightly different: Henry's principal concern in 1610 seems to have been the preservation of his influence in Germany, which had waned since the formation of the Protestant Union (his formal offer of protection had actually been refused). A brisk campaign in Cleves to support the Protestant cause would, Henry felt sure, demonstrate French power to his former clients. Certainly, it would also prevent any increase in Habsburg and papal influence in the area, but that was not France's primary objective. Henry's other alleged motive for a war with the Habsburgs in 1610 – the flight of the prince of Condé (first prince of the blood, and heir apparent if Henry's sickly children should die) to Brussels and the refusal of the Spanish authorities to repatriate him – was certainly not the *casus belli*. On the contrary, since 1608 Henry had been negotiating for the marriage of his eldest son, the future Louis XIII, to a Spanish princess.

It would thus seem most likely that Henry IV's intention in 1610 was to save Cleves-Jülich from falling under Habsburg control by aiding the Evangelical Union, and then to redress the balance by a Spanish match for his son and heir. In fact, this was precisely what the regency government did after his death: Jülich was cleared of Habsburg troops by September 1610 and the two Lutheran claimants installed (but see page 152–3); and the double marriage of Louis XIII to Anne of Austria (daughter of Philip III) and of Louis's sister to the future Philip IV was agreed in April 1611 (it took place in 1615). The continuity between the reigns of Henry IV and his son was thus seemingly perfect. But there was one crucial difference: once the strong hand of Henry was removed, French influence abroad was undermined by weakness at home.

After almost 40 years of civil war, passions in France ran deep and wide, and many a cause (thanks to the diffusion of printing presses) could command so many supporters that royal authority might be compromised. On one occasion, Henry IV observed that scandalous political and religious tracts were published in France in such numbers that 'If I cut off every slanderous tongue, I would have a lot of mute subjects'; but, in truth, France needed a stricter censorship than the government chose to provide. Foreign observers, like the English traveller Thomas Dallington in 1604, regarded the abusive language of the French on political matters as their greatest vice:

> It is incredible to beleeue, and odious to heare, how the Frenchman will talke, and impudently vtter what hee foolishly conceiueth, not onely of all forraine States and Princes of the world, but euen of their owne State and King himselfe; of whome hee will not spare to speake whatsoeuer hee heareth, and sometimes also more then the trueth; which insufferable vice of theirs, I heere put in the first place, because I holde it of all others the most disloyall and vnlawfull.[2]

This criticism naturally increased after 1610, when the direction of royal policy was controlled by a trio of inept Italian immigrants: Marie de Medici (queen regent with full powers until Louis XIII's majority, on 2 October 1614, and then president of the royal council), Leonora Galigai (who had been brought up by the same wet-nurse as the queen and became her lady-in-waiting), and Leonora's husband Carlo Concini (a Florentine noble who had served Henry IV and was soon made marquis of Ancre). The trio dismissed Sully in 1611, and dominated the surviving ministers of Henry IV (Villeroy, Sillery and Jeannin); but they could not dominate the magnates, who bitterly resented their exclusion from a role in the minority government. At first *les Grands*, led by Condé, were kept in line by pensions paid from Sully's accumulated treasure in the Bastille; but in 1612–13 they began to oppose the crown's pro-Spanish policies, which also irritated the Huguenots; and when, in January 1614, with some Huguenot support, the grandees began to raise an army in order to compel the crown to convene the States-General, the regent had to give way (treaty of Sainte Ménehould, 15 May 1614). But, having done so, she successfully orchestrated a campaign to keep her critics from being elected.

As the selection of deputies took place over the summer, perhaps a thousand political pamphlets were published, almost all of them hostile to the grandees; and in the end, few even of the noble representatives were supporters of Condé's programme – indeed 40 per cent of them were officers of the crown, easily open to government persuasion. Outside the noble estate, support for Condé was even thinner. Many were alienated by the self-seeking of the aristocratic petitions, such as the one from the nobles of Normandy: 'Let the hereditary nobility be preferred to all others, not only for offices and commissions in the royal household and for judicial offices in all courts and jurisdictions, but also in all bishoprics and benefices of the church, seeing that they are suitable to hold and discharge them.'[3]

Although almost one thousand separate grievances were tabled by the States-General (the first to be held since 1593 and the last before 1789), the critics were so divided that the regent was able to dissolve the assembly in May 1615 without redressing a single one. Perhaps this was unwise, for the grandees felt deceived and resolved in 1616 to use their private armies again, once more with some Huguenot support, to gain a voice in government and to stop the Spanish match. Hostilities began in August 1615 and, although they did not prevent the marriage in November of Louis XIII to a Spanish princess (and of Philip IV to a French one), in May 1616 they succeeded in getting Condé and some others on to the royal council. Concini was dismissed. On 1 September, however, Condé was arrested and sent to the Bastille on the orders of the queen mother. In his place she put the conduct of public affairs in the hands of a group of her own advisers, including Concini and when other grandees took up arms against her she declared them to be guilty of treason and sent three armies against them. The war effort was directed by the secretary of state of the new administration, Armand-Jean Duplessis de Richelieu, bishop of Luçon, with such effectiveness that by the spring of 1617 the position of the rebels seemed hopeless. But Marie de Medici's own position was also perilous. Since October 1614 she had no longer been queen regent, only president of the royal council. The sovereign ruler of France was now Louis XIII and he bitterly resented the changes in his ministers decreed by his mother without reference to him. On 24 April 1617, the king, advised by one of his courtiers, Charles d'Albert later duke of Luynes, sanctioned the murder of Concini as he walked to the Louvre Palace. The other members of the government were disposed of equally swiftly: Leonora Galigai was condemned to death as a witch by an obliging supreme court (executed 8 July); the queen mother and Richelieu were banished to Blois.

These events prevented the extinction of the threat posed by the grandees: all of them were pardoned by the king and lived to fight another day (when their exclusion from the royal council under Luynes proved as irksome as their former exclusion under Concini). The only differences after the coup of April 1617 were, first, the existence of the court-in-exile of Marie de Medici at Blois which served as a permanent focus for opposition and a potential alternative government; and, second, the outbreak of a rebellion in Bohemia in 1618, which threatened to spread to the Empire after 1619. Initially the devout Louis XIII wished to send military assistance to the Emperor (in the event he did intervene to neutralize Protestant Germany: see page 167 below) but he was prevented by another rising of the grandees, supported by Marie, in 1619–20. Only when it was ended, by a military encounter at Ponts-de-Cé in Normandy (7 August 1620) and by the reconciliation of Marie and Richelieu on the one hand with Louis and Luynes on the other (13 August), was the French crown free to attempt a thorough solution of all the problems which had beset it since 1589 – the Huguenots, the nobles, the Habsburgs. The year 1620, as the Soviet historian Mme Lublinskaya has written, was a turning point in French political history: Ponts-de-Cé began the crucial phase in the development of French absolutism. But by 1620 it was almost too late.

2. *The Netherlands Divided*

Towards the end of his life, Philip II of Spain became convinced that his policy of meeting the Dutch revolt with implacable military force was unlikely to succeed. After 25 years of continuous campaigning, at vast cost, Spain controlled considerably less territory in 1597 than at the end of 1572, most of it lost in the ten years since the defeat of the Spanish Armada in 1588. The United Provinces (as the areas in revolt against Spain were known) had improved their position in three ways during the 1590s: they conquered a solid bloc of territory north of the rivers Maas and Waal which was relatively easy to defend; they began to trade with the Mediterranean lands (where severe famines in the 1590s were relieved only by Dutch vessels bringing Baltic grain), with the Atlantic ports of Europe, and with Spanish America; and the succession of political disagreements which had fragmented the rebel cause ever since 1576 came to an end, creating a stable nucleus of seven provinces firmly united in their opposition to Spain – Gelderland, Holland, Zealand, Utrecht, Groningen, Overijssel and Friesland. However, everyone realized that these successes were due as much to Spanish ineptitude as to Dutch skill. As early as 1593 a papal observer in Brussels noted that 'the progress of the Protestants stems more from their diligence and energy than from their military strength; but even more it stems from the absence of any obstacle.'

It was in a final effort to create an 'obstacle' to the further success of the Dutch that Philip II decided to turn the Catholic Netherlands, which included the Franche-Comté of Burgundy as well as the Netherlands south of the Maas and Waal, into a separate sovereign state under his daughter Isabella, instead of his son Philip III who was to rule the rest of his monarchy. Isabella was to marry her cousin, the Archduke Albert of Austria, who had been governor-general of the Netherlands since 1595. 'The Archdukes', as they were known, assumed power in August 1598. At first, however, the new regime was little more than a satellite of Spain: the Archdukes could not make peace or war without Spanish consent; Spanish garrisons controlled directly from Madrid occupied the key towns; and a large Spanish army was permanently quartered in the country (60,000 men in wartime, of whom only 10,000 were paid from Brussels). Although the fiction was maintained that the Archdukes were autonomous, everyone knew that when they died their 'state' would revert to Spain, and their diplomats were treated accordingly. At the negotiations in London for a peace with England in 1603–4, the Archdukes were allowed to appoint their own representative, but he was instructed to accept whatever terms the chief Spanish negotiator, the Constable of Castile, could secure. The Constable and his colleagues, complained the Archdukes' representatives, 'behaved themselves more as our masters than as our companions'. It was the same at the truce talks with the Dutch in 1607–9: Philip III saw to it that everything was dealt with by his own representatives, even though they experienced extreme difficulty in understanding the French and Dutch in which the talks were conducted, rather than trust the Archdukes' advisers. The Archdukes were even more impotent in military matters. Although commands were issued in their name, all strategic decisions were taken in Spain and were implemented by the commanders appointed by Philip III.

The most important decision in this sphere was, of course, whether or not to continue the war against the Dutch; and in this Madrid constantly overruled the Archdukes, who longed for peace. In 1599, taking advantage of the forces freed by the conclusion of peace with France, Philip III decided to launch an invasion of the Republic – the first since 1589. At first all went well, and the important Bommelerwaard, an island between the rivers Maas and Waal, was overrun; but during the winter the Spanish garrisons mutinied and either sold their posts to the enemy or fled. In 1600 the Dutch decided on a counter-attack: 10,000 men under Maurice of Nassau, commander-in-chief of the Republic's armies, landed in Flanders with instructions to capture the towns of Nieuwpoort and Dunkirk. But the Dutch were ill-prepared and were forced to fight a battle on unfavourable terrain on the beach outside Nieuwpoort, in which only their superior artillery saved them from serious defeat. As it was, they had to retreat with heavy losses, having achieved nothing. Although from 1601 to 1604 there were some conquests (Rheinberg, 1601; Grave, 1602; Sluis, 1604) while the Spaniards laid siege to Ostend, in 1604 the Archdukes did at last capture the town, which had proved a most useful Dutch outpost in Flanders. Worse still, in the same year the new English sovereign, James I (James VI of Scotland), concluded a peace with Spain (treaty of London, 19 August 1604). Now the Dutch faced the power of Spain alone and almost at once the military position turned against them. In 1605, the Spanish army of Flanders invaded the north-eastern provinces lost in the 1590s and captured several important towns (notably Oldenzaal and Lingen). The Archdukes had a new commander-in-chief, the Genoese banker Ambrogio Spinola, who combined great military skill with the ability to finance the army during the frequent periods when the king of Spain's coffers were empty. The Dutch became fearful that, in 1606, Spinola might lead his forces deep into their territory; and at great expense they constructed a fortified rampart for 150 miles along the River Ijssel, from the Zuider Zee to Arnhem and from there along the Waal to Gorinchem. In spite of this, in 1606 the Spanish army did force its way across the Ijssel line, besides capturing the towns of Groenlo and Rheinberg. At the same time, embargoes placed by Spain on Dutch shipping reduced a profitable source of trade severely, while energetic moves against Dutch traders in the Caribbean in 1605 brought that lucrative commerce, which occupied 100 and more vessels a year, to a temporary stop. For the Dutch, therefore, the war since 1598 had brought, in the words of their leader Johan van Oldenbarnevelt, 'little glory and great expense';

and it began to seem that the 1607 campaign would bring even worse fortune. In December 1606, therefore, the Republic let it be known that she would be prepared to make a peace with Spain.

To the councillors of Philip III, the timing of this offer seemed little short of miraculous. The state of Castile's treasury, and of her economy, had forced the government reluctantly to decide to halve the military establishment in the Netherlands, sending only enough funds for the year 1607 to keep the Archdukes' territory from being totally overrun. There was no other alternative. In 1596 all the short-term debts of the Spanish crown had been consolidated into a funded debt, at low interest, which totalled 85 million ducats (almost £20 million sterling); but in every year after that, expenditure far exceeded revenue and the deficit was only bridged by anticipating through bank-loans the income of future years. By the beginning of 1607 a total of 22·7 million ducats in short-term loans was outstanding and all revenues until 1611 had been used up. The crown therefore had to decree the forcible conversion of its loans, once again, to non-redeemable consolidated stock, with the consequence that no bankers were prepared to lend money again. Little could be raised in taxes because the government had virtually driven all silver and gold coins in the peninsula out of circulation with the issue of some 22 million ducats (about £5 million sterling) of cheap copper-alloy (*vellón*) coins. The effect on trade was catastrophic: the overvalued *vellón* coins circulated at a discount of up to 30 per cent of their face value, which meant that foreign merchants either had to barter their wares and avoid coin altogether, or else see their profit eaten up in exchange rates when they tried to exchange their copper for silver. *Vellón* was worthless outside Spain.

Spain therefore welcomed the chance of putting an end to the fighting almost as much as the Dutch, and an armistice was signed on 29 March 1607, coming into force a month later. It was not so easy to agree on a formula for permanent peace, however. Some ministers such as the count of Fuentes, governor of Spanish Lombardy, found the whole idea of negotiating with rebels demeaning and base. 'I cannot refrain from pointing out to Your Majesty', he wrote, 'that it will appear good neither to God nor to the World if Your Majesty goes about begging for peace with his rebels.' The king was not unmoved. As soon as he heard that talks had been started, in May 1607, Philip III instructed one of his councillors to go to Brussels and inform the negotiators that 'if the Dutch were made absolute sovereigns of the lands they occupy, it will be clearly seen as damaging for our reputation'. It certainly was: no sooner was a truce of twelve years signed in 1609 than foreign powers (Venice, France, England) sent permanent ambassadors with full powers to reside at the Hague. And Spain had obtained nothing in the talks (except an end to hostilities in the Low Countries). Everything Philip III's negotiators were instructed to insist on had to be abandoned: they failed to secure further toleration for Dutch Catholics, or the opening of the River Scheldt to trade, or an end to hostilities at sea. They were even obliged to recognize the United Provinces 'as if they were a sovereign power' at the truce of Antwerp (9 April 1609).

The Republic, however, was not the only beneficiary of the twelve years' truce. The Archdukes, who had consistently put pressure on Philip III to reach an agreement with his 'rebels', made good use of the opportunity afforded by the suspension of hostilities.

The Low Countries' wars, which had continued almost unbroken since 1572, involved widespread destruction and devastation, especially in the south. In 1609 the English traveller Sir Thomas Overbury wrote the following description of 'the Archdukes' Country' just after the fighting had stopped:

> As soon as I entered into the Archduke's country, which begins after Lillow [Lilloo], presently I beheld . . . a Province distressed with war. The people heartless; and rather repining against their Governors than revengeful against their enemies. The bravery of that gentry which was left, and the industry of the merchant, quite decayed.

> The husbandman labouring only to live, without desire to be rich to another's use. The towns (whatsoever concerned not the strength of them) ruinous. And, to conclude, the people here growing poor with less taxes, than they flourish with on the States' side.[4]

Other evidence confirms this dismal picture. Perhaps 100,000 people abandoned the South Netherlands between 1567 and 1609, taking their wealth and their skills to the north, to Germany and to England. In addition people and property were wantonly destroyed: many communities in Flanders and Brabant lost between one-third and one-half of their populations between 1570 and 1600; many villages disappeared entirely and in others the amount of cultivated land shrank to almost nothing. Yet as soon as the fighting ended, recovery began. The number of baptisms recorded in parish registers surged upwards and continued to climb until (in most cases) the 1660s. Trade and industry also recovered. Antwerp merchants began to trade again with Italy and Spain and even with the Spanish and Portuguese overseas empires. Almost 600 South Netherlands merchants are known to have traded with the Iberian powers and their empires between 1598 and 1648. Silk, sugar and other colonial goods flowed into Antwerp in considerable quantities after 1589, while the vast sums spent by the king of Spain on his army in the Netherlands, most of it sent from Castile, also brought prosperity to some bankers, sutlers and military contractors in the 'obedient provinces'. There was considerable industrial recovery too. The main textile centre of Hondschoote produced almost as many broad-cloths in the 1620s as in the 1550s: nearly 60,000 pieces were turned out in some years, most of them exported to Spain through Ostend and Dunkirk. Ghent too produced large quantities and many varieties of textiles in the first half of the seventeenth century: 29,000 linen cloths were brought to market in 1636, of which 20,000 were exported to Spain. In many towns new activities grew up to compensate for the demise of the old – silk, lace, tapestries, glass-making, jewellery, diamond cutting and printing flourished – whilst in general there was a shift of emphasis from quantity to quality. The profits made from these enterprises are reflected to this day in the rich town houses of Antwerp, Ghent, Brussels, Bergues and elsewhere constructed between 1600 and 1670. In the countryside too there was recovery (possibly aided by the enforced fallow of the 1590s). The improvements in farming methods became legendary and an English observer, Sir Richard Weston, wrote in 1644–5 that between Dunkirk and Bruges 'I saw as rich a countrie as ever my eies beheld, stokt with goodly wheat and barlie, and excellent meadow and pasture.'

The regeneration of the South Netherlands under the Archdukes was spiritual as well as economic. On the one hand the government, aided by the papal nuncios (in permanent residence since 1596), tried to improve episcopal and clerical standards: new churches were built (not only in towns, as with the great Jesuit churches of Brussels or Antwerp, but also in villages such as Scherpenheuvel in Brabant, which has a magnificent baroque domed church dating from this period); old churches were restored; and the educational and moral standards of the parish clergy were raised. The 'crusading orders' were also encouraged: the strength of the Jesuits in the South Netherlands increased from 17 convents in 1598 to 46 in 1640, the Capuchins increased from 12 houses in 1595 to 42 in 1626. On the other hand, the government also attempted to extirpate Protestantism. An edict of the Archdukes issued on 31 December 1609 ordered the expulsion of all non-Catholics, and over the years the covert Protestant minorities that remained dwindled into insignificance in most places. There were exceptions (especially near the Dutch border, where the Republic prevented any priests from residing in some twelve Catholic villages north of Antwerp), but on the whole the problem of the Catholic clergy in the seventeenth century was, as in Protestant areas, to combat the superstition, indifference and ignorance of their parishioners, not to ward off the seducers from another faith.

Nevertheless, the Catholic clerical elite expended a great deal of missionary zeal, and some of their best men, in the

'Hollandse Zending', an attempt by about 200 missionaries to supply the Catholics of the north with priests, services and religious literature. Presses all over the South Netherlands printed pamphlets and history books, as well as Bibles and devotional manuals, to set out what a good Catholic should believe in politics as well as in religion. The revolt was portrayed as the work of a few wicked men, the disasters of the war were seen merely as God's punishment on the Netherlands for their former opulence and luxury. Every deed of the Protestants was denigrated and ridiculed. At first only Netherlands affairs were covered, but after 1609 events elsewhere came in for scrutiny: the revolt of Bohemia in 1618–20, the war with England in 1624–30 and so on. Gradually a consistent attitude emerged, a sort of collective identity which was able to resist the inroads, intellectual as well as military, of both the Dutch (especially during the crisis of 1632) and the French.

This embryonic national identity was an impressive monument to the government of the Archdukes, and it survived almost 40 years of gruelling warfare (1621–59) and later the invasions of Louis XIV. The 50,000 inhabitants of Lille, who became perforce Frenchmen in 1667 when the city was ceded to Louis XIV, remained faithful to their former rulers until at least 1700, drinking the king of Spain's health, celebrating the births and marriages of the House of Habsburg, and aiding French garrison soldiers to desert to join the Spanish forces. The areas of Brabant, Limburg and Flanders that were captured by the Dutch after 1621 have remained staunchly Catholic to this day.

The creation of this distinctive national consciousness in the South Netherlands during the reign of the Archdukes (which lasted, in effect, until Isabella's death in 1633 even though sovereignty returned to Spain at Albert's death in 1621) was a fact of enduring significance, since one of the long-term problems of modern European history had been the refusal of the Catholic area known today as Belgium to be absorbed into any larger political unit. In the seventeenth century it was this sense of patriotism that prevented the

Dutch and the French from annexing the South Netherlands in the 1640s, when Spain was virtually unable to send any relief.

It is ironic that the Archdukes, who sacrificed so much at the truce of Antwerp, derived so much profit from it; whereas the Dutch, who secured all the concessions they desired by the peace, were weaker when it ended than when it began. They were by no means united even in 1609, however.

The provinces in revolt against Spain were not, for the most part, united by history or tradition. Friesland and Gelderland had spent much of the fifteenth century fighting Holland and Zealand, with Overijssel and Utrecht as both prize and battleground. The landward provinces had only come under Habsburg rule during the reign of Charles V and they all brought their local rights, laws and liberties with them. They even had their own languages: whereas the western provinces spoke Dutch, Friesland had (and still has) its own language, and the other eastern provinces spoke either Oosters (which Hollanders could understand only with great difficulty) or Low German. The family of Orange-Nassau and their entourage spoke mainly French, as did many of the refugees who arrived in the North Netherlands from the south. In 1607 arrangements for a National Synod of the Reformed church were made in 'the two languages of the Netherlands: French and Dutch'; and in 1613 Maurice of Nassau built a special theatre for the company of resident French actors who entertained his court.

The religious complexion of the Republic was as varied as its languages. In a sweeping but famous generalization, a Swiss observer in 1672 estimated that one-third of the population of the United Provinces was Calvinist, another third was Catholic, and the rest were either Anabaptist or indifferent. There was doubtless some truth in this, but the strength of the various religious (and irreligious) groups was not the same in all areas. The Anabaptists, for example, constituted more than half the total populations in some areas of Friesland, and in 1580 it was estimated that 25 per cent of the whole province was Anabaptist. In 1660 the Anabaptists still numbered 13 per cent of the Frisian population, and the Catholics only 10. In the town of Rotterdam in 1622 there were 20,000 people, of whom about 1500 were Catholics (7½ per cent), and the rest either Calvinists, atheists, Jews or something else – in seventeenth-century Rotterdam there were ten different religions, and there were still many people who belonged to none of them. Thus neither religion nor language nor history could provide a basis for the lasting union of the North Netherlands provinces. Survival depended on the participants finding some concrete political or economic advantage in their continued association.

The trade of the northern provinces had prospered both by land and sea since the 1590s, accompanied by a growth in population, commerce and industry, especially in Holland. The clothworks at Haarlem and Leiden, the shipyards at Zaandam, the sugar refineries along the Maas all testified to the wealth of the province. The expanding opportunities for profit attracted immigrants from all parts of Europe, but above all from the South Netherlands. Many of these refugees were rich: about one-third of the wealthiest Amsterdammers in 1631 were of South Netherlands origin. However, few of the benefits of this economic miracle were felt by the inland provinces of the Republic. Gelderland was regularly ravaged by Spanish troops; 20 per cent of the agricultural land of Overijssel was abandoned in the early seventeenth century; even Utrecht province was not safe from military attack (see also pages 189–91 below). The revolt against Spain had brought prosperity to some areas but misery to others, and this divergent economic experience often led to political divisions.

Some cohesion was provided by the House of Orange-Nassau. William the Silent's second son, Count Maurice of Nassau, was already stadholder of Holland and Zealand. In 1590–1 he was elected stadholder of Gelderland, Overijssel and Utrecht as well, thus creating a measure of unity at the top of the administrative hierarchy; and Maurice's cousin William-Louis was stadholder of Friesland and, from 1594 onwards, of Groningen and Drenthe too. In addition, there were certain institutions which served the Union, rather than any individual province: the Council of State (for military matters), the mint, the admiralty boards and the audit office. But executive power rested with the provincial estates of each of the seven provinces in the Union, whose delegates sat in the States-General. This supreme assembly was a surprisingly small body, seldom consisting of more than twelve deputies, and often of no more than four or five. Even the provincial estates were small, with the clerical estate often abolished and only one or two representatives of the nobles. Effective power now rested with the councillors of the 57 towns represented in the provincial estates. These councillors, 2000 or so in number and known collectively as the 'regents', constituted the entire ruling class of the Republic.[5] Their grip on public affairs was only loosened twice in the seventeenth century, in 1618 and 1672, when the princes of Orange instituted a purge to remove their opponents from the leading towns, replacing them with new men more favourable to Orangist policies. At other times, the government of each major town (at least in the maritime provinces) was in the hands of a closed patriciate that excluded all other families either by formal agreements to ensure that offices rotated fairly within the closed circle, or (after 1650) by reducing the number of offices whenever it fell below the total of eligible families. The patricians were thus well shielded from popular opinion or democratic stirrings; and they could also effectively oppose autocracy, for they themselves deputed and instructed the colleagues who represented them at the provincial estates and, in turn, at the States-General. It was a world made safe for oligarchs, a world where they could grow rich in safety.

This complex structure, although far from democratic, involved the consent of too many people to be effective and harmonious at all times. Friction could easily develop over a wide range of issues, and particularly over financial, religious and foreign policy. There was normally prolonged opposition to war-taxation from Holland (which paid more taxes than any other province); and equally determined opposition to peace with Spain from the Calvinist clergy (whose influence counted for something in the estates, not least because many oligarchs were either the sons or fathers or brothers of ministers) and from the province of Zealand (which prospered from piracy at Spain's expense and from the Dutch blockade of the river Scheldt). The fact that unanimity was preserved over almost all issues up to and including the twelve years' truce of 1609 was due largely to the pressure of war, which encouraged some turbulent spirits to accept compromise rather than make the Republic more vulnerable to Spanish attack. But it also reflected the skill of the Advocate of the estates of Holland, Johan van Oldenbarnevelt.

The Advocate, whose role was to prepare, introduce and execute the business of the estates, had shown outstanding skill in handling both the foreign and domestic policy of his province during the war with Spain. But after the war ended, in 1609, Dutch politics came to be dominated by issues with which Oldenbarnevelt was less familiar and over which he had less control. Profound differences had developed among the Calvinist faithful in the 1600s, particularly concerning predestination and the right of civil magistrates to intervene in clerical disputes. At the centre of the controversy was one of the Amsterdam pastors, Jacob Hermans or Arminius. In 1592, in 1602 and again in 1608 he was accused of heterodoxy and challenged to a public disputation, but on each occasion the quarrel was settled by the civil authorities, who felt that an open schism in wartime was to be avoided at all costs. In 1609 Arminius died peacefully in his bed, but the coming of peace in the same year removed much of the restraint from the other protagonists in the dispute. The Arminian debate became far more passionate and almost everyone of political consequence was eventually forced to choose a side. The discussions over whether or not there should be a truce with Spain had already created two determined political parties: Oldenbarnevelt, who favoured a settlement, was supported by most of the regent class of

Holland; Maurice, who did not wish for peace, was supported by the Calvinists, the southern exiles and the city of Amsterdam. This division of opinion was kept alive and made sharper by the barrage of pamphlets issued by the supporters and opponents of the late Arminius, all appealing for support. On the whole the Calvinist establishment, the House of Orange, the exiles from the south, and the landward provinces sided with the anti-Arminians (known as Counter-Remonstrants or Gomarists), while the regent class of Holland sided with the Remonstrants (as the Arminians were known). The situation steadily worsened. The writings of Catholic theologians like Bellarmine against predestination (which Arminius had also attacked) opened the Arminians to accusations of being pro-Catholic. Their churches were attacked and their ministers mobbed, while Prince Maurice and the Gomarist magistrates and militia companies stood aloof and refused to protect them.

In 1616 there was a major riot at Delft against an increase in the corn excise duty: the town house was besieged for two days, barricades were erected and the houses of patricians were stoned by the mob. Although unconnected with the religious problem, it added to the general tension and in August 1616 Prince Maurice told his intimates that he believed that the unrest could only be settled by force of arms. Over the winter of 1616–17 attitudes hardened further, with Maurice and Oldenbarnevelt exchanging harsh words at a public meeting on 13 January 1617 and the stadholder openly siding with the Gomarists for the first time. From that point onwards the Arminians, and any politicians who tried to defend them, were doomed.

Yet Oldenbarnevelt still did not see this. He was deceived by Maurice's extreme reluctance to come to blows into thinking that the stadholder did not dare to attack him. So, since public order appeared to be threatened, in August 1617 the estates of Holland, led by Oldenbarnevelt, decided to authorize any town to raise troops of its own if it judged them to be necessary to preserve law and order; these troops, known as *waardgelders*, were to swear allegiance to the town which raised them. This move, although justified by the refusal of both Maurice and the militia companies to protect the Arminians from attack, proved unpopular with the other provinces and with the House of Orange. Oldenbarnevelt was reliably reported to have ordered the *waardgelder* officers to obey the estates of Holland 'even against the orders of the States-General and His Excellency' – a rumour that was to cost him his head.

In September 1617, outraged by this challenge to his military authority, Maurice began a political campaign designed to unseat the seventy-year-old Advocate. He methodically toured the landward provinces, purging them of their Arminian magistrates until by August 1618, all the provinces except Holland had been dealt with. Then battle was joined in the States-General where it was decreed that all the *waardgelder* units should be dissolved. The delegates from Holland, outnumbered and isolated, agreed; every town complied. Next Maurice purged the Holland towns of those Arminian magistrates who had challenged his authority; he agreed to convene a National Synod for the Dutch Reformed church at Dordrecht (Dort) to purge the Arminian ministers from its midst (300 were eventually expelled); and he permitted the States-General, now solidly anti-Arminian, to have Oldenbarnevelt tried for treason. He was found guilty, mainly because he had raised the *waardgelder* units without proper authority and had called on them to serve against Maurice if required. He was executed on 13 May 1619.

The constitutional crisis of 1617–19 in the Dutch Republic attracted considerable contemporary notice. The surrender of the *waardgelder* units was commemorated in paintings and prints as if it were a great victory and, in London, Fletcher and Massinger staged a play, *The Tragedy of Sir John van Oldenbarnevelt*. The execution of the Advocate was condemned by later generations, although it would have been folly to leave such an able adversary alive after his disgrace (it was not long before his family organized a plot against Maurice). But at the time, many observers, especially Protestants abroad, were not sorry to see him go: they much preferred Maurice's militancy in the cause of religion. Foreign merchants likewise had few regrets for the Advocate, whose monopolistic stand on Dutch overseas trade they resented. And Oldenbarnevelt's fellow-countrymen tended to see him as the dupe of a papal or Arminian plot. But it was the Habsburgs who had the greatest cause for rejoicing. The Advocate's fall, coinciding with the cautious foreign policy of France under Luynes, delivered the fate of Europe into the hands of Spain at a critical juncture – and at a moment when Spain was able and ready to seize the initiative.

3. Spain under Philip III

'The King of Spain', according to the English traveller Owen Feltham in 1652, 'hath now got a command so wide, that out of his Dominions the *Sunne* can neither rise nor set.' Although it appeared in a somewhat scurrilous work about the Low Countries (which Feltham described as 'the great Bog of *Europe*; . . . the buttock of the World, full of veines and bloud, but no bones in't'), this late tribute to the might of Philip IV serves as a reminder that the Spanish Habsburgs might sometimes seem to be down, but they were seldom out.[6] There have been suggestions that Spain's decline began in the 1590s and continued inexorably until the extinction of the Habsburg dynasty in 1700: such a view is too simplistic. The Spanish Empire appeared far stronger at the death of Philip III in 1621 than at the death of Philip II in 1598; Spain still seemed mightier than France as late as 1652 – when Feltham wrote – with the rebellions in Catalonia, Naples and Sicily suppressed but the Fronde still keeping the adolescent Louis XIV out of his capital. Philip IV still controlled absolutely an overseas Empire that was eight times the size of Castile and larger in extent than those of all other European powers put together.

Philip II passed on to his son an inheritance that was

larger than the one he had received from Charles V in 1555–6, for although the North Netherlands continued the rebellion they had begun in the 1570s, the extensive Portuguese seaborne empire was now securely in Habsburg hands. The overseas possessions of Castile (Mexico, Peru, the Caribbean islands and the Philippines) were complemented by those of Portugal (Brazil in America, Angola and Moçambique in Africa, and a chain of factories and fortresses stretching around the northern shores of the Indian Ocean and into the Pacific). The Atlantic islands and many North African ports were also firmly under Iberian control; and Spanish preponderance was assured in the South Netherlands, in Franche-Comté (to the east of France) and in Lombardy, southern Italy and Sicily.

However, weakness underlay almost every part of this impressive structure. In Spain itself an outbreak of bubonic plague in 1598–1602, following a run of poor harvests and high food prices, appears to have reduced the population of Castile by about ten per cent: some 600,000 people died. Apart from the capital, Madrid, the towns were particularly hard hit, as Table 6 shows. The loss of urban population seriously weakened both the demand for, and the production of, industrial goods, and was coupled with a drift away from the countryside of serious dimensions. As early as 1591, one of Philip II's ministers warned his master: 'The population is failing, and in such a way that many reliable people who have come from various parts of this kingdom are saying that it is a marvel to meet anyone in the smaller villages. In this way agriculture will very soon fail. It is to be feared that everything here will collapse . . .'[7] The heavy mortality, disruption and discomfiture caused by the plague and famine, coming as it did after a decade of political and military reverses (from the defeat of the Spanish Armada to the peace of Vervins), gave rise to pessimism and disillusion among Spain's ruling elite. The first modern novel to be written in Europe, Mateo Alemán's *Guzmán de Alfarache* (two parts, Madrid 1599 and 1604) was suffused with the spirit of impotent desperation that gripped the unfortunate Spaniards who were trapped between 'the plague that came down from Castile and the famine that rose from Andalusia'. The same spirit was reflected in the Memorial published in 1599 by a perceptive officer of the Inquisition of Valladolid, Martin González de Cellorigo, who invented the term 'decline of Spain' but offered few realistic cures for it. Despite this, Cellorigo's tract was followed by, literally, hundreds of others: although only 165 have survived from the reigns of Philip III and Philip IV, many others have been lost (often

Table 6. The Demographic Decline of Certain Castilian Towns, 1580–1650 (in households)

Town	1587–94	1601–11	1640–50
Avila	2826	—	1123
Burgos	2247	1528	800
Cádiz	900	400	—
Cuenca	3095	—	800
León	1086	—	600
Medina del Campo	2760	—	650
Palencia	2561	1143	800
Salamanca	4953	—	2965
Segovia	5600	3100	1625
Talavera de la Reina	2035	1804	1512
Toledo	10,933	—	5000
Valladolid	8112	6000	3000

because they were never printed). These writers, normally known as *arbitristas* (people who offered *arbitrios* or remedies; the term was coined by Cervantes in 1613), concentrated their attention upon political economy and diagnosed the 'Spanish disease' as being the country's rigid economic and social structure. They even employed – anticipating their modern counterparts – a special vocabulary of technical terms which made their proposals difficult to comprehend. By the 1630s they had become the butt of satirists and even of playwrights, portrayed either as misguided eccentrics or as enemies of the state.

The obsession with Spain's malaise and with finding remedies for it arose from the patent failure of the Madrid government to suggest solutions of its own. Philip III ruled by delegation: most of the decisions sent out in his name were in fact made by the fourteen advisory councils sitting in the royal palace at Madrid. Even in the field of foreign affairs, the king endorsed virtually without comment nine-tenths of the recommendations made to him by the relevant council (the council of state). A co-ordinating role might have been exercised by Don Cristóbal de Moura or by Don Juan de Idiáquez, who between them had held the central government together during the last years of Philip II; but Moura was sent from the court into honourable exile as viceroy of Portugal, and Idiáquez was too busy with foreign affairs until his death in 1612. Informed observers believed that the administration of Philip III was controlled by his favourite, the marquis of Denia (duke of Lerma from 1599) but they appear to have been mistaken: the council of state met 739 times between 1598 and 1618, but Lerma only attended on 22 occasions. While he could initiate or terminate policies at any time, Lerma seems to have shown little interest in doing so. His energies, such as they were, centred on securing advancement for his relatives and friends and riches for himself: his annual income rose from 8027 ducats in 1598 to 932,073 ducats (about £200,000 sterling) in 1625.

A reform committee (*Junta de Reformación*) was created to propose remedies for Spain's ills only after Lerma's fall in 1618, when it was really too late (and by the time it made its recommendations in 1623, it was certainly too late). Nevertheless the committee's findings were sensible and well informed. Two causes of decline were picked out as being of supreme importance: depopulation and poverty. The two phenomena, it was realized, were related and others besides the ten wise men on the committee could see it. In 1619, a shrewd friar from Toledo, Sancho de Moncada, studied the parish registers of the city for the three preceding years and noted that the number of marriages had declined by 50 per cent. He concluded that the reason for this was the poverty:

'people no longer get married because they have no money to buy food and set up a house together,' he suggested, adding that the heavy weight of taxes kept down the standard of living. The magistrates of Burgos agreed. In 1624 they informed the king that high taxes kept the city 'so depopulated that the people who live here are leaving because they can no longer make a living'. The tax quota of Burgos, for example, which was shared between 2247 households in 1595, was only shared between 915 households in 1618. And the total tax burden increased in the interim. Burgos declined to 823 households in 1624, to 800 in 1638 and to 700 in 1669 (see also Table 6).

Everyone realized how serious the loss of population was for Spain. 'What is a kingdom without people?' asked the *Discourse* of Pedro de Valencia in 1610: 'they are its wealth, its strength and its reputation'; 'Nothing is more necessary for keeping a kingdom strong and wealthy than an abundant population,' repeated Cristóbal Suárez de Figueroa in 1617; 'Without people there is no kingdom because people *are* the kingdom,' echoed Sancho de Moncada two years later. In time, even the government seemed convinced by the new orthodoxy: 'The sole foundation of a state', Philip IV informed the *Cortes* (Parliament) of Castile in 1622, 'is its population . . . and the greatest danger now facing this monarchy is its shortage of inhabitants.'[8] Yet such verbal recognition did not lead to practical action. On the contrary, certain government policies in the early seventeenth century tended directly and intentionally towards depopulation. The classic case was the decision, taken on 9 April 1609, to expel all Moriscos from Spain.

Morisco was the name given to persons of Arab descent who remained in Spain after the collapse of Moorish power and embraced the Christian faith (hence their other name: New Christians). There were several attempts in the sixteenth century to eradicate Moslem practices amongst the Moriscos. Twice government decrees had forbidden them, and twice there had been a revolt in the kingdom of Granada, where the Moriscos made up over one-half of the total population.

After the second revolt, in 1571, the surviving New Christians of Granada, about 90,000 in number, were plucked from their ancestral homes and forcibly resettled in small groups all over Castile. But even here, the Islamic practices continued and the close family networks remained intact. In Aragon and Valencia, to the east, the Moriscos were not resettled and made up about twenty per cent of the population. Philip II had created a special committee for the religious instruction of the Valencian Moriscos in 1596, which directed the activities of a team of twelve missionaries appointed to every diocese in the kingdom of Valencia, each team headed by a friar with experience of evangelism in the New World; but the task was too great. There were over 100,000 Moriscos in Valencia, many of them concentrated in all-Morisco villages, and almost as many again lived in Aragon. By 1609 it had become clear that evangelism and patience were not achieving the integration of the New Christians, and the government decided to accept the suggestion of the *Cortes* of Castile (which had also been offered in 1592) that the entire heterodox population should be expelled. A regiment of veterans was brought over from Naples to supervise the hunting down of those who – like Ricote the Moor in *Don Quixote* – either did not want to leave or else tried to come back; and by 1614, some 275,000 people had been deported, most of them going to France or North Africa. Most of the villages which the Moriscos abandoned were never recolonized; many of the complex irrigation schemes which they had tended fell into disrepair; much of the industrial output, especially silk which they had produced, was lost. Few landowners escaped serious financial loss: rural indebtedness increased. The expulsion was a demographic and economic blow from which the crown of Aragon was slow to recover. It was ironic that a measure which was so deleterious should have been carried out with such exemplary efficiency, when more valuable domestic policies were prosecuted so half-heartedly.

Foreign affairs, too, seldom gave cause for self-congratulation. Although peace was concluded with France in May

1598, Philip II bequeathed two long-standing wars to his son: one with England (begun in 1585), the other with his rebellious subjects in the Netherlands (begun in 1572 and extended after 1577). Both wars were fought not only in Europe but also on the high seas, where English and Dutch privateers sought to break the monopoly of the Iberian powers on trade with Asia, Africa and America. There were direct attacks (Spanish invasions of England were attempted in 1588, 1596 and 1597, and a landing was made at Kinsale in Ireland in 1601; Anglo-Dutch expeditions attacked Lisbon in 1589 and Cadiz in 1596). There were also bloody combats in American and Asian waters: between 1598 and 1635 the Portuguese government ordered all Dutchmen caught in the Indies to be hanged, while the crews of a dozen or more Dutch vessels in the Caribbean were hanged in 1605 alone. But the main theatre of the conflict was, naturally, the Netherlands, where an army in the south paid largely by Spain opposed another in the north paid in part by France. In addition, even after the Anglo-Spanish Peace of London was signed in August 1604, regular units of James I's army remained among the forces of the Republic, albeit at Dutch expense, holding the strategic ports of Flushing and the Brill until 1616.

The cost of these two conflicts was enormous. Apart from the expense of aggression, the threat of seaborne attack by her enemies made it essential to repair the coastal fortifications of Spain and Portugal, to mobilize a militia for coastal defence, and to maintain an Atlantic warfleet. There was also the direct damage inflicted by privateers on Portuguese and Spanish shipping, which cost between £100,000 and £200,000 every year in direct losses and a larger but unquantifiable sum via disruption to trade and discouragement to traders. Finally came the crippling outlay required to maintain an army in the Low Countries: every year, about 3 million ducats (some £700,000 sterling) in wartime, and perhaps half of that in peace, were sent from Castile. Some of it came from the crown's share of the silver mined in the New World and remitted back to Seville, but increasingly this treasure was required to improve the defences of America and the Philippines against the risk of a Dutch attack. There was even talk of abandoning the Philippines because of the cost of defending them, but the government feared that the Dutch might then use the archipelago as a base from which to complete the destruction of Portuguese shipping in the west Pacific. So between 1618 and 1621 the government of Spanish Mexico sent 1·65 million pesos (about £400,000 sterling) to the Philippines and only 1·5 million pesos to Spain.

This diversion of Spanish resources was precisely what the Dutch had intended. Warfleets were sent from the Netherlands in 1598–1600 (under Mahu and Cordes), in 1599–1601 (under van Noort), in 1615–6 (under van Spilsbergen) and in 1622–4 (under Lhermite) specifically to make as much trouble for Spain and Portugal overseas as was humanly possible. As soon as France signed the peace of Vervins in 1598, the leaders of the Dutch Republic realized that they needed to avoid becoming Spain's only enemy, left alone to face the greatest Empire of the world. They therefore sought to make alliances with every potential enemy of Philip III and Philip IV in the hope of causing them trouble in some part of the globe other than the Low Countries. Treaties were signed with the Sharif of Morocco in 1608, with the Ottoman Sultan in 1611, and with Algiers in 1612: the Dutch soon became the principal supplier of arms to North Africa and the chief ally of the Islamic rulers in their opposition to the Iberian powers. Among Christian powers, the Republic allied with the Palatinate (1604), Brandenburg (1605), the German Protestant Union (1613), Sweden (1614) and the Hanseatic towns (1616); regular ambassadors were exchanged after 1609 with France and Britain, and after 1615 with the Venetian Republic.

This diplomatic offensive meant that, even when open war between Spain and the Dutch in Europe ceased in 1609, the two enemies regularly found themselves opposing each other whenever there was an international crisis. The first such confrontation occurred over the Cleves-Jülich succession. Although French intervention in 1609–10 enforced an interim settlement unfavourable to Spain without much Dutch involvement, when the problem re-emerged in 1614 Henry IV was dead and the Republic felt obliged to intervene. The crisis began when the elector of Brandenburg, one of the two claimants, who had become a Calvinist, in May 1614 occupied the duchy of Jülich with Dutch assistance. The other claimant, the count of Neuburg, retaliated by becoming a Catholic and marrying the sister of Maximilian of Bavaria, head of the German Catholic League; and the Spanish army of Flanders moved in and occupied Düsseldorf, Wesel and several other towns of Cleves in Neuburg's name. For some time a new war seemed likely, but in November the treaty of Xanten apportioned the larger but less prosperous duchies of Jülich and Berg to Neuburg and the more attractive duchies of Cleves and Mark to Brandenburg. In 1616, moreover, the elector of Brandenburg placed the local administration and defence of his new lands in the hands of the Dutch, in return for a loan of 100,000 thalers – about £20,000 sterling. Spain was outmanœuvred again, although she retained the valuable right to cross the Rhine at Wesel.

At least in this case the Dutch were operating within their own sphere of influence. Italy was a different matter: Spain was used to having her own way there, not least during the first decade of the seventeenth century while the energetic count of Fuentes was governor of Lombardy for Philip III. A nephew of the great duke of Alva, who had advised Charles V and Philip II, Fuentes had proved an efficient minister in Portugal (1588–92) and a highly successful commander-in-chief in the Netherlands (1592–6). In Lombardy he exploited the indecision and delays of the government in Madrid to act on his own initiative a great deal: in 1601 he sent a veteran regiment into Savoy to garrison all strategic points along the Spanish Road linking Lombardy with the Low Countries; in 1602, without direct royal orders, he occupied the small marquisate of Finale which gave Lombardy a direct outlet to the sea; in 1603 he invaded the Valtelline, on the northern border of his province, and constructed a fortress known as the Fuentes Fort on a hill commanding the valley which connected Lombardy with Austria; and in 1604 he browbeat the Catholic Swiss cantons into permitting the passage of Spanish troops through their lands between Milan and Alsace. Finally, in 1607, he offered to invade Venice in order to enforce papal authority over the Republic.[9]

The ability of Spain's proconsuls to act in this high-handed manner, however, was short-lived. At a popular level, the Spanish presence in Italy was accepted because only Spain seemed capable of defending the peninsula from the Ottoman Turks. As late as 1600, Turkish successes in Croatia brought their forces within 100 kilometres of Trieste; as late as the 1590s reputable Italian statesmen, like Scipione Ammirato of Tuscany (1531–1601) were writing tracts which portrayed Spanish hegemony as Italy's only shield against Islam. But already the Turkish maritime threat had abated and after 1606 the danger of a land attack receded too. It became safe to question Spain's right to dominate.

In 1609, even before Fuentes's death, Duke Charles Emanuel of Savoy ordered the Spanish garrisons in the Alpine valleys to return to Lombardy, and he signed a treaty of alliance with France in April 1610 which guaranteed military assistance if either signatory were attacked by Spain. Even though the assassination of Henry IV the following month made this agreement (the treaty of Bruzzolo) worthless, both France and Savoy strove to undermine Spanish preponderance in the area. In 1613 France persuaded the Catholic cantons to repudiate their treaty of 1604 with Spain, while Savoy raised an army with which to defy Spain over the succession to the neighbouring duchies of Mantua and Monferrat, joined together since 1536 under the Gonzaga family and containing some 230,000 subjects. The conflict was, perhaps, unnecessary. It arose when Duke Francis IV died in 1612, leaving only a daughter and two brothers in holy orders, the elder of whom at once succeeded. The duke of Savoy argued that the daughter (who happened to be his own granddaughter: Duke Francis had been his son-in-law) should ultimately inherit the duchies. Spain, supported by the

Emperor (titular suzerain of both Mantua and Monferrat), claimed that when the late duke's brothers were dead, the Gonzaga family would be extinguished and the imperial fief would come under direct Habsburg control. In April 1613 Savoy invaded and occupied Monferrat in the name of his granddaughter; the duke of Mantua called in Spanish support to dislodge him. Hostilities began, after abortive attempts to negotiate a settlement, in June 1614; but Spain mismanaged her campaign, getting bogged down in sieges, while Savoy mobilized popular opinion by posing as the champion of Italian liberty against the yoke of Habsburg subjugation – Tassoni's vituperative 'Philippico' of 1615 set the tone. In June 1615 France negotiated an armistice (the peace of Asti) which restored the *status quo ante bellum* – but this, under the circumstances, was a serious reverse for Spain: a minor Italian prince had challenged her power and survived.

As peace came to one part of northern Italy, it departed from another. War broke out in 1615 between the Archduke Ferdinand of Styria (later to be Emperor Ferdinand II) and the Republic of Venice. It began because Venetian merchants had grown tired of losing ships to the piratical attacks of Balkan Christian refugees (the uskoks), based in the Croatian port of Zengg (or Segna), and living under Habsburg patronage. From time to time, piracy at Venetian expense proved so lucrative that the inhabitants of Zengg crawled from the harbour to the main church on their knees to offer thanks for their uninterrupted good fortune. Nothing the Venetians could do seemed able to stop them or reduce their success, and so in desperation the Republic began to attack the lands of Archduke Ferdinand in the hope of encouraging him to discipline his uskok vassals (although in fact they were subjects of the crown of Hungary, not of Styria). Ferdinand, not unreasonably, counter-attacked and the Republic retaliated by laying siege to the Inner Austrian town of Gradisca. It also promised support, withheld in 1615, to the duke of Savoy, if he should choose to defy Spain again, for Ferdinand of Styria was receiving considerable military aid from Spain. At the same time, promises of support came to Savoy from

France, where the aggressive ministers of Marie de Medici (with Richelieu in charge of war and foreign affairs) welcomed a chance to humiliate Spain; while the Venetian ambassadors in the Dutch Republic and in England secured firm promises of military aid. The duke of Savoy invaded Monferrat again in September 1616.

These developments caused grave consternation at the court of Spain. Even Lerma was affected, and made a rare visit to the council of state while it discussed the correct action for Spain to take. Speaking first, he pointed out that although political collusion between the Dutch, England, Venice and Savoy was serious enough, introducing Calvinist troops to Italy was far worse. 'Should we therefore stop these reinforcements from the North?' And how should we do it? And is it more important to maintain the [Catholic] religion and faith in Italy than to break the truce with the Dutch?' he asked his colleagues. The reply was firm and clear: if the Dutch sent help to Savoy, war would have to be declared against the Republic forthwith so that the army of Flanders could invade the North Netherlands. 'Religion and reputation . . . are the two great matters which sustain states,' the council reminded the king, and when they were involved there neither could nor should be any compromise.[10] In the event, papal mediation brought the fighting over Mantua to a halt before Dutch aid could arrive: the peace of Pavia (9 October 1617) again restored the *status quo* and postponed a decision on the succession question until the death of the reigning duke and his brother (which in fact only occurred in 1626–7). But in May 1617 2500 Dutch troops landed in Venice, and a second contingent of 2000 men arrived in the autumn, together with some English volunteeers. It is true that the Dutchmen mutinied and proved poor in action, and that (according to the English ambassador, Sir Henry Wotton) the English were too addicted to 'the three B's – beef, beer and bed'; but there was no overlooking the ten English and twelve Dutch ships which sailed into the Adriatic and opposed the fleet which Spain had loaned to Ferdinand.

A major crisis appeared to be brewing, but suddenly the

Archduke became deeply involved in the succession to the Holy Roman Empire. He lost interest in the uskok war. At the peace of Wiener Neustadt (1 February 1618) he obligingly agreed to move the pirates out of Zengg and resettle them in Croatia (Ferdinand had become king-designate of Hungary in 1617). But a general European conflict had only just been avoided, and the general political situation was still tense. The closer alliance of Ferdinand and Spain, matched by the military contacts of the Dutch with the Habsburgs' other opponents, had created two rival axes: one based on Vienna, Brussels, Madrid and Milan, with tacit support from Rome and Munich and Warsaw; the other anchored in London, the Hague, Turin and Venice, with tacit support from Paris, Stockholm and elsewhere. They linked the four sensitive areas where political tension had built up over the years and could easily erupt into open war. First, in the Netherlands, the truce between Spain and the Dutch was due to expire in April 1621. Second, in the Empire, the two confessional leagues in Germany and the conflict between Protestant estates and Catholic prince in the Habsburg lands seemed poised on the edge of violence. Third, a similar religious division, reinforced by dynastic differences, pitted Lutheran Sweden against Catholic Poland. Finally, there was the rivalry of France and the Habsburgs which made all areas of strategic value to both sides – Lorraine, Savoy, the Swiss cantons, the independent duchies of northern Italy – into potential trouble spots. Many argued that, with so many points of tension and so many international alliances linking them, a major European war could not be long averted. They were soon proved right.

CHAPTER V

The Apogee of Habsburg Imperialism

1. The Revolt of Bohemia, 1618–21

'The month of May will not pass away without great difficulty . . . because everything has already been prepared, especially in those places where the community has great power.'[1] The prediction for the year 1618 made by Johannes Kepler, the most famous astrologer of his day, proved uncannily correct: a 'great difficulty' occurred in Bohemia that was to last for thirty years, destroying both the prosperity of the kingdom and the power of its estates. But Kepler was not casting horoscopes in the dark: he did not hold the office of Imperial Mathematician for nothing. It was clear to all at the Emperor's court that the religious situation in the Bohemian lands had not been entirely settled by the Letter of Majesty of 1609 and the religious charter of 1611. Above all, there was no agreement about the Protestants' right to build churches on ecclesiastical land, or on land that had belonged to the crown in 1609 but had subsequently been alienated to the Catholic church (the question was important: Matthias alienated 132 parishes to the archbishop of Prague alone during his brief reign). By 1614, serious controversy had arisen in two towns where the new Catholic ecclesiastical lords attempted to close down Protestant churches built under the terms of the Letter of Majesty: Broumov (Braunau) and Hroby (Klostergrab), both near the mountainous northern frontier of the kingdom. The Bohemian estates regarded these as test cases and in 1614 and again in 1615 condemned the attempt to terminate Protestant worship in the two towns. The government, however, ignored all protests and in 1617 ordered the leading Protestants of Broumov to be arrested and authorized the lord of Hroby to pull down the Protestant church there. In addition, during the winter of 1617–18, the regency government (composed of seven Catholics and three Protestants) established a censorship of printed literature, prohibited the use of Catholic endowments to pay Protestant ministers, and refused to admit non-Catholics (who made up 90 per cent of the population) to civic office.

These measures were alarming. They appeared to presage an all-out attack on Protestantism in Bohemia and the Defensors created by the Letter of Majesty decided to convene a Protestant assembly in Prague on 5 March 1618. The assembly duly met and petitioned the Emperor (in Vienna) to redress the injuries done by his regents; they also wrote to the estates of Moravia, Silesia and Lusatia (which were joined to the Bohemian crown in a federal union) asking for support. On 21 March, as expected, Matthias rejected this petition; but he also, unexpectedly, declared the assembly to be illegal and he forbade it to meet again. This was certainly unconstitutional – the right of the Defensors to convoke an assembly was guaranteed in the charters of both 1609 and 1611 – and the Defensors felt justified in recalling their supporters to Prague for 21 May. The government again called on them to disperse, but the deputies refused. Instead, on 23 May they invaded the royal palace and hurled out of the window two of the Catholic regents whom they found there, on the grounds that they had advised Matthias to reject the assembly's petition in March. Two days after the Defenestration of Prague the assembly elected a committee of thirty-six directors, twelve from each estate in the Diet (nobles, gentry and burghers), to form a provisional government, and gave authority for them to raise an army of 5000 men to drive out the few garrisons in the country loyal to the Emperor. They also set about winning European public opinion over to their side: an *Apology* published in May presented their stand as one of tolerance and constitutionalism against bigotry and absolutism (by Matthias's wicked councillors, of course, not by the sovereign himself), and called for financial and possibly military support. Various towns of the Empire – Hamburg, Erfurt and so on – were asked to provide loans; sympathetic princes such as Christian of Anhalt, who had proved so helpful during the crisis of 1609, were requested to supply military equipment. Appeals were also sent out to the estates of the other Habsburg provinces, and in the summer of 1618 Silesia and Lusatia agreed to support Bohemia, sending troops to help repulse the army of 14,000 men sent in by the Emperor. In August the directors authorized all lords in Bohemia to explain to their vassals the reasons for the rebellion, in the hope of winning popular support (although, given the brutally repressive system of serfdom which prevailed in most areas, it was unlikely that lords and peasants would stand united for long).

At first, however, the Bohemian estates achieved some military success. In November 1618 their army captured Pilsen, one of the two remaining imperial strongholds in the kingdom, and before long negotiations began between the Emperor and his rebels. Even the death of Matthias on 20 March 1619 did not prevent the conclusion of a cease-fire and the opening of informal talks in April between the estates and the Archduke Ferdinand, who as king-designate of Bohemia automatically took over the reins of authority when Matthias died.

In many ways the Bohemian leaders had chosen a good moment for their new defiance. The death of Matthias left the imperial title vacant, and there was no agreement among the seven electors on his successor: the electors of Cologne, Trier and Mainz favoured Ferdinand of Styria, the Habsburg candidate; but Brandenburg, Saxony and the Palatinate favoured Maximilian of Bavaria; and Bohemia was now 'vacant'. In 1617, when it was clear that Matthias had not long to live, there had been some discussions among the spiritual electors concerning Maximilian's candidacy (the Elector of Cologne was his brother), but no decision had been reached. Ferdinand had, it is true, gained the support of Spain for his cause (by the treaty of Graz), but the Madrid government seemed to be preoccupied with organizing a campaign against the pirates of Algiers and preparing for the expiration of the twelve years' truce with the Dutch in 1621. Ferdinand even managed to forfeit some support. The excesses committed by his army in Moravia under the command of Albrecht of Wallenstein provoked such outcries that in May 1619 the non-Catholic members of the estates decided to expel all Ferdinand's officers and to ally with the rebels of Bohemia. In July the estates of Lower Austria did the same, creating a standing committee to govern the country until such time as the Archduke should confirm their liberties. In August, at the suggestion of their veteran leader Tschernembl, they entered into alliance with Upper Austria and with Bohemia. Now Ferninand only controlled Inner Austria and Hungary.

The confederates were also at first fortunate in their search for foreign supporters. From June 1619 the duke of Savoy offered to contribute towards the cost of a regiment of 2000 Germans raised in the Palatinate by Count Ernest of Mansfeld. Letters written on 16 June to the Dutch, the English, the Venetians and the German Protestants seemed likely to bear similar fruit. It seemed that Ferdinand would be forced to negotiate, and there seems little doubt that the confederate leaders expected to win with scarcely a blow being struck, as they had in 1609 and 1611. But the international climate had changed to their detriment. Although they commanded plenty of goodwill abroad, their supporters were no longer in control of policy. From 1617 until the spring of 1619, the Dutch Republic was paralysed by the deadly feud of Oldenbarnevelt and Maurice of Nassau (pages 142–5 above): every Bohemian appeal for aid was turned down or deferred. In August 1618 the States-General responded to the Bohemian appeal of 16 June by asking the German Protestants to help instead; in November they refused a Bohemian request for 600,000 florins and instead wrote to James I suggesting that he might help. But here, too, the Bohemians proved unlucky. Although James had signed a treaty of alliance with the German Protestant Union at Wesel in 1612, married his daughter to the Union's leader in 1613, and renewed the treaty of Wesel early in 1619, neither he nor his principal advisers were sympathetic to rebels, especially republican rebels. In the words of Lord Chancellor Francis Bacon in March 1617 (a full year before the Bohemian crisis broke) the English government deprecated the current 'creeping disposition to make popular estates and leagues to the disadvantage of monarchy'. In September 1619, James formally declared that he would send no aid to Bohemia; instead he offered to mediate in the dispute between Ferdinand and his subjects.

James's refusal of support was crucial, for none of the other powers sympathetically disposed towards Bohemia was prepared to act alone. France stood aloof, as did Venice, Sweden and Denmark; the duke of Savoy, discovering that he stood out of line, stopped paying for Mansfeld's troops in April 1619. After that, the only ally still prepared to provide aid to the Bohemians was Bethlen Gabor, since 1613 prince of Transylvania, who dreamed of conquering the rest of Hungary as his predecessor Stephen Bocskay had almost done during the revolt of 1604–6.

Nevertheless the rebels almost won, single-handed. Ferdinand too had received little aid from his supporters: Spain sent only money – 300,000 ducats (£75,000 sterling) in the course of 1618 – and Poland, the Papacy and the Archdukes in the Netherlands did not even send that. When the confederate troops marched on the imperial capital in May 1619 they met with no resistance and by 5 June they stood before the gates of Vienna. Even as they smelled victory, however, their cause was shattered by the arrival of a detachment of Ferdinand's regular soldiers in the capital and the news that on 10 June Mansfeld's home army had been defeated by imperial forces at Záblatí, leaving Bohemia undefended (and also delivering to Ferdinand all Mansfeld's correspondence with the Dutch and Savoy, discrediting both). The confederates reacted strongly to their defeat: in July they confiscated the property of the crown, Catholic institutions and loyalist subjects; and in August they deposed Ferdinand and elected Frederick of the Palatine king of Bohemia in his place.

Although these moves caused shock and surprise across much of Europe, they had been long prepared. Since at least 1614, some of the leading Bohemian Protestants had resolved that when Matthias died they should choose a sovereign who was not from the Habsburg dynasty. Unfortunately for them, when Matthias called a Diet in 1617 to designate his successor, plans for an alternative were still vague – some opponents of the regime favoured the elector of Saxony, others the Elector Palatine – but the pre-election of Ferdinand did not end the search for a suitable candidate. On 26 August 1619 the leaders of the movement put the matter to the vote: 146 were for the Palatine, 7 for Saxony. Two days later, 250 miles away at Frankfurt, the electors (unaware of Ferdinand's deposition) chose him to be Holy Roman Emperor.

Everyone realized the potential danger of the conflicting double election. 'If it is true that the Bohemians are about to depose Ferdinand and elect another king,' wrote Count Solms (Palatine ambassador at Frankfurt) to his master, 'let everyone prepare at once for a war lasting twenty, thirty or forty years. The Spaniards and the House of Austria will deploy all their worldly goods to recover Bohemia; indeed the Spaniards would rather lose the Netherlands than allow their House to lose control of Bohemia so disgracefully and so outrageously.'[2] Shortly after the election, the duke of Bavaria (who was a cousin of the Elector Palatine) warned Frederick that acceptance of the Bohemian offer would ruin him since the Habsburgs would be sure to take their revenge on the Palatinate as well as on Bohemia. Finally, the Evangelical Union at its meeting in September also advised him not to meddle in Bohemia, as did Frederick's own councillors: they advanced fourteen reasons for refusing the Bohemian crown and only six for accepting. Venice was also against acceptance. Only in England was there genuine enthusiasm. Although the king favoured mediation not intervention, there were many who favoured the Palatine cause, led by the archbishop of Canterbury, George Abbot. British intervention, he prophesied, 'will comfort the Bohemians, will honour the Palsgrave [Frederick], will strengthen the [Evangelical]

Union, will bring on the States of the Low Countries, will stir up the king of Denmark . . .; and Hungary, I hope (being in that same cause) will run the same fortune.'[3] This apocalyptic vision, in which Frederick was to lead the forces of godliness (the Protestants) to overthrow Antichrist (the Catholics), was taken up in the voluminous pamphlet literature of the time (most of it printed in Holland for distribution abroad). There was a public collection for Bohemia (which King James did his best to sabotage) and a recruiting drive (which only produced about 2000 men); but neither assistance was ready until the autumn of 1620. Dutch aid, too, was tardy and small. Although the States-General raised 5500 men and sent almost 250,000 florins (£25,000 sterling) between May and September 1619, thereafter the Dutch subsidies tailed off: only 300,000 florins more were sent between the autumn of 1619 and the spring of 1621. The only ally who actually provided substantial support for Frederick was the prince of Transylvania, Bethlen Gabor, who began the conquest of Habsburg Hungary in August 1619.

On political grounds, therefore, accepting the Bohemian crown was inadvisable: promises of support were few. But Frederick did not consider his politics to be purely secular. The Bohemian election, he told one of his uncles, 'is a divine calling which I must not disobey. My only end is to serve God and His Church.' And on 28 September he notified the Bohemian estates that he was prepared to accept the kingdom that they had offered. He was crowned in Prague on 4 November 1619, eighteen months after the Defenestration and eight after the death of Matthias.

It is possible that Frederick of the Palatinate would have thought more about obeying his 'divine calling' had he appreciated the significance of certain changes which were taking place in the government of Spain. On 4 October 1618, one of the duke of Lerma's favourites, Don Rodrigo Calderón, who held high government office, was arrested for murder.[4] His style of life had long been a source of envy and embarrassment, and his disgrace gave Lerma's enemies an opportunity to bring the patron down with his protégé. In the autumn of 1618, after a reign which had lasted twenty years, Lerma, who had taken holy orders and become a cardinal in March (to avoid a worse fate, no doubt), relinquished his influence over royal policy and patronage to others. Foreign affairs were taken over by Don Baltasar de Zúñiga, a veteran of the crown who had survived the Spanish Armada to become ambassador in Brussels (1599–1603), Paris (1603–8) and Vienna (1608–17). From the moment of his return to Madrid, where his nephew Olivares was already firmly entrenched as head of the household of the heir apparent, Zúñiga argued that Spain's first priority was to support the Austrian Habsburgs' authority, whether against Venice or against the turbulent estates. On 18 July 1618, even before the fall of Lerma, Zúñiga managed to persuade the king to send 100,000 ducats (about £25,000 sterling) to the Emperor, and to allow the Spanish-paid units in Istria to be used against the Bohemian rebels; on 2 August a further 200,000 ducats were dispatched. Over the following winter Zúñiga convinced his master that further measures were required and in May 1619, on Philip III's orders, 7000 troops left the Spanish army in the Netherlands and marched to Austria, while over the course of the summer a further 10,000 Spanish and Italian soldiers marched from Lombardy to join them. At the same time, more financial assistance – 500,000 ducats – arrived. The Papacy too provided subsidies: 60,000 Rhine florins (£10,000 sterling) in July 1618, with the promise in August of a regular monthly subsidy of 10,000 florins, raised in March 1620 to 20,000. By the end of 1620, the Pope had sent 380,000 florins to the Emperor, and a further 255,000 florins to the duke of Bavaria as head of the German Catholic League. In the years 1621–3 further subsidies of 1·3 million florins were sent to the Emperor, almost 700,000 to the duke of Bavaria, and more to Poland.[5]

However, both papal and Spanish aid almost came too late. In October 1619 Bethlen Gabor, having completed the conquest of Hungary, marched on Vienna, supported by the Bohemian confederate army and some troops raised by the

Austrian estates. For the second time in six months the imperial capital seemed about to fall. As the besiegers prepared for victory, however, news reached Bethlen that a cossack army, sent by the king of Poland to assist his brother-in-law Ferdinand, had crossed the Carpathians and was ravaging Transylvania. Poland was to pay a high price for this action – it provoked a full-scale Turkish invasion in 1620 because Transylvania was under Ottoman protection – but it saved Vienna and the Habsburg cause, for Bethlen at once withdrew his forces and thereby forced his allies to withdraw theirs. On 16 January 1620 he concluded a nine months' truce with Ferdinand.

The withdrawal of Frederick's last real ally left the confederate cause dangerously isolated: all he had now from abroad was empty promises. A Jesuit play in Antwerp contained a scene in which a courier announced to the Elector Palatine that 100,000 herrings had just arrived from Denmark, 100,000 cheeses from Holland, and 100,000 ambassadors from England. Rather more, however, was to come from Ferdinand and his friends. On 8 October 1619 the new Emperor held a strategic conference at Munich with Duke Maximilian of Bavaria, his university companion at Ingolstadt and his brother-in-law, at which it was agreed that the duke would use the army of the Catholic League to occupy the Upper Palatinate, which the Emperor would declare escheated in view of Frederick's behaviour. In return, the Emperor promised to reimburse the League's expenses, to allow the duke to retain any lands that his troops conquered, and to transfer Frederick's electoral dignity to Maximilian (Frederick's cousin). With these promises in his pocket, Maximilian in December persuaded the members of the Catholic League to help him recruit a force of 25,000 men for imperial service. He could easily afford it: his personal fortune already stood at 5 million Rhine florins (see page 84 above) and, in any case, the costs of the campaign were to be recouped later from Ferdinand.

On 30 April 1620 the Emperor issued his ultimatum that unless Frederick withdrew from Habsburg territory by 1 June, war would be declared on him; and on 9 May the government of Philip III sanctioned the dispatch of a large army from the Spanish Netherlands to occupy the Rhine Palatinate as soon as the Emperor gave the signal. A great deal depended on the attitude of the Evangelical Union, and here James I and Louis XIII came to the rescue. The former, adopting the recommendation of the pro-Spanish members of his council and always loath to encourage rebels, threw his influence with the Union on the side of neutrality. Louis XIII did the same, partly because of his fervent desire to advance the interests of the Roman church and partly in order to leave himself free to deal with his own Protestant problem (page 198 below). On 3 July, with the imperial ultimatum to Frederick expired, French and English envoys persuaded the Evangelical Union, meeting at Ulm, to remain neutral and to provide no assistance to their erstwhile director. Already the leading Lutheran prince, John George of Saxony, had agreed to invade Lusatia in the Emperor's name (on the understanding that he would be allowed to keep it once Frederick had been defeated).

After the agreement at Ulm, the imperial campaign was ready to be launched. The Union looked on while the army of the League crossed into Lower Austria on 24 July and the small imperial army overran Upper Austria. The Dutch, who in September 1619 had boasted that they would 'make such a course by way of divertion that the Spanish troops in these provinces under the Archduke shall not be spared or have commoditie to be employed into Germanie', stood by and watched in August 1620 as Spinola led 22,000 troops across the Rhine on pontoon bridges at Koblenz, invaded the Rhine Palatinate and captured thirty towns in six months. The army organized the first contributions system of the Thirty Years' War and found the living as easy 'as if we were in Toledo'. The Saxon army meanwhile began its advance into Lusatia and Silesia.

The confederate main army still remained intact; with about 24,000 men it indeed slightly outnumbered the Catholic forces. But the confederates were demoralized, the Dutch units were mutinous, and their commanders counted on the approach of winter to save them. Realizing this, the veteran Catholic commanders (both Bucquoy, who led the Spanish imperial army, and Tilly, who commanded the troops of the League, had over thirty years of active service behind them) decided to risk a battle and on 8 November 1620 they attacked the confederates in their hastily dug trenches on the White Mountain (Bílá Hora) outside Prague. The engagement lasted only an hour, but it proved decisive: the confederates were routed and fell back on Prague in disorder. Frederick and his court evacuated their capital the same day, leaving Prague in such haste that Queen Elizabeth did not have time to count her children and feared, for some time, that she had left one behind. And with the collapse of the central government, resistance elsewhere was doomed.

For most inhabitants of the Bohemian lands, there had never been much point in fighting for 'the Winter King', a rigid Calvinist who cared little for the Hussite beliefs of the majority of his subjects. Although 'elected', Frederick in fact owed his throne to a small group of noblemen who enjoyed little support either from the towns, which were required to pay higher taxes after the Defenestration, or from the peasants, who had to endure the excesses of the ill-paid soldiery. By the summer of 1620, large areas of Bohemia were lost to Frederick either through peasant revolt or by peasant defection to towns loyal to the Emperor. Observers at the court of the Winter King, men who were by no means democrats, were astounded by the indifference or cruelty shown by Frederick and his entourage towards the 'wretched peasants'. Only the Austrian leader Tschernembl argued that if 'the serfs be freed and serfdom abolished . . . Common people will then be willing to fight for their country.' He even believed that the peasants would fight more effectively than the troops raised abroad. But he was overruled: the confederate leaders depended upon the systematic exploitation of their peasants, and any reduction in labour services or social control threatened their well-being. They fought badly, as the English said, for a good cause.

Perhaps Tschernembl was a little hard on the foreign troops. Some of them resisted the Habsburgs long after the White Mountain: Mansfeld's officers held on to Pilsen until March 1621, while the Scottish and Dutch troops sent by the States-General retained Tabor until November 1621 and Trebon until October 1622. In the Rhine Palatinate the English garrison of Frankenthal held on until ordered to surrender in May 1622 by James I. All of Frederick's domains were now under Catholic control; the west bank of the Rhine in the hands of Spain, the east bank and the Upper Palatinate in those of the League. By this time, Silesia, Lusatia and Moravia had also surrendered, and Bethlen Gabor had withdrawn from Hungary. The whole of the Habsburg lands lay at Ferdinand's feet.

2. *Years of Victory, 1621–3*

The Habsburgs' victory over the confederates and their foreign supporters was thus secured comfortably before the expiration of the twelve years' truce with the Dutch on 9 April 1621. Spinola returned to the Low Countries at the end of April with half his army of conquest, leaving a subordinate to complete the siege of Mannheim, Frankenthal and Heidelberg, the only towns still holding out for Frederick (they all surrendered in 1622). As late as 1 April Spinola was able to use his Palatine troops to browbeat the Protestant Union into an agreement to disband their troops in return for a guarantee that Spain would respect their neutrality (the Mainz Accord). The march of events could hardly have been better timed from Spain's point of view.

Nevertheless, the decision not to renew the Dutch truce in 1621 was surprising, since few in Madrid had anticipated such an easy victory in Germany and no one wished to fight on two fronts at once. But there was invincible opposition among Spain's ruling elite to prolonging the truce with the

Dutch on the same terms. There had been active discussion of the issues involved since March 1618, when a circular letter from the king's secretary invited the central councils to give their views on the correct policy to be followed towards the Netherlands after 1621. The Council of Finance was, predictably, opposed to any move – such as a declaration of war – that might increase public expenditure, especially when funds were already deeply committed in Germany. This was also the view taken by the Archdukes in Brussels. However, the councils of Portugal and the Indies were insistent that the truce had ruined the Iberian overseas empires by permitting the Dutch to expand their trade to an unprecedented degree: there were now Dutch forts at Arguim in West Africa, at Pulicat in India, at Batavia in Indonesia and at the mouth of the Amazon in America. There were Dutch traders on every sea. Of course, some of this clandestine trade was inevitable. America, Asia and Africa all produced goods that were attractive to the Dutch, and they produced them in greater quantities than the Spanish and Portuguese fleets could handle. In addition, certain areas (such as the Caribbean) produced commodities of large bulk and low value that Spanish shippers found it unprofitable to handle – and with no outward cargoes, no European goods were brought back. Neglected areas of the Spanish system like the Caribbean were therefore sitting targets for Dutch interlopers, and they were welcomed by the local communities: both sides were happy to exchange cheap colonial raw materials for European manufactures. Over 150 Dutch ships every year visited the Caribbean after 1594, 25 more traded annually with West Africa, 20 with Brazil and (after 1600) 10 with the Far East. In each area, the number of Dutch ships involved increased after the signing of the twelve years' truce in 1609. If that had been all, perhaps the Spanish government would have been prepared to tolerate the Dutch presence overseas. But there was more. Dutch expeditions also set out to foment rebellions against Spain among the native tribes of America and there were direct attacks on Spanish colonial outposts (see pages 151–2 above). So Philip III's councillors were able to argue not only that the truce had made Holland rich, but that continuing the *status quo* would make the Iberian powers poor, through the appropriation of their overseas empires. The Council of State also feared that unless war were renewed in the Netherlands, the Dutch would be free to support Spain's enemies in Italy again, as they had done in the case of Savoy and Venice in 1617–18.

The ministers of Philip III were thus faced by an impossible dilemma: on the one hand the monarchy's prestige, strategic position and commercial prosperity made war necessary; on the other, the lack of money and the over-extension of her resources dictated prudence. Even when all the advice had been received, in April 1619, the king's chief minister Don Baltasar de Zúñiga could see no solution:

> . . . we cannot, by force of arms, reduce those provinces to their former obedience. Whoever looks at the matter carefully and without passion, must be impressed by the great armed strength of those provinces both by land and by sea, their strong geographical position ringed by the sea and by great rivers, lying close to France, England and Germany. Furthermore that state is at the very height of its greatness, while ours is in disarray. To promise ourselves that we can conquer the Dutch is to seek the impossible, to delude ourselves. To those who put all blame for our troubles on to the Truce and foresee great benefits from breaking it, we can say for certain that whether we end it or not we shall always be at a disadvantage. Affairs can get to a certain stage where every decision taken is for the worse, not through lack of good advice, but because the situation is so desperate that no remedy can conceivably be found.[6]

It was highly significant that although Zúñiga and his fellow-councillors were very clear about what constituted defeat for Spain, they were unable to imagine what would constitute victory.

Eventually it was resolved that the truce might be renewed

only if certain clauses of the original agreement were changed in Spain's favour. Zúñiga hoped for four things: that the Dutch should grant full toleration for Roman Catholics in the Republic; that navigation down the Scheldt to and from Antwerp should be free of all control and taxation by the Dutch; that Dutch trade to America should cease; and that Dutch trade to Asia should be restricted. Realizing that these demands were unlikely to be met, the Madrid government made preparations to resume the war on a more economical footing than that prevailing before the truce. Far greater economic pressure was to be placed on the Dutch, via embargoes, piracy and naval action, with the Army of Flanders restricted to a defensive role.

The Dutch, of course, were not prepared to dance to Spain's tune. The fall of Oldenbarnevelt muted the political voice of his supporters, the oligarchs of the West Netherlands towns who, like Spain, favoured renegotiation of the truce. Instead, in August 1619 the Orangist-dominated States-General authorized the construction of a special war-fleet which was to sail to Peru and capture (or destroy) the silver with which Spain hoped to finance the war in the Netherlands. Without the active support of the western towns, however, more expensive preparations were not possible: the Holland oligarchs contributed half the Republic's taxes. The States-General's leaders therefore had to go through the motions of serious negotiation, even though they intended to fight, in order to convince the peace-party in the Republic (as well as foreign powers) that agreement with Spain was impossible. A very complex quadrille therefore took place in 1620 and 1621 in which Spain (and, to a lesser extent, the Archdukes) were encouraged to raise their demands by false reports circulated by the Dutch that they were hopelessly divided and were prepared to renew the truce on almost any terms. These leaks were supported by similar rumours, equally mischievous, from England and France. England wished to see the fighting recommenced because it might aid James I's son-in-law, Frederick V, to recover the Palatinate from the Spanish army of occupation. France, too, wished

Spain to resume the war against the Dutch, because it would divert Spanish resources from Italy, where France was attempting to re-establish her influence; and on 11 January 1621 the French ambassador in Brussels was instructed to seek 'the opportunity dexterously to manage the situation over there in accordance with His Majesty's intention that the truce should be broken'. In the end, despite an elaborate secret diplomatic service, the Habsburgs appear to have been totally taken in by their enemies and when a formal mission was sent to the Hague to renegotiate the truce in March 1621, it demanded that the 'rebels' should recognize Spanish sovereignty again. No one in the States-General could tolerate that, so the Orangists were able to secure universal support for the renewal of war.

There was, however, a price to be paid. More than 800 Dutch vessels traded profitably with ports in the Spanish and Portuguese empires every year; perhaps two-fifths of all the Republic's seaborne commerce, measured in terms of tonnage, was with the Spanish monarchy. But in April 1621 all Dutch ships were expelled, together with the Dutch merchants resident in Spain and Italy, and an embargo was placed upon the import of Dutch goods. There was an immediate slump in Dutch trade, and at first the Spaniards seem to have hoped that this economic pressure might force concessions from the beleaguered Republic. Certainly a stream of secret envoys crossed the frontier from Brussels to the Hague and back. When nothing happened, early in 1622 military pressure was added: the strategic fortress of Jülich, held by the Dutch since the emergency of 1614, was captured in February; the stronghold of Steenbergen, in North Brabant, was taken in July. Then, rather misguidedly, the victorious army of Flanders was sent to besiege the seaport of Bergen-op-Zoom. In spite of every effort, the canal that linked the town to the sea remained open, so that victuals and reinforcements were able to arrive throughout the siege. Meanwhile, the losses among the besiegers were catastrophic: of the 20,000 men who surrounded Bergen in July, only 13,000 remained in October. In the end the siege had to be abandoned because not enough men were left to resist the approaching relief army.

Philip IV, who at the age of sixteen had succeeded his late father as king of Spain and Portugal in March 1621, was not impressed by this performance. Neither were his ministers. At a debate of the council of state in April 1623, an experienced adviser contended that 'The war in the Netherlands has been the ruin of this Monarchy' and that 'The manner in which the war is waged at the moment is the worst that could be': Spain could not afford to support an army of 63,000 men costing £100,000 a month which scored few successes. Subsequent meetings of the council concluded that besieging Dutch towns like Bergen was nothing but a waste of men and money, and that economic warfare should replace sieges. Expenditure on the fleet in the Netherlands therefore trebled in the course of the year (and the increase was deducted from the army's budget), while in Spain regular checks on neutral shipping were commenced. In 1623 over 150 British, French and German vessels in Spanish ports were given a surprise search by special commissioners from Madrid, and those found to be carrying Dutch goods were subjected to fines and confiscations. From 1624 this economic warfare was coordinated by a new 'Admiralty for the North' (the *Almirantazgo del Norte*).

It was perhaps unfair to generalize from the army of Flanders's failure before Bergen-op-Zoom, for Spinola and his troops had been defeated by totally unforeseen developments in Germany. After the White Mountain, Frederick of the Palatinate made attempts to rally his supporters in Lusatia (December) and to secure assistance from Denmark (February 1621) before finally taking asylum with the Dutch, where he set about organizing a new campaign. On 27 April the elector signed a treaty by which the States-General agreed to subsidize a campaign to reconquer his patrimonial lands. James I also sent 2000 men and some money, although he insisted that his son-in-law should not ally with Bethlen Gabor, a vassal of the Turk whose victories (whether scored against Poland or the Emperor) would advance the cause of Islam at the expense of Christendom. Instead, Frederick was to concentrate on finding German allies. Christian of Brunswick (Protestant administrator of the diocese of Halberstadt and cousin of the queen of Bohemia) and the margrave of Baden-Durlach both agreed to raise an army for the Palatine cause, while Mansfeld succeeded in extricating some of the survivors of the Bohemian campaign and leading them to Alsace. In April 1622 Frederick left the Hague to join Mansfeld.

The Habsburgs and their allies, however, were fully prepared. There were 4000 Spanish troops in Alsace and 5000 more in the Alpine valleys that linked Alsace and Austria with Spanish Lombardy; the army of the Catholic League under Tilly was fully mobilized; and Spain and the Papacy continued to send funds to both the League and the Emperor. Thanks to their superior state of readiness, the Catholic army was able to prevent Frederick's supporters from effecting a union. Instead they were defeated individually: the margrave of Baden at Wimpfen on the Neckar (6 May); Christian of Brunswick at Höchst on the Main (20 June). Only the army of Mansfeld lived to fight another day: after the rout of his allies he led his troops north towards the Netherlands, and it was their surprise arrival before Bergen-op-Zoom that forced Spinola to abandon the siege on 4 October.

This, however, was small consolation for Frederick and his supporters. 'Madame my dearest and most beloved Queen,' Brunswick grovelled to the queen of Bohemia on the morrow of his defeat at Höchst, 'the fault is not that of your most faithful and affectionate servant who ever loves and cherishes you. I entreat you, most humbly, not to be angry with your faithful slave for this disaster.' But it was impossible not to be dispirited. 'There ought to be some difference made between friend and enemy,' Frederick complained from Mansfeld's camp on 8 July, 'but these people ruin both alike . . . I think these are men who are possessed of the devil and who take pleasure in setting fire to everything. I should be very glad to leave them.'[7] A week later he could stand it no longer, and returned to the Hague, cancelling his commissions to Mansfeld and Brunswick.

The Emperor did not give up so easily. The few Protestant

princes who had rashly joined Frederick in the course of 1622 – the dukes of Weimar as well as Christian of Brunswick and Baden-Durlach – were systematically hunted down and their forces destroyed at Stadtlohn, as they tried to escape into the United Provinces (6 August 1623). An attempt by Bethlen Gabor to support this new Protestant challenge was defeated at the same time. Meanwhile all remaining pockets of resistance in the Palatinate and in Bohemia were liquidated. The time had come to settle scores with those who had rebelled. Although Ferdinand was not the tyrant that his enemies made him out to be, no early modern monarch could afford to leave open armed rebellion unpunished: chastisement was unavoidable.

The work of pacification was begun almost immediately by the armies of occupation (Bavarian in Upper Austria, imperialist in Bohemia and Moravia, Saxon in Lusatia and Silesia). Some of the rebels were executed out of hand; some saw their property looted or burned; some had their estates confiscated at once. Even before the White Mountain, by a decision of 6 August 1619, Ferdinand began to transfer the possessions of the rebels to his army commanders in lieu of pay, thus ensuring that their armies kept in the field. A fortnight after the White Mountain, an imperial proclamation confiscated all rebel property and created a judicial commission to ascertain who had been involved in the revolt. On 21 June 1621, 27 persons (including the rector of Prague University) were executed, and in the course of the year some 486 landed estates (over half the total of all estates) and numerous merchants' fortunes were confiscated.

Those who survived the scrutiny of the judges were punished in a different way: by the rapid devaluation of the currency. Towards the end of 1621, the Emperor decided to pay off his forces by selling all the confiscated estates for 30 million florins. To assist the purchasers to raise this sum quickly (the army had to be paid until it was demobilized) Ferdinand issued a licence to a consortium of the principal buyers which allowed them to mint new debased silver currency and distribute it at the old higher prices. Since coins worth 42 million florins were minted during 1621 and 1622, and since the consortium managed to strike twelve times as many coins for the same amount of silver as before, the operation was a great success: the buyers all became very rich and were able to pay cash for their new lands very soon. But for the populations of Bohemia, Moravia and Austria, where the new currency circulated, the Emperor's policy brought ruin.[8] Until 1623, only those who had been actively involved in the rebellion found it prudent to take refuge abroad, but after the great debasement more and more people – perhaps 120,000 in all – left the country. In 1628 the imperial decree expelling all Protestant nobles turned this exodus into a flood. Many of the refugees came to neighbouring Saxony, where the Czech church in Dresden had 74 members in 1623, 400 in 1629 and 642 in 1632. They brought wealth and expertise with them, and retained their customs, language, religion and organization – including printing presses which published such important works as the first Czech edition of Comenius's *Labyrinth of the World* (Pirna 1631: a sad and bitter exposure of the futility of men's ideals and aspirations, contrasted with the security of God's protection). Before long, the Lutheran clergy of Saxony began to fear the corrupting influence of so many committed Calvinists and Hussites in their midst; by 1630 they were printing Czech texts themselves to explain Lutheran doctrine in the hope of converting some of the newcomers.

Few of these exiles ever went back, except during the brief occupation of Prague by the Saxon army in 1631–2. They would not abandon their religion and the Habsburgs were no longer prepared to rule over heretics. The patrimonial provinces might be less prosperous and less populous (Bohemia's population fell by 50 per cent in 1615–50; Moravia's by 30 per cent); but the Habsburgs considered the devotion of the surviving inhabitants to church and dynasty to be ample compensation.

Ferdinand took steps to detach his newly purified hereditary lands from the rest of the Empire, turning them into a sort of entail. In 1621 he decreed that his various patrimonial provinces should remain joined in all time coming and should pass by primogeniture. He introduced special institutions for them: a common chancery (*Hofkanzlei*) was created in 1620 and the competence of the war council (*Hofkriegsrat*) and Aulic council was extended to cover the entire patrimonial lands. The constitution of Austria was revised in 1625, that of Bohemia in 1627 (the process included the ceremonial revocation of the Letter of Majesty, which Ferdinand symbolically tore with two strokes of his dagger). Moravia was given its 'renewed constitution' in 1628. In all these areas German became the official language of government; and the national language, like the national religion, was by-passed whenever it conflicted with that of the sovereign. The independence of the estates was terminated, the authority of prince and Diet giving way to that of prince alone. Only in Hungary did the old dualist system survive: with Bethlen Gabor still anxious to expand his territories, Ferdinand had no intention of repeating the errors of 1604–5.

The same policies of enforcing religious, political and linguistic uniformity were also followed by the new landlords who bought up the confiscated property that flooded the market in the 1620s. The measures implemented by the Czech nobleman Albrecht of Valdstejn, or Wallenstein as he became known, in the compact duchy of Friedland, acquired in 1622–4 and covering 100 square miles in the north of Bohemia, may serve as an example. It yielded the duke a revenue of £70,000 sterling (four times Charles I's receipts from Scotland). Wallenstein's government was conducted entirely in German ('You must have a German clerk in the chancery, for I do not wish anything to be handled in Czech') and 99 per cent of his own letters were now written in German. He was assisted, at the height of his power, by a household of 899 persons (including a private hangman) costing 20,000 thalers (more than £4000 sterling) a month to maintain in salaries, clothes and food. Most of these servants, and their sustenance, came from Wallenstein's own estates and thus provided valuable employment. The duke's new subjects also benefited from his economic policies: he bought exemption from billeting and military transit for his domains (most of the other soldier landlords, who knew how effectively their troops could destroy, did the same); he purchased as much as he could inside his duchy for his household and, after 1625, for the imperial armies that he commanded ('I would sooner that Friedlanders have it than outsiders rob me'); he encouraged prospecting for natural resources and provided the capital to develop them; in 1628 he ordered a twenty-one-point *Economic System* to be published, explaining how his lands were to be exploited. And those who did not participate in the system were punished by Wallenstein's own private judicial system from which, by imperial decree, there was no appeal after 1627. Thus indwellers could be compelled to drink only beer made at the ducal breweries, and failure to do so involved fines for them, for the publican, and for the lord of the village in which the outrage occurred. Moreover the beer was to be of good quality: one brewer whose beer left a nasty taste on the ducal palate was sentenced to 100 lashes. This absolutism at local level was not confined to economic matters. While the *Reformationskommission* in the rest of Bohemia expelled all Protestant ministers in 1622 (and from Moravia in 1624), and then all Protestants in 1628, Wallenstein carried out his own purges in Friedland, but at a slower rate. He set up a Jesuit college at Gitschin, his capital, in 1623, and made plans for a separate ecclesiastical organization under a bishop (a plan that, like the proposed constitution and Diet for the duchy, fell through because Wallenstein died before it could be implemented); but Protestants were allowed to reside, and some even held office until 1628.

Elsewhere in Bohemia, the new landlords were neither as restrained in religion nor as gifted at economics, but the burden of their demands was just as high. Eventually, the combination of religious persecution and ruthless exploitation of labour services, aided by the currency disorders, produced widespread popular revolts. There were three in Bohemia and eastern Moravia in 1622, 1624–5 and 1627, but the most dangerous one occurred in Upper Austria in 1626. The

Austrian lords had for some time employed trained administrators to run their estates on more efficient principles – increasing labour services and taxes, acquiring the judicial rights to enforce them, and controlling the movement and consumption of their subjects. After the major peasant revolt of 1595–7 there was some relaxation of the pressure, but after 1620 confiscation, inflation and persecution created a serious new situation. In particular, Ferdinand's *Reformationskommission* began to take away the church property and school endowments that had been administered by Protestant parish councils, to their considerable profit and prestige, and they also deprived Protestants of local office. Catholic creditors were encouraged to foreclose on Protestants and force the sale of their lands. In July 1626 the various grievances provoked the outbreak of the most important popular rising in the German-speaking lands since the Peasants' War of 1524–5. The popular leaders were all Protestants from well-to-do peasant families that had provided local magistrates in the past and enjoyed a natural status in the community, a status that seemed doomed under the New Order of Ferdinand.

Yet the rebellion, which was suppressed by the army of the Catholic League after pitched battles in November 1626, was not directed against Ferdinand, because Upper Austria was under Bavarian administration. The Emperor, lacking adequate funds with which to pay the costs of Maximilian's army during its service against Bohemia, had allowed the duke to administer Upper Austria both as a partial reimbursement and as a guarantee that Bavaria would eventually receive the rewards promised at Munich in October 1619 (see page 166 above). The administration therefore was Bavarian, but it was made to carry out Habsburg policies: although Maximilian wished to preserve the *status quo* in order to keep revenues flowing in, Ferdinand wished to extend his economic and social control. It was the Emperor's policies that caused the revolt of 1626 and thereby led Maximilian to hand Upper Austria back in 1628, having received only one million florins in revenue instead of the six million he had expected, the twelve million Ferdinand owed him or the twenty million he had spent on the army of the League. But by 1628 Maximilian had received other, non-financial rewards and Ferdinand was fully able to complete the subjugation of Austria by himself.

Frederick V had been declared an outlaw by the Emperor in January 1621. Many people in Germany, supported by the kings of Spain and England, at first believed that the ban should be lifted and Frederick restored to his ancestral possessions. But his invasion of the Empire in 1622 cut the ground from under this position: Frederick was clearly a rebel now, and he made no secret of his plans to break the imperial peace in 1623 as well. The Emperor therefore decided that the moment was ripe to settle scores. In January 1623 he convened a meeting of the leading princes of the Empire at Regensburg, where he proposed that Frederick should be deprived of his electoral dignity as well as of his lands, and that both should be transferred to Maximilian of Bavaria. It was argued that the electorate at least was Bavaria's by right, since in 1329 it had been agreed that the dignity should alternate between the Bavarian and the Palatine branches of the Wittelsbach family, but the Palatines had never relinquished it. But this argument cut little ice at Regensburg. Opposition to the transfer had to be overcome in other ways. Saxony was placated by the cession of Lusatia; Brandenburg (the other Protestant electorate) received extensive rights over East Prussia from Ferdinand's brother-in-law, the king of Poland; and the Catholic princes, already warm in the support of their League's leader, had any further scruples removed by the able diplomacy of the papal envoys who pointed out that the transfer would give the Catholic electors a majority of five to two, instead of four to three (an aim of papal diplomacy since at least May 1621). At last, all objections and difficulties (in Spain as well as in Germany) were overcome and on 25 February 1623 Maximilian was finally invested with the electoral dignity and the Upper Palatinate (the Lower, or Rhenish Palatinate remained for the time being in Spanish hands). The papal agents (who became so numerous at Regensburg that it was considered prudent to withdraw some) asserted that the transfer would save the Catholic cause from defeat in Germany and both Maximilian and Ferdinand claimed to believe that it would terminate the troubles which, since 1618, had threatened to engulf the Empire. But all this was merely rhetoric, for in February 1623 the Catholic League voted to raise more taxes in order to keep their army in being and in March Ferdinand and Maximilian renewed their defensive alliance. Everybody recognized that the ceremony at Regensburg constituted an open challenge to the general Protestant cause which linked not only Dresden and Berlin, but London, Copenhagen, Stockholm and the Hague as well.

3. Rise and Fall of a Coalition, 1624–9

Late in 1621, a detachment of Frederick V's army intercepted an imperial courier carrying a package of highly secret letters from the Emperor and the nuncio in Vienna. They revealed in embarrassing detail the plans of the Habsburgs and the Papacy for the reorganization of the Empire, including the transfer of the electorate (which until now had been a closely guarded secret); and in March 1622 Frederick's councillor, Ludwig Camerarius, published the letters in a series of pamphlets, together with a witty yet damning commentary. The most popular tract, entitled 'The Spanish Chancery' (*Cancelleria hispanica*: 173 pages) revealed the full extent of papal plotting in Spain, Italy and Germany to secure both the electorate for Maximilian and the re-Catholicization of the Empire. For some time it was not believed, because the Catholics maintained it was a forgery (it was not; neither was 'the Anhalt Chancery', a Catholic pamphlet of 1621 composed of documents captured at the fall of Prague, on which 'The Spanish Chancery' was modelled); but after February 1623 it was clear that everything Camerarius had said was true. The pamphlet was reprinted with additions and enjoyed even greater success, and Camerarius began to exploit the support that he had mobilized. From the Hague he directed the efforts of Frederick's government-in-exile towards the formation of a great anti-Habsburg coalition, which would recover the Palatinate and Bohemia for his master. His efforts continued unceasingly until, in 1631, many of those who had fled so precipitately from Prague after the battle of the White Mountain were able to return.

The Palatine government-in-exile had two distinct objectives: to fight unceasingly '*pro causa communi*' (that is, for the restoration of a religious peace in the Empire favourable to Protestantism) and '*pro rege bohemiae*' (that is, to regain Bohemia and the Palatinate for Frederick). It was the precise mirror-image of the papal programme. The Palatine protagonists also employed the opposite methods: where the Papacy sought to work through autocratic princes to establish confessional absolutism, Frederick's advisers wished for aristocratic constitutionalism to secure a measure of toleration. This made Camerarius, in particular, careful to choose allies who tended to support his constitutional principles (like the Dutch and, to some extent, England), and it led to a split with Frederick's other senior councillor, Christian of Anhalt, who favoured Denmark and Sweden in spite of their rulers' autocratic leanings. But in the end the exiles had to accept every offer of help that came their way. Frederick himself was sometimes a problem. 'Our king languishes in idleness,' Camerarius once complained, 'and begins to shy away from any worthy, strong or heroic action'; and on another occasion: 'The "king of Bohemia" is totally confused and very depressed in spirit.' Not until the end of 1625, with the completion of a full anti-Habsburg coalition, did his spirits rise again.

The first and staunchest ally of the Winter King was the Dutch Republic. Frederick was the nephew of both Maurice of Nassau, who died in March 1625, and of Maurice's half-brother and successor, Frederick-Henry, and this personal bond was strengthened when Frederick-Henry married Amalia von Solms, daughter of one of the leading Palatine councillors. The military position of the Dutch at this time was not good. Although little happened in 1623 (except an attempt by Oldenbarnevelt's family to assassinate Maurice), early in 1624 the Spaniards launched a major raid across the frozen rivers, laying waste much territory and almost reaching Utrecht. In August they laid siege to Breda, an important town in North Brabant: in June 1625, thanks to the arrival of reinforcements from the Emperor, it was forced to surrender. This defeat caused a serious loss of prestige for the Republic, and it came at a time when tax increases (imposed to finance the war) had provoked serious rioting in many towns, including Amsterdam, Haarlem, the Hague and Delft. The unrest was exacerbated by widespread economic disruption generated by the Spanish blockade.

The creation of the Spanish *Almirantazgo* in October 1624, with a fleet of 24 ships to enforce its ban on Dutch shipping using Spanish ports, was having considerable success. The surviving registers of the Atlantic ports all show that French, English and Hanseatic ships were able to acquire an important share of Iberian trade and almost monopolized the short runs between the Cantabrican ports and Bordeaux, Nantes and St Malo (where Dutch ships could take over in safety). The Spanish authorities were convinced that 'Taking away the trade [of the Dutch] is the most important thing we can do to aid the war in the Netherlands and bring about a favourable settlement', and royal decrees were issued in April, June, July and October 1625 to reinforce the embargo and to extend it to the rivers controlled by the army of Flanders – Scheldt, Maas, Lippe and Rhine – and those controlled by Spain's allies – Eems, Weser and (after 1627) Elbe. Prices in the Dutch Republic began to rise; supplies of timber, vital for ship-construction, ran short; salt could not be imported in sufficient quantities; and herring catches were down (partly because the blockade cut off some of the markets but also through Spanish attacks on the herring fleet in 1625 – 80 herring-boats sunk – 1626 and 1627). The Gelderland patrician, Alexander van der Capellen, could be forgiven for recording pessimistically in his diary: 'The plague of God lies on this land.'

The only Dutch successes occurred overseas, and even they proved ephemeral. Under the aegis of the Dutch West India Company, formed in 1621, a succession of state-subsidized fleets sailed into American waters for trade, piracy and plunder. In 1623, a fleet of 5 heavily armed ships was sent to Chile and Peru with the intention of provoking a native rising against the Spaniards. It failed, but later in the year a fleet of 26 ships, carrying 3310 men and 450 guns, was sent to capture Portuguese Brazil. The colonial government could not match this show of force and its capital, Bahía, fell in May 1624. Just one year later, however, a Luso-Spanish fleet appeared in irresistible strength (52 ships, 12,566 men and 1185 guns), recaptured Bahía and drove off a Dutch relief expedition.

Dutch efforts to divert Spain's resources from the war in the Netherlands having failed, the Republic therefore looked the more favourably upon the efforts of the Palatine diplomats to build their anti-Habsburg coalition in Europe. Camerarius was sent to secure the support of Sweden, and he was deeply impressed by the personality of Gustavus Adolphus ('Gideon', he called him): 'I cannot praise adequately the heroic virtues of that king: piety, prudence, resolution. He has no equal in all Europe. If the king of England had his spirit, our Frederick would now have not only the Palatinate but the kingdom of Bohemia as well.'[9] But such enthusiasm was premature: in the end, Gustavus refused to join any coalition that he could not control, and invaded Poland instead (see page 211 below), while James I surprised everyone by sending troops to Holland. His pliability in the Habsburg interest had stemmed principally from the hope (dexterously dangled before him by Philip IV's able ambassador in London, Count Gondomar) of a Spanish bride for his son. When it became clear, in the autumn of 1623, that Spain had no intention of allowing a 'Spanish match' (look what happened last time, the council in Madrid argued, when Catherine of Aragon married Henry VIII!) James entered into a new defensive alliance with the Dutch (15 June 1624). Already, five days earlier at Compiègne in France, the Dutch had also signed a treaty with France which guaranteed them 1·2 million livres (£100,000 sterling) for 1624, and 1 million for each of the two following years, to help defray the cost of fighting Spain; in return a Dutch fleet was to be sent to assist Louis XIII to reduce the rebellious town of La Rochelle. In October the Dutch also signed a closer alliance with Brandenburg.

As this alliance-building in the west was going on, there was similar activity in the north. Christian IV of Denmark was no friend of the House of Habsburg. He resented the existence of the *Collegium Nordicum* at Olomouc in Moravia, from which Jesuit missionaries were dispatched to Denmark and Sweden; and he feared an expansion of the Roman Catholic offensive into Scandinavia if Ferdinand were to be victorious in the Empire. In March 1621 he sent a formal mission to Vienna to protest that it was not Frederick of Bohemia but the Spaniards in the Palatinate who were the source of unrest in Europe: he urged Ferdinand to expel them. He also took more positive steps. In the winter of 1620–1 he lent 300,000 thalers (£75,000 sterling) to Frederick V (whose wife, Elizabeth Stuart, was his niece) and before long he was also sending loans to other German opponents of the Emperor: almost 1 million thalers had been advanced by the end of 1622. The king also intensified the policy he had followed since 1605 of buying up land, particularly secularized church land, in North Germany, so that by 1620 he possessed extensive properties in the Lower Saxon Circle. He tried to persuade his new neighbours there to lend their support to the Palatine cause, again offering subsidies if they agreed, and pointing out that a total imperial victory would imperil the rights of all who held secularized church lands (including himself). In February 1625 Christian signed an alliance with the dukes of Saxe-Weimar, who had fought for Frederick and been outlawed for their pains, and in May he bribed the princes of the Lower Saxon Circle to elect him their president and to allow him to raise an army for service there. Duke John Ernest of Saxe-Weimar became quartermaster-general and led the new army to Hanover, where they came up against the troops of the Catholic League under

Tilly, spread out along the Weser in order to close it to Dutch shipping.

Although Christian was able to finance the opening gambits of his aggressive foreign policy from his private fortune, which totalled 1·5 million thalers (£375,000 sterling) by 1625, he faced opposition at home from his aristocratic council, who had begun to realize that the king's activities in Germany were about to precipitate Denmark in a major war. Negotiations were already far advanced with the new rulers of the United Provinces (Maurice died in April 1625 and his half-brother Frederick Henry succeeded him) and the British Isles (James VI and I died in March 1625 and his son Charles I, Christian's nephew, succeeded). In the autumn of 1624 James had indeed agreed to allow an army to be raised in England by Count Mansfeld, in the name of the Elector Palatine; but he would not countenance an open breach with Spain. Charles, however, had no such scruples and within weeks of his accession an expedition to attack the Habsburgs was prepared. An Anglo-Dutch alliance against Spain was signed in September and the fleets of both countries set sail at once. But the expedition failed to take Cadiz and failed to capture the vital Indies treasure fleet. Nor was this the only foreign policy failure: France refused to associate herself with the Protestant cause, even though Charles had married Louis XIII's sister, Henrietta Maria, in May 1625, and had received informal assurances that French support for his Palatine relatives would be forthcoming. On 9 December 1625, therefore, only Denmark, England and the Dutch Republic signed the Hague Convention with Frederick V. However, the coalition's plans were still impressive on paper: Christian was to lead one army, partly subsidized by England; Mansfeld was to lead a second, partly subsidized by the Dutch; and Frederick was to create a new Protestant Union which would provide a third army inside Germany.

These developments did not go unmarked by their intended victims. The Spaniards were warned about the impending attack on Cadiz: of 88 English ships and 12,000 troops who set out in October 1625, only 50 ships and 5000 men returned at the end of the year. The duke of Bavaria, whose army was left facing Christian's troops along the Weser, urged the Emperor early in 1625 to raise troops who could assist his own forces should Denmark attack. 'Tilly cannot gain superiority alone,' he warned. 'The Danes hold great advantages: they will act first and overwhelm us.' In May, Ferdinand accepted this advice: he authorized his commandant in Prague, Wallenstein, to create and command a new force of 50,000 men. The general, with his vast Bohemian estates to provide munitions and his profits from the recoinage to hire soldiers, quickly obliged. In August the new imperial army assembled at Eger, on the Bohemian border, and then moved north to positions east of Tilly's force. While the army of the League waited on the Weser, keeping an eye on Mansfeld's army on the Dutch border, Wallenstein camped on the Elbe to prevent Christian IV's troops from breaking out of Lower Saxony. The four armies remained locked in these positions until April 1626 when Mansfeld tried to force a crossing of the Elbe at the bridge of Dessau, which the imperialists had carefully fortified. Mansfeld lost 5000 men and was forced to retire. Shortly afterwards he led the remainder of his army through Silesia and Moravia to join Bethlen Gabor, who had invaded Habsburg Hungary, while Tilly stayed in the north to oppose Christian. Wallenstein, however, followed Mansfeld south-eastwards, driving Bethlen back in late September and gradually wearing down Mansfeld's forces until their despairing commander gave up and abandoned them. He died shortly afterwards.

No better success attended the forces commanded by Christian in person. Hoping to profit from Wallenstein's departure in pursuit of Mansfeld, in August the Danish army moved south against Tilly. But Christian was badly defeated at Lutter, twenty miles south of Wolfenbüttel (27 August): half his army and all his field artillery was lost; all his German allies hastened to make peace with the victors, except the dukes of Mecklenburg (an omission that was to cost them dear); and the king retreated ignominiously to Holstein to reorganize his forces. While he did so, Wallenstein and Tilly used their overwhelming numerical superiority to defeat all the other Protestant forces remaining in the Empire.

Christian's position was now serious. He had no German allies, and England's aid was slow to arrive. Charles I had managed to antagonize his Parliament so much that, even though they approved of the Protestant alliance in principle, they refused to vote the funds needed to honour the government's commitments. In the end, the 5000 soldiers promised to Christian could only be provided by drafting the troops sent in 1624 to the Netherlands. They had not been paid in Holland; they were not paid in Denmark either. Inevitably many men mutinied, and many more deserted and went home. When, in April 1628, the survivors of the enterprise surrendered to Tilly, there were less than 2000 left.

The surrender of the English contingent virtually completed the Catholic reconquest of the rebellious areas west of the Elbe. East of the river, the war was conducted by the imperial army under Wallenstein, who was rewarded for his spectacular advance to the Baltic in April 1628 by possession of the duchy of Mecklenburg, confiscated by the Emperor from its hereditary rulers for their continued support of King Christian. The supreme commander was now lord of 300,000 subjects and he moved into the ducal palace at Güstrow in order to direct the final stages of the war. He routed Christian's forces at Wolgast when they attempted to invade Mecklenburg (September 1628); he sabotaged a French attempt to negotiate a separate peace between the League and the defeated Protestants (April 1629); and he occupied the entire Jutland peninsula while he waited for Christian to accept his terms (the peace of Lübeck was signed on 7 June 1629).

Only one of the signatories of the Hague Convention of December 1625 had gained: the Dutch Republic. Although the blockade directed by the Almirantazgo still damaged trade, as did the disruption of Baltic trade by the various wars fought along its shores, Habsburg pressure on the Republic was considerably reduced as the Emperor and his allies concentrated on Denmark. In any case, Spain was herself beginning to suffer financial exhaustion after keeping her armies fully mobilized in Germany and the Netherlands for so long: payments from Spain to the army of Flanders fell ever further in arrears until on 4 February 1627 the government of Philip IV declared a state bankruptcy and froze all its debts. As it happened, the effects of this measure were softened by the offer from a consortium of Portuguese bankers to provide immediate loans to the crown in the Netherlands via their contacts (mostly Jewish) in Lisbon and Amsterdam, thus breaking the near-monopoly held by the Genoese bankers since 1575; but the new financiers were seriously affected by the capture of the treasure fleet from New Spain, with £800,000 aboard in silver alone, by a Dutch fleet under Admiral Piet Heyn, in September 1628. No money arrived from Spain for the army of Flanders between October 1628 and May 1629 and during the rest of the year the total receipts from Spain were less than half the normal provision. It was impossible for Philip IV's troops in the Netherlands to operate effectively in these circumstances, and in 1626 the Dutch captured Oldenzaal, followed by Groenlo in 1627, thus completing the reconquest of the north-eastern territories taken by Spinola in 1605–6. The aged marquis was recalled to Madrid to explain these reverses, and there he attempted to convince the king that terms should be made with the Dutch before any other important towns were lost.

There had been a number of half-hearted attempts at negotiation since the twelve years' truce expired in 1621 – one intermediary, Madame t' Serclaes (a relative of Tilly and one of the few female diplomats of the century) shuttled across the frontier more than 38 times between 1621 and 1625; another envoy was the painter Pieter-Paul Rubens – but Spinola in 1628 insisted on starting peace-talks in earnest. He argued that the Spanish Netherlands were being devastated by the troops of both sides, and by the effects of the embargo on Dutch trade which prevented raw materials from reaching the manufacturing centres of Flanders and Brabant. Before long, he argued, the Netherlands would not be worth defending. A similar report came from Rubens in Antwerp: 'This city languishes like a consumptive body which is gradually wasting away. Every day we see the number of inhabitants decreasing, for these wretched people have no means of supporting themselves either by manufacture or by trade.'[10] Gradually the 'hawk' members of Philip IV's council were worn down. In April 1628 they favoured peace provided the Dutch guaranteed toleration for Catholics in the Republic, opened the Scheldt to trade, desisted from all commerce with America, and recognized Spain's protection (though not necessarily her sovereignty) over the Republic; but in September, Spinola persuaded his colleagues to accept any peace or truce that would safeguard 'religion and reputation' (that is, toleration for the Dutch Catholics and some token concessions in other matters). However, the religious demand was totally unacceptable to the Republic and the talks were broken off.

The events of 1629 fully vindicated the defeatism of Spinola. Although a Spanish force crossed the rivers, marched towards Holland and even captured the town of Amersfoort, it was forced to withdraw in late August when the Dutch gained control of the Rhine crossing at Wesel, through which all their supplies had to come. Then, on 14 September, the main Dutch army, swollen to 120,000 men, forced the surrender of 's Hertogenbosch, a city of great strategic importance in North Brabant which also served as the headquarters of Catholic propaganda and missionary work to the Republic. The city and 170 villages around it were occupied by the Dutch. The Spanish blockade of the great rivers was broken.

The advisers of Philip IV had made a major miscalculation. They had counted on the Emperor's forces, so close to victory over Denmark, to save 's Hertogenbosch. And, indeed, Wallenstein was willing to co-operate: a force of 20,000 men was detached in June and sent in the direction of Brussels. But in July the order was countermanded: the imperialists were ordered to march south to Italy where war had broken out again over the Mantuan succession. The Dutch were indeed fortunate: shielded for three vital years by Denmark, they were now saved for another two by Mantua. Spain's new peace offers could be rejected.

4. The Cold War for Italy

The Italian peninsula in 1600 was the most densely populated and most highly urbanized area in Europe. Its 13 million inhabitants were concentrated at a density of 42 per square kilometre; and there were 32 cities with more than 10,000 inhabitants, including five with more than 100,000. Naples was, with the exception of Istanbul, the largest city in Europe at that time. However, Italy was politically fragmented to an extraordinary degree. Although Spain controlled almost half the peninsula (the states of Lombardy, Naples, Sicily and Sardinia), with a combined population of 5 million, the rest was split up among more than a score of sovereign states. Even so, the most important of these petty states were still large by the standards of the day, at least in terms of population (which in early modern times was the index by which most contemporaries measured economic and political power): the Republic of Venice had 1·8 million Italian subjects, the Papal States about the same; the duke of Savoy had about 1 million subjects, the Grand Duke of Tuscany some 750,000; the Republic of Genoa (which also ruled Corsica) had about 450,000 citizens, the duchy of Mantua-Monferrat only a few less. The relative importance of these populations stands out when they are compared with those of the north European states: Sweden and the Dutch Republic, each with 1·25 million; Scotland with only 1 million.

Nowhere was political fragmentation greater than in the north, on the plain of Lombardy. The three dominant powers – Venice, Milan, Savoy – were each composed of a number of smaller units annexed in earlier centuries, and they were anxious to expand further at the expense of their smaller neighbours. In particular, Lombardy (which meant Spain) and Venice both wished to dominate the Alpine valley known as the Valtelline, which had belonged to Lombardy until 1386; and Savoy and Lombardy vied for the succession to the united state of Mantua-Monferrat, still undecided after the wars of 1614–15 and 1616–17 (see pages 154–6 above). It was the Valtelline which erupted first into the forefront of European politics.

The Alpine valleys to the south-east of the Swiss cantons contained a population of only 80,000, but they constituted an area of immense political and religious complexity. They were ruled by an elected diet, but effective power lay with the leaders of three associations of landlords known as the Grey Leagues (*Grisons* or *Graubünden*: see Figure 7). The Leagues jointly administered the Valtelline as a vassal state, selling offices to the highest bidder and leaving the incumbents to recoup their outlay from the local inhabitants. The Reformation added religious division to this political grievance: most of the Grey Leagues' own land was won over to Zwinglianism, but the Valtelline remained staunchly Catholic. Its inhabitants bitterly resented the Protestantizing policies of their rulers, who sometimes diverted Catholic church property to the support of newly founded Protestant schools, and sometimes just appropriated it to their own use. The diocesan visitation records of the later sixteenth century reveal an appalling scale of neglect, with many parishes lacking a priest and several lacking even a pulpit or church furnishings.

Through this volcano of political, linguistic and religious instability, which had already erupted into a bloody peasant revolt around Sondrio in 1572, ran several international highways. Some connected Venice with the Grey Leagues, the Swiss cantons and France; others linked Lombardy with Alsace, Austria and the Netherlands. The area was one of the cross-roads of European politics, where the messengers, troops and treasure of the Habsburg-Catholic axis going one way met those of the anti-Habsburg-Protestant axis going the other.

Figure 7. The Valtelline

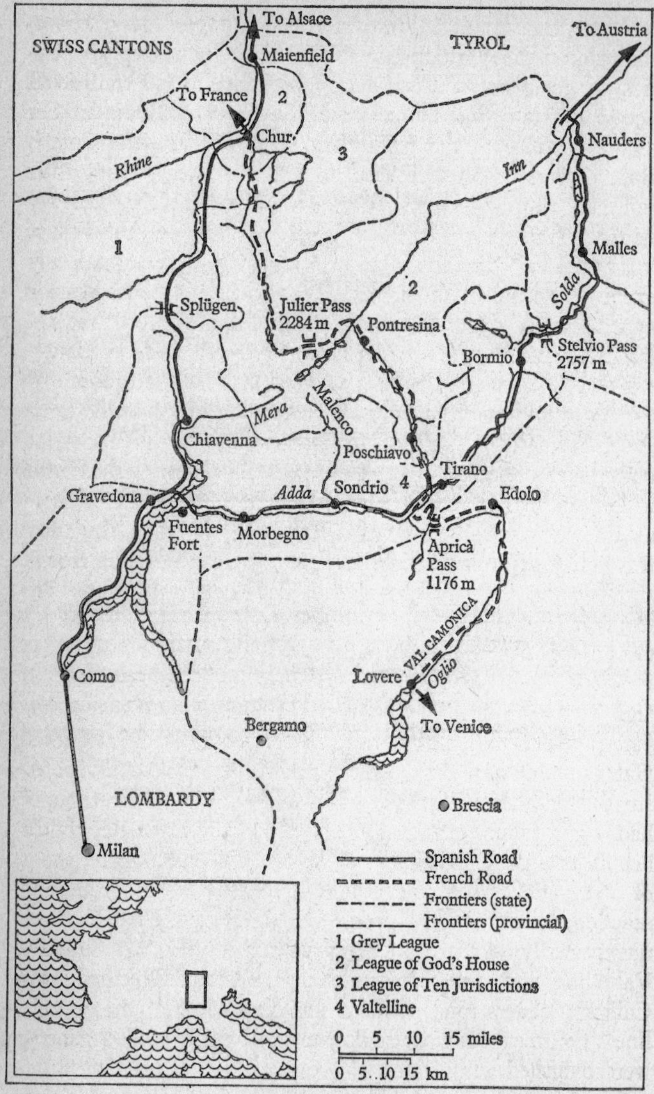

It was the war of Saluzzo in 1600–1 (pages 122–3 above) that placed the Valtelline in the forefront of European politics, for the peace of Lyon deprived France of her traditional access to Italy (via Saluzzo and Savoy) and Spain of her secure corridor to the Netherlands and the Franche-Comté. Both powers began to search for a new route to carry their imperial communications. France was first, securing a treaty with the Grisons in December 1601 that reserved the valleys 'for her alone' in military matters, and despite the apparently exclusive nature of this concession, Venice secured a similar agreement in 1603. Spain, however, had her overtures rebuffed and in retaliation the Spanish governor of Lombardy, the count of Fuentes, built a powerful fort at the mouth of the Valtelline and prohibited all exports from Lombardy to the Grisons' land. He also began the liberal distribution of bribes to the Catholic leaders in the valley 'since self-interest is the best hold one can have over that nation [the Swiss]' as Fuentes cynically informed Philip III in 1604. In 1607 this policy paid off when a Venetian attempt to march troops through the Grisons provoked a popular uprising by the Catholic communities which seized Chur, capital of the Grisons, and blocked the passages to Italy. Eventually the Protestants regained control, executed two Catholic leaders and restored order, but the basic problem was not solved: the valleys could not remain neutral, yet adherence to either Habsburgs or anti-Habsburgs would produce fatal divisions. In 1618 another disturbance occurred. The Grison Protestants had begun to lend clandestine aid to Venice in the Republic's hostilities against Ferdinand of Styria. Understandably, some of the valleys' Catholic leaders objected. The Protestant reaction, led by a fiery pastor called George Jenatsch, was unexpectedly violent: an army marched into the Catholic Valtelline and arrested, tried, tortured and executed two Catholic leaders (one of them the Archpriest of the Valtelline). Fourteen other Catholics, most of them landed gentry, were banished.

These actions alienated France, as did the Grisons' decision to expel Louis XIII's ambassador in an attempt to maintain strict neutrality in the European power struggle. And at the same time the revolt of Bohemia made the Valtelline more crucial than ever to both Spain and the Austrian Habsburgs, anxious to create a reliable military corridor between Lombardy and the Tyrol so that men and money could be sent to help Ferdinand. In 1619 two regiments, the vanguard of Spain's assistance, were sent over the St Gotthard pass and through the Catholic Swiss cantons to the Rhine at Baden, but from there they had to march overland to Vienna. The Valtelline was far more convenient, and so in 1620 the governor of Lombardy lent a favourable ear when the Catholics of the Valtelline requested support for a proposed rising against their Grison overlords, who since the purge of 1618 were enforcing Protestantization ever more energetically. Even on religious grounds, Spanish support was advisable, since the Catholic Valtelline provided both a barrier to the spread of Protestantism into Italy and a guarantee that the Grisons (like the Swiss Confederation as a whole) would remain divided and therefore weak; but the escalating conflict in the Habsburg lands made intervention militarily imperative. In July 1620, therefore, Spanish troops moved into the mouth of the Valtelline and blocked it against any possible Grison counter-attack, while the Catholics in the valley massacred some 600 Protestants, most of them their Grison overlords. Simultaneously, a detachment of imperial troops moved into the north end of the valley in support of those Catholics from the Valtelline, exiled in 1618, who had taken refuge at Innsbruck. Civil war between supporters of the two creeds began in 1621, the Protestants looking to Venice, France and the Protestant cantons for military aid, and the Catholics looking to Spain and Austria.

The outcome was a foregone conclusion. The troops from Lombardy were already on the scene, and they were soon joined by Tyrolean forces sent by Bishop Leopold of Passau. By the end of 1621 they had overrun the entire Grisons lands and forced its Diet to grant independence to the Valtelline, which now remained under Spanish protection. Four thousand soldiers were garrisoned in the valleys, and a

Protestant rising in the summer of 1622 was brutally suppressed; 3600 Spaniards were stationed in Alsace, and 5000 more in the Rhine Palatinate. In the words of the English ambassador to Venice, Sir Henry Wotton, the Spaniards were 'now able to walk (while they keep a foot in the Lower Palatinate) from Milan to Dunkirk upon their own inheritances and purchases, a connexion of terrible moment in my opinion'.[11] In 1623 Wotton's opinion was confirmed when a Spanish army of over 7000 men marched via Chiavenna and Chur through the heart of the Grisons land to South Germany and the Netherlands.

It was the very completeness of the Habsburg success that betrayed them: capturing the Valtelline alone might have been permitted by the other powers; occupying the entire Grisons lands as well could not be. In February 1623 France, Venice and Savoy signed an alliance (the treaty of Paris) pledged to expel the Habsburgs from their new conquests. The Spaniards reacted by surrendering the Valtelline to the papacy, which sent its own forces in. But this still left the Austrians in possession of the other valleys, and allowed Spain to continue sending her forces through the Valtelline; so, after several ultimata, France sent an army and in the course of 1624 all the Grisons lands, including the Valtelline, were occupied. After a while, however, France agreed to allow the papal garrisons back into the Valtelline, whose independence from the Grisons was confirmed (treaty of Monzón, 5 May 1626). The Habsburgs were again able to use the passes as they pleased, sending a Spanish army to the Netherlands in 1631 through the Grison heartland and sending two to Germany through the Valtelline in 1633 and 1634; in the opposite direction, several regiments from the imperial army marched through the Valtelline to Lombardy in 1629–31.

The halting rhythm of French intervention in Italy was dictated by the tergiversations of internal policy. The reconciliation between the queen mother and her son in August 1620 (page 130 above), negotiated by Richelieu (for which he was rewarded with a cardinalate two years later), heralded a series of pro-Catholic measures in French foreign and domestic policy. At home, the king determined to re-Catholicize his father's ancestral province of Béarn in the Pyrenees, which Henry IV had promised to do in 1595 as a condition of his absolution by the Pope, an absolution which was a vital preliminary to his overall victory in France. But Henry had only appointed two bishops. He had not even given them possession of the temporalities attached to their sees, and when his son decreed in June 1617 that they should be admitted to their lands, the general assembly of the Protestant church defiantly ordered its members in Béarn to keep the bishops out. In 1620, after the end of the aristocratic opposition, the king in person led an army southwards and restored full Catholic worship in the province. At once the Huguenot assembly ordered a full mobilization to defend its territorial integrity, and civil war began in 1621. When neither side was able to gain an advantage, in October 1622 a compromise was reached whereby the Huguenots retained their fortified strongholds, of which La Rochelle was the largest, but the Catholics kept Béarn (the treaty of Montpellier).

But there was a price to pay for this success. Louis and his ministers, in their anxiety that no group of foreign Protestants should be free to provide aid to the Huguenots, had offered assistance neither to the German Protestants nor to the Dutch Republic in their struggle against the Habsburgs. They had also succeeded in enmeshing James I in both conflicts, by encouraging him to commit himself with cautious promises of support which were broken as soon as England had advanced too far to retreat. Louis, however, had not expected the Habsburgs to make such rapid progress, and he became alarmed by their success. He therefore resolved, once he had signed the treaty of Montpellier, to adopt a more positive foreign policy. Unfortunately, he could find no one capable of devising one: Luynes had died in December 1621, and the survivors of the Concini regime (including Richelieu, who had conducted military operations with great skill in 1616) were still in disgrace. The only acceptable ministers were the septuagenarian Nicholas Brûlart and his son, but their foreign policy failed either to save the Valtelline from Habsburg occupation or to prevent the transfer of Frederick V's electorate to Maximilian of Bavaria. Early in 1624 the Elector of Saxony asked bitterly of the French resident at his court: 'Is there still a king of France?' It was the sort of aspersion to which the prickly and conceited Louis was particularly sensitive. Morose, unhappy, irritable, a stammerer – he was also intensely proud and possessed a great awareness of his own importance. 'Remember that the greatest honour you have in this world is to be my brother,' he once arrogantly informed the older (illegitimate) duke of Vendôme. Louis would not long tolerate a foreign policy that brought him only discredit. In February 1624 he therefore dismissed the Brûlarts, and in April he swallowed his dislike of a man tainted by association with the hated Concini and appointed Richelieu to the direction of foreign affairs. The cardinal was given special responsibility for the Valtelline question; and as that increased in importance, so did Richelieu's power.

The queen mother rejoiced at the promotion of her trusted adviser to the royal council, for through him she expected to recover her influence over the king and his policies. But in this she made a serious miscalculation, which she tried for six years to undo, for Richelieu immediately declared his total allegiance to Louis. The king was well satisfied, and in August he dismissed most of his other advisers, making Richelieu president of the council. The cardinal lost no time in filling the administration with his own servants (such as Bouthillier – see page 58 above) and his confidents (like Father Joseph, provincial of the Capuchin Order in Poitou and one of the first to perceive Richelieu's exceptional gifts).

Louis XIII, despite the dislike and distrust he had shown for the cardinal since the events of 1617, had a great deal in common with him. Richelieu was as zealous for the Catholic faith as Louis and, like the king, he was personally pious, fasting regularly. Both men were physically weak; both took their duties seriously and worked at them indefatigably; both were of a nervous, inflexible temperament and were happiest when they were alone. Neither regretted leaving the world at the hour of their death, prematurely aged by their ailments and the almost daily purges and clysters prescribed for them. But the partnership of king and cardinal, which was only broken by death, was fragile. After 1633, when the last senior councillor opposed to him died, Richelieu's ascendancy appeared to be complete, and he dazzled contemporaries with his arrogant display of wealth, his patronage of the arts, his nepotism and his omniscience in public affairs (which led the literary luminary Malherbe to exclaim one day: 'I swear there is something superhuman about that man.'). But the cardinal's power rested entirely on the king's favour. He needed to keep in constant touch with those about his master (who travelled round the kingdom while Richelieu had to keep close to the other ministers in Paris), in order to keep track of any *mauvaises humeurs* that might undermine his position of confidence. He also had to arrange for unpleasant news or decisions to be kept back until the king was in a suitable mood to receive them. Keeping on the right side of Louis was never easy, and Richelieu was lucky to survive the policy failures of his first seven years.

An influential group on the council, led by Cardinal Pierre de Bérulle and supported by the queen mother, the queen and the Catholic *dévots*, maintained a steady opposition to Richelieu's policy of compromise with the Huguenots and intervention against the Habsburgs abroad. They insisted that suppression of the Huguenot troubles (there was another revolt in 1625) should come first and portrayed Richelieu as 'the cardinal of La Rochelle' when he bought off the Protestants with concessions yet again. In 1626 they managed to convince Louis to give way over the Valtelline and sign the treaty of Monzón; and in 1627, when La Rochelle rebelled for the third time in ten years, they engineered an alliance with Spain to crush the city's resistance. For almost two years, in spite of Richelieu's misgivings, the siege of La Rochelle came first.

The fate of the city was determined, to a large extent, by the strange policy followed by the duke of Buckingham, who exercised complete control over England's foreign affairs. He saw La Rochelle as a pawn with which to secure French support for the cause of the Elector Palatine in Germany. All his encouragement to the magistrates of La Rochelle, even his ill-fated expedition to the Ile de Ré, cruelly deceived the besieged: all the time Buckingham was negotiating with Richelieu, offering to withdraw English aid in return for the longed-for French declaration in favour of Frederick V. Richelieu, however, gambled on taking the town without making a bargain with anyone, and it was while he tried to raise a second expedition for La Rochelle that Buckingham was assassinated (August 1628). The city surrendered in October.

Buckingham's fumbling foreign policy played right into the hands of the Habsburgs: with England's fleet and troops tied down at La Rochelle, nothing could be spared for Christian of Denmark, and the imperialists advanced into Jutland virtually unopposed. Spain, too, profited from England's preoccupation with the Huguenots to arrange a cease-fire in the war begun in 1625 (the agreement was negotiated in 1627 by the painter Pieter-Paul Rubens; a full peace was signed at Madrid in November 1630). This left Spain free to engage in the long-deferred conquest and partition of Mantua, after the death of the last Gonzaga duke on 26 December 1627. Philip IV laid claim to the duchy of Mantua, and agreed that Savoy should annexe Monferrat; both parties refused to recognize the claim of the French-born duke of Nevers, the nearest surviving male relative of the last duke, to succeed. Spain realized that she could not afford to fight another long and indecisive war in Italy, but with France tied down at La Rochelle it was expected that Nevers could be defeated and made to yield concessions in return for recognition; and the committee of lawyers and theologians who were asked to consider the justice of the new war agreed in January 1628 that such gunboat diplomacy was both legitimate and worthwhile. Troops were therefore mobilized, and in July an expedition of French volunteers was defeated. But the key fortresses of Casale and Mantua still held out for Nevers, and the Spanish and Savoyard armies had to prepare for a long siege.

This was the point at which Habsburg fortunes began to decline, for a siege required time, and time they did not have. In October 1628, La Rochelle surrendered, its 28,000 inhabitants reduced to 5400 'ghosts, not people'. Although pockets of Huguenot resistance continued to defy the crown for twenty months more, the state-within-a-state created by the Edict of Nantes and the *brevets* of 1598 was at an end. The Edict of Grace, signed by the king at Alès on 28 June 1629, confirmed religious toleration for the Huguenots but abolished their right to hold a separate assembly, to raise troops and to garrison towns.

At once, Louis and Richelieu led an army into Savoy, forced the duke to come to terms, and pressed onwards to relieve Casale. A French garrison was left to hold the town for Nevers, and the rest of Monferrat was cleared of Spanish troops. The independent states of Italy hastened to send envoys to the French camp to hail Louis as their deliverer, and as the champion of Italy against Habsburg; but they were to be bitterly disappointed. Before long, France's diplomats were forced to agree to the withdrawal of all their troops from Italy (peace of Regensburg, 13 October 1630, and accord at Cherasco, 19 June 1631). Only Pinerolo remained as a French enclave across the Alps: France still held far less territory in Italy than in 1559.

Four factors had defeated France's first effort at imperialism since Cateau-Cambrésis. First, her efforts at recruiting and maintaining an army had been hampered by the widespread outbreak of plague in southern France and Italy in 1630–1. People died in such numbers that crops could not be harvested, so that the soldiers who escaped the plague nevertheless starved for lack of provisions. The Habsburg armies were, of course, also affected by this catastrophe (which was used with graphic effect as the background to the nineteenth-century novel by Alessandro Manzoni, *The Betrothed*), and a truce was called to the fighting in 1630 because neither side had enough men left for operations. Second, thanks to the pacification of Germany, the Emperor had sent a steady flow of troops through the Valtelline to Lombardy to fight for Spain: more than 30,000 men crossed in 1629–30 under Wallenstein's deputies Collalto, Gallas and Piccolomini. In March 1631 there were still 12,000 imperialists and 25,000 Spanish troops in northern Italy: it was a concentration of front-line troops that France could not yet equal, since her troops were needed to garrison the conquered towns of Savoy (only evacuated in June 1631), to defeat the remaining Huguenot forces (until June 1630) and to intimidate the duke of Lorraine who had allied himself with Richelieu's opponents led by the king's brother, Gaston of Orleans. But the final and most important reason for France's failure in Italy was the bitter policy disagreement between Richelieu and the *dévots* which culminated in November 1630 in the Day of Dupes.

The siege of La Rochelle was very popular with the *dévots* – Father Joseph even composed a verse epic in Latin hexameters to celebrate its progress – but it was also extremely expensive. Taxes, above all direct taxes, had to be increased, and Richelieu also resolved to raise the contributions demanded from the *pays d'états* (those provinces on the periphery of the kingdom where taxes were voted and apportioned by the local estates). The cardinal felt that the estates were not carrying out their work properly, and in 1628 he ordered the provinces of Burgundy, Dauphiné, Languedoc and Provence to be divided up into *élections*, each with a team of *élus* appointed from Paris to assess the correct tax obligation of each parish. Since it was notorious that *pays d'élection* paid far more than *pays d'états*, few were surprised that Richelieu's proposal provoked bitter resistance. However, the cardinal had not anticipated such a ferocious response. In Languedoc there was a tax-strike, in Burgundy a fearsome popular revolt, in Provence a series of uprisings encouraged and unpunished by the provincial estates and law courts. Only in Dauphiné was there no serious opposition. There was also a wave of anti-fiscal riots in 1629–30 in other areas.

It was against this background of serious domestic unrest

that the *dévots* made their final attempt to defeat Richelieu: once again, he had made concessions to the Huguenots (they were allowed public worship by the Grace of Alès) in order to fight the Habsburgs in Italy. Led by Bérulle, the opposition argued that Louis had 'acquired enough glory already' and that unless France withdrew from all foreign commitments and allowed time for retrenchment and reform, the monarchy would be overwhelmed. There were many who sympathized with this view, even among Richelieu's own supporters. Father Joseph, for example, dreamed of a peace amongst Christians followed by a new crusade against the Turks, and he composed a verse epic of Vergilian dimensions – the *Turciade* – about it. But at a crucial juncture, in October 1629, Bérulle died, and a voice which the king always heeded was silenced. The *dévot* spokesman was now the keeper of the seals, Michel de Marillac, whose papers of advice to the king insisted that 'Everywhere in France is full of sedition, but the courts punish no one. The king has appointed special judges for these cases, but the appeal courts [*Parlements*] prevent the execution of the sentences so that, in consequence, the rebellions are authorized. I do not know what we should hope or fear in all this, given the frequency of revolts, of which we have word of a new one almost every day.'[12] Marillac, who was sixty-seven years old in 1630, could remember clearly the French religious wars in which high taxation and religious innovations had produced factionalism and revolt.

Richelieu did not dispute these facts, and he accepted the need for reform. Indeed, the years of his ministry from 1624 to 1630 were the most fertile in projects for retrenchment: a navy was created, under the cardinal's direct supervision, for both Atlantic and Mediterranean service; trading companies were formed in 1626–7 to exploit the successful private efforts to colonize the Antilles, Senegal and Canada; and French trade with the rest of Europe was patronized. But Richelieu was prepared to sacrifice all these ventures, like the fiscal and other reforms that the government had proposed to an *Assemblée des Notables* in 1626, in the interests of opposing Habsburg power before it became too great. In order to 'halt the process of Spanish expansion' and 'protect Italy against the pretensions of Spain' it was necessary 'to abandon all thought of peace, economy and retrenchment in this kingdom', he warned the king in a succession of pungent papers of advice.

At each escalation in the Mantuan crisis – after Nevers's defeat in July 1628; after the relief of Casale in April 1629; after the seizure of Pinerolo in March 1630 – there was a full-dress debate between Richelieu, who favoured conciliating the Huguenots and invading Italy, and the *dévots*, who advocated the reverse. In September 1630, with Mantua in imperial hands and Casale about to fall, Louis fell seriously ill and the queen and queen mother tried to convince him that it was a punishment for neglecting the interests of the Catholic church (which would be best served by adopting Marillac's policies). The king gave the impression that he would dismiss Richelieu and, although he continued to delay actually doing so, the government of France was totally paralysed. It was during this hiatus of power that the Mantuan war was terminated by the French ministers left in Italy without any instructions, and therefore open to persuasion by the papal mediator who later entered French service, Giulio Mazzarini. Heartened by this success, which constituted a reverse for Richelieu's hard-line policy, the queen mother determined to force her former servant's dismissal. On 10 November 1630 she created a scene in her Luxembourg palace before her son and forced Richelieu, in tears, to his knees before her. Louis, who hated to be confronted with this sort of decision, fled from the Luxembourg, apparently leaving the cardinal to his fate, just as he had abandoned Concini in 1617. The court immediately rallied to the queen mother and Richelieu contemplated flight. But Louis, who spent the day sitting on his bed petulantly pulling the buttons off his waistcoat, eventually sent his valet to summon Richelieu to his presence. The news swiftly spread: next day the Luxembourg palace was deserted.

The Day of Dupes, as contemporaries called it, was a turning-point of European history. The queen mother and Gaston of Orleans, who had supported her, fled abroad;

Marillac spent the rest of his life in prison, and his brother was tried and executed; the group's supporters were either imprisoned, exiled or confined to their estates. There was now no serious obstacle in the way of Richelieu's dream of checking Habsburg expansion and the cardinal lost no time. Italy might have been lost, but Germany might yet be saved. In January 1631 France signed the treaty of Bärwalde with the king of Sweden by which, in return for regular subsidies, Gustavus Adolphus would lead 36,000 men against the Emperor and destroy the Habsburg hold on Germany. A major European war was about to begin.

CHAPTER VI

The Defeat of the Habsburgs, 1629-35

1. *Sweden and Poland*

The reduction of Poland to the rank of a second-rate power in eastern Europe was a crucial development, but it must not be antedated. Although the elective kingship, the over-mighty magnates and the unco-operative Diet all suggest paralysing impotence after the extinction of the Jagiellonian dynasty in 1572, for at least another seventy years the Polish-Lithuanian state retained political vigour and economic prosperity; and it remained the cultural leader of slavonic Europe for almost a century. It was the secession of the Ukraine in 1648 (bringing in its wake a costly war with Russia) and the Swedish invasions of 1655–60 (devastating large tracts of Poland), which all but led to partition in the 1660s. Before 1648 the comments of foreigners about Poland's political and economic structure were rarely adverse: Giovanni Botero, Jean Bodin and Francis Bacon all wrote at length about its unique political system (without having been there), and even first-hand observers like William Bruce or Fynes Morison were no ruder about their experience of the Polish economy than about their sufferings elsewhere on their travels.

Nevertheless, the decline of Poland as a great power began in the 1620s. Her Russian pretensions were finally abandoned; there was a sharp defeat at the hands of the Turks; and she experienced a series of failures in the war against the invading Swedish forces of Gustavus Adolphus. This unhappy history is sometimes blamed on the political and social structure of the country, or on the decline in grain production and export; but neither was as important as the military inferiority of the

Polish army. This army was still recruited by the indenture system favoured by European states in the fifteenth century: the crown engaged a 'master in the military art' to raise a group of associates (six for cavalry, twelve for infantry) to accompany him to the war at set salaries. The teams thus formed were normally also bound together by family ties, and whole military dynasties were created, especially in the south where a permanent defence force (known as the cossacks) was needed against the Tatar raiders. The masters also, after about 1600, formed themselves into a military trade union which met annually and elected negotiators who would secure a salary agreement with the crown for the whole army. If the crown failed to pay the agreed scales, the union (calling itself a *confoederatio*) refused obedience and made its own arrangements for discipline and finance until state funds were again provided. The power of the military *confoederatio* was a major weakness during the Moscow campaign, but it was not the only one. A number of masters were attracted from the royal army into the service of the magnates by offers of higher wages, so that the crown could no longer call up some of its best veteran troops. Moreover, the troops who were left were not supplied with up-to-date equipment: the Polish army failed to emulate the great increase in firepower (and the ability to use it more effectively) among western armies, so that when the cavalry of Sigismund Vasa met the army of his cousin Gustavus in the 1620s, they were massacred by gunfire before they could reach their target. Although immediate steps were taken to introduce western-style reforms (companies and regiments; field artillery and muskets; new fortifications and military cartography), they came too late to save Poland from losing territory to the Swedes along the Baltic coast in the north and to the Turks and Tatars in the south.

The Turks won their successes in their habitual way: with vastly superior numbers. When, in the winter of 1619–20, Sigismund III sent one army to ravage the Ottoman vassal principality of Transylvania (which supported the Bohemian estates against his brother-in-law Ferdinand II) and another to raid deep into Ottoman territory (in fact to Varna, only 200 miles from Istanbul), the Turks retaliated by invading Poland in overwhelming force and totally destroyed Sigismund's army at Cecora on the Pruth (20 September 1620). The following year, the Sultan himself led another huge invasion and besieged a second Polish army at Chocim on the Dniester. Sigismund's generals were very fortunate to secure a cease-fire in October 1621, at the end of the campaigning season. It came just in time, for Gustavus Adolphus of Sweden, aged just twenty-seven, took advantage of the Turkish threat in order to invade Livonia.

Gustavus could not draw upon enormous human and material reserves like the Sultan; instead, important reforms were undertaken in order to maximize the resources that Sweden did possess. More nobles were encouraged to become professional civil servants – ambassadors, administrators, advisers – and each of the five main offices of state was expanded into a full government department or 'college': treasury, chancery, war office, admiralty and mines. There was also a supreme court, created in 1614. The leading administrators were also present in the highest college of all, the *riksrad* or council of state, where the king and his advisers discussed major matters. The full minutes of the deliberations of the council, which are printed, reveal the body acting in almost every way like a modern cabinet, whether the king was present or abroad (and between 1621 and 1632 he spent less than six full years in Sweden). In each province, the orders of the king and his ministers were carried out by a governor who supervised a team of local bailiffs. The entire system was given the force of law in a comprehensive piece of administrative legislation, the Form of Government (July 1634), which made permanent the arrangements evolved in Gustavus's last years (arrangements which gave little scope to the Diet, an omission that later led to trouble). It was thanks to this stable administrative system that the king found it possible to spend so much time winning wars abroad, and that after his death the regents for his daughter Christina were able to fight on for sixteen years in order to secure a satisfactory peace.

Gustavus had, of course, other sources of strength to sustain his military enterprises besides a sound government. Foreign investors had long been at work in Sweden, organizing production of its raw materials – especially iron and copper – for the market. Both were crucial to the war effort because of their direct use in the production of military hardware (especially artillery), and also because their export and sale on the Amsterdam market produced foreign exchange which Gustavus could use as collateral security for the loans needed to pay his troops. It was unfortunate for Sweden that, just when she needed to sell as much copper as possible, first Spain abandoned her minting of copper-alloy coinage (no *vellón* was minted after 1626 until the 1640s), and then an alternative source of supply, Japanese copper, came on the Amsterdam market and depressed prices. Nevertheless, Sweden's copper exports in the 1620s, organized by the able Liégeois exile, Louis de Geer, averaged 737 tons annually; and Sweden's armies were supplied with enough bronze field and siege guns to assure them of constant superiority of fire-power. De Geer was only one of a large colony of Netherlanders in Sweden, based on Göteborg (where at first Dutch was the official language): they were encouraged by the crown to settle, to introduce new technology and new skills, and generally to increase the wealth of Sweden. In this, they achieved much success.

The new technology and the new expertise were quickly applied by Gustavus to military reforms. He pioneered the use of field artillery, often concentrating the fire of 150 cannon against his enemies, and he provided his troops with a new type of light three-pounder cannon using leather as well as bronze around the barrel in order to make it lighter. From the Dutch he borrowed the mortar (invented 1588), grapeshot (devised *circa* 1600), the standardization of weapons (decreed by the States-General in 1599) and finally the linear battle formation (instead of the pike square) in which successive ranks of musketeers fired their pieces and retired to reload, producing a continuous barrage of fire. He also copied the smaller tactical formations of the Dutch army and their economical logistical organization which enabled an army to move rapidly with a minimum of wagons and baggage. In 1623 he introduced a conscription system for his infantry, the first in Europe, to augment the volunteers recruited abroad (especially in Scotland). Finally he created a new fleet of warships and transports with which to guarantee communications and trade between Sweden and her Baltic empire.

The first use to which these innovations were put was the siege of Riga, the principal city of Livonia, in 1621. Many observers admired the creeping barrage, traverses and trenches employed by Gustavus during the siege; and they were all struck by the discipline of his forces, both before and after the victory. This success gave Sweden control of an entrepôt which since 1581, when the city became Polish, had handled almost one-third of the kingdom's entire seaborne exports, mostly in the form of flax and hemp and mostly destined for western Europe. At first Riga was left as a Swedish outpost, while Gustavus negotiated with the German Protestant leaders over the terms of his support for their cause (page 185 above); but in June 1625, with Denmark installed as leader of the Lower Saxon Circle, Gustavus recommenced the conquest of Livonia. The new offensive began in June 1625 and its outcome was settled by his major victory over the Polish army at Wallhof in January 1626: the rest of the province was swiftly overrun. Sweden now controlled some 500 miles of the south Baltic coast and its hinterland, from Viborg on the frontier of Finland (a Swedish province) to Riga on the Düna River, and Gustavus was determined to make the most of it. As early as 1617, when the peace of Stolbova with Russia gave him control of Ingria and Estonia, the king began to study the economic advantages offered by the new lands. He informed the Swedish nobles, even as he announced the terms of the peace:

> I say to you . . . who clamour for grants of land – what do you here, treading on each other's toes, quarrelling and

> wrangling for a few wretched farms? Be off with you to these new lands and clear for yourselves farms as big as you like, or at least as large as you can manage! I will bestow privileges and immunities upon you; I will give you assistance; I will show you every favour.[1]

Shortly afterwards, Gustavus authorized the deportation to the new provinces of unruly peasants, and those guilty of poaching and theft on crown estates, to serve as colonists. In 1627 a royal commission was sent to all the Baltic provinces to reform the church there, to found high schools (*gymnasia*) and a university, and to assess the opportunities for immigration. By 1650, over 40 per cent of Livonia was owned by Swedish aristocrats, and all government posts were either in their hands or in those of Livonians who had spent at least two years in the exclusively Swedish-speaking university of Dorpat (which opened its doors in 1632).

As soon as Livonia was safely under Swedish control, Gustavus decided to continue the long-standing war with Sigismund by attacking another fief of the Polish crown: ducal Prussia (the coast between Memel and Elblag, with its hinterland and the great port of Königsberg, now Kaliningrad; recognized as a Polish fief since 1466, but since 1618 administered by the elector of Brandenburg). The king landed at Pillau, near Königsberg, in May 1626 and steadily moved along the coast towards the Vistula, which he closed to traffic. The Poles, however, had learned their lesson: they declined all opportunities of battle, and instead kept up a constant pressure to deny the Swedish garrisons as much freedom of action as possible. Gustavus was far from being able to emulate the majestic march of Wallenstein and Tilly to the Baltic in 1627 and 1628: he and his army were bogged down in Prussia and he was unable to respond to the appeals of the despairing Protestants in North Germany, except to send a small column under Alexander Leslie to relieve the besieged port of Stralsund in Pomerania.

The relief of Stralsund, however, was extremely important: it thwarted a well-prepared attempt to create a Habsburg fleet in north European waters. The idea of a North Sea fleet, based on the ports of either East Friesland or the Hanseatic League, had been advanced in 1598 and 1624, but the German traders had refused to co-operate. Then in 1626, an offer arrived in Spain from Sigismund III proposing a joint Habsburg-Polish fleet to dominate the Baltic, using ships purchased from the Hanse. Philip IV sent negotiators and a credit of £50,000 to start work on the creation of a navy of 24 ships, but naturally the work was not easy: few ports carried such a stock of serviceable vessels and by the spring of 1628 not one ship had been built or purchased. Herein lay the attraction of taking Stralsund, for her commodious harbour did contain such a fleet. But Stralsund was not taken. Instead, Wallenstein, who had become interested in the project, offered his new port of Wismar in Mecklenburg as a base for the new fleet. Both in Vienna and Madrid, ministers became excited about the plan, Olivares expressing the hope that the fleet (when constructed) would support Sigismund in his war against Gustavus and prevent 'that most valorous prince, who enjoys so much Dutch help, from stepping over the king of Poland and attempting greater things'. He also pointed out that the Baltic trade was to the Dutch economy what the Indies trade was to Spain: a source both of profit and of vital raw materials, including every commodity from tar to timber which the Dutch required to build their ships. So, Olivares argued, any naval presence in the northern seas that interrupted the prosperous flow of Dutch commerce with Danzig and the other Baltic ports would, in theory at least, incline the United Provinces to conclude a peace with Spain on almost any terms.

One must admire this bold strategic vision, for a pirate fleet in a safe harbour like Wismar or Stralsund would have been able to inflict yet more damage on Dutch shipping than the privateers from Dunkirk. As it was, the Swedish blockade of the Vistula pushed up grain prices and reduced profits in the Republic between 1626 and 1629, and the number of Dutch ships leaving the Sound fell from 2133 in 1618 to 817 in 1625 and 966 in 1626. But by the time Philip IV had allocated money for the new fleet, Poland was defeated and the few ships purchased already from the Hanseatic ports had to be sent to the Netherlands. Thus Spain lost perhaps her best chance of bringing the Dutch to an early settlement.

After the initial successes of 1625–6, Gustavus proved unable to enlarge his hold upon Prussia, even though he possessed substantial advantages: the Habsburgs were fully occupied in Germany, and Dutch and Transylvanian pressure secured invasions of Poland by the Crimean Tatars in 1626 and 1627. Perhaps surprisingly, the Polish army managed to defeat these attacks, and as the Tatars retired to lick their wounds their energies were diverted into a succession dispute. In the meantime, Sigismund (having studiously avoided pitched battles with the Swedes since 1626) became bolder as he received reinforcements from the west. Following the subjugation of Denmark, Wallenstein sent a force of 12,000 veterans to assist Poland against the Swedish invaders, who were sharply defeated at Stuhm (or Honigfelde) on 17 June 1629. Gustavus was lucky to escape with his life.

The victory, however, was won by Wallenstein's Germans; Sigismund's subjects were reluctant to join in. As the generalissimo gloomily observed: 'The Poles are by nature hostile to the Germans. The Polish magnates reckon that the more powerful the Emperor becomes, the sooner they will have their wings clipped by their own king.'[2] And, indeed, the demand of the Polish Diet for peace became irresistible. Sigismund, old and demoralized at last, was willing; and Gustavus, unaccustomed to defeat and anxious to intervene in Germany before the creation of a Habsburg fleet made a landing difficult, was not opposed. With the assistance of French mediators, likewise keen to expedite the Swedish invasion of Germany, the Vasa cousins signed the truce of Altmark, which suspended hostilities for six years, on 25–6 September 1629. Sweden's gains were modest: her possession of Livonia, recognized in 1622, was now confirmed, but all other conquests from Poland or Brandenburg had to be restored. Her only reward in Prussia for four expensive years of war was the grant for the duration of the truce of all the tolls on shipping using the ducal ports (extended, following a separate agreement in February 1630, to include Danzig). These customs receipts, paid on the spot and in silver, produced (while they lasted) one-fifth of the revenues of the Swedish crown – 663,000 out of 3·2 million imperial thalers in 1633 and even more in the two subsequent years – and it was partly the possession of this new source of military finance that gave Gustavus the opportunity of acting immediately after Altmark to break the Habsburgs' hold on North Germany. It had long been contemplated.

As early as January 1628 a select committee of the Swedish Diet had resolved that intervention in Germany was justified, both to protect Swedish interests (by preventing the formation of a Habsburg fleet in the Baltic) and to restore the fortunes of the Protestant cause; they were content for their king to determine the correct moment. In 1629 he had almost moved from the Vistula to the Oder, but Wallenstein's aid to Sigismund prevented him. Now, in June 1630, at peace with all his old enemies, with more land and a greater revenue than any Swedish king had ever possessed, Gustavus Adolphus landed in Germany, at Peenemünde in Pomerania, and quickly collected an army of 80,000 men. He intended to inflict a crushing defeat on the imperial forces which would not only drive them away from the Baltic, but ensure that they never came back. And in this aim, recent events in the Empire gave him a decisive advantage.

2. *Gustavus Adolphus and Wallenstein*

In the autumn of 1629, for a brief moment, most of Europe was at peace. The Protestant cause in Germany was shattered, and its allies defeated; the Polish-Swedish conflict was temporarily resolved; England and France had made up their differences (treaty of Susa, April 1629); England and Spain were on the point of doing so (treaty of Madrid, November 1630). But the breathing-space in the wars was short, and the peace was undermined by the Habsburgs, both in Mantua and in the Empire.

Even before the defeat of Denmark and the peace of Lübeck, Ferdinand II had taken steps to translate his victory into harsh practical terms. In 1623, Calvinist preachers were expelled from the Rhine Palatinate and a programme of forcible re-Catholicization was initiated. The same happened in the Upper Palatinate (under Bavarian control) and the other Protestant areas conquered by the armies of Ferdinand or the League. These haphazard efforts were eclipsed, however, on 6 March 1629, when the Emperor signed the edict of Restitution. This measure (drafted in 1627) sought at a stroke to recover all church property acquired by the Protestants since 1552. Wallenstein's army was to enforce the decision of special commissioners in the two Saxon circles, where twelve archbishoprics and bishoprics and over 500 abbeys were to be restored. In addition, Calvinists were to lose all political rights. Within eighteen months, six bishoprics and their lands were back in clerical hands, as were 100 convents (with more than 80 more in the process of restitution), while countless parishes, both rural and urban, were reclaimed for a Catholic incumbent. No distinction was made between rebellious (usually Calvinist) and loyal (mostly Lutheran) Protestant states and it was clear that the edict was but one of a series of intended measures aimed at extirpating Protestantism.

Discontent both with the edict and with the method of enforcement was widespread:

> All the trouble is caused by this untimely and strict catholic Reformation and also by the Imperial Edict concerning the restitution of church lands and the expulsion of the Calvinists.

> The Imperial Edict has turned all the non-Catholics against us . . . the entire Empire will be against us, aided by the Swedes, the Turks and Bethlen Gabor.[3]

These extracts from two letters written by Wallenstein to his military colleague Collalto during the winter of 1629–30 were a trifle disingenuous. For, as the general himself boasted, he had done little to enforce the edict of restitution outside the rebellious lands of Lower Saxony; nothing was done in Württemberg until summer 1630; and nothing had been (or ever would be) done in the two great Protestant electorates of Brandenburg and Saxony. Most of the opposition was not to the edict itself, although few apart from the Catholic clergy liked it, but to the instrument chosen to implement it: Wallenstein himself and his army. With almost absolute power, the general directed, supplied and supported an army of 134,000 men spread out over all Germany, from Stuttgart in the south, through Halberstadt, where his headquarters were, to Kolberg on the Baltic. His troops were garrisoned in, and drew heavy contributions from, all conditions of people – Catholic, Lutheran, Calvinist – and all types of territory – lay, ecclesiastical, imperial. Only the general's own duchy of Mecklenburg was safe. This was the role in which Wallenstein excelled: the entrepreneur, the manager, who made sure that supplies and funds came in on time, were of suitable quantity and quality, and were properly appointed. He dictated or wrote scores of letters a day, ranging from ample dispatches to explain the situation to the Emperor, to curt reminders to his quartermasters that pairs of boots should be supplied firmly tied together to make distribution easier. But not everyone was impressed by these managerial skills. After all, they had a price: the monthly assessments levied by the army's commissioners were exacted in full and in cash at a time when trade was slack and agricultural output disrupted by the recent hostilities.

It was the Catholic princes who began to campaign for a reduction in Wallenstein's army and, since he seemed reluctant to carry out the edict, for the general's recall. At meetings in February and December 1629 the members of the Catholic League, led by the electors of Mainz and Bavaria, resolved to press for both these changes at the meeting of the major princes that the Emperor was known to be planning to call: it eventually met in Regensburg in June 1630. The Emperor desired the electors formally to recognize his son as heir apparent to the Holy Roman Empire, and to agree to send the League's army to fight for Spain in the Netherlands; but the electors refused even to consider these matters until Wallenstein was dismissed (and stripped of his duchy of Mecklenburg) and his army reduced. The wrangling went on throughout July and August, with the general in close attendance at the nearby town of Memmingen, perhaps awaiting a summons to justify his conduct. But it never came. Instead, with mounting fury, Wallenstein impotently observed the vendetta waged against him by the men on whose lands his troops were quartered: 'If they want to wage a war in which affairs are arranged and managed in such a way that quartering gives the Empire pleasure and not displeasure,' he thundered to one of his lieutenants, 'let them appoint God himself to be their general – not me!'[4] But such outbursts were in vain. On 13 August the Emperor decided to dismiss Wallenstein and replace him not with God, but with the League's general, Tilly. In addition, the imperial army was to be reduced by two-thirds and the edict was to be submitted to a full imperial Diet. The ex-general retired, dejected, to his ducal estates at Friedland; his chief financier, Hans de Witte, committed suicide.

All this was a great triumph for Maximilian of Bavaria, the new elector, and he and his supporters followed it with another. Aided by French diplomatic offices, they managed to avoid recognizing Ferdinand's son as heir apparent ('King of the Romans') and they refused outright to send military aid to the Spanish Netherlands, as Philip IV had requested. The Emperor was completely outmanœuvred: he had sacrificed Wallenstein in the expectation that this would lead at least to the recognition of his son; but he gained nothing and instead lost his army.

The French diplomats, led by Richelieu's confidant Father Joseph, who were at Regensburg in order to negotiate an end to the war of Mantua, were overjoyed by the turn of events. Their master, however, was not: much to his annoyance,

Father Joseph and his colleagues had given an undertaking not to ally with the Emperor's enemies, even though they knew that the cardinal was already deeply committed to supporting the German invasion of Gustavus Adolphus.

The final terms of Franco-Swedish co-operation had not yet been settled. Gustavus was anxious to restore the Palatinate and the electoral title to Frederick V, and halt the loss of Protestant lands, whereas Richelieu wished to exalt Bavaria and the Catholic League as a third force in German politics. Even when Gustavus invaded Germany in June 1630, Richelieu haggled over the terms on which French support would be offered; but on the same day that he heard of the agreement at Regensburg, the cardinal instructed his agents with the Swedish king to conclude an alliance at once, on Gustavus's terms. France could not take the risk that Gustavus might achieve, without her help, a position of dominance from which the map of Germany might be redrawn. The king was at Bärwalde in Brandenburg when the French envoys arrived, and a treaty was signed there on 23 January 1631 which promised Sweden 1 million livres (£83,000 sterling) annually for five years, to finance a war for 'the safeguarding of the Baltic and Oceanic Seas, the liberty of commerce, and the relief of the oppressed states of the Holy Roman Empire'. The treaty, which was published immediately, together with a note that France had paid 300,000 livres on the spot, created a sensation – for it openly proclaimed French support for the Protestant cause, and indirectly constituted a declaration of war against the Emperor. It was widely acclaimed as a masterstroke for Swedish diplomacy. It was not the only one. An arrangement was also made with the Tsar of Muscovy whereby grain was exported from Russia to Sweden at a subsidized price, allowing Gustavus's agents to sell it in Amsterdam at a profit. In 1629–30 this procedure realized some 400,000 thalers (£90,000 sterling) – rather more than the French subsidy, although in later years the sale of Russian grain brought Sweden little profit. There was also a promise of financial support from the Netherlands. In Germany itself a proclamation in five languages was published, explaining the king's reasons for landing; and a series of diplomatic missions to Protestant potentates was dispatched. But after the defeats of the 1620s, few were rash enough to risk a second rebellion. Apart from the already dispossessed dukes of Saxe-Weimar and Mecklenburg, only the city of Magdeburg (1 August) and the landgrave of Hesse-Cassel (11 November) declared for Sweden. Both of them were too far away from Gustavus's base in Pomerania for their own good. Those who were closer showed greater prudence.

In February 1631, a meeting of the Protestant princes assembled at Leipzig in Saxony formally demanded a revocation of the edict of restitution. But nothing further was proposed: the princes felt confident that they could use the Swedish invasion as a bargaining counter with which to extract concessions from the Emperor. The princes would not need to mobilize themselves. They could not afford to: the public debt of Brandenburg stood at 18 million thalers (£3·75 million sterling) in 1618; that of Saxony totalled 5·3 million Rhine florins in 1621 and 7·1 million (£1·2 million sterling) in 1628. So, supported by none of the major Protestant states, Gustavus marched impatiently up and down the Baltic coast, conquering Mecklenburg and Pomerania so that Swedish control was now complete from Denmark right round to Finland: the Baltic was a Swedish lake. Gustavus had achieved the first of the objectives of his invasion. Now he had to secure a settlement that would guarantee Sweden's gains for the future, and for this he required the active support of the two Protestant electors.

He began with his brother-in-law of Brandenburg. He moved down the Oder and his army captured and brutally sacked the town of Frankfurt on 13 April. From there he planned to cross westwards and relieve his allies in Magdeburg, closely besieged by the imperialists, but first he felt it was essential to secure an alliance with Brandenburg which would protect his lines of communication with the Baltic ports. Alas, the elector refused every bribe offered by Sweden and while Gustavus wasted time negotiating, the Catholic forces took and sacked Magdeburg with even greater brutality than the Swedes at Frankfurt (20 May). Of almost 40,000 people in the city on the eve of the siege, at least three-quarters perished and most of the houses were destroyed by fire. The Protestant world wept, for Magdeburg had been a leader of the Lutheran faith since the 1520s. Even Catholics were appalled: the imperial general Pappenheim, who led the final assault, commented that such an awful visitation of God had not been witnessed since the Romans under Titus destroyed Jerusalem. And a new verb entered the German language: *Magdeburgisieren*, to 'make a Magdeburg' of somewhere.

Gustavus had warned the elector of Brandenburg in February that 'The circumstances of the moment were always the basis of his plans . . . [He] adapted his policies in the light of the enemy's actions, the circumstances of the moment, and the conduct of his friends.' The capture of Magdeburg freed the main imperial army for operations again, and so Gustavus decided to march upon Berlin, where he compelled the quaking elector to surrender all his fortresses to Swedish garrisons and to pay a monthly contribution of 30,000 imperial thalers (22 June 1631).

The scale of Gustavus's penetration of Germany in 1631 took everyone by surprise: he himself had marched out of the area covered by the maps he had brought with him. The Emperor feared an invasion of his patrimonial provinces, and recalled his forces from Italy after the Mantuan campaign. The key to the situation was now Saxony. Elector John George's dominions were large, and they dominated the eastern part of the Empire. If Saxony declared for Ferdinand, the adjacent Habsburg provinces would be cushioned against the Swedish onslaught; but if Saxony declared for Sweden, Bohemia and Moravia would become the front line and face renewed devastation (see Figure 8). The elector, his treasury empty and his debts huge, still hoped to preserve neutrality by talking to both sides. The Swedish invasion of his neighbour, Brandenburg, forced John George to raise an army of 18,000 in order to defend his territories, but in the event it

Figure 8. The Thirty Years' War

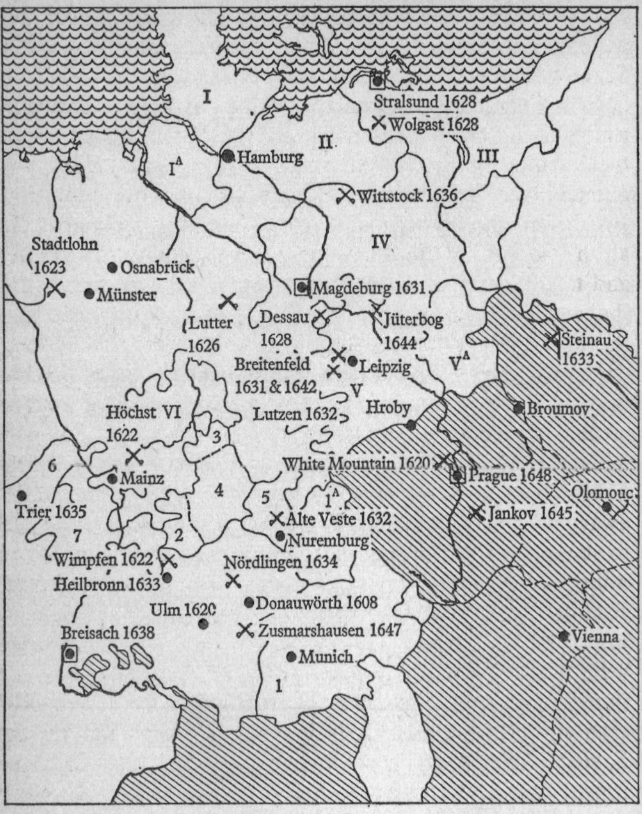

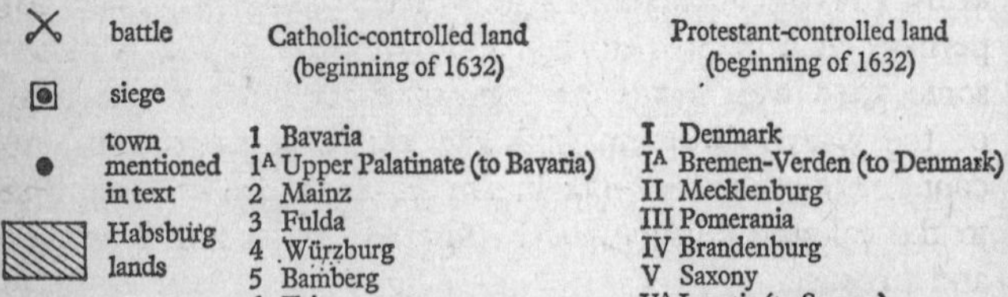

was the imperialists who struck first. On 4 September, his patience exhausted, Tilly led the imperial army across the Saxon border and advanced rapidly to Leipzig.

John George now had no alternative but to join Gustavus, which he did on 11 September, and the Saxon troops joined the Swedes, forming a field army of 40,000 men. Tilly was outnumbered, and his troops were also in poor condition. Just before the invasion of Saxony, he had complained: 'In all the days of my life, I have never seen an army so suddenly and totally deprived of all that it needs, from the greatest to the smallest requisite . . . And I am utterly astonished that the poor soldiers remain so long in such necessity.' Indeed, one of his reasons for invading had been the pressing need to find better quarters for his troops: Saxony was one of the few areas of Germany that had not been fought over. But now Tilly's veterans were weighed down with booty, and the army of his enemies, in superior strength, was only twenty miles away and closing in for battle. Tilly dared not retreat: he had to stand and fight, hoping that the inexperience of the Saxon militia would give him an advantage and, perhaps, victory. It almost did. When the two great armies met at Breitenfeld, just north of Leipzig, on 17 September 1631, the Saxons were indeed routed and fled early from the field. Only the iron discipline and the new tactics of the Swedes enabled them to redeploy their men to cover the gaps left by the Saxons. After many hours of hard fighting, in which the imperialists lost heavily, the superior firepower of the Swedish army proved decisive: Tilly's forces crumbled. They lost perhaps 20,000 men during and after the battle, of whom some 7000 were made prisoners and later joined the army of the victor. Gustavus had lost just over 2000 men, not counting the Saxons who, in any case, gradually came back to the colours. Gustavus also captured his enemies' artillery and treasury.

The victory of Breitenfeld, the first major Protestant success since the war began, was immediately followed up. The reorganized Saxon army was sent into neighbouring Silesia and defenceless Bohemia: Prague was occupied on 15 November, allowing the exiles of 1620 to return. The Swedish army, for its part, extended its control west of the Elbe, moving through Germany's Catholic heartland – the bishoprics of Würzburg, Mainz and Bamberg – to the Rhineland. Gustavus spent the winter in splendour at the city of Mainz.

The military situation was now totally transformed. Sweden and her allies held almost all of the Empire north of a line from Mannheim on the Rhine to Prague in Bohemia. The only exceptions were in the west: Westphalia, where an imperialist army under Pappenheim campaigned throughout the winter in conjunction with the Spanish army of Flanders; the west bank of the Rhine, where French troops occupied the electorate of Trier and the duchy of Lorraine; and the Palatinate and Alsace, which were still occupied by Spanish troops with imperial support. South Germany was a sort of no-man's-land stretching to the River Danube, behind which lay the shattered remnants of the Catholic army under Tilly, whose headquarters were at Ingolstadt in Bavaria.

France had neither expected nor wished for Swedish success on this scale, and at all costs Richelieu now wished to protect the German Catholics from Swedish attack. On 9 December the council of Louis XIII debated the best way to preserve the third force that they had so carefully created at Regensburg the previous year. The best they could think of was to offer French protection to any German prince who asked for it; but with the Swedish headquarters at Mainz, in the French sphere of influence, only one prince dared to move – the elector of Trier (and even he only accepted French protection in April 1632, after the Swedes had occupied his capital). Nevertheless, French troops moved into the electorate in the course of the summer, occupying the bridgeheads over the Moselle at Trier and Koblenz and across the Rhine at Philippsburg and Ehrenbreitstein. Richelieu was satisfied with this. He did not, as is so often claimed, seek to control the Rhine basin or to advance France's frontier to the river. He merely wished to be free to intervene in Germany to sustain the princes under French protection against the Habsburgs (or, if necessary, against another foreign power such as

Sweden). It was for the lack of similar French bridgeheads farther south that Richelieu was compelled to watch impotently while Bavaria was devastated.

Duke Maximilian had brought destruction on his own head. He did not believe French assurances that Sweden would spare his lands: he realized that, since Gustavus would take orders from no one, French guarantees for his good behaviour were worthless. Instead he begged the Emperor to save him, urging Ferdinand to raise another army under Wallenstein to replace the one lost at Breitenfeld.

Ever since the great battle, the general had expected to receive such a summons. When it came, in December 1631, he knew just what to do: he accepted the supreme command for three months only, during which time he agreed to raise a large army. He was confident that, with an army to command and with the Swedes about to advance, he would be ideally placed to impose on the Emperor, and on those who had secured his dismissal in 1630, the conditions under which he was prepared to continue in command when the three months were passed. He did his work well, collecting and equipping almost 40,000 men and creating an efficient general headquarters at Znaim in southern Moravia to shield Vienna against the Saxons in Bohemia: there was a treasury, a hospital, a military court, a chancery (with fourteen secretaries and a field printing-press) – all the normal but necessary machinery with which to govern an army. On 13 April 1632, at an interview with Ferdinand's senior advisers at Göllersdorf, half-way between Znaim and Vienna, Wallenstein was persuaded to continue in his supreme command in return for three concessions from his master: that there would be regular subsidies for his troops paid by the Emperor and by Spain; that he would be given full compensation both for Mecklenburg and for his present services (but the 'reward' was left unspecified); and that he was free to negotiate a separate peace between Saxony, or any other German prince presently in arms, and the Emperor. Although Protestant propaganda made much of the Göllersdorf agreement, seeing it as a sort of satanic pact to subvert the Empire, it appears to have amounted to no more than oral assurances on these three practical points; and on the strength of it Wallenstein set about increasing his army to 100,000 men.

The Emperor had hoped that Wallenstein would not fight alone. His brother-in-law, Sigismund of Poland, seemed ready to break the truce of Altmark and declare war on Sweden again, an event which would immediately recall Gustavus to the north and save Bavaria from devastation. But the Swedes too had foreseen this move. The armistice of Deulino (page 113 above) was due to expire in 1633, and both Poland and Russia prepared in 1631 for a war to determine the fate of Smolensk, captured by Poland in 1611. Sweden did everything she could to hasten the advent of this war, providing the Tsar with military advisers (including Alexander Leslie), and military supplies; but still Poland collected an army of 20,000 cossacks with which to aid the Emperor. Then in April 1632 Sigismund died, and there was a hiatus while the Diet laboriously proceeded to elect his son, Wladislaw IV (the only possible candidate) as king. This effectively stopped all military operations by the Poles, whether in attack against Sweden or in defence against Russia, whose armies began in August to invade the lands occupied during the time of troubles. The siege of Smolensk began in December 1632, but it failed, so in June 1634 the two sides made a peace which confirmed to Poland all her territorial gains made before 1618. Wladislaw only surrendered his title to be Tsar. It was a considerable triumph for the new king, but it came two years too late to save the Catholics of the Empire: there was to be no second front to divert the Swedish onslaught in 1632.

Moscow was not the only target for Swedish diplomacy during the winter of 1631–2. Gustavus's military advances led him to think of achieving long-term security for Sweden by creating a league of German princes, under his direction, which would continue after the war as a guarantee against the recurrence of danger. His treaties with new German allies (Anhalt, Brunswick, the restored dukes of Mecklenburg) now contained clauses acknowledging that a Swedish protectorate existed over them, one that was to persist after the fighting was over. The territorial claims made in 1630 – mainly for Pomerania – now became not just Sweden's security (*assecuratio*) but also her recompense (*satisfactio*) for the expenses and risks of liberating the Empire. For the occupied territories that did not ally with him, Gustavus created a 'government-general' at Frankfurt, under Chancellor Oxenstierna, which organized the collection of funds, equipment and munitions for his 120,000 troops, using the existing administrative machinery. Everything was made ready for the new campaign, on the outcome of which the fate of all Europe was generally expected to depend.

Operations began in March 1632 when Tilly, perhaps foolishly, attacked and expelled the Swedish garrisons in the diocese of Bamberg. This provoked Gustavus to invade Bavaria, which was ravaged with exemplary thoroughness in April and May. The passion play still staged by the people of Oberammergau commemorates their village's escape from devastation by the Swedes; but some 900 other settlements were destroyed, their richer inhabitants fleeing to the towns, their poorer ones to the woods – the normal pattern in the Thirty Years' War. There was little resistance, for peasant vigilantes were only successful when there was a friendly army nearby, on which they could fall back when need arose. And in Bavaria, there were now no regular units. Tilly, who was seventy-three years old and had commanded troops for fifty of them, died as he retreated before the victorious Swedes. Maximilian, although only fifty-nine, 'crept with a stick . . . like a shadow, so cast down that he was scarcely recognizable'.

Duke Maximilian had expected Wallenstein to save his duchy in recompense for his support of the Emperor since 1619 (which had already cost him 15 million Rhine florins); but the general preferred to look after the interests of his own master first, driving the Saxons out of Bohemia while Gustavus was fully occupied in Bavaria. Then he made a feint towards Saxony, which drew the Swedes towards him, and the two armies closed for combat just west of Nuremberg. But the battle never took place: Wallenstein retired with his forces into a carefully fortified camp, the Alte Feste, and challenged the Swedes to drive him out. He relied on the long distance separating Gustavus from his supply bases to cause a gradual attrition which would compel his adversaries to withdraw. On 18 September, after two months of unsuccessful siege, Wallenstein's patience was rewarded: the Swedes retreated northwards, away from the Catholic lands of Maximilian and Ferdinand. In October they tried to return, but Wallenstein forced them again to withdraw by invading Saxony: on 1 November he captured Leipzig. Then, unaccountably, the general began to send his army into winter quarters, so that when Gustavus attacked the imperialists' headquarters at Lützen, south-west of Leipzig, on 16 November, Wallenstein, outnumbered, could not do more than force a draw. In the night following the battle, both armies withdrew. The imperialists retired to Bohemia, where 17 people were shot for cowardice in the face of the enemy and 330 more had their property sequestered for their part in the return of the exiles in 1631–2. The Swedish army wintered in garrisons all over Germany. But Gustavus Adolphus did not. He was killed at Lützen, like 15,000 or so other combatants, leaving the government of the Empire he had created to the team of ministers and generals he had trained, just as Alexander the Great's conquests had passed to the *Diadochi*.

Opinions differ concerning Sweden's greatest king. In his early years, his charm captivated all whom he met; after his death, his achievement was respected, if not admired, by all Europe. But during his invasion of Germany, a new harshness of speech and rudeness of manner became apparent. The king no longer attempted to disguise his contempt for his German allies, his indifference to the wishes of his foreign supporters, his resentment of any outside interference with his plans. Having achieved his victories in 1631 almost without help, pride seems to have got the better of him in 1632: the man who had won a battle like the Breitenfeld no longer needed to compromise, either in domestic or in foreign policy. Gustavus had become a force that no one could control. Although his death at Lützen, shot in the back at short range, was lamented by almost all Protestants, it was welcomed by most politicians.

The campaign of 1632 had thus failed to change the military situation in the Empire: Bohemia had been regained by the Emperor, but otherwise the Habsburgs and the Protestant allies were left in possession of almost the same areas at the end of the year as at the beginning. Only Bavaria had lost. In this situation, the German princes on both sides began to favour peace, led by Saxony and Brandenburg (always reluctant combatants), who saw in the death of the formidable king of Sweden an opportunity to end the conflict. Even the Swedish government, acting in the name of Gustavus's infant daughter, Christina, began to consider the terms on which they might disengage from Germany. As early as 14 January 1633, barely two months after the king's death, Chancellor Oxenstierna proposed to the council of regency in Stockholm that Sweden should make peace if she could secure two things: possession of Pomerania as her *satisfactio* for war expenses; and the creation of a strong Protestant union, already mooted by Gustavus, as *assecuratio* that she would not be threatened again by imperial power. The council approved this plan and the chancellor was sent back to Germany to achieve it: in April a new association of Protestant princes, the Heilbronn League, was formed, with Oxenstierna as director. But Brandenburg and Saxony refused to join the league, and Brandenburg also refused to accept Sweden's claim to Pomerania (to which the elector had a legitimate title once the reigning duke, the last of his line, should die). The army, too, gave cause for concern: it spent most of the summer in idleness, mutinous for its pay; and in October, Wallenstein encircled and captured a Swedish force at Steinau in Silesia and advanced towards Pomerania. The financial situation was even more alarming. Although the cost to Sweden of the war in Germany had fallen from 2·4 million thalers in 1630 to only 130,000 in 1633, it began to rise again to around 2 million. The Dutch subsidies dried up after 1632 (and only £50,000 had been sent anyway) and the French subventions were now diverted into the treasury of the Heilbronn League. The truce with Poland was due to expire in 1635 and Wladislaw was scoring success against Muscovy. In diplomatic, military and financial terms, Sweden was no longer winning the war.

The regency government of the infant Queen Christina was ill-equipped to cope with these reverses. Chancellor Oxenstierna, now aged fifty and at the height of his powers, certainly enjoyed a commanding position on the council, since almost two-thirds of its members were either related to him or to his close political allies (to be precise, of the 72 councillors appointed between 1602 and 1647, 54 belonged to the Oxenstierna faction). But the chancellor himself was forced to stay in Germany from the spring of 1633 until July 1636, and in his absence a group of councillors began to oppose his policies. To them, it seemed desirable to disengage both from Poland and from Germany as soon as possible, surrendering the Prussian port tolls to the Poles, and even offering to return Pomerania in return for a cash payment from the Empire (6 million thalers was the figure mentioned in March 1634).

This disposition to settle was frustrated by two things: the curious behaviour of Wallenstein and the intervention of Spain. About the first there is no certainty, in spite of countless books and copious archive material. The general was empowered by the Göllersdorf agreement to undertake negotiations for a separate peace with any of the Emperor's German enemies, and in January 1633 he began peace talks with the Saxons. But he also sent envoys to Sweden and France, which he was not authorized to do. Later writers, drawing on the hostile press which followed the failure of these peace initiatives, condemned the liaisons as treasonable; but it might equally be true that Wallenstein was trying to divide his enemies one from another. That is certainly how the perceptive French ambassador Feuquières saw it in the end, after being deceived all summer: 'His game is too subtle for me. From his silence in the face of all that I have offered him, I can only assume that what he really wants is strife between Your Majesty [Louis XIII] and his allies.'[5] The

Swedes and the Saxons saw their error at about the same time, and broke off negotiations; whereupon Wallenstein sent his army into action in Silesia (see above), while a Spanish army arrived in Alsace to relieve the besieged imperial cities of Konstanz and Breisach.

The Emperor and his advisers, however, were not impressed. They had maintained Wallenstein's army for almost a year, at vast expense, yet it had neither fought a battle nor cleared the enemy from their lands: the Swedes were still in Bavaria and the Catholic south. If the general had gambled on suspending the war in order to gain a settlement, there too he was open to criticism, for the peace initiative had clearly failed. In December 1633 the Emperor therefore began to reassert his control over Wallenstein. First he ordered the general to attack and expel forthwith the Swedish and Protestant troops from South Germany; second, he forbade the general to bring his troops back to be billeted in the patrimonial provinces – they were to winter in the Protestant areas of the Empire. To make sure he was obeyed, the Emperor gave orders to his commanders in Austria to raise extra troops who could keep Wallenstein's men out. Although after a while Ferdinand relented, allowing the army to winter at Pilsen in western Bohemia, it was clear that the general's command was all but over. Imperial confidence, undermined by the failure of the 1633 campaign, had been shattered by the revelations concerning the secret negotiations with Saxony, Sweden and France (most of them leaked from Swedish headquarters in Frankfurt). It was clear that Wallenstein would have to go, and in January 1634 Ferdinand and his council concluded that the only wholly safe way to remove him from his command was by assassination.

The labyrinthine process by which Wallenstein's end was accomplished defies description. As one of the chief conspirators said: 'Put briefly, dissimulation is the alpha and omega of this business.' But gradually all the general's supporters were detached, until only four were left and they, and their master, were murdered by the Emperor's agents on 25 February 1634. He had outlived his usefulness. He had betrayed so many people and ravaged so many countries, starting with his native Bohemia, that few had sympathy for him. Too much has been written about his supposed desire to bring peace to the Empire in his last year: a king without a kingdom, he had little chance of achieving that. Wallenstein was sacrificed not because of the radical solutions he might have imposed on Germany, but for losing a campaign and defying his master's orders. In any case, in the spring of 1634 the general was expendable because of the firm promise from Philip IV that a large Spanish army would be sent to replace that of Wallenstein and sweep the Swedes from South Germany.

3. The Cardinal-Infante

The almost miraculous appearance in Germany of the king of Spain's brother at the head of an army of 15,000 men in July 1634 was the product of the vision of one man: Don Gaspar de Guzmán, count of Olivares and (after 1625) duke of San Lúcar la Mayor. The Count-Duke, as he was always known, both in state papers and in conversation, came from one of Castile's oldest and best noble families. Born in Rome in 1587, he returned to Spain in 1599 and went to Salamanca university, where he was student rector in 1604–5. He became attached in 1615 to the household of the crown prince, later Philip IV and then aged ten, and he steadily increased in influence over his young charge. Meanwhile his uncle, Don Baltasar de Zúñiga, became chief minister to Philip III in 1619. The position remained the same after Philip IV's accession on 31 March 1621: Zúñiga continued to direct state policy until he died in October 1622, leaving the roles of both favourite and chief minister to his energetic nephew. In his early years of power Olivares rose at five, confessed, roused the king from his slumbers and discussed the day's programme with him. Then he would spend the rest of the day (until eleven at night or later) giving audiences, reading papers, dictating orders. Although he often accompanied the king while hunting, or in his carriage, he worked on the way, giving audiences from the saddle or dictating letters to the coachful of secretaries who followed him. With state papers stuffed in his pockets and even stuck in his hat, 'from his bedchamber to his study, from his study to his coach, out strolling, in the corner, on the stairs, he . . . would hear and deal with an infinite number of people'. Four of Olivares's secretaries were killed by this hectic routine, and the Count-Duke himself suffered alternately from acute lack of sleep when he needed it and an inability to sleep when he had the opportunity. But he never stopped: the ox-like constitution which looms out of his portraits sustained him for 22 years of tireless dedication to his sovereign's service. Until 1640, moreover, his grasp of affairs was remarkably good: he made a collection of maps and reference works to enable him to assess the progress of his policies and wars abroad; and he drew on the advice of a wide range of specialist advisers for areas where his own knowledge was thin. His papers of advice and his speeches at the council table were always forceful, incisive and persuasive: they are instantly recognizable by historians today. Towards the end of his career – when his obesity made him look ridiculous, his rages already presaged the insanity which clouded his last two years of life, and his policies had evidently failed – he could safely be caricatured as a figure of fun; but in the 1620s and '30s he unquestionably inspired awe and respect from all who knew him. As a ministerial colleague wrote of him in 1629: 'It is true that the ship is going down, but under other captains we should have perished much sooner.'

At the death of Philip III, no time was lost in driving out the relatives of Lerma, who had monopolized royal patronage for over twenty years, to make room for the families of Olivares and Zúñiga. The new ministers criticized everything done by the former regime, declaring that their intention was 'to restore everything to the state it was in during the time of King Philip II'. 'The king wishes to model his government on that of his grandfather King Philip II, and to this effect . . . he has appointed ministers to all departments who held office under his grandfather.'[6] In order to turn the clocks back, the indispensable prerequisite was a thorough reform of the society, economy and government of Spain. In a memorandum presented to the king on Christmas Day 1624, Olivares asserted that 'the state in which these kingdoms are now is, for our sins, perhaps worse than has ever been seen'. The risks of doing almost anything were less than the risks of doing nothing at all. He therefore proposed new social policies to reform morals and achieve sobriety and austerity. Industry, trade and agriculture were to be stimulated, and taxation reduced (in Castile at least). Most important of all, the different provinces of the Empire were to be brought into a closer association, to be known as the Union of Arms, in order to spread some of the cost of Spain's military budget to other states besides Castile.

The Union was the most important attempt at reform made by Olivares, and he expended much time and energy on it. His model was the Circles of the Holy Roman Empire, and Olivares claimed that his scheme only aimed at ensuring closer military co-operation between the various units of Philip IV's monarchy, and at sharing the costs of imperial defence. The ease with which the Anglo-Dutch fleet had attacked Cadiz in the autumn of 1625 showed how necessary it was to improve Spain's state of readiness. But both Olivares and the political elites in the provinces realized that the Union would do rather more than that: it would 'familiarize' (the word used in government circles) the inhabitants of the various states with each other, and might thus provide the basis for a closer union. The Count-Duke had already stated the need for a unified Spain in his Great Memorial of Christmas 1624: the Union of Arms was to form the first step towards achieving it.

Olivares believed in scientific government and he collected statistics and reports which convinced him that Castile was paying too much, and the rest of the empire too little, towards the cost of imperial defence. He placed particular emphasis on the population figures which he had to hand for each area. The Italian dominions carried out regular censuses; Castile had been surveyed in the 1590s (for the *millones* tax); the lands of the crown of Aragon in 1603–9. Unfortunately, these Spanish estimates were misleading, especially for Catalonia. By a careful reconstruction of scattered local data (most of it not used by the government) it has been shown that the principality's population in the early seventeenth century was about 400,000, and rather less after the plague of 1630–1. But contemporaries – whether ministers, merchants, or members of the Catalan estates – assumed that the figure was 1 million. It was on this basis that in 1626 Olivares and the king made a personal visit to the eastern provinces with the Union of Arms project and demanded taxes worth 3·7 million ducats from the Catalan estates whereas Aragon (with perhaps 300,000 inhabitants) was only asked to provide 2 million ducats, and Valencia (with 350,000 people) was called on for 1 million. Although payment of these taxes was to be spread over fifteen years, and although the sums requested were intended for imperial defence, the Catalans flatly refused to vote a penny. They complained that the province was too poor to raise so much, and they complained even more that in recent years the government had attempted to initiate policies which went against the provincial constitutions (or *furs*). The king and Olivares rode back to Castile empty-handed. For the Count-Duke, 1626 was also to bring personal disasters. In June, his favourite nephew and chosen successor died; in July, his only daughter died in childbirth, and the baby soon followed. The now heirless Olivares himself fell seriously ill and barely survived the purges and blood-lettings prescribed by his doctors. He seems to have lost confidence in his political gifts, for he offered his resignation to the king. It was refused. Philip IV put a brave face on his misfortunes and on 25 July issued an edict putting the Union of Arms into effect, and shortly afterwards couriers were sent to Italy, Portugal, the Netherlands and America, detailing the higher contributions required for imperial defence. But they came too late to prevent some severe losses in Spain's possessions abroad.

The loss of 's Hertogenbosch in the Netherlands, in 1629, and the failure to regulate the Mantuan succession were bad enough. Far worse were the successes of the Dutch in America. The fleets sent out by the West India Company were getting larger every year. Although Bahía, the capital of Brazil, had been recaptured after a year of Dutch occupation (1624–5), in 1627 another expedition burned and plundered shipping there again, and in 1628 a fleet of 31 great ships, carrying 689 guns and 4000 men, tried once more. Commanded by the redoubtable Piet Heyn, they in fact captured an entire treasure fleet off Havana, taking £800,000 in silver and £1·2 million in goods, so Brazil was left alone; but everyone knew that the Dutch would be back in even greater force before long. They already had a lively trade with the Portuguese colony, with about twenty ships sailing every year to collect the sugar produced in the north-western province of Pernambuco. The Dutch also had a Fifth Column in most Brazilian ports: Jews who feared Catholic persecution and, according to the Dutch mariner Dierick Ruiters, who had been in Brazil himself, 'would rather see a Dutch flag than a couple of inquisitors'. The Dutch were already adept at exploiting any Jewish presence among their trading partners. Dutch Jews carried on a lively trade with Spain and Portugal during the truce, to the alarm of the Inquisition (who greatly exaggerated their numbers), and the role of the Portuguese Jews in Brazil was accurately predicted in Lope de Vega's play *Brazil Regained* (completed in 1625) in which the province's capital, Bahía, is betrayed to the Dutch by its Jewish residents. Whether this particular episode was true or not, when a Dutch West India company fleet of 67 ships, 1170 guns and 7000 men arrived off Recife, the capital of Pernambuco, in February 1630, the local Jewish community welcomed them (and in return the Dutch allowed them a rabbi, a synagogue and even their own printing press – the first Jewish books printed in America were published at Recife in 1636). Later, many Portuguese Jewish exiles in the Netherlands came out to settle in Brazil for, before long, most of the coastal plain of Pernambuco was in Dutch hands.

The impact of these Dutch successes on Castile was at first dulled by the roaring inflation of the years 1626–8, caused by a new, massive issue of worthless *vellón* coins. Criticism of the government mounted, and both in 1627 and in 1629 a court faction (led by disgraced supporters of the late duke of Lerma) challenged Olivares for control over the king. But the Count-Duke survived, and before long he had formulated a grandiose proposal to restore Spain's fortunes. The plan he put forward in February 1631 hinged upon the dispatch of Philip IV's two brothers (known as the *Infantes* or princes) to the chief trouble spots of the Empire: Prince Charles was to go to Lisbon where he would organize the necessary fleets and armies to recover Pernambuco, and Prince Ferdinand (who had been promoted cardinal of Toledo at the age of ten and was therefore known as the Cardinal-Infante) was to go via Lombardy to the Netherlands, where he was to take over the government from Philip II's aged daughter, the Archduchess Isabella. 'If the news that two members of the royal family are being sent out does not inspire the nation to do its duty,' Olivares claimed, 'we may despair of ever being able to stiffen our sinews as we ought if we are to beat the enemy . . . and to restore Spain's reputation.'[7] Of course such plans were easier proposed than executed: Prince Charles died in 1632 and the relief fleet only left for Brazil in 1635 (where it was defeated); and although the Cardinal-Infante left Madrid in April 1632, he only left Spain in April 1633 and did not reach Brussels until December 1634.

During the delay, however, various developments in the Netherlands made the plan more difficult to achieve. In 1632, despite the efforts of an imperial army under Pappenheim in Westphalia, the Dutch had invaded Limburg and captured a whole string of towns along the Maas. The fall of Roermond, Venlo, Maastricht and the rest cut the Spanish Netherlands off from the Empire; it also provoked the most serious crisis of confidence in the 'obedient provinces' since the general revolt of 1576. With French help, two Walloon noblemen, Count Warfusée and Count van den Bergh, raised the standard of revolt against Spain in the autumn of 1632; the prince of Orange, still in Limburg, prepared to assist them; and there were anti-Spanish riots in the cities of Brabant and Flanders against the effete government that had allowed so much territory to be lost. But the rebellion was nipped in the bud. Neither France nor the Dutch acted promptly, and the conspirators were all arrested (their names were betrayed to the Spanish government by the English agent, the artist Sir Balthasar Gerbier). Meanwhile, Spain sent a large provision to the Netherlands and made some timely concessions: a States-General of the southern provinces was called, and it was allowed to begin peace talks with the Dutch. There was no basis for agreement, however, as long as the Dutch remained in Brazil; and in the campaign of 1633 more towns were lost. The death of the Archduchess Isabella in December 1633 ended all pretence of autonomy for the South Netherlands, for she was to be replaced by the Cardinal-Infante and, until he arrived, the government was placed in the hands of a Castilian grandee, the marquis of Aytona. His military achievements in the 1634 campaign were encouraging – one or two places were recovered – but the cost was crippling.

It may seem strange that the enormous and continuing cost of the indecisive war in the Netherlands, which seldom came to less than £750,000 sterling a year from Castile alone, never led to serious consideration in Spain of abandoning the northern outposts. It was accepted as axiomatic in government circles that: 'Although the war which we have fought in the Netherlands has exhausted our treasury and forced us into the debts that we have incurred, it has also diverted our enemies in those parts so that, had we not done so, it is certain that we would have had war in Spain or somewhere nearer.' And although there was not actual rejoicing when news arrived in Spain that France had increased her subsidies to the Dutch Republic, the Madrid government drew comfort from the expected reduction in French resources available for a possible war in Italy or in the Empire. Spain's strategic thinking at this time resembled the structure of a house of cards, in which any reverse sustained by the Habsburg cause in Germany threatened Spain's hold on Lombardy and the Netherlands, which in turn exposed the Indies and the Iberian peninsula to direct attack. At its simplest, the theory ran: 'The Netherlands cannot be held if the imperialists are defeated in Germany' and 'If the Netherlands are lost, neither the Indies, nor Spain, nor Italy can be defended.' At its most complex, the vulnerability of the whole Habsburg edifice was inter-connected:

> The first and greatest dangers are those that threaten Lombardy, the Netherlands and Germany. A defeat in any of these three is fatal for this Monarchy, so much so that if the defeat in those parts is a great one, the rest of the monarchy will collapse; for Germany will be followed by Italy and the Netherlands, and the Netherlands will be followed by America; and Lombardy will be followed by Naples and Sicily, without the possibility of being able to defend either.[8]

Thus, saving the imperial cause in Germany began to seem to be as important to Spain as the recovery of Pernambuco, and the same strategy could be employed to achieve both: sending a large army to the Low Countries via Italy and Germany. This would restore imperialist fortunes in the Empire and then, by constant military pressure, force the Dutch to concentrate all their resources on home defence and thus abandon Brazil. Furious troop-raising began in Spain and Spanish Italy, and in 1633 an advance guard was sent through the Valtelline (still under Habsburg control) into Alsace, where the sieges of Konstanz and Breisach were raised, and the Swedish army was shifted out of the south-west. But in 1634, with Wallenstein out of the way and Bavaria ravaged, the Emperor needed more than a few thousand Spanish troops in Alsace to defend his interests. Already in June 1634 the Saxon army had invaded Bohemia yet again, and the remnants of Wallenstein's imperial army, now commanded by the Emperor's son Ferdinand, was trapped between the need to defend the patrimonial provinces and the desire to join with the promised Spanish army coming up from Italy to clear all southern Germany of Protestant troops. In the end, the latter prevailed, and on 2 September, despite all the efforts of their enemies, the Spanish and imperial armies joined forces outside the town of Nördlingen, north of Donauwörth, which the imperialists had under siege. The Protestants could not afford to abandon Nördlingen – they had already lost Regensburg and Donauwörth the previous month – and on 6 September their main field army, consisting of Swedes under Gustav Horn (Oxenstierna's son-in-law) and German Protestants under Bernard of Saxe-Weimar (partially in French pay), made a major attempt to drive the Spanish-imperial army off. They were, unknown to them, outnumbered by 25,000 men to 33,000, and the battle of Nördlingen proved a catastrophic defeat: fifteen desperate charges failed to dislodge the Habsburg army; and when the shattered Protestant battalions tried to withdraw, they were destroyed. Horn and about 4000 men were taken prisoner; perhaps 12,000 others lay dead on the field.

Even though the Spanish army moved off immediately in the direction of Brussels, South Germany was lost to the Heilbronn League: Saxe-Weimar ordered all his garrisons to retreat across the Rhine and winter in Alsace. Only Augsburg continued to resist the rising imperial tide, her obduracy perhaps stiffened by the brutal treatment inflicted on the areas that surrendered. In Württemberg, as the imperialist army advanced, the local administration fled, and between 1634 and 1638 the duchy was a prey to uncontrolled plunder: 42 million florins (about £7 million sterling) of damage was done by the occupying Spanish and Bavarian troops. A survey of twelve small towns of the duchy in 1655 revealed only 1874 buildings where in 1629 there had been 3004; in the countryside there were 41,000 destroyed houses – more than the total of inhabited ones; and one-third of the agricultural land was uncultivated. Most of this damage was done during the years of anarchy between 1634 and 1638.

The duchy's population fell from 450,000 in 1620 to less than 100,000 in 1639; it had only recovered to 121,000 in 1645 and 166,000 in 1652, when the last foreign garrisons withdrew.

However, there were other consequences to the Habsburg victory at Nördlingen. Young Ferdinand took advantage of the discomfiture of the Swedes to open negotiations with the Protestant princes who had not joined the Heilbronn League, notably Saxony and Brandenburg. On 28 February 1635 he concluded a truce with Saxony which promised the immediate repeal of the edict of restitution and an amnesty for everyone except the Bohemian exiles. In return, Saxony recognized Bavaria's electoral dignity, and accepted a prohibition on all alliances between princes and the exclusion of all Calvinist rulers from the right to hold ecclesiastical lands. On 30 May 1635 these terms were published as the peace of Prague, and all were invited to accept them and join their forces against the foreign powers (unspecified) who perturbed the Empire's peace.

It was never supposed that all the Protestant princes would accept this peace: it had been designed specifically to attract those like Saxony (demoralized by defeat) and Brandenburg (alienated by Sweden's claim on Pomerania) who were already estranged from the Heilbronn League. And in this it was successful. Henceforth the Saxon army, and the puny forces of Brandenburg, fought for the Emperor. But most members of the Heilbronn League did not accept the peace of Prague. The landgrave of Hesse regarded it as a 'monstruous peace . . . [which] aims to subjugate all Germany and extirpate liberty and the Reformed religion'; while even the government of Brandenburg feared that 'if the peace of Prague is confirmed, the Reformed religion will not survive'. There was some justice in this unfavourable judgement, since article 24 of the peace created a joint imperial-Saxon army of 80,000 men to enforce the terms agreed between the two powers. It was to be commanded by Ferdinand III. In June this force was increased still further by its junction with the army of the Catholic League to form a 'Haupt-Armada'. It was not one in which Calvinists at least could place much hope.

If the Emperor relied on the reinforced army to compel his opponents in Germany to make peace, his strategy towards Sweden was more sophisticated. Here, his hopes were pinned on Poland, whose truce with the Swedes was about to run out: if Poland attacked, Sweden would be forced to withdraw from Germany, and perhaps Saxony could exploit her contacts with the *riksrad* to open negotiations. But here, Sweden's defeatism actually frustrated the Emperor's design: she conceded almost everything that the Poles demanded – even surrendering the Prussian port tolls – and tamely renewed the peace at Stuhmsdorf (12 September 1635).

The Swedish council dared not provoke Poland. They could not ignore the mounting evidence of domestic distress and discontent occasioned by the wars of the past decades. Conscription was beginning to affect all classes of society: some 55,000 men in Sweden and Finland were raised for military service between 1621 and 1632 alone, of whom perhaps half were killed or wounded. The social costs of losses on this scale were extremely severe. In smaller hamlets, almost every adult male was conscripted; even in larger villages the losses could be catastrophic. In the parish of Bygdea in northern Sweden, for example, 230 men were conscripted between 1621 and 1639, of whom 216 died in service, a further 5 returned home crippled, and 6 were still in the army in 1640 – but there was little prospect of them surviving until the peace of 1648. Conscription thus seems to have been almost the equivalent of a death warrant, and the number of men aged between fifteen and sixty in Bygdea, who were eligible for conscription, decreased from 345 in 1620 to 152 in 1639.[9] Many of those recruited resisted (and were deported); others mutinied after they had joined the army. In July 1635, Oxenstierna was arrested by mutinous units of his army and held prisoner at Magdeburg. And, on top of all this, in October, Saxony declared war on Sweden. The Swedish council now began to panic. They instructed Oxenstierna to 'obtain any territory' that could be had by making peace; 'if not, to take satisfaction in money; and if he cannot get that, to try every means consistent with reputation and safety to extricate ourselves from the German war: if it cannot be done on honourable terms, then let us content ourselves with whatever terms we can get; for the resources of the country are not adequate to the maintenance of great armies' (23 October).[10]

These events were of crucial importance for France. On the one hand, Sweden's defeat and the resulting panic among the council of regency in Stockholm left the anti-Habsburg cause leaderless; on the other, the imperialist successes made it more essential than ever to protect France's remaining allies in the Empire from reprisals. Richelieu therefore convinced his king that steps must be taken at once to break (or to get others to break) each of the physical links which held the Habsburg alliance together. First, the Dutch were given larger subsidies, so that their armies would confine the energies of the Cardinal-Infante to the Netherlands and their fleets would cut communications between Madrid and Brussels (the treaty signed on 8 February 1635 even contained a clause concerning the way in which the South Netherlands should be partitioned if Franco-Dutch forces overran them). Second, the links between Lombardy and the Low Countries, already threatened by the occupation of Lorraine, were finally severed by the occupation, during the winter of 1634–5, of several key towns in Alsace. Third, in March 1635 a French army overran the Valtelline and prevented all military contacts between Milan and Vienna. Fourth, in order to avert the signature of a general peace in Germany, in November 1634 Richelieu concluded a preliminary agreement with the Heilbronn League, offering them the services of an army of 12,000 men, paid by France, during the 1635 campaign. On 28 April, a full treaty of alliance was signed with the League, including Sweden, which incorporated an undertaking that France would declare war on Spain at the earliest possible opportunity and make no separate peace without her allies. Finally, in Italy, Richelieu prepared for the coming war by signing treaties with the dukes of Parma and Savoy (June and July 1635).

In the space of six months, therefore, France had skilfully

isolated her enemies before launching a simultaneous attack on several fronts. There was even a reasonable excuse to hand for declaring war. The elector of Trier, who had been a French pensioner since 1627 and under French protection since 1632, was arrested and imprisoned by Spanish troops from the Netherlands on 26 March 1635. At the same time, Spanish forces occupied the principal cities of the electorate: Philippsburg, Landau and Trier itself. The seizure of a ruler and his capital while under French protection was a challenge which Richelieu and his haughty master could not afford to overlook, even had they wanted to. So a French herald delivered a declaration of war on Spain to the Cardinal-Infante in Brussels on 19 May. Although the formal breach with the Emperor was delayed until March 1636, it was a foregone conclusion.

These were momentous events, whose consequences were to be felt for years. The elector of Trier was kept in prison until 1645; the war between France and the Empire was to last until 1648, the war between France and Spain until 1659. These conflicts merged with the others already afoot – in the Netherlands and in the Empire – until a genuinely European conflict was being fought. And the strain of war on so many fronts at once was to bring most of the states involved to the brink of dissolution and revolution.

CHAPTER VII

War and Revolution

1. *On the Edge of Disaster, 1635–40*

In the debates of 1628–9 on the need for French intervention in Italy, Richelieu had told his king that breaking the Habsburg encirclement of France took precedence over reform and retrenchment at home; in his 'Great Memorandum' of 1624, by contrast, Olivares had placed the need for domestic renewal above foreign aggrandizement (although defence against foreign aggression was, of course, permitted). In the end Richelieu got his way, Olivares did not; and Richelieu has also had his way with the historians. The tone was set by Guillaume de Vallory's preface to his (fairly worthless) *Anecdotes du Ministère du Comte-Duc d'Olivares*, published at Paris in 1722, in which the subject's character and achievements were unflatteringly compared, point by point, with those of Richelieu. But few contemporaries, except for patriotic reasons, saw a clear difference between the two men. They both combined the roles of favourite and chief minister, absolutely dependent on a fickle master's favour (and Louis XIII, at least, flirted with other men). They were born at almost the same time and they rose to power and retained it for more or less the same time (Richelieu, born in 1585, entered the king's council in April 1624 and died in December 1642; Olivares, born in 1587, succeeded his uncle in October 1622 and was dismissed in January 1643). Finally, although very different in appearance and style (Philippe de Champaigne's sphinx-like cardinal in scarlet versus Velásquez's gross grandee in black), contemporaries seem to have found neither man lovable: diligence, competence, omnipotence and arrogance was not a combination to warm many hearts. Times, however, were hard. There were serious problems facing the leaders of European states in the mid-seventeenth century and politicians needed to be intransigent if they were to survive.

In 1635, neither France nor Spain was ready to fight another war. They were exhausted before the conflict began, both by wars already fought and by the adverse economic situation. As early as 1626, Olivares only saw gloom ahead: '[Spain's] sickness is serious and has become chronic,' he wrote. 'We have lost our prestige; the treasury (which is the basis of authority) is totally exhausted; and our ministers are lax, accustomed either not to act or to act slowly and ineffectively.' There was certainly wealth in Spain – the 1000 coaches which clogged streets of Madrid, the new noble palaces, the 6000 slaves owned by the citizens of Seville all testified to it; the problem was to tap it for the treasury. The situation facing Richelieu was much the same. A city like Amiens in Picardy, for example, had seen its population and its textile trade expand rapidly from 1600 to 1630, with many immigrants from the South Netherlands and much cloth exported to Spain; but after the harvest failure in 1630–1, the onset of plague, and then the closing of the frontiers in 1635, production and population both fell off. When new taxes were imposed to pay for the war in 1636, the unemployed weavers of Amiens staged a revolt. In this they were not alone, for a wave of popular uprisings shook France in 1636–7, from the rebellious peasantry – the *Croquants* – of Saintonge and the neighbouring provinces (whose protest, led by the Seigneur of La Mothe la Forêt, challenged a regular army before it was suppressed) to the urban proletariat of dozens of towns.

These anti-fiscal revolts, which fortunately for the government were largely unco-ordinated, only died down when Richelieu promised to remove the more obnoxious taxes; but the war would not permit a reduction in revenue for long, and until 1645 the overall tax-burden demanded from France was constantly rising, as Figure 9 shows. A great deal of this

Figure 9. The Finances of the French Monarchy, 1600–50

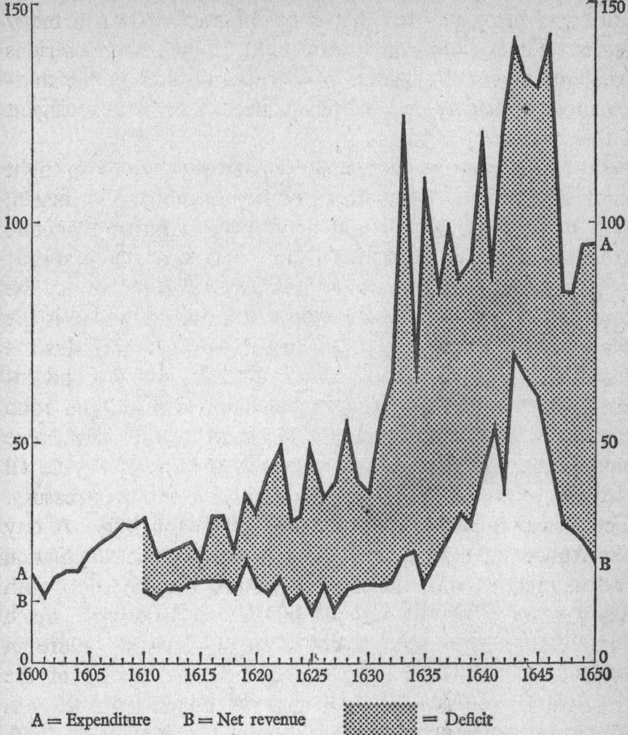

Source: A. Guéry, 'Les finances de la monarchie Française', *Annales ESC*, XXXIII (1978), 236–7.

ncrease came from raising the principal direct tax, the *taille*, whose annual yield rose from 36 million livres in 1635 to almost 73 million in 1643. The incessant fiscal pressure alarmed ministers. As the governor of Guyenne put it as early as June 1633, after a wave of disturbances had been suppressed:

I know very well that the great and important affairs of His Majesty oblige him, in spite of his reluctance, to tax his subjects more than he wishes; but I can assure you that misery [here] is so general in all areas and among all classes that unless there is an immediate reduction it is inevitable that the people will be driven to some dangerous course of action.

Richelieu did not know what to do. His policies were expensive, but he did not understand the machinery of finance well enough to minimize the burden. 'I confess fully my ignorance of financial matters,' he told one of his colleagues with touching candour in 1635. He had learned little more by 1642. Only ten months before his death he claimed to be unable to assess the advisability of a new fiscal expedient because of 'the little experience that I have in financial matters'. And when he had to persuade the king to sanction some new tax, he could only agree to present the arguments prepared by his treasury colleagues 'if we talk about it before [seeing] the king and I am well instructed beforehand'.[1]

So the popular risings recurred, in the south-west and elsewhere, and in 1639 there was another group of rebellions in Normandy, 37 in number, known as the *Nu-pieds* (bare-feet) risings, which (like the Croquants) only ended after a pitched battle between the peasants and a royal army (30 November 1639).

Olivares was not faced by popular revolts on this scale. Every European country had some – it was, in that undemocratic age, the only means by which the people could register their discontent with government policies. Yet Spain had, if anything, rather less than its share before 1646 (when several towns staged anti-fiscal riots), even though the *per capita* tax burden in Castile, at least, was no less than in the French *pays d'élection.* There are several probable explanations for this strange contrast. First there was the existence of a tradition of revolt: the areas of France which rebelled in the 1630s and '40s were much the same as those which had rebelled in the 1590s and earlier. There was an arsenal of precedents and experience available to those who wished to organize violent protests (see also pages 31–2 above). Second, Castilian peasants, especially those in the south, had the chance of escape to the New World: perhaps 5000 Castilians sailed for America every year during the seventeenth century, and they doubtless included (to judge by their conduct in the colonies) some of the more turbulent, enterprising and determined members of society – the potential leaders of popular unrest. Third, and more important, a greater proportion of Castile's taxes were indirect than in France: there was no Spanish equivalent of the *taille*, a direct property or personal tax (according to region), which produced more than half the total French revenue every year; instead, the mainstays of the Castilian exchequer were the *alcabala* and the *millones*, both of them levied as excise duties on selected goods. Any increase in direct taxes bore immediately upon every taxpayer; increases in individual excise duties, however, except for staples such as bread, did not affect all groups to the same extent. The risk of a general revolt was thus diminished.[2] Finally, even in the administration of the hated direct taxes, there was an important difference between France and Spain, despite the fact that collection in both countries was often entrusted to tax-farmers who had advanced the anticipated yield of a tax to the treasury and needed to recover the full sum, and more, as quickly as possible. In Castile, although from 1637 more arbitrary methods were employed to secure overdue tax debts (in some case they were fifteen years in arrears), every taxpayer had the right of appeal to the law courts against his individual assessment – over-assessment, misfortune, changed circumstances and so on – and the courts appear to have acted sympathetically, often judging against fisc and tax-farmer. But in France there was no appeal against over-assessment for sums of less than 30 livres – the equivalent of 50 days' wages for most working men – except to the courts run by the *élus*, whose corruption and idleness were proverbial. The *élus* of Gascony preferred to reside at Toulouse and knew little of the area whose taxes they apportioned; the *élus* of Saintes, who did reside, knew all too much of their area, for they managed to pocket over 81,000 livres (roughly £6500 sterling) in only two years; and the *élus* of Amiens refused to issue receipts for taxes paid, specifically 'to prevent exact accounts from being drawn up'. And so on. Such men had no interest in ensuring that individual taxpayers were fairly assessed. The poor were thus virtually defenceless in the face of unfair or excessive tax-demands by the private collecting agencies – defenceless, that is, except for revolt.

The pattern of anti-fiscal rebellion in France was therefore almost the reverse of that in Spain. Except in 1631–2, revolts tended to occur in areas where the government's control was greatest, for that was where the impact of increased taxation was felt most severely. Direct taxes in Normandy were fourteen times heavier than in Provence (with half of Normandy's population) and eleven times heavier than in Languedoc (which had a somewhat larger population). Small wonder that the most serious popular uprising of the period, the *Nu-pieds*, occurred in Normandy. In Spain, by contrast, the main anti-fiscal troubles occurred in those areas which, ironically, provided least to the royal treasury: Vizcaya, Portugal, Catalonia. Like Charles I in Scotland and Ireland, and like Louis XIII in the *pays d'états*, Philip IV would have done better to have left the peripheral provinces alone. They were so poor, yet so protected by privilege and tradition, that they always produced more trouble than taxes.

Olivares, however, did not see matters in this light. He had never really understood why the Catalans refused demands for taxes which to him, thanks to his false statistics (page 235 above), seemed so eminently fair and reasonable. So, in 1632, he tried again. The king made another personal visit to convoke the Catalan estates and request the aid due under the Union of Arms. But, once again, there was a humiliating failure: the Catalans would not vote a penny, despite dark threats by ministers about the consequences of royal displeasure. Perhaps the Catalans were saved by the outbreak of anti-fiscal unrest elsewhere, which made Olivares more cautious. In Portugal, there were riots against new taxes at Oporto in 1628 and at Santarem in 1629. More seriously, a major opposition movement began in Vizcaya province in September 1631 in protest against a new tax on salt imposed two years before (although the government secured the consent of the provincial estates, this was only achieved by depriving the Basque-speaking majority of their votes). The opposition was not overcome until May 1634. Then, in 1637, trouble again flared up in Portugal, at Evora, and rumours circulated that it might spread to the other towns. The cause was again fiscal: the efforts of the Madrid government to raise new taxes to finance the recovery of Brazil from the Dutch (page 236 above). Although Olivares made a show of nonchalance, claiming that 'normally we take very little notice of such things, because popular tumults occur every day without causing anything untoward', he nevertheless made preparations to send in troops if necessary, and he sent a special envoy, Don Miguel de Salamanca, to make sure that the duke of Bragança (Portugal's premier noble) kept the aristocracy loyal to Spain.[3] On this occasion, Bragança remained Philip IV's faithful vassal, but the situation was clearly unstable and the government was worried. It was above all the unrest in the peripheral Iberian provinces that led Olivares to send the same Don Miguel de Salamanca to Compiègne in April 1638 with instructions to negotiate a cease-fire with France.

The three years of war had not gone well for the Habsburgs. In 1635 the French had invaded the Low Countries as far as Leuven, which they failed to take. The Cardinal-Infante devoted most of his efforts to recovering some of the places lost to the Dutch in Limburg and Cleves, but broke little new ground. Olivares, however, had more grandiose plans in view. In June 1635, almost as soon as he had heard of the French declaration of war, he began to arrange a triple invasion of France for the following year: one army under the Cardinal-Infante from the Low Countries, a second under an imperial general from Franche-Comté, and a third under the king himself from Catalonia. Olivares was aware of the desperate nature of this effort, which would be crippling in financial terms and might cause a political crisis with the Catalans, but he was prepared to take the risk. With his eyes 'so tired that they cannot bear the light of a candle or of the window', the indefatigable minister concluded his explanation of the strategy for 1636: 'To my mind, this will lose everything irremediably or be the salvation of the ship . . . Either all is lost, or else Castile will be head of the world.'[4] But the plan misfired. Catalan opposition to the plan, aided by the reluctance of the court at Madrid to travel to Catalonia a third time, prevented the launching of an offensive against France in the south. And without it, the invasion of the Cardinal-Infante from the north petered out after an encouraging start: the Spanish army from the Netherlands crossed the frontier on 3 July 1636 and at once captured La Capelle and Câtelet; then it crossed the Somme on 4 August and took Corbie on the 15th. Advance parties reached Pontoise, only 25 miles from Paris, and refugees streamed out of Picardy towards the capital, whence they and many Parisians set off for the Loire.

Louis XIII and Richelieu did not leave, however. Although Paris was full of seditious talk about him, the cardinal travelled about the narrow streets in his coach with fewer guards and retainers than usual, talking to people in his path and restoring respect by his cold but calm courage. When the goverment's hold on Paris was secured, the king and his minister moved north to Compiègne to direct operations in person. At the end of August, the Spaniards began to withdraw. By the time the third Habsburg army, under the command of Count Gallas, crossed from the Empire into Burgundy on 15 September, French forces were free to oppose them. But, in the event, this proved unnecessary. On 4 October, Sweden regained the reputation lost at Nördlingen when her army defeated a larger force of Saxons and imperialists at Wittstock and went on to occupy the electorate of Brandenburg. Gallas was recalled to Germany. His mighty invasion had achieved only devastation. Burgundy was virtually turned into a desert: 86 villages were laid waste; no crops were planted; plague spread in the wake of the troops. Of the 244 inhabitants of Blagny near Dijon, 217 died in 1636. As the main army withdrew, small guerilla bands kept up hostilities, and between 1636 and 1643 (when a local truce was arranged) all the records are silent, as if the entire province had ceased to exist.

This devastation brought little benefit to Spain. In 1637, his gamble having failed, Olivares had to face a massive counter-attack. On the Catalan front, the refusal of the principality to raise troops for its own defence led to an ignominious defeat of the Spanish forces engaged in the siege of Leucate (27 September). In the north, the imperialists were tied down in Germany by the Swedish army (heavily subsidized by France) on the Oder, and by the army of the Heilbronn League (under Bernard of Saxe-Weimar and entirely paid by France) in Alsace. The Spanish Netherlands were also subjected to heavy pressure: Landrecies, Damvilliers and La Chapelle fell to the French; Breda, with its seventeen bastions and great prestige value, was lost to the Dutch. The Madrid government was dumbfounded: 'What has happened this year is not to be believed,' wrote one minister, while another advised Olivares to introduce the Ottoman custom of executing town governors who surrendered. The only consolations were the capture of Venlo and Roermond on the Maas, which cut off Maastricht (taken by the Dutch five years before) from the rest of the Republic, while a popular rebellion in the Valtelline again delivered that strategic corridor into Habsburg hands. The most serious development of all, in Spain's eyes, was the dramatic expansion of Dutch power overseas. In October 1636 the West India Company sent a new fleet to Pernambuco under the command of the energetic grand-nephew of William the Silent, Count John Maurice of Nassau. He rapidly extended the area of the coast under Dutch control until it covered 300 miles, from Sergipe to Ceará, and he sent an expedition to Angola which captured Luanda in August 1641 and thus provided access to the Negro slaves required to cultivate the sugar plantations of Brazil. Another Dutch expedition began the conquest of Ceylon at the request of the local ruler.

It was largely in the hope of regaining Brazil, whose economy was vital to Portugal, that Olivares began serious negotiations with France. In 1636 and 1637 the Count-Duke had been approached informally by agents of Cardinal Richelieu, anxious to achieve a respite in the war that would enable him to deal with the Croquants of the south-west; but the overtures had been rejected. War had been declared publicly by France, and Olivares therefore insisted that France should also beg publicly for peace: 'Let those who broke the peace, sue for peace,' he told Richelieu's envoy in June 1637. But even if Richelieu had himself been ready, he could not speak for his allies. Although almost all the European powers were anxious to end the war in 1638, fighting continued in most theatres for another decade, and in some for another two, because it was impossible to negotiate bilateral agreements. The talks at Compiègne between Richelieu and Don Miguel de Salamanca, and those at Hamburg between the parties to the German war both broke down because, on the one hand, there were too many independent states to be accommodated, and, on the other, fighting continued throughout the negotiations so that one power was for ever gaining a military advantage which caused it to raise its diplomatic demands. At Compiègne, it was the need to deal with both France and the Dutch that thwarted all chance of a separate agreement between France and Spain. The points at issue between the two states were, in fact, few: the restoration of the parts of Alsace and Lorraine occupied by France, and the exchange of captured frontier towns. A separate peace would have been easy. But Richelieu would not desert the Dutch, and they were not prepared to hand back Pernambuco, Breda and Maastricht – not even for the 5 million ducats offered by Olivares. As a perceptive Venetian ambassador wrote in October 1638: Brazil in Dutch hands was 'more damaging than the continuance of the Low Countries' Wars' to Spain's imperial position, for it might entail in time the loss of Portugal too. Separate talks with the Dutch at Roosendaal also failed to reach agreement on these points: the Republic, after all, had little to lose so long as France continued to absorb the greater part of Spain's attention.

In 1639, however, it appeared that the two super-powers might indeed settle their differences. Bernard of Saxe-Weimar had taken Breisach, the key to Alsace, in December 1638. At first he refused to surrender it to his French paymasters, demanding instead that he should be recognized as autonomous ruler of Alsace; but after his death in July 1639 his army accepted French authority and Breisach, with its commanding position on the middle Rhine, came under Richelieu's control. Olivares became more anxious than ever to call a halt to the fighting: 'We have to think of bending in order to avoid breaking,' he warned the king. At first the *Nu-pied* rising in Normandy (July-November 1639) seemed to offer hope for a settlement. Even though his forces captured Salces in Catalonia and Hainaut in the Netherlands, Richelieu agreed to extend a local cease-fire arranged by the French and Spanish commanders in Italy: as long as the Norman emergency lasted, he was prepared to talk, and Olivares became more optimistic. But once again the Dutch disrupted these developments: they scored two decisive victories over Spain, both of them at sea.

Ever since he made peace with Charles I in 1630, Philip IV had made increasing use of British shipping to transport Spanish troops to the Netherlands and Walloon troops to Spain. Experience had shown that expatriate soldiers were far more reliable than men raised locally, and over 18,000 Spaniards were transported to Flanders between 1631 and 1637. After 1632, money too was shipped in almost the same way: a consortium of bankers, mainly Portuguese, arranged to advance money to the Spanish army in the Netherlands by shipping cash from Spain to England and sending bills of exchange from there to Dunkirk. The specie was sent to the London Mint, whose burgeoning coinage issues reveal the scale of this operation. But all the shipments, whether of men or money, were clandestine and risk-laden: the ships could only set sail at the rare moments when the sea was clear of Dutch squadrons. In 1639, for example, two small flotillas (one of them English) set sail from Spain carrying some urgently needed troops to the Netherlands; but the Dutch were forewarned and the troopships were intercepted and their human cargo was imprisoned in Normandy (until the *Nu-pieds* released them later in the year). It was to break the Dutch grip on the chief military supply route that Olivares made his last desperate gamble: to send a fleet of 80 warships into the North Sea, there to attack and destroy the Dutch navy. The new Armada, which included almost every available ship in Spanish service, put to sea in September 1639. No sooner had they entered the Channel than the Spaniards were outmanœuvred, being forced to take refuge off Dover in the roadstead known as The Downs. Trapped, while the Dutch built up their strength to overwhelming proportions, the Spanish admiral, Don Antonio de Oquendo, appealed for English protection. But the English fleet was no match for the Dutch, commanded by their redoubtable admiral, Maarten Tromp, and on 21 October 1639, the Dutch destroyed 60 or more Spanish ships. The battle of The Downs was one of the greatest Dutch victories at sea, even though a small squadron of Dunkirk ships carrying 9000 men and perhaps 2 million ducats did manage to escape to Flanders, for it all but destroyed Spain's Atlantic fleet, and she could no longer build another. More losses followed in January 1640: after years of preparation, a joint Luso-Spanish fleet had been collected for the reconquest of Brazil and it crossed the Atlantic in 1639, but there it was defeated and scattered by a far smaller Dutch squadron and the flag of the United Provinces continued to flutter over Pernambuco.

So, by the beginning of 1640, Spain's position had indeed deteriorated. In January, Olivares advised the king that any terms, 'provided they are not too bad, must be accepted.' 'In our present position, not only do we need a peace, truce or cease-fire, but we cannot go on without one.' And he could expect no assistance from the Emperor (since 1637, Ferdinand III, the co-victor of Nördlingen), who appeared to be staggering from defeat to disaster, 'With no government, no order, no means of achieving it, without the obedience of his vassals . . . In effect,' Olivares concluded, 'everything is lost.'[5] In April 1640 Spain sent four envoys to Paris to begin serious negotiations for a peace with France and the Dutch, with instructions that everything could be sacrificed except

Brazil and Spain's monopoly of influence in Italy. But it was now too late. In May 1640 Catalonia rebelled, to be followed in December by Portugal, and the future of the Spanish monarchy threatened to be short indeed. France and her allies decided to wait and see what would fall into their lap.

2. *The Collapse of the Spanish Monarchy, 1640–3*

There are few clearer examples than the revolt of Catalonia of the role of war in turning a tense political situation into open rebellion. The relations between the Madrid government and the Catalans had been worsening since 1600, mainly because the government was misinformed about the taxable capacity of the province and demanded more taxes than could reasonably be met. The Catalans, through their representative institutions (and especially the *Diputació* or standing-committee of the estates), took refuge behind certain grievances, most of them concerned with attempts to enhance the power of the viceroy, and refused to vote taxes until after they were redressed. But such confrontations between government and estates were common in early modern Europe. They rarely led to revolution unless the spur of war compelled the executive to break the traditional constitution and introduce a measure of 'war absolutism' in order to raise the money needed to defend the province from invasion.

The French had tried unsuccessfully to penetrate Spain's defences at the western end of the Pyrenees in 1637 and 1638, but the key fortress of Fuentarrabía had not fallen. In 1639, therefore, it appeared inevitable that the main theatre of operations would shift eastwards, to the Catalan gap between the Pyrenean mountains and the sea, where the poor defensive state of the frontier towns and the presence of a large immigrant French population seemed to offer Richelieu valuable advantages. Surprisingly, the Madrid government welcomed the prospect of waging war there. Whereas the

Basque lands had been a difficult military terrain, poor economically and unable to supply either men or munitions in quantity, Catalonia was 'a rich province, abundant in men and supplies, and the most unburdened [with taxes] of all these kingdoms'. A direct French invasion would force the Catalans to utilize their resources, and to become 'directly involved, as up to now they seem not to have been involved, with the common welfare of the Monarchy'. An army was therefore raised in Castile to defend the Catalan frontier, and the people of the principality were forced to pay for them in kind – with food, billets and contributions – whether they wished to or not. 'Better that the Catalans should complain, than that we all should weep,' Olivares wrote smugly in June 1639 to his viceroy at the Catalan front. But the Catalans did not stop at complaints: citing the 'constitutions', which prohibited all exaction without parliamentary consent, they steadfastly refused to provide any money or supplies for the army (except when the troops were too close to risk defiance). Thanks to this intransigence, the French captured the important frontier post of Salces (19 July) and the Spanish army was crippled by desertion.

Olivares was rapidly losing his patience: 'By now I am nearly at my wits' end, but I say, and I shall still be saying on my deathbed, that if the constitutions do not allow this, then the Devil take the Constitutions.' He began to consider how to 'settle matters in Catalonia in such a manner that no obstructions are placed in the way of Your Majesty's service', and his gaze fixed upon the local customs which had so often thwarted him in the past: 'We always have to look and see if a constitution says this or that,' he protested. 'We have to discover what the customary usage is, even when it is a question of the supreme law [of necessity], of the actual preservation and defence of the province.'[6]

Early in 1640, therefore, the viceroy of Catalonia was authorized by Olivares to disregard the laws and customs of the province, if it seemed necessary, in order to provision and pay the troops that defended it. Those who advocated non-co-operation, or who insisted on the strict observation of the constitutions, were to be imprisoned and, in March, two obstreperous Barcelona councillors and a member of the Diputació were indeed incarcerated.

The king and his ministers were encouraged when this provocative move produced no general outcry, and they proceeded to order the levy of 6000 more troops in Catalonia, at the province's expense, and to decree that the entire cost of feeding the army thenceforth should also be paid by the province. At a time when a severe drought threatened to ruin the harvest, this was foolishly provocative. A Castilian observer sent to rural Catalonia to deal with complaints against the soldiers composed an urgent warning of impending trouble:

> This province is very different from [the] others. It contains a villainous populace, which can easily be excited to violence, and the more it is pressed, the harder it resists. For this reason, actions which would be sufficient to make the inhabitants of any other province submit to orders of any kind from above, only succeed in exasperating the inhabitants of this province, and in making them insist more stubbornly on the proper observance of their laws.[7]

Just over a month later, on 30 April, the rural population around Gerona, 60 miles north of Barcelona, began a series of attacks on royal regiments marching by. When the troops retaliated by razing to the ground the obstreperous village of Santa Coloma de Farners (14 May), they provoked a general rising. There were three distinct social groups involved: first the poor labourers, known as *segadors*, who came down from their upland homes every summer to work on the harvests of the Catalan plain; second the villagers of the plain themselves; and third, the outlaw bands. All three groups had suffered at the hands of the Castilian soldiers during the winter of 1639–40, and the burning of Santa Coloma served to unite them and to spur them to action. They marched south towards the provincial capital, Barcelona, and managed to gain entrance on 22 May. First they freed the magistrates imprisoned in March. Then they spread out in armed bands to 'liberate' the other towns of the principality, aiding local sympathizers to kill and plunder the royal servants or loyal inhabitants who had helped to carry out the harsh policies decreed by Madrid. Fortified by local triumphs, on 7 June the insurgents returned to Barcelona and murdered any royal ministers they could find there, including the viceroy himself. Next they turned to looting the property of the wealthy citizens of Barcelona, a pursuit from which they were only distracted five days later by the need to drive off the royal troops still in the area. All over the principality, violence and social revolution flared up, with the poor attacking the rich; everywhere, magistrates, town oligarchs and village landowners were either murdered or driven into hiding, and their property was plundered or destroyed.

This anarchic situation provided Olivares with his last chance to regain control of the province: had he made soothing overtures to the terrified ruling class of Catalonia in June and July, he would probably have met with a favourable response. Certainly the provincial elite, led by the Diputació, had no alternative policy. There was indeed some informal contact between certain prominent Catalans and one or two French gentlemen; but with so many people of recent French descent in the province – over ten per cent of the entire population – such contacts were inevitable and not necessarily treasonable.[8] Clearly the elite at least had as yet no definite policy of rapprochement with France.

Olivares was soon to change that: instead of concessions to the elite, he announced his intention of sending a large army to restore royal authority in the province and of abolishing the laws that so restrained the power of the executive. Alarmed, the Diputació now encouraged one of its supporters to use his private contacts in France to explore the possibility of securing French support should Catalonia be invaded by a royal army from Castile. The response was favourable, and in September a formal petition for aid was sent to Louis XIII. The problem was that the Diputació was no more able than Olivares either to restore law and order or to persuade the

Catalans to raise an army for national defence: when an official representative of Louis XIII arrived in Barcelona, late in October, to co-ordinate the province's defences he found the towns and countryside plagued by roving bands of unemployed vagabonds, fully armed; and he found virtually no troops mobilized to oppose the royal army preparing to invade from the south. The troops of Philip IV crossed the frontier at the end of November and moved slowly northwards towards Barcelona, meeting with no real resistance from the Catalans. Even the French were disgusted and began to withdraw. Yet again, a conciliatory approach from the crown might have secured the support of the Catalan ruling class, few of whom now supported the Francophile Diputació; but no offer was made. So in January 1641 the Diputació and their remaining supporters placed Catalonia under the authority of the king of France, and it was in his name that a combined Catalan-French army inflicted a major defeat on the advancing royalist troops and drove them back at Monjuich, on 26 January 1641.

By this time, Olivares already had another cross to bear: Portugal, too, renounced her allegiance to Philip IV on 1 December 1640. The Portuguese revolution was accompanied by none of the social upheaval and violence of the Catalan troubles. The country's ruling class never lost control and in the duke of Bragança, who was proclaimed King John IV by his aristocratic colleagues, they had a valuable focus for popular loyalty which the Catalans lacked. Although there is no doubt that the timing of the Portuguese revolt was governed by events in Catalonia – in the autumn of 1640 Bragança and the rest of the nobles received orders from Philip IV to join the army massing on the Catalan frontier: the break with Spain therefore had to be made before they left Lisbon – there were many deep-seated reasons for the rebellion. Taxes, troop-levies and the increased Castilianization of government all played their part: they had already provoked riots in Setúbal, Oporto and Evora during the 1630s. But the revolt of 1640 was led, not by tax-payers and men in danger of conscription, but by merchants and nobles;

and their grievances were somewhat different. They resented above all the collapse of their overseas empire. The loss of the spice trade and the commerce of Asia to the Dutch and English after 1600 had been serious; but it had been counterbalanced by the development of sugar production in Brazil. However, when the Dutch captured Pernambuco, the principal sugar-producing area, in 1630, the prosperous exploitation of the colony ceased. Every effort to drive out the Dutch failed: even a great fleet sent out in 1638 was defeated by a Dutch squadron half its size in January 1640. Furthermore, just at the time when the Portuguese were urgently looking for help in one part of South America, Castile began to move against Portuguese traders in another. From about 1600, a lively overland trade had developed between southern Brazil and Upper Peru: goods were exported from Portugal to one of the Brazilian ports and hauled by mule-train or slaves across the Pampas and over the Andes where they were sold for Peruvian silver. Goods arriving by this route were always cheaper than those brought via Seville and Panama because they paid neither customs duty nor convoy dues; and the *peruleiros* (as these Portuguese merchants were known) also brought with them valuable slaves from Angola. From the 1620s onwards, as the health of the Seville trade deteriorated, Spanish officials cast around for scapegoats: the Portuguese, who appeared to be prospering at the expense of Spaniards, were prime targets, and their property was subjected to heavier taxes, their trade was disrupted by official malevolence, and the Inquisition began to harass the many merchants with Jewish ancestors involved in the trade.

By 1640 it began to seem that Portugal's only chance of recovering a measure of colonial prosperity was to come to terms with the Dutch. So no sooner had John IV been proclaimed king, than he began negotiations with the Republic. A ten-year truce was secured on 12 June 1641 (although it was not implemented in Brazil until 1642 and not in the Far East until 1644), and the Dutch sent a squadron of warships to defend Lisbon against the threat of a Spanish counterattack. Trade began to revive and, with its profits, Portugal was able to finance effective resistance to Spain and to import grain for the population of Lisbon. The Portuguese revolt succeeded where so many other rebellions of the 1640s failed because it could draw on the wealth of Brazil: the colony was, in John IV's phrase, a *vacca de leite*, a milch cow.

It was soon realized in Madrid that the success of the two peninsular revolts in gaining foreign aid so soon – Catalonia from France; Portugal from the Dutch – would make the restoration of Philip IV's authority no easy matter. An attempt to invade Catalonia was defeated at Lérida in October 1642, with heavy losses; at the same time, Perpignan surrendered to the French. These defeats, which occurred while the king himself was at Zaragoza to take personal charge of the war, encouraged Olivares's enemies to launch a campaign for his dismissal. Alienated by the taxes that they were now required to pay, the nobles stayed away from court in increasing numbers: on Easter Day 1641 only one grandee accompanied the king to the royal chapel. Some aristocrats passed from passive into active opposition, and the duke of Medina Sidonia responded to the king's call to raise troops for the Catalan campaign by plotting to make himself the independent ruler of Andalusia with their aid (in imitation of his brother-in-law, Bragança). Although this conspiracy was betrayed and prevented, the continuing boycott of the court by the grandees began to make its impact on Philip: a king shunned by his nobles stood in grave danger of deposition, and by the time he returned to Madrid from his lonely vigil in Zaragoza, Philip had come to accept that Olivares would have to go. The all-powerful minister was dismissed on 17 January 1643. He died two years later.

At first the king attempted to rule without a chief minister, taking advice from such unlikely figures as the mystic nun, Sor María de Agreda. Philip went to see her, for consolation, in May 1643 and between then and her death in 1665 (a few months before the king's), over 600 letters were exchanged between them. In almost every letter, the king begged the nun (whose mystical experiences suggested unusual divine favour) to pray to God on behalf of himself, his family and his monarchy; he also asked forgiveness for his moments of weakness, especially with women (Philip fathered at least eight bastards); and he tried hard to convince her that he was doing his best to govern well. 'I, Sor María, do not shirk from any form of work,' he told her in 1647, 'and as all can witness, I am more or less continually seated in this chair, with my papers before me and my pen in my hand, working on all the papers sent to me by the councils and the despatches from abroad.'[9] But the affairs of the Spanish empire were too numerous and too complex to be handled by a monarch of mediocre gifts like Philip IV, however well-intentioned and industrious. By the end of 1643 Philip was leaning increasingly on his childhood play-mate, Olivares's nephew Don Luis de Haro, who before long became recognized as chief minister. He succeeded to an unenviable inheritance. Although the grandees were placated by the fall of Olivares, the change of ministers did little to improve Spain's military position. The Portuguese carried out raids against Castile; the army of Catalonia melted away through desertion and, despite the desire to carry out exemplary punishment on some of the fugitives, none could ever be captured. Foreign aid continued to arrive for the rebels, often in unorthodox ways. Thus in spring 1646 the frontier guards in Navarre became suspicious of the large number of French pilgrims entering Castile with the intention of going to Santiago de Compostella (amazingly, the war had not been allowed to interfere with this tradition). The 'pilgrims', 4000 in all, travelled in groups of six to ten persons, wearing fine clothes beneath their pilgrims' garbs and receiving money along the way from regular paymasters. At last the white, delicate hands of the leader of one group caused suspicion and he was identified as the lord of St Pol, leading French reinforcements to Portugal (only 50 miles from Compostella). The 'pilgrims' were sent back and the frontier was at last closed.

But unfortunately for the Portuguese – and, even more, the Catalans – French aid was never regular and constant: virtually nothing was sent to Catalonia in 1643–4 and Philip

IV's forces recaptured Monzón and Lérida. The cost of the war fell increasingly on the local population, who also had to bear the ravages of the royal army and the economic exploitation of the French merchants who followed the troops into the province: Catalonia's trade came to be handled exclusively by French merchants, just as her administration came to be monopolized by a small Francophile faction. Struck by famine in 1647–50 and plague in 1650–1, the principality seemed content to see the French and their few remaining Catalan supporters (probably less than 700 people) driven back to Roussillon in 1652, whence they carried on a bitter frontier war until the peace of the Pyrenees in 1659 gave Roussillon and Cerdagne to France and left Catalonia to Spain.

The Catalans' misfortune was that they lacked a 'milch cow' of their own and lived too far away from Paris to be valuable to France in themselves. Fomenting a rebellion within Spain was one thing; protecting distant allies from attack was another. Keeping a Spanish army tied down in Catalonia was enough to serve France's ends; tying an army of her own down was counter-productive. In any case, after 1640, France had no resources to spare: with the revolt of Normandy barely suppressed, the troubles in Catalonia came as a deliverance to the beleaguered ministers of Louis XIII. After the rebellion, according to Richelieu's agent in Barcelona: 'Our affairs (which were not going well in Flanders, and still worse in Piedmont) suddenly began to prosper on all sides, even in Germany; for our enemy's forces, being retained in their own country and recalled from elsewhere to defend the sanctuary, were reduced to feebleness in all the other theatres of war.'[10]

The figures of the Spanish army paymasters abroad bear this out. The armies in Germany received 1·9 million crowns between April 1637 and August 1641, an average of 453,000 a year (about £100,000 sterling); but between August 1641 and March 1643 only 553,000 crowns, an average of 350,000 a year. The fate of the Spanish army in the Netherlands was even worse: it received an average of almost 4 million crowns a year from 1635 to 1641, 3·3 million in 1642, but only 1·5 million in 1643. Not surprisingly, when the bankrupt army of Flanders invaded France it was defeated decisively, by a larger force, at Rocroi on 19 May 1643: the Spanish field army was cut to pieces where it stood, the paymaster lost his treasure and the commander-in-chief lost his papers. It was, according to Philip IV's new chief minister, Don Luis de Haro, 'Something which can never be called to mind without great sorrow; . . . [it is] a defeat which is giving rise in all parts to the consequences which we always feared.' The French took Thionville and Sierck (in Luxemburg) in August, and their navy defeated Spain's principal Mediterranean fleet off Cartagena in September. In 1644 French forces overran all Alsace and achieved mastery of the left bank of the Rhine from Basle to the Dutch border. In 1645 they captured ten major towns in the South Netherlands – more than the Dutch had taken in more than two decades of fighting. Even in Italy, where Spain's grip was most secure, the French made headway: their forces continued to occupy certain strongpoints in Piedmont and Monferrat, and the support of Savoy kept the Alpine passes open to France and closed to Spain. No progress was made against the Spanish garrisons in Lombardy, but the cost of defending the province, which was paid for overwhelmingly by the other major Spanish possessions in Italy – Naples and Sicily – caused widespread unrest. The kingdom of Naples, according to its own viceroy in 1640, provided more men and money for Spain's wars than did the Indies. Almost all the proceeds of taxation were exported, and collection was almost entirely alienated by the treasury to tax-farmers. It was indeed an explosive situation and, by 1644, a popular revolt was clearly probable: there had been two in living memory, in 1585 and 1620. Mazarin sent an agent to Naples in the hope of stirring up popular discontent, and of encouraging fear of popular unrest among the nobles of the kingdom. Plans were made among the Francophile barons to declare a French client, Prince Thomas of Savoy, their king. In March 1644, Mazarin mediated a peace between the duke of Parma and the Pope (a sordid conflict which began in 1642 with Urban VIII's attempt to seize the duke's possessions within the papal states: the papal forces were routed and Urban VIII, a broken man, died shortly afterwards). Then in 1646, two fleets commanded by Prince Thomas captured and garrisoned the Spanish bases in Tuscany and Elba, providing France with a valuable springboard for the enterprise of Naples. But before matters could be properly arranged, Palermo in Sicily rose against its Spanish governors in a furious anti-fiscal riot (18 May 1647).

Sicily had been taxed, proportionately, less heavily than the rest of Spanish Italy (bearing out the famous proverb: 'In Sicily the Spaniards nibble, in Naples they eat, and in Lombardy they devour'): from 1620, when the island was required to raise 1 million ducats for the war against Bohemia, until the revolt of 1647, Sicily's 1 million or so inhabitants paid taxes worth at least 10 million ducats for overseas wars; whereas the kingdom of Naples, with 3 million people, was forced to export at least 40 million ducats over the same period. It is not surprising, therefore, that the revolt of Palermo was swiftly followed by a similar uprising in the city of Naples (7 July), before Mazarin's plans were completed. France lost contact with the nobles, and the aristocratic plot misfired.[11]

Nevertheless, even without Naples, French gains between 1640 and 1647 in the north, south, east and south-west were very considerable. They constituted virtually her first territorial expansion since the 1550s. It was therefore ironic that the government which secured these gains, all at Habsburg expense, was directed by an Italian cardinal, educated at the Spanish university of Alcalá, and the sister of Philip IV.

3. France Resurgent, 1643–6

Richelieu did not live to see France victorious. He died on 4 December 1642, in his bed, having hung on to supreme power for eighteen years. But his tenure of office had not been easy. Even after the Day of Dupes in 1630, there were six major attempts to break his grip on France and her king, most of them engineered by other members of the royal family. In 1632, Louis XIII's mother and his brother Gaston (who until 1638 was heir apparent) persuaded the governor of Languedoc to lead the rebellion of the province against Richelieu's misguided attempt to abolish the estates (but the rebellion was easily crushed and the governor executed); in 1633 the queen, Anne of Austria, managed to replace Richelieu, during one of his serious bouts of illness, with her own servant Châteauneuf (but he was exiled for revealing state secrets to the queen's lady-in-waiting, who in turn betrayed them to a foreign power); in 1636, Gaston arranged to have Richelieu murdered by a 'hit-man' (but in the end Gaston failed to give the agreed signal); in 1637, the queen persuaded Louis's mistress and his confessor to emphasize the sinfulness of the war with Spain and the alliance with Protestant powers advocated by Richelieu (but the confessor was replaced by one of the cardinal's creatures). These four conspiracies were all fairly amateur affairs and none of them stood much chance of success. The last two, however, were different. In 1641 the count of Soissons (a member of the Bourbon family exiled for his part in the plot of 1636), and the duke of Bouillon issued a manifesto at Sedan which promised 'to restore everything to its former place: re-establishing the laws that have been overthrown; renewing the immunities, rights and privileges of the provinces, towns and personages that have been violated; . . . ensuring respect for churchmen and nobles'. The conspirators had an army, which included

Spanish troops, and it defeated a royalist force at La Marfée; but, luckily for Richelieu, Soissons foolishly lifted his visor with a loaded pistol and inadvertently pulled the trigger as he did so. 'If monsieur the count had not been killed, he would have been welcomed by half of Paris. Indeed such is the general feeling of all France that the whole country would have rallied to his side,' was the opinion of even the cardinal's own agents. The conspiracy of 1642, led by Louis's young companion, the marquis of Cinq-Mars, had a good deal in common with the Soissons plot: the marquis also aimed to turn the clock back in terms of domestic policy and saw a peace with Spain as the inexcusable preliminary to reform at home. It was the discovery that Cinq-Mars had made a secret treaty with Spain, promising to place Gaston on the throne in place of Louis, that caused the failure of the plot and the execution of the royal favourite: 'I throw him up [*je le vomis*],' Louis told Richelieu. But, three months later, the cardinal was dead.

There must have been many persons at court who expected a radical change of policy after Richelieu's death, especially since the king's health was itself not good: wasted away with tuberculosis, he died on 14 May 1643. He was glad to die, if his last words are to be believed: 'Let God be my witness that I have never enjoyed life and that I am overjoyed to be going to Him.' (Louis never doubted the correct destination of French kings in the afterlife.) He left the government of France to a council of regency (for Louis XIV was aged only four-and-a-half years) headed by his wife, Anne of Austria, and one of Richelieu's disciples, Giulio Mazzarini (born in Rome in 1602 but usually known by the French version of his name: Mazarin), who had entered French service in 1639 as a special diplomatic representative.

Given Anne of Austria's implacable hostility to Richelieu, and her known opposition to the continuation of the war with Spain, it is remarkable that she accepted the cardinal's creature and his policies so enthusiastically. In 1646 she even made him director of her son's education, a task that Mazarin superintended with the greatest care and to the entire satisfaction of both Anne and his charge. Mazarin, who became a cardinal himself in 1641, soon became not only the minister of Anne of Austria, but also her intimate friend. Where Richelieu's letters to Louis on affairs of state ended with a request for decision, Mazarin's reports to Anne tended to justify decisions already taken. And her letters to him were openly love-letters which breathed a passion untarnished by the political cares she had to bear. The exact nature of the liaison between these two foreigners in France will probably never be known: no proof exists, outside hostile gossip, of a marriage or of carnal dealings; and although they spent long hours alone together in which the passion of Anne's letters may have been put into practice, the Habsburgs were renowned for their sexual coldness (Philip IV being the exception and not the rule) and Anne, now in her forty-third year, had lived most of her conjugal life segregated from her husband.[12] Speculation on wild, romantic attachments between the middle-aged couple, however, is largely irrelevant; the important fact is that their personal ties were unshakeable, and everyone could see it. Even though the political opponents of Richelieu were allowed to return from exile in 1643, they did not hatch court plots against Mazarin (apart from the half-hearted *cabale des importants* of 1643) because it was generally recognized that only armed rebellion, along the lines of the Soissons conspiracy, would dislodge him. And at first, this seemed unnecessary because French troops began to score major victories on all fronts, starting with the triumph of Rocroi only five days after Louis XIII's death (page 266 above).

'To a gentleman, any country is a homeland,' wrote Mazarin in 1637, and after his rise to pre-eminence in France he found no difficulty in putting down roots in his adopted fatherland. He built a splendid town residence, which now houses the French National Library, not far from the royal palace; there he kept his books, his artistic collection, and his seven nieces, popularly known as the Mazarinettes, one of whom completed Louis XIV's education by becoming his mistress. The cardinal increased, both by his example and by his encouragement, Italian influence on French culture: he imported Italian religious orders, Italian singers, Italian opera and Italian theatre. But appearances were deceptive. Beneath the bland, cultivated, worldly prince of the church lay a calculating, ruthless and insensitive politician. Mazarin decided early in 1643 that if France maintained a heavy military pressure on Spain for a few years, Philip IV would be compelled to surrender on unfavourable terms. He realized that the cost of the effort to France would be extremely high, but he gambled on forcing Spain to her knees before major domestic protests distracted him, and as long as there was a chance of winning the war with this strategy, Mazarin was prepared to sanction every available expedient in order to raise the taxes and the troops required for success, if necessary putting into practice the theory of French royal absolutism propagated in Cardin Le Bret's *Of the Sovereignty of Kings* (Paris, 1632):

> If a man's conscience tells him that what the king orders him to do is unjust, is he bound to obey? Yes: he must follow the king's will, not his own . . . If it is an occasion when urgent assistance is required for the public good, resistance . . . would be pure disobedience. Necessity knows no law.

The machinery for implementing these ideas was already to hand. The civil service of the French crown was the largest in Europe: 45,000 officials spread all over France in financial and judicial institutions, either collecting the king's revenues (the *Cours des Aides* and *bureaux des finances*) or administering his justice (the *Parlements* and *bailliage* courts). But the control of the central government over this bureaucracy was imperfect, mainly because most civil servants were allowed to purchase their posts and pass them on to a nominee of their choice. The sale of offices was systematized in 1604 with the introduction of the *droit annuel* or *paulette* (page 121 above), payment of which guaranteed the office-holder's right to nominate his successor. The idea was introduced in order to save money – the *droit annuel*, of course reduced the salary payable to each officer – but it also made possession of public office more attractive so that there was never any shortage of purchasers. By 1613, therefore, almost all the crown's servants had become part of the new system. There was, naturally, opposition from those who were now deprived of all promotion prospects by this closed-shop principle; and during the administrations of Concini and Luynes sales of office declined (although the process was reversed during the troubles of the 1620s, when the government needed to conciliate its officers and also to raise cash through more sales). Richelieu made another attempt to halt the *paulette* in 1629, but it was subverted by the unrest caused by the campaign against the provincial estates in 1630–2 (page 203 above), which again forced the government to restore the sale of offices. The crown was too poor to live without it: almost a quarter of Louis XIII's income came from this source in the 1620s.

The government was more concerned with the right of the civil service legally to refuse to carry out orders. The ten *Parlements* and the *Cours des Aides* (regional courts of appeal in, respectively, legal and fiscal matters) had two important constitutional powers: first, they had the right to interpret (sc. to modify) a government order when a specific legal case arose from it, and the *arrêt* or *ordonnance* so issued might not be in accord with the government's original intention; second, because no new edict (for instance creating or increasing a tax) could be enforced in a province until it was registered by the local tribunals, these bodies could delay, modify or reject the edict sent to them by the king. There was little that the crown could do in the face of this entrenched bureaucracy. If it attempted a trial of strength with one tribunal on an issue, others might immediately send letters of support or issue an *arrêt* themselves, associating their tribunal with the controversial decision taken by their fellows. Within each body, moreover, there existed trade unions. The *trésoriers de France*, who handled the revenue accounts of each fiscal area (*généralité*), founded their trade union (*syndicat*) in 1599 and kept two deputies permanently at court (by the 1640s they held annual general meetings and supported a standing committee of six from their union dues). There were also annual general meetings of the union of *élus* (who apportioned the taxes between parishes and judged all legal cases arising from taxation), and they used their annual union dues to maintain a permanent secretary in Paris. Such solidarity discouraged the crown from victimizing individual trouble-makers when there was a disagreement. It is true that the king in person could always override the obstructiveness of a *Parlement* by making a personal appearance in court to supervise the registration of the law or edict he had issued, a process known as the '*lit*' or 'bed' of justice; but such behaviour in a monarch was unseemly and could cause embarrassment. At a *lit de justice* in 1629, when the king forced the registration of an edict abolishing the sale of certain offices, the *Parlement* of Paris informed Louis XIII that 'Great in the law though he is, the king will not wish to overturn the basic laws of the kingdom . . . *Our* power is great too.' In the provinces, opposition to this edict was taken to even greater lengths: in Languedoc, the sovereign courts seized royal funds held by tax-collectors and used them to pay their own wages; in Dauphiné, they ordered the grain prepared for the army to be sold to the people; in Burgundy and Provence, they encouraged popular riots against royal policies and refused to punish those who took part.

With non-cooperation on this scale from its own immovable bureaucracy, the central government could either admit defeat and abandon war altogether, or else create an alternative civil service. Under the ministries of Richelieu and Mazarin, it did the latter. The chief agents of the new system were the *intendants*, many of them recruited from the *maîtres de requêtes* (advocates) in the sovereign courts whose promotion was blocked by the venality of higher offices. At first the new commissioners were given only temporary authority to investigate the affairs of a limited area, but between 1633 and 1637 the government made all the commissions permanent until every one of the 23 *généralités* of

France had its own intendant of justice, police and finance.

The principal duty of the intendants was to ensure that the government received the taxes it imposed. At first (until the outbreak of war in 1635), they merely reported on the refusal of the established civil service to levy taxes unregistered by the *Parlements*, noted the unequitable distribution of registered taxes, and recorded the corruption with which collection was organized. After 1635, however, the central government could no longer permit such delay, inefficiency and graft in tax-raising. The yield of most taxes was now paid to the treasury in advance by financiers, and in return they required every assistance in recovering their loan from the tax-payers. The central government was anxious to please its creditors (in the hope that they would lend more), and it therefore gave the intendants special responsibility for arranging the prompt payment of taxes. To make sure there was no interference, any case involving the intendants or the financiers was 'evoked' from the local courts to the royal council. In August 1642, while Richelieu was still in power, the local officers were ordered to obey their intendant in all matters: he was to be supreme in fiscal affairs and they were to give advice and assistance only when he called on them to do so. But Richelieu was reluctant to go further, for fear of the consequences. He had been shaken by the *Nu-pieds* rising, rebuking his financial advisers at one point for their unrealistic attitude: 'I have to say that I do not understand why you do not give more thought to the consequences of the decisions you take in the council of finance. It is easy to prevent misfortunes, even the worst; but when they strike, no remedy can be found.' Two years later, the cardinal feared a further 'misfortune':

> If the council of finance continues to allow the tax-farmers and financiers full liberty to treat His Majesty's subjects according to their insatiable appetites, certainly France will fall victim to some disorder similar to that which has befallen Spain . . . By wishing to have too much,

we shall create a situation where we shall have nothing at all.'[13]

This advice was not heeded by Richelieu's successor, Mazarin, because of his gamble on a rapid victory. In 1643 he took the fateful step of farming out the *taille* to financiers, thereby placing it under the direct control of the intendants.

This decision entirely ruined the livelihood of the crown's fiscal officers. The *taille*, as noted above, produced over half the government's revenue, and as long as it remained under the administration of the officers, their salaries could be deducted before the proceeds were remitted to the treasury. But when this tax was farmed out, their whole way of life, which they had long paid the *paulette* to secure, was destroyed. Mazarin had created a powerful class of men who now had nothing to lose by opposing the government, even by posing as defenders of the people against the fisc. They published pamphlets and statements defending their view, appealing not only to their colleagues in the law courts but to the people at large. Mazarin did not stop them, even though Richelieu had taken care to employ pamphleteers to put the government's point of view as well as employing censors to suppress those of his opponents, since: 'Arms uphold the cause of princes, but well-tempered books publicize their equity and orient public affections to regard them as epiphanies of justice.' Instead, Mazarin laughed as he read the innumerable attacks on him (the *Mazarinades*). Perhaps his brief period of residence in France before he was appointed chief minister in 1643 did not provide him with a sufficient understanding of how the country was governed: certainly, after 1643, he took little trouble to find out. His letters, to judge by the published corpus (8000 pages in nine fat volumes), rarely revealed any interest in home affairs before the summer of 1648, when it was too late. Until then, he concentrated upon foreign policy, as Richelieu had done, without seeming to realize that during a minority, especially a wartime minority, domestic developments could not be left to others – especially not to men like the Italian adventurer, Michel Particelli d'Emery, superintendent of finance 1640–8, whose inventive schemes to raise money alienated one social group and one geographical area after another; or like Pierre Séguier, chancellor of France 1635–72, who issued implacable orders to the intendants for the suppression of one protest after another, some of them major rebellions extending over several provinces (like the Croquants' uprising in the south-west in 1643–4). There were many who saw the danger of a general revolt, and warned the government to seek peace in order to reduce taxation. From the peace conference at Münster the duke of Longueville, wrestling with Mazarin's instructions on how to achieve the best results for France, wrote in August 1645: 'The awful misery which the people have suffered during so many years of war oblige their rulers to provide them with some respite, so that they will not despair and revolt.' In January 1648 one of the leaders of the *Parlement* of Paris warned: 'The honour of battles won and the glory of provinces conquered cannot nourish those who have no bread.' But these prophets, like others who tried to point to the impending storm, were ignored: the cardinal did not want to hear.

For five years, Mazarin's luck held. After the suppression of the Croquants, armed with a royal edict of 11 July 1643 which declared refusal to pay taxes to be treason, the intendants under Séguier's direction managed to restore calm and orderly government to almost all of France. There were no further serious popular revolts (not even during the Fronde, except at Angers, Bordeaux and Paris); taxes began to reach the royal treasury regularly again; and financiers once more anticipated the yield of future revenues, enabling French troops to extend their conquests in Flanders, Germany, Italy and Catalonia. Between 1645 and 1647, the crown made 107 loan contracts worth a total of 115 million livres (almost £10 million sterling) and anticipating all future income up to the end of 1648. Thus, no sources of revenue were left for the new year, but Mazarin set about creating fresh ones: he sought permission from the *Parlements* to anticipate the yield of future revenues up to the end of 1650; he raised the level of the *paulette* (and threatened to abolish the system altogether if the civil service refused to pay the higher rate); and he created a large number of new offices for sale to the highest bidder. The last measure caused serious opposition from those who already held office and were obliged to work less – and therefore to earn less – when the new posts were introduced. It may seem at first sight surprising that takers were still to be found. But, in spite of poor salaries, uncertain hereditary rights and popular obloquy, the purchase of public office remained an attractive proposition: the salary was at least paid more regularly than the interest on government bonds, there was no risk of dismissal, and acquiring judicial offices conferred immediate noble status (and therefore, in most provinces, exemption from the *taille* and other direct taxes). So the sales went on until, in the 1660s, it was calculated that the government would have to spend 419 million livres (equal to six years' revenue) to repurchase all hereditary posts: the policies of Richelieu and Mazarin could not have been financed without the revenue from selling offices.

However, discontent among the office holders was reaching dangerous levels. At Aix-en-Provence, for example, Mazarin's new fiscal expedients doubled the number of councillors in the *Parlement*, the new men and the old each to work six months of the year. The officers in post thus saw their fees and salaries cut by half. Passions ran high, and in March 1648 the first man to purchase one of the new offices was stabbed to death in a tavern and posters were affixed all over Aix warning other prospective purchasers to expect the same. The financiers whose loans were to be repaid from the proceeds of office-sales began to be alarmed.

And still total success eluded Mazarin. With every month that passed, it became clearer that his gamble of squandering all France's resources in the hope of gaining a complete victory had failed. Indeed, the prospect of dictating terms to the Habsburgs was receding, for in January 1648 the Dutch Republic made a separate peace with Spain. Their reluctance to fight had long been apparent. As early as 1639,

Richelieu had reduced the level of France's financial support to the Republic because so little military effort was made to tie down the Spanish army of Flanders; and although matters improved somewhat thereafter (with a major Dutch campaign in 1644 and an undertaking not to make a separate peace), the French army's victories in 1645 profoundly alarmed the Dutch. While they spent the entire campaigning season taking the stronghold of Hulst in northern Flanders, the French overran all the rich south-western part of the province. It became obvious that two more campaigns would see the entire South Netherlands overrun, and a common frontier between France and the Republic. This prospect was not welcomed by the Dutch: 'France, enlarged by possession of the Spanish Netherlands, will be a dangerous neighbour for our country,' declared the estates of the province of Holland, and they pointed to the advantages which would accrue from negotiating a peace with Philip IV before his monarchy collapsed. In 1646, therefore, as the French conquest of Flanders continued, serious negotiations for a peace between Spain and the Dutch began at Münster (where the French were already negotiating with the Emperor). The various obstacles to a settlement had all disappeared. Spain was prepared to swallow her pride and recognize Dutch sovereignty in return for a peace that might allow her to win wars elsewhere. Philip IV, on his own admission, was prepared by 1646 'to give in on every point that might lead to the conclusion of a settlement'; indeed, according to an unsympathetic observer, he was so desperate for peace that 'if necessary he would crucify Christ again in order to achieve it'. Even the question of Brazil, which had prevented peace in the 1630s, was now open to solution, since it had followed Portugal into rebellion and renounced obedience to Philip IV early in 1641: why should the king now fight on to help recover the colony of a rebellious province? The Dutch, by contrast, were far more worried about saving Brazil. In 1645 their position in Pernambuco had been almost destroyed by a revolt among the Portuguese settlers who produced their sugar, and only four coastal towns remained under their control. The rebels' forces were growing as they received aid both from Bahía, the capital of Portuguese Brazil, and from Portugal itself. It was therefore imperative to cut off this source of assistance, and it seemed to many Dutch merchants and politicians that the best policy was to make a peace with Philip IV that would allow him to intensify his attacks on Portugal, and thus prevent her from sending reinforcements to Brazil. On these grounds too, a swift settlement of the Low Countries' wars seemed desirable.

A cease-fire was therefore agreed in June 1647, despite the opposition of the Dutch Calvinist clergy and of the French, who liberally financed an opposition group in the Republic, and created 'an artificial labyrinth, constructed in such a way that those who allow themselves to be led into it can never find the exit'. But after several attempts at sabotage, the final peace was signed at Münster on 30 January 1648. A special relationship almost immediately developed between the former enemies: Philip IV calculated that the South Netherlands could only be preserved with Dutch assistance; the Republic, for its part, was still anxious to maintain the existence of a weak Spanish buffer between herself and France. So the financing of the Spanish army of Flanders and the trade between Spain and Holland was now undertaken largely by the Jewish community of Amsterdam, whose numbers perhaps doubled between 1648 and 1660. They converted letters of credit from Madrid into cash paid in Antwerp; and with the profits, to Spain's chagrin, they endowed yeshivas and synagogues.

The peace of Münster was a serious reverse for Mazarin, and it could not have come at a worse time. The *Parlement* of Paris had proved unwilling to register the edicts containing his new fiscal measures – anticipating the income of 1649 and 1650; increasing the *paulette* and so on – and on 15 January 1648 the Cardinal had taken the young Louis XIV to the court in person to hold a *lit de justice* and thus force the registration of the edicts. But there was unprecedented opposition to this step by the *Parlement*, especially since some argued that no *lit* could take place until the king reached the age of majority. The unrest spread to the other sovereign courts in Paris, and to the provinces, where the increase in the *paulette* (at a time when the intendants were taking away much business) was also bitterly resented, and on 13 May 1648 the various courts in Paris issued an *arrêt d'union* (a declaration of solidarity) against the government's policies and refused to authorize any new fiscal measures. This made the financiers more cautious: afraid that repayment might be delayed, they refused to lend further. Mazarin, with no money for independent action until the sovereign courts endorsed the new taxes, was compelled to allow them to formulate grievances and to meet in a special joint assembly in Paris to articulate them: the Chambre St Louis (from 30 June). Since the financiers still refused to lend, Mazarin also had to accept the demands of the Chambre, even agreeing to recall the intendants on 18 July, a move which destroyed all chance of securing more loans, because the financiers realized as clearly as everyone else that without the intendants there would be no repayment. The government therefore declared a state bankruptcy. At the same time, a maladroit attempt to arrest the leaders of the Chambre St Louis provoked an uprising in Paris (20 July), which the capital's militia captains, one-quarter of whom themselves worked in the sovereign courts, did little to quell. Within a month, there were 1300 barricades in the streets around the royal palace. The royal family kept a team of horses constantly saddled and ready to flee; Chancellor Séguier was almost stoned to death as he left his lodgings; and the Paris coachmen intimidated their recalcitrant beasts with the threat, 'Mazarin will get you.' The *Fronde* had begun.

At last, the cardinal had to pay attention to the domestic affairs he had neglected for so long. Without money, he had to appear to accept the Chambre's programme and start peace talks, thereby encouraging his opponents to approve the new taxes that would allow him to fight on if negotiations failed. He correctly surmised that Philip IV of Spain would not be keen to negotiate, now that France was so weak that she could not defend her conquests in Catalonia, Italy and the

Netherlands, so he concentrated on securing peace in Germany. On 14 August 1648 the cardinal reluctantly instructed his negotiators at Münster to make peace at once, and on almost any terms that could be had, since: 'It is almost a miracle that, amid so many self-made obstacles, we can keep our affairs going, and even make them prosper; but prudence dictates that we should not place all our trust in this miracle continuing for long.' The cardinal proceeded to survey the opposition of the law courts, the enforced reduction in public expenditure, and the tax-strike which was spreading over the country, forcing the government into bankruptcy. He regretted, 'shedding tears of blood', that it had all happened at a time when 'our affairs had never been in a more prosperous state', but concluded: 'The end of this long discourse is to convince you of our need to make peace at the earliest opportunity.' The peace of Westphalia was signed on 24 October 1648 and, at last, the Thirty Years' War came to an end.[14]

4. *The End of the Thirty Years' War*

In 1618 there had been four major tensions within the European political system: the struggle between Spain and the Dutch; the confrontation of largely Protestant princes and estates with the Catholic Habsburgs in the Empire; the enmity of Sweden and Poland; and the rivalry of France and the Habsburgs. One of the reasons why all of the conflicts lasted so long was the alignment of groups involved in one conflict with those involved in another. Thus the war in the Empire lasted for almost thirty years, with very few interruptions, mainly because the enemies of the Habsburgs outside Germany were too numerous and too well co-ordinated to permit an imperial victory, and they could always muster some support within the Empire because of its fragmented political and religious structure. A memorandum drawn up by the imperial privy council in January 1633 sadly observed that all the battles and sieges won by Ferdinand II's armies, from the White Mountain to Magdeburg, had achieved nothing; but a single defeat, at Breitenfeld, had involved the loss of almost all of Germany. In November of the same year much the same point was made by Wallenstein, near the end of his career, in an interview with an imperial councillor: even if the Emperor were to win ten more victories, the general observed, his enemies would keep mobilizing new forces to continue the war; but another defeat like Breitenfeld would compel unconditional surrender, for no further armies would be found to defend Vienna. Although this advice was disregarded, because Ferdinand preferred to make a military alliance with Spain rather than a compromise peace with his enemies, the aftermath of the battle of Nördlingen proved Wallenstein and the pessimists right, for France came into the war and shored up the defeated anti-imperial coalition. Although numerous princes of the Empire subscribed to the peace of Prague in 1635 (page 241 above), France and Sweden were still able to make alliances with the rulers of Trier, Hesse, Brunswick and Saxe-Weimar against the Emperor (albeit all four were exiled from their patrimonial lands). It was not much, but it sufficed to support an army that routed the imperialists at the battle of Wittstock in Brandenburg (4 October 1636). This defeat was followed by others: the Spaniards lost Breda and other towns in the Netherlands in 1637, and the French-subsidized troops of Bernard of Saxe-Weimar overran Alsace in 1638. In the hereditary provinces, there were serious peasant revolts in Styria and Upper Austria.

The victory at Wittstock and the conquest of Alsace encouraged Sweden and France to turn their thoughts towards negotiating a settlement that might secure their new conquests for the future. The machinery for such activity was already in existence. Since 1634, Pope Urban VIII (1623–44) had been pressing the Emperor, France and Spain to send plenipotentiaries to a congress to make a universal peace. Although France's declaration of war on Spain in May 1635 was a serious reverse to this project, the Pope continued his efforts undaunted, studiously avoiding bias for one side or the other. Although an implacable autocrat in his own domains – persecuting dissident intellectuals like Galileo, ostracizing artists who would not conform to his stylistic requirements, and annexing neighbouring states when he could – outside central Italy Urban fully appreciated the diminished influence of his office. Even with the annexed duchies of Ferrara (from 1597) and Urbino (from 1626), the papal states only contained 2 million inhabitants; while the Pope's revenues, though very substantial, were squandered on ostentation and nepotism (see page 344, note 5 below). There was not enough left to pursue an aggressive foreign policy, even in Italy: the interdict against Venice (1606–7), the occupation of the Valtelline (1622–4), and the attempt to seize Parma (1642–4) all failed totally. Outside Italy, the Popes of the seventeenth century did not even try. Urban VIII repeatedly stressed to the nuncios responsible for arranging the peace congress: 'Never forget that the Pope is not a mediator: he may not command. You must always guard against irritating the parties.'

Eventually this cautious persistence paid off. After a year's argument, in July 1636 the Catholic parties at war accepted the papal invitation to send plenipotentiaries to an international peace congress (the first of its kind) to be held at Cologne. But the Protestants would not attend, and the project foundered. Ferdinand II therefore decided to try to settle at least the German conflict himself, and he called a meeting of the electors to Regensburg in September 1636 (there were only five: the Emperor, who was king of Bohemia, did not sit; the elector of Trier was in prison; and the elector Palatine had been replaced from 1623 by the duke of Bavaria). Although the Emperor succeeded in persuading the electors to recognize his son, Ferdinand III, as heir apparent (something the previous assembly, in 1630, had refused to do), there was little progress in finding a formula for peace. Sweden demanded more lands and money than the princes could countenance (Brandenburg insisted that the Swedes 'must not keep a foot of imperial soil, still less a place, fortress or province') and the Protestant electors demanded amnesty and restitution for too many outlaws.

Nevertheless, in 1637 and 1638 talks took place between representatives of the Emperor (Ferdinand III after his father's death in February 1637) and the envoys of Denmark, England, France and Sweden, who were assembled at Hamburg to sign further treaties among themselves. But again, no common ground for a settlement materialized. In 1640, Ferdinand III decided to try another approach and summoned a full Diet of the Empire (*Reichstag*) to meet at Regensburg and find a solution to the internal disputes involved in the war. The Catholics predominated heavily in the gathering: of the five electors, three were Catholics; of the 58 voting princes, 30 were Catholics (and about one-quarter of the votes were controlled by the electors); and of the 52 towns, 19 were Catholic. But despite this, the Protestants – or at least, those of them who were not outlawed – attended, and between September 1640 and October 1641, over 150 sessions were held to settle the great issues of war and peace within the Empire. Even the bombardment of the city by the Swedish army in January 1641 failed to interrupt the discussions, and by the time the assembly broke up, almost all the internal problems had been settled, while talks with France and Sweden were beginning again at Hamburg.

There might have been more progress still but for two obstacles. First, the Emperor was reluctant to make an immediate peace with France because it would intensify French pressure on Spain; second, the elector of Brandenburg died in December 1640. To the last, George William had adhered to the peace of Prague, even though it had involved the occupation of most of his lands by the Swedish army. But his successor Frederick William would have none of this. Educated in the Hague, he was on good terms with the Protestant powers and he was determined to end military operations in his possessions. In May 1641, after preliminary talks with the Swedish commanders, he sent ambassadors to

Stockholm who arranged, in July, an armistice: peace was restored to the electorate, although there was serious disagreement over possession of Pomerania which was claimed by both parties. It was to prevent other princes from conducting their own foreign policies that Ferdinand III authorized his representatives at Hamburg to sign, on Christmas Day 1641, an undertaking with France and Sweden that a general peace congress, on the lines proposed since 1634 by Urban VIII, should be held in the neighbouring Westphalian towns of Osnabrück and Münster. The imperial plenipotentiaries arrived in July 1643.

Unfortunately for the cause of peace, the parties refused to stop fighting while negotiations went on. All of them believed that continuing the war would bring them further advantages. At first, the strange behaviour of the Swedish army in Germany gave Ferdinand cause to hope that the anti-Habsburg coalition might fall apart. First, the field commander, Johan Banér, seemed disposed to make a private peace with the Emperor in return for lands in Silesia; then, after his death, the troops mutinied for their pay and discipline was not restored until the formidable Lennart Torstensson arrived at army headquarters in November 1641 with 7000 new Swedish soldiers and some money for the veterans. Although crippled by arthritis – most of his orders were issued from a litter or sick-bed – Torstensson was a skilful general and a strict disciplinarian: he ruthlessly exacted absolute obedience from his troops and total co-operation from civilians. Any failure was instantly punished by floggings or hangings. After reorganizing his army over the winter of 1641–2, Torstensson led his men straight towards the Habsburg heartland, occupying all of Moravia and much of Saxony. While they were besieging Leipzig, an imperial field army rashly challenged the Swedes to battle: the result was the second battle of Breitenfeld on 2 November 1642 – as brilliant a Swedish victory as the first, the imperialists losing 10,000 men, 46 field guns, and their pay chests.

Any hope that the Spaniards would appear again, as at Nördlingen, to make good this loss was dashed by the destruction of the army of Flanders at Rocroi the following spring. But still the Emperor was anxious to delay participating in a general peace conference, once again encouraged by a reduction in Swedish pressure: in May 1643, the month of Rocroi, Sweden went to war against Christian IV of Denmark.

Christian, never a friend of Sweden, had undoubtedly provoked the new attack. For some time, his customs officials, anxious to raise money for their master, had made life difficult for Swedish merchantmen sailing through the Sound: they and their cargoes were embargoed, and ships sailing from the ports of North Germany brought under Swedish control by Gustavus Adolphus were denied the preferential customs rates accorded to Sweden at the peace of Knared in 1613. Christian, however, could not afford to be generous. The peace of Lübeck in 1629 had not brought security: on the contrary, defence spending had been increased lest any of the armies operating in Germany should turn against Denmark. Extraordinary taxes doubled between 1629 and 1643, but still expenditure regularly exceeded revenue so that the healthy surplus of 1625 changed into a heavy deficit. The king was compelled to turn for financial assistance to his council; they, for their part, saw the king's need as an opportunity to regain the control that they had exercised over his policies twenty years before. They therefore agreed to authorize new taxes worth 1 million thalers (over £200,000 sterling), but only on condition that they handled both collection and distribution. Christian refused to accept this insulting restriction on his power, and threatened not to ratify the peace with the Emperor unless the money were voted unconditionally. In the end, the council gave way – its members all owned land in Jutland which would be devastated if the war continued – but in 1637, with the 1 million thalers all spent, the king at length accepted the principle that further taxes should be administered by the council. It was in order to minimize his dependence on this conciliar income that Christian attempted to raise more revenue from the tolls levied on ships passing through the Sound, thus antagonizing the Swedes. But this was not their only grievance. In 1640

Christian had added another, by aiding the escape of the Swedish queen mother to Copenhagen, which created a potential focus for opponents of the regency, and in 1641–2 he began to intervene again in the affairs of North Germany. First he persuaded the Emperor to recognize him as mediator in all negotiations with Sweden, with the tacit understanding that if the Swedes proved obdurate, Denmark would join forces with the Emperor. In return, Christian wished to gain control over Hamburg and the mouth of the Elbe, and in the spring of 1643 his fleet began to blockade the port. At the same time, he began to mobilize an army and to send envoys to the Emperor, to the Tsar and to Poland to seek an offensive alliance against Sweden. On 25 May, the Swedish council decided to act before matters went any further and, in September, Torstensson (still in a litter) led his troops towards Jutland, where they spent the winter in the rich farms and villages of a country untouched by war since 1629. The Emperor expected hostilities to spread, relieving the pressure on his own dominions; but they did not.

Christian's efforts to enlist Polish support failed completely: King Wladislaw wished to direct his forces, especially the cossacks (who had rebelled against him in 1637–8), against the Turks and was anxious to avoid new commitments in the Baltic. Russia, too, remained neutral. The Tsar, still Michael Romanov, was indeed in close touch with Christian IV, because he wished to marry his daughter to Prince Waldemar of Denmark, who arrived in Moscow in January 1644 and became engaged to the Tsarevna. But the young man refused to embrace the Orthodox faith and was kept under house arrest (and away from his betrothed) until the Tsar died in July 1645. Waldemar was then allowed to go home, but without any alliance for his father. Muscovy was fully committed elsewhere: in the east, expansion in Siberia continued, aided by a civil war in China, until in 1648 Russian colonists founded Othotsk by the Pacific; in the south, the cossacks captured Azov on the Black Sea in 1637 and surrendered it to the Tsar, but he preferred to hand it back to the Ottoman vassals from whom it had been seized rather than face the inevitable war with the Sultan and his Tatar allies which retaining Azov would entail (1643). In addition, the Tsar's ministers were spending all available funds on the construction of a heavily fortified line of defence against Tatar raids in the south, stretching from Belgorod in the south-west through Voronezh and Kozlov to Nizhni Lomov. The cost of the work, which was begun in 1638 and completed in 1650, helped to deter the Tsars from intervening in any foreign conflict. Denmark's other potential allies were also incapacitated: France was allied to Sweden, and Christian's nephew Charles I was fully committed in the civil wars in England, Scotland and Ireland.

So, in the end, only the Emperor came to Denmark's aid. An imperial army moved towards Holstein in the summer of 1644, in the hope of strengthening Danish resistance, but Torstensson won another victory at Jüterbog which sent the survivors scuttling back to Bohemia. In the meantime a fleet chartered in Amsterdam by Louis de Geer captured the Danish islands of Oesel and Gotland and drove the Danes off the sea, although de Geer's ships failed to ferry the main army across from Jutland to capture Copenhagen. The Dutch Republic now negotiated a settlement between Denmark and Sweden in her own interests (the peace of Bromsebro: 25 August 1645): neither state was given full control of the Sound, but Sweden gained the province of Halland (on the Swedish side) for 30 years, and the Norwegian provinces of Jamtland and Harjedalen (on the Swedish side of the Kjolen mountains) and the islands of Oesel and Gotland in perpetuity. The Dutch, for their part, secured virtual exemption from the Sound tolls for all their ships, which ruined the tolls as a source of revenue for the Danish crown since 60 per cent and more of all ships passing through the Sound were Dutch. The peace of Bromsebro, indeed, marked the death of Denmark as a major European power: the depredations of the Swedes caused a drop in agricultural production and a shortage of capital; the Swedish withdrawal was followed by harvest failure and plague (1647–51); and the total population loss by 1660 has been estimated at 20 per cent. Politically speaking, the crown was totally discredited. Christian was compelled in 1647–8 to agree to tight aristocratic control of every aspect of government, and when he died in February 1648 the nobles spent some months bargaining with his son before they agreed to elect him king.

The collapse of Denmark was so evident by the end of 1644 that the Swedish council decided that it would be safe to return to the German war in the following year, making a final effort to defeat the Emperor and bring him to terms. An alliance was made with the prince of Transylvania, George Rakoczy (1630–48), who began an invasion of Habsburg Hungary, while the Swedish army moved once more through Saxony into Bohemia. There, on 5 March, the imperialists were routed by the Swedes yet again, at the battle of Jankov: even their generals were captured, and the Emperor retreated first to Vienna and then across the Alps to Graz, whence his father had been called to the imperial crown a generation before. In the west, the French followed up their successful campaign of 1644 (which had secured the right bank of the Rhine) by a considerable victory over Ferdinand's Bavarian allies at Allerheim, near Nördlingen (3 August 1645). These two victories convinced most German princes that the imperial cause was irretrievably lost. Brandenburg had already made a separate peace with the Swedes; Saxony now followed (September 1645) and, after another campaign in which the French ravaged the Catholic south-west of Germany, on 14 March 1647, Mazarin agreed to conclude a truce with the rulers of Hesse, Cologne, Mainz and Bavaria (although Duke Maximilian broke it briefly in the winter of 1647–8). Spain, with rebellions in Italy and the peninsula, and facing the worst plague epidemic since the Black Death (1647-52), was plainly no longer a force to be reckoned with in Germany.

The misfortunes of war had also thinned the ranks of the sometime anti-imperialists. Prince George Rakoczy of Transylvania had been ordered back by the Sultan (August 1645); Denmark had been defeated; and the German princes who had fought against the Emperor were either dead or had made terms with one side or the other. By the time the chief imperial negotiator, Count Trautmansdorff, arrived at the peace conference in Westphalia in November 1645, there were only two major protagonists left to deal with: France, whose negotiators were at the town of Münster, and Sweden, whose agents were at nearby Osnabrück.

Because of the separate agreements noted above, and the compromises already worked out at Prague in 1635 and Regensburg in 1640–1, there was already much common ground between the various parties concerning the internal settlement of the Empire's affairs.[15] The only major problem remaining was the *satisfactio* demanded by the two foreign powers still in arms. Sweden, which in 1635 and 1636 had been ready to settle for a relatively modest cash indemnity of 5 million thalers and little or no German territory, by 1643 was seeking either 26 million thalers in cash, or else 13 million in cash and possession of Pomerania (despite Brandenburg's claim), Verden and Bremen (two secularized bishoprics formerly held by Christian IV of Denmark). The Swedish government calculated the annual cost of its war effort at 2 million thalers, hence 26 million for the thirteen years 1630–43. The French, for their part, asked for no money; but they demanded possession of Lower Alsace, of the bishoprics of Metz, Toul and Verdun, and of certain Rhine fortresses – areas already in French hands. In addition, France insisted that the duke of Bavaria should retain both his electoral title and the Upper Palatinate, conferred in 1623; and Sweden demanded that the elector Palatine, the duke of Brunswick, the landgrave of Hesse and all other subjects in rebellion against the Emperor should be restored to their estates.

Most of these outstanding points were settled in 1646. The territorial claims of France were admitted; an amnesty was agreed for all rebels; and Pomerania was partitioned between Sweden and Brandenburg (the elector was compensated with the ecclesiastical states of Magdeburg, Halberstadt and Minden, which lay between his patrimonial lands and the Rhineland territories of Mark and Cleves, acquired after the succession dispute of 1609–14). There was even agreement on Sweden's cash *satisfactio*: 5 million thalers were offered and accepted. But still Ferdinand III hesitated, hoping that somehow God would divert his enemies and allow him to improve the terms of his surrender. For a moment, success seemed possible, for in the autumn of 1647 Bavaria abandoned her agreement with France and once again entered an alliance with the Habsburgs. It was too late. The Bavarian army was routed by the French at Zusmarshausen, near Augsburg, on 17 May 1648, while in July the Swedish army invaded Bohemia and captured the suburb of Prague where the treasures of Rudolf II were still housed in the Hradschin. Now, 570 paintings, innumerable books and works of art, and even a lion from the half-forgotten imperial zoo were sent back to Stockholm, where they joined the treasures of Munich (captured in 1632) and other places looted in the course of Sweden's wars in Poland, Russia and the Empire. The threat of losing all Bohemia, if Prague fell, finally forced Ferdinand's hand: the peace of Westphalia was signed on 24 October.

Paradoxically, the Papacy, France and Spain, all professed to be disappointed by the settlement. Innocent X refused to ratify it; Philip IV urged the Emperor to break it; Mazarin wished it could have been made at some other time. 'It might perhaps have been more advantageous for the conclusion of a universal peace had the war in the Empire continued a little longer,' he wrote in characteristic vein to his envoy at Münster, and he regretted that France had 'hurried on the settlement of matters as we did' on account of the *Fronde* rebellion. In doing so, he claimed, the position of the Emperor was saved since 'his total collapse, considering his sad situation, was imminent and ineluctable'. The cardinal could not resist adding tartly: 'It is clear that the greatest aid for the Emperor has thus come from France, in that we forced him into making peace; for otherwise his total ruin seemed inevitable.'[16]

The Emperor had not emerged so badly from the peace, at least on paper. He had recovered all his hereditary dominions, most of them occupied by foreign powers (only Lusatia, ceded to Saxony in 1620, was not restored); he had avoided giving an amnesty to any rebellious subjects from the patrimonial provinces (despite strong pressure from Sweden to do so); and he had saved his patrimonial provinces from the obligation of contributing to Sweden's war indemnity. Finally, in return for sacrificing Alsace (where imperial rights were nebulous) to France, he had recovered some valuable lordships along the Upper Rhine previously occupied by the French. Overall, perhaps unwittingly, Ferdinand had sacrificed German territory in the north and west in return for gains in his Austrian lands. None of the territorial concessions to Sweden or France touched him personally; the acceptance of a new political and religious settlement in the Empire merely recognized the decline in imperial power which had taken place since the fifteenth century and which his father had sought, unsuccessfully, to reverse. The peace which he had negotiated lasted for almost a century, and the religious settlement which it incorporated lasted for even longer.

By 1648, general excitement about the peace had grown almost to fever pitch. A popular pacifist literature had grown up in Germany, with hymns, poems, satires and plays calling for an end to the war. The peace plays were particularly effective, since they coupled the vocabulary of Lutheran pietism (often reinforced by Lutheran church music) with a powerful emotional message expressed in the vernacular. One of the most popular, The *Victory of Peace* (*Friedens Sieg*) was written by a pastor's son, Justus Schottel, who was a councillor to the duke of Brunswick, and the duke's children took part in the first performance of the play in 1642 while Frederick William of Brandenburg looked on. The plays formed part of an early manifestation of German patriotism which reached its crescendo as the foreign occupying forces moved out of their billets and camps, receiving either cash or bonds in settlement of their wages. The diary of a peasant craftsman near Ulm, who had been forced to flee to the city 22 times during the war, reflected the nervous, almost incredulous enthusiasm which spread as the last of the troops finally left: 'On 24 August [1650] . . . a thanksgiving feast was given in Ulm and all the villages around the city. There were sermons, songs, prayers, and holy communion was joyfully celebrated, since all the garrisons of troops had now left their billets and towns, and we now had full and total peace by the grace of God Almighty.'[17]

But the deliverance was not extended to everyone. The struggle between Spain and France continued; so did the rivalry of Poland and Sweden. Only the tensions in the Netherlands and the Empire were settled in 1648, and even there the harvest of 1649 was the worst of the century, causing widespread starvation and numerous popular revolts. A sustained pogrom in Poland led to the death of 100,000 Jews during the decade 1648–58. Bubonic plague swept through many areas, decimating the Italian and Iberian peninsulas with especial severity. Those who dreamed of achieving a universal peace among men, like Jan Amos Comenius, exiled after the Bohemian revolt, saw their hopes dashed time after time and their idealist, ecumenical approach stigmatized as treason. Far more attention was paid by contemporaries to the millenarians – whether Quakers, mystics or Jews – who proclaimed that the times in which they lived were accursed, an Iron Century, the years of Antichrist which (according to the Bible) would precede the end of the world. The fear of imminent destruction, which reached its peak as the numerologically alarming year of 1666 approached, imparted that febrile, anguished quality to much of the culture of mid-seventeenth century which was, perhaps, its most distinctive feature.

CHAPTER VIII

The Culture of Post-Renaissance Europe

1. Popular Culture

It has been suggested that the last scholar to be acquainted with the whole body of knowledge current in the Europe of his day was Joseph Scaliger, a French luminary of Italian extraction who died in 1609. The scientific discoveries and the general cultural advance of the seventeenth century made it impossible for a single man to keep abreast of all learning after Scaliger's death. Few people tried. Most, indeed, could not try, because they could not read: the culture of most early modern Europeans was not written, but oral.

'Ears are the only organ necessary for the Christian man,' wrote Martin Luther, because the Word of God was more often heard than read. The same could be said of most other forms of wisdom. Knowledge of nature came from parents or older brothers and sisters; knowledge of religion and morals was learned, perhaps by rote, from the parson at catechism; knowledge of how to build and how to make was taught by a master during a long apprenticeship; knowledge of how to run a house or a farm was acquired by becoming a servant; knowledge of stories, folk-lore and legend was absorbed during evenings spent by the fire or at the ale-house. This essentially oral popular culture was both rich and varied. Every community had its own songs and stories, and its own specialists in telling or singing them (often blind or crippled persons who found it hard to make a living in other ways). Every community above a certain size also had its own craftsmen to paint or to carve the artifacts that they needed, and the towns also had their craft guilds and professional societies which regularly staged plays or spectacles. Large towns, finally, also had their own theatres where travelling professional players and entertainers would perform. There were also popular recreations in which the public could participate: handball and tennis, archery and bowls, skittles and quoits, cards and dice. In some regions there were special sports, such as ice-hockey in the Netherlands and golf in Scotland (Charles I was playing golf on Leith Links outside Edinburgh when news of the Ulster Massacres was brought to him in December 1641: like a true Scot, he of course went on to finish his game). Besides these games for small groups, there were others that involved teams, the most popular being mass-sports like 'choule' (a sort of cross-country hockey, very popular in Normandy, in which large groups from neighbouring villages or rival guilds fought – literally – for possession of a ball) and football (a game 'meeter for laming rather than making abler the users thereof' according to James I; 'a bloody and murderous practice' and 'nothing but beastly fury and extreme violence', according to others).

The list of popular recreations was not long, however, and the ones noted above were often the subject of complaint and opposition from the authorities. Mass activities like choule or football were the commonest targets for attempted suppression, but criticism was also directed at dancing (because it was said to lead to debauchery), street-singing (which lent itself either to smutty or seditious songs), and theatres and taverns (which allegedly encouraged indecency). Enjoyment of any kind on a Sunday was discouraged and, in Calvinist countries at least, fined: the records of the parish courts abound with punishments meted out to ordinary people for drinking, singing, fishing, working and even for walking outside or going to sleep on the Sabbath. Few of those arraigned and fined complained, for most people were obliged to accept arbitrary authority of many sorts. Women and servants, for example, were permanently subject to the head of the household. Religious manuals composed around 1600, such as those of Jean Benedicti, Francisco de Toledo and Fernandes de Moura, all emphasized the subordination of a wife: 'She must do nothing against her husband, to whom she is subordinate by human and divine law.' To oppose him or challenge him was a mortal sin, and it was generally agreed that insubordinate or quarrelsome wives should be beaten. One English author in 1650 held that the only limit to the level of punishment was the sixth commandment (Thou shalt not kill). Even in the Netherlands, where wife beating was regarded as the English disease, those who wrote about domestic matters – such as Jacob Cats, who wrote 120,000 hexameter verses on marriage, ranging from 100 on the virtues of breast-feeding to a four-page verse prayer to be said by young couples before getting into bed on their wedding night – enjoined the wife to be obedient, submissive and silent. Husbands who failed to get the better of their wives were subjected to ritual ridicule by the young people in their annual festival or *charivari*, or in a specially arranged demonstration of disapproval (still known in rural Spain and called a *vito*). Some of the earliest strip cartoons for children, printed in the Netherlands in the 1650s, made fun of 'Jan de Wasser' (John the Washerwoman), a hen-pecked Dutch husband who was beaten by his wife when he failed to get the house cleaned quickly enough. Of course children also came in for their fair share of brutal treatment: Bartholomew Batty in 1581 praised the wisdom of the Almighty who had made the human posterior in such a shape that it could take much correction without suffering permanent damage.

Europe's rigid hierarchy was only overturned completely during the two slack times in the rural year: during Lent (when most charivaris took place) and at Christmas (when the Feast of Fools placed the humble and oppressed in temporary positions of authority). Both exercises were accompanied by elaborate rituals, which reassured the establishment that the reversal of roles was only temporary; but sometimes the fun got out of hand. In 1638, in the Rouergue area of France, a cavalry company from the regular army was harassed by the local bachelors to such an extent that they were forced to shift their lodgings; while at Agen in 1635, at Barcelona in 1640 and at Bordeaux in 1651 a popular carnival turned into a political revolt. Small wonder that the authorities sometimes prohibited or postponed a carnival or procession at a time of political sensitivity.

The Christian churches also had their problems with popular culture, and especially with the superstitious beliefs which the medieval church had failed to overcome. In Protestant areas there was a marked reluctance to abandon the Romish ceremonies and religious practices which had become almost ingrained. As late as the 1640s, the principal Catholic shrines in the Dutch Republic – holy wells and the like – were still attracting pilgrims of almost all denominations. In Saxony, the avowedly Lutheran people still revered Saints' days. Even the Calvinists could not eradicate veneration of Christmas. But by the side of these forms of superstition (to Protestant eyes) lay another far more serious: clergymen of all denominations became increasingly concerned about the existence of an alternative popular religion of devil-worship involving organized covens of witches and the systematic use of diabolic means to spread evil and ignorance in the world.

The existence of a European witchcraze between 1580 and 1640 is now taken for granted; but its precise nature and its geographical distribution are still sometimes misunderstood. It seems clear that magical traditions existed at all times and in all areas of Europe, with most communities of any size possessing a person who claimed to have (or really did have) a sixth sense which allowed him or her to cure sickness (by herbal or other means), to locate lost objects (often with the aid of divining rods), and to identify the source of a misfortune or misadventure (normally by placing suspicion on another person hostile to the victim). After the fourteenth century, however, a number of cases of magic were brought before the law courts with the additional accusation that the witches had sold their souls to the devil in order to acquire their supernatural powers. In 1398 the university of Paris defined witchcraft as a heresy and in 1484 the papacy confirmed this. In 1487 two German inquisitors compiled and published a handbook of the sort of practices they claimed to have uncovered while interrogating suspected witches: the *Malleus maleficarum.* It was reprinted sixteen times before 1520 and a host of books and pamphlets on demonology followed: 345 were published in France alone between 1550 and 1650, creating the impression that a comprehensive alternative religion existed, posing a major threat to Christianity.

There were few educated people who dared to express doubt about this. All the evidence was against them, as the French judge, Henri Boguet, pointed out (in one of the 345 treatises):

> It is astonishing that there should still be found today people who do not believe that there are witches. For . . . they are refuted by Canon and Civil Law; Holy Scripture gives them the lie; the voluntary and repeated confessions of witches prove them wrong; and the sentences passed in various places against the accused must shut their mouths.[1]

And yet sorcery trials did not take place at all times and in all places, nor did they take place on the scale which one might expect. The *Parlement de Paris*, the appeal court for 500 inferior courts covering half of France, heard less than 1300 cases of witchcraft between 1565 and 1640; and many of those it dismissed. In Spain there were few, if any, sorcery trials after 1611; in Geneva no witches were burnt after 1626; in Luxemburg none after 1630. But the situation was very different farther east. In Germany, 600 people were burnt for sorcery in Bamberg alone between 1628 and 1633; while in Poland the persecution of witches only gathered momentum in the 1650s, continuing at a high level for over a century, just as the witchcraze in western Europe was dying out.

The explanation of this curious chronological contradiction lies in the different local strengths of the principal Christian creeds. A witchcraze normally occurred in areas which had experienced a period of religious upheaval during which Christian teaching was somewhat neglected, especially in outlying regions (for instance, mountainous or isolated lands).

And the persecution tended to coincide with the moment at which one of the warring Christian churches emerged as the victor, and was intent on turning mastery into monopoly: Scotland after 1590 in the case of the Calvinists; south-west Germany after 1625 and Poland after 1650 in the case of the Catholics. Not unnaturally, the dark corners of the land presented a special challenge to the new church triumphant, for there it found heterodoxy of all kinds. It is true that many of the accusations were lodged in years of dearth and against marginal members of society whose continued presence in a small community was inconvenient – old, single women dependent on charity (75 per cent of all the witches accused were women); men without an obvious occupation; a diviner who had accused some local notable of theft or malevolence – but economic explanations do not necessarily exclude intellectual ones. A population needed to be confessionally conditioned and partially (but not totally) literate, as well as poor, before a witchcraze could get under way.

The most effective weapon employed by the ruling elite of Europe to emasculate and, eventually, to eradicate popular culture and superstition was undoubtedly the campaign waged by both church and state to bring the ordinary people into contact with the written culture of their betters. Schools were founded in great numbers in order to teach children to read and write. More than 800 schools were endowed in England and Wales alone between 1580 and 1650, and the pace of new foundations grew even faster thereafter. It was the same elsewhere (see Table 7). Some of these schools were grammar schools where a wide range of courses were available to pupils. Some of the most famous, in Catholic countries at least, were run by the Jesuit Order, which maintained about 520 colleges across Europe by 1640, where at least 150,000 children (all boys) were taught every year – 40,000 in France, 32,000 in the South Netherlands and so on. Certainly, conditions in these colleges were not always ideal. Discipline was brutal (some children were threatened with the thumbscrew) and classes were large. At the Jesuit college of Rouen, for example, 1800 children were taught in only 7 classes in

1603. But on the other hand, up to half the intake of the Jesuit schools were the children of local peasants and artisans, who were taught free of charge. In Protestant countries too there were many scholarships for the poor, and the number of 'plebeians' entering the universities during the sixteenth and seventeenth centuries rose until in some cases they formed the largest single group. In England, 50 per cent of all students admitted to the university of Oxford between

Table 7. Distribution of Schools in Seventeenth-century Europe

Area	*Date*	*Number of parishes*	*Number of schools*	*Percentage with schools*
England				
county of Kent	1620s	266	133	50
France				
diocese of Toul	1690s	1036	613	59
Verdun	1690s	269	113	42
Paris	1670s	127	111	87
Poland				
diocese of Poznan	1620s	390	179	46
Scotland				
five Lowland shires	1690s	179	160	89

1570 and 1640 were described as 'plebeians' and many held a college scholarship which paid for their fees.

Not all countries went to these lengths, however. The educational revolution tended to take place only in those countries where the conflict of incompatible religious creeds made it advisable to educate congregations to distinguish between the truth of their own church and the falsehood of everyone else's. Thus in Germany, some 3600 students were admitted annually to the twenty or so universities in existence, but few of the matriculants were 'plebeian' except at Ingolstadt in Bavaria (where many Catholic priests were trained) and at Wittenberg in Saxony (seminary of Lutheran pastors): there, between 10 and 25 per cent of the students enrolled were said to be 'poor'. The educational opportunities in Castile were even less favourable to the non-noble. Although almost 20,000 young men were at university at any one time during the reign of Philip III (1598–1621), scarcely any were not of gentle status or above: indeed, perhaps one-quarter of the Castilian aristocracy in this period was receiving a university education. Some people thought it was too much. No new universities were founded in Spain between 1620 and 1830; the university population was allowed to fall to 6000 by 1650; some institutions were allowed to close. At the same time, a current of anti-intellectualism was directed against the grammar schools, of which there were perhaps 4000 in Spain in 1621, the year in which an official report advised Philip IV that:

> It would also help to close down some grammar schools newly founded in villages and small towns, because with the opportunity of having them so near, the peasants divert their sons from the jobs and occupations in which they were born and raised and put them to study, from which they benefit little, and leave for the most part ignorant because the preceptors are not much better.[2]

The king responded in 1623 with an edict ordering all grammar schools to close unless they had an endowed income of 300 ducats a year (which very few did) or unless they were in one of the 70 or so towns governed by a royal *corregidor*. A specific order was added to prohibit the teaching of Latin to children in foundling hospitals and orphanages; instead, the inmates were to be taught more practical skills.

Schools were not, however, indispensable to formal education, as the example of Sweden shows. The Lutheran church there was able to insist in the later seventeenth century that all its members should be able to read: unless they could pass their reading examination, they could not be confirmed and therefore could not marry in church. Aided by his parish council, each vicar held regular tests of his parishioners, and the progress of each one of them towards fluency was recorded annually in examination books. There were so many categories of fluency that there can be no doubt about the accuracy of the measurements, even though these show scores of 100 per cent among the adult population of Vesteras diocese in the 1690s and 80 per cent at Uppsala. But this achievement was unique: few other groups – not even aristocracies – could match the Swedish literacy score. It seems unlikely that any other state even came near, although we cannot be certain because no other government or church attempted to measure literacy as such, and the historian is driven to calculate the ability to read and write from records which were compiled for other purposes. The chief source to be utilized is the number of signatures and marks appended to marriage registers, notarial acts, testaments, and oaths of loyalty. Although the use of such evidence has been criticized on several grounds (see page 334 below), there seems to be a reasonable correlation between the ability to sign and the ability to read (at least); so the data presented in Table 8 may be compared with the Swedish scores above.

The geographical variations in these literacy scores are interesting, and they are confirmed by other more fragmentary data collected by various teams of historians. It would appear that in areas where literacy as such was of little use beyond the comprehension of religious texts, the score amongst adult males was in the region of 20 to 25 per cent. This, therefore, was the contribution of the church's insistence on individual knowledge of the Bible; but it could not by itself push literacy rates much above 25 per cent. If they were to rise further, other stimuli were needed: either moral pressure and tests, as in Sweden, or economic benefits, as in Amsterdam. If such inducements to literacy were removed, the scores declined; and if a local disaster closed a school for some years, an illiterate generation might grow up in a village where once high scores had been registered. Outside Sweden, at least in the seventeenth century, there seem to have been few places with a tradition of self-taught literacy.

The imperfect penetration of literacy into the population of Europe created great disparities in reading abilities: by the side of those who could read fluently in many languages resided those who could only make out one word at a time. By the side of the traditional, weighty Latin tomes (not for nothing did the erudite Janus Gruter address a vast work of 1614 to 'the persevering reader') printers brought out more and more brief ephemera. Some 25,000 tracts or pamphlets were published in England between 1640 and 1661; nearly 2000 were printed in the year 1642 alone, more than five a day. In Germany, 1800 broadsheets and pamphlets were published in 1618; in France, at least 4000 attacks on Cardinal Mazarin were printed between 1649 and 1652, so that 'One half of Paris prints or sells pamphlets and the other half writes them.' The subject-matter of almost all these publi-

Table 8. Literacy Scores in Seventeenth-century Europe

Country	*Dates*	*Percentage able to sign*	
		Men	*Women*
England			
East Anglia	1580–1640	35	5
Surrey	1642	33	
Sussex, Berkshire	1642	27	
Westmoreland, Yorkshire	1642	17	
Devon, Cornwall	1642	17	
France			
national average	1686–90	29	14
Netherlands			
Amsterdam	1630	57	32
Amsterdam	1660	64	37
Amsterdam	1680	70	44
Poland			
Little Poland	1630–50	17·5	4

cations was politics and such was the desire to know of current events that a most important literary invention was made: the newspaper. The Dutch writer Pieter Corneliszoon Hooft observed in 1640: 'Let the news be good or bad, it is always welcome to me because it tells me of the world.' And by 1640 Hooft had a choice of two weekly *corantos* from Amsterdam (one founded in 1618, the other in 1619), three from Antwerp (the earliest dating from 1620), and one from Bruges. Each contained a section on domestic and foreign news, and some even maintained permanent war correspondents.

No government could afford to leave uncensored this flood of printed mass-produced literature, so easily available from shops in towns and from peddlars in the countryside. Sometimes those who acquired hostile material were prosecuted, but mostly criticism was controlled at source by censoring the printers. Even in the Dutch Republic, where 'people believe that freedom of speech is a part of liberty', the government suppressed a few books and broadsheets and occasionally stifled a tiresome preacher; but the federal structure of the Republic's government made stricter supervision impossible, with the result that many seditious or scandalous tracts which could never have been published elsewhere were printed in the North Netherlands for distribution abroad. Life for printers outside the Republic was not so free. The authorities of the Holy Roman Empire established a body of commissioners at Frankfurt to examine books before they were printed in order to guard against the dissemination of seditious material. In Spain and in Venice the Inquisition censored literature (although in Venice the inquisitors were joined by a deputation of magistrates for this purpose). In France, Richelieu established a board of censors (there were 50 of them by 1700, 179 by 1789) and authorized the university of Paris to draw up an Index of prohibited books. Such control was considered essential because 'The little books which are widely distributed among the common people attract them like Manna. Since they are captivated by whatever is new, they take what they read so much to heart that it is impossible thereafter to eradicate the impression books make, especially where religion is concerned.'[8]

Many of the 'little books' belonged to a new genre, a literary invention of the seventeenth century almost as important as the newspapers: the 'chapbooks', known collectively in France as the *bibliothèque bleue.* Most of the items of this type were simple broadsheets, containing news of recent crises, government proclamations, predictions for the future, jokes (most of them obscene) and satire. The most common type was a striking print with an explanatory commentary – much like the devotional pictures of the Middle Ages – and sometimes, in the case of a satire, with a key to explain the allusions. The repertoire of prints remained restricted and its style was heavily stereotyped: often the same illustration was used for several different topics and the same iconographic conventions (the 'stone of folly' being exorcized and so on) were repeated over and over again. But in France a new development began in the early seventeenth century. A printing family called Oudot, in the town of Troyes, began to publish popular stories in cheap booklets which were sold by peddlars for a few pennies. The print runs – up to 100,000 of some editions – indicate the popularity of the new genre, which was soon imitated elsewhere. The works were printed in large type, with short chapters and numerous illustrations. *The Hystoire de Guerin Mesquin*, for example, printed by Oudot in 1628, consisted of 104 folios with 50 woodcuts; the *Adieu de Tabarin au peuple de Paris*, a gallows speech printed in 1623, had only eight folios (one printer's gathering: the commonest denomination). Apart from stories and news, the *Bibliothèque bleue* also included religious tracts in simple language (often the lives of saints, or counsels on preparing body and soul for death), and practical advice. In 1650, *L'escole de Salerno* ('The school of Salerno', a famous medical faculty) was published at Paris: its 74 quarto pages in burlesque verse (for easier memorization) contained some useful advice about curing oneself of illness. In 1645, Oudot published the rather longer but far more useful *Le médecin charitable* (220 pages) which taught 'the way to prepare in one's own house, with little cost, the correct remedy for every illness . . . together with a list of all the instruments and medicines, both simple and compound, which should be kept in the house'. Those who failed to heed this advice were not forgotten, for the title concluded: 'Also containing an account of how to embalm corpses.'

Here, then, was a bridge between the 'two cultures' which had grown up in early modern Europe. It was not the only one. There was considerable cultural seepage from the poems, chivalric romances, and art of the elite to that of the people (by means of parody as well as by emulation); conversely the art and drama of the elite often took its inspiration or its subject from a popular art-form. Further, the elite regularly participated in popular culture. The Dutch magistrate, Pieter Corneliszoon Hooft, whose castle at Muiden near Amsterdam was a centre of poetry and letters, liked listening to popular ballads, folksongs and entertainments; Philip IV and his courtiers attended public carnivals and spectacles; and the plays of Shakespeare, Jonson and the rest were watched in London by the aristocracy in their boxes and the populace in the 'pit'. The European elite of early modern times, it has been observed, participated in both cultures equally, just like the Europeanized black elites of modern West Africa.

But perhaps the surest bridge between the two cultures was the one unaffected by literacy: music. Popular music was performed at court, and it was incorporated into more complex compositions; popular songs and dance tunes were printed and sold. A great deal of the best baroque church music, especially in Germany where the tradition of choral singing was particularly strong, was composed for audience participation. Many city churches in Germany commissioned organ concerts open to the public, and later in the century many cities maintained their own opera house, also open to the public. Governments saw music as a vehicle for proclaiming their glory and power, using it to impress as well as to entertain their subjects and their visitors. In Venice, for example, composers were encouraged by the senate to experiment with various combinations of solo voices, choirs and instruments in order to achieve the greatest impact. The results could be electrifying. When Thomas Coryat, an experienced traveller, attended the patronal festival at the Scuola di San Rocco in Venice in 1608, he was overwhelmed by the music 'which was both vocall and instrumental, so good, so delectable, so rare, so admirable, so super-excellent, that it did even ravish and stupify all those strangers that never heard the like . . . For mine owne part . . . I was for the time even rapt up with St Paul into the third heaven.'[4]

2. *Elite Culture*

Thomas Coryat was fortunate. He was able to enjoy, at no expense to himself, an entertainment that had cost a great deal to produce – and he knew it. Early modern connoisseurs had an even keener awareness of the value of the arts than our own society. Travellers like Coryat always recorded the price as well as the description of a work of art, often entering more detail about costs than appearance: and where it was hard to give a firm price (as with a large building), the approximate worth was calculated from the time taken in construction and the quality of the materials used. Works of art were seen as valuable capital assets, to be hoarded as well as enjoyed, and to be disposed of in case of need. Thus when the Marquis Boniface Doria, living in Danzig, lost part of his fortune in a shipwreck in 1593, he sold his considerable library to the city in return for free lodgings and an annuity: Doria's investment in culture in fact paid better dividends than his last commercial venture. Admittedly, the magistrates of Danzig were more art-conscious than most. In 1604 they decided that the series of 'grotesque' canvases painted on commission twelve years before by Jan Vredeman de Vries for their town hall were unworthy of the city, and they had them removed, ordering instead a new series of 25 allegorical pictures by Isaac van den Blocke which depicted the apotheosis of Danzig and glorified the patricians who ruled it.

The Danzig city fathers patronized art because it was beautiful, of course; but they also liked its capacity to influence others and to indicate the status and wealth of the patron and owner.

This mercenary attitude towards art may seem distasteful, but it was important: without it, during the turbulent years of the mid-century, it is unlikely that so many cultural activities could have been supported on a troubled continent. Instead of being disrupted by war, European art (at least) seemed to be stimulated by it: countries which were mostly at peace, like England and France, produced few great artists; while the Netherlands, Italy and Spain, which were at war for most of the first half of the century, produced some of the greatest works of European painting – many of them on martial subjects: Velásquez's *Surrender of Breda*, Rubens's *Horrors of War*, and many others. Almost every major victory occasioned one or more works of art: Spinola's capture of Breda in 1625 inspired not only Velásquez but also Snaeyers and Callot to produce pictures, and Calderón to produce a play. Only in the Holy Roman Empire does war seem to have crippled art, although the extent of this must not be exaggerated. Few of the princely courts of Germany possessed a flourishing artistic school on the eve of the Thirty Years' War. Although a ducal *Kunstkammer* (a 'gallery of culture') had been established in most princely courts (Bavaria's possessed 3407 items by 1598), few of the objects in the collection were produced by local artists; most were gathered abroad – which was cheaper than maintaining an atelier of one's own. The major exception in the pre-war Empire was in Prague during the reign of Rudolf II, where a team of artists, smiths and engravers worked under the Emperor's personal daily supervision in the newly constructed 'Spanish wing' of the Hradschin. But after Rudolf's death in 1612 the workshops were abandoned, the carefully planned gardens were neglected and the menagerie of rare animals was dispersed. What was left of the Rudolfine collection was plundered like the collections of other dead princes of the mannerist age in Heidelberg and Munich, by Spanish, Italian and Swedish armies. The choicest works of German mannerist art were sent back to Madrid, Rome and Stockholm.

The great musical tradition of Germany survived the war rather better, although there was considerable disruption. Many of the numerous town music societies which had been modelled on those of Italy – the *Musikkränzlein* at Wörms (1561) and Nuremberg (1568), the *Convivia Musica* at Görlitz (1570), the music 'colleges' at Frankfurt (1588) and Mühlhausen (1617) – were forced to close during the war. Even the princes were obliged to reduce their musical patronage. As early as 1623, one composer lamented that the war had placed a spear in the hand of princes with which to kill musicians, just as the Devil had given Saul a spear to kill the harpist David: 'Saul's spear is . . . in the hands of court finance ministers who lock their doors when they hear musicians approach.' Heinrich Schütz, court musician of Electoral Saxony and probably the finest composer of his day, was compelled to arrange short choral pieces of religious music for only 'one, two, three or four voices with two violins, 'cello and organ' because the war left him neither choirs nor orchestras for anything grander. Schütz left Saxony altogether in 1628–9 and 1633–40 because 'the times neither demand nor allow music on a big scale . . . It is now impossible to perform music on a large scale or with many choirs'.[5] In 1641, the musical director of Hamburg, Thomas Selle, complained that he had only four good singers of each voice – and Hamburg was a city relatively unaffected by the war. But in Lübeck, in 1646, Franz Tunder began a series of lunchtime and Sunday evening concerts in St Mary's Church to entertain the Lutheran business community, and the musical culture of Germany recovered quickly to become the strongest in Europe after 1700. Schütz returned, joining Buxtehude, Hammerschmidt and Froberger, and before long there were Bach, Handel, Telemann and a host of others.

The greatest musical innovation of this period was not made in Germany, however, but in Florence, by a group of musical enthusiasts led by Vincenzo Galilei and known as the *Cammerata*. From the 1580s, they began to experiment with new techniques of composition and performance, gradually evolving into the Opera, an attempt to resurrect the multi-media theatre of ancient Athens: orchestra, chorus and solo voices were combined to provide a stage spectacle of impressive proportions. The first known opera is Peri's *Eurydice* of 1597, and the new genre was soon perfected by the Venetian Claudio Monteverdi, whose *Orfeo* (1607) is still regularly performed. This work required a cast of over a hundred, an unprecedented figure for the time, and subsequent operas required even more. The invention and popularity of this new musical form was important (and, despite the expense of production, it flourished and developed throughout the period). Operas encouraged princes to maintain a larger corps of performers, for whom other types of mass music could then be composed (such as the *concerto*).

Perhaps the major innovation to take place in European literature at this time was the growing popularity of the novel. The genre began in Spain as a reaction to the chivalric romances still favoured by many writers at the end of the sixteenth century (the anti-chivalric reaction is particularly evident in the most famous novel of the period, *Don Quixote*, published in two parts in 1605 and 1615). From Spain the new literary form quickly spread, encouraged partly by the Counter-Reformation church which preferred the apparently truthful realism of the novel (in which the wicked received punishment, saw the error of their ways, and were redeemed) to the escapist and 'untrue' chivalric and pastoral romances (but see also page 335 below). Eighteen separate translations of Mateo Alemán's *Guzmán de Alfarache* (two parts, 1599 and 1604), the first full-length novel, were published in France during the seventeenth century. The same work, like most other picaresque Spanish novels, was translated into German and printed in Munich (centre of the German Counter-Reformation). Plagiarism of these works was also common: the *Guzmán de Alfarache* clearly shaped the form of Grimmelshausen's *Simplicissimus* (1669) and probably influenced John Bunyan's *Life and Death of Mr Badman*

(1680); López de Ubeda's *Pícara Justina*, published in Spain in 1605, may or may not have inspired Defoe's *Moll Flanders* (1722), but it certainly determined much of Grimmelshausen's *Mother Courage* (even the titles were the same in German: *Die Landstörtzerin Justina*, 1627; *Die Landstörtzerin Courasche*, 1670). Nor was plagiarism of Spanish originals confined to novels: over twenty Jacobean plays derive from Spanish sources, and the plays of Calderón and Lope de Vega were performed, in translation, in many parts of Europe. Likewise, the mystical books and poems of St Teresa of Avila, St John of the Cross and others were welcomed in France and played an important role in the Catholic revival there, directed by Pierre de Bérulle (page 52 above).

There were several reasons for this primacy of Spanish literature in the first half of the seventeenth century. First, there was its undoubted quality: Spain's political decline seems to have given a distinctive cutting edge to her prose and drama and an allusive mystical resignation to her poetry. Don Francisco de Quevedo, one of the greatest Golden Age writers, once described a collection of essays – *La Hora de Todos* – as 'making one laugh with anger and desperation'; and it is that acerbic quality, caused by frustration at Spain's growing impotence, which marked out Spanish literature from the rest.[6] But there was more to the matter than simple excellence. The works of the Englishmen Milton, Donne, Jonson and Shakespeare were by no means inferior; neither, perhaps, were those of the Dutch writers Hooft, Bredero and Vondel. But these luminaries were less influential because they wrote in languages which were read by relatively few people. Spanish was the language of a world empire and a Spanish-reading public existed outside Spain: in the South Netherlands (where almost 400 Spanish editions were printed during the period from 1598 to 1648), in the New World, in the Habsburg *Erbländer* and in Italy. The only comparable popular language was French, but until the mid-century French literary figures failed to find a market, even in France: the first successful modern French play, Corneille's *Le Cid* (typically, based on a Spanish original), only received a performance in 1637; and in 1645 lack of demand forced even Molière to leave Paris and take his theatrical company on a thirteen-year tour of the provinces. The most popular French novels of the day – Madelène de Scudéry's *Le Grand Cyrus* (in ten parts with 15,000 pages, 1649–53) and *Clélie* (also in ten parts with 8000 pages, 1654–60) – owed their popularity to the author's satirization of contemporary society. *Clélie*, set in ancient Rome, made fun of French bourgeois life; *Cyrus* was a thinly veiled portrait of the leading French aristocratic families of the day (Cyrus himself was obviously Condé, and so on). Madelène de Scudéry owed her popularity – and, despite their length, both books were almost immediately translated into English (five volumes each) – to the fact that she was writing in a major European language and about a country that was already able to influence the rest of European culture. Writing in 1648, the cultivated Lucasz Opalinski regretted that even Poland was affected: 'France seems to be the only country, excluding Spain, that sets the tone for all European peoples in decoration and clothes. And whatever she invents or introduces is considered beautiful and fashionable . . . She arbitrarily demands that others observe her customs and condemns those who oppose her.' Opalinski lamented the uniformity – 'the French way of life should not be binding on everybody else' – but it nevertheless increased (while that of Spain waned), until in 1688 the German professor Christian Thomasius advised his students to imitate the French 'for they are the cleverest people these days, and know how to give everything a special sort of life. They make their clothes well and comfortably . . . They are able to prepare their meals so well that both taste and stomach are satisfied . . . Their language is graceful and seductive.'[7]

One area where France failed to establish cultural superiority before 1650 was the fine arts. Spain failed too: the fame of the great Spanish painters – Velásquez, Ribalta, Zurbarán, Murillo – was almost entirely confined to Spain; only José de Ribera was famous outside the peninsula during his own lifetime, and that was because from 1611 until his death in 1652 he painted in Italy. By contrast, the artists of the Netherlands were known all over Europe: the Breughel family, Rubens and van Dyck from the southern provinces; Rembrandt, Hals, Vermeer and a galaxy of others from the north. The difference was not so much one of quality – few would care to adjudicate between Velásquez and Rembrandt – as of subject-matter and patronage. In the later Middle Ages religious subjects had predominated in the output of all painters, but with the spread of Renaissance learning secular subjects became more common. Of 2239 dated Italian paintings which are known from the years 1420–1539, 87 per cent (or 1796 canvases) were religious in subject – half of them depicting mainly the Virgin, one-quarter Christ and one-quarter the saints; and 13 per cent (237 canvases) were secular, one-quarter of them portraits. In the Netherlands, of 271 canvases produced by the eight leading Dutch artists active between 1460 and 1533, no more than 16 dealt with non-religious subjects. The number of secular paintings increased with the passage of time, with some later artists producing virtually no religious art. Outside the Low Countries, however, religious subjects predominated in the repertoire of almost all artists. The exceptions were few: the peasant pictures of the Le Nain brothers, the landscapes and classical scenes of Poussin or Claude Lorraine. Even the acknowledged eccentrics – Caravaggio and El Greco – painted mainly religious subjects (and the former lived in the houses of cardinals for much of his career, while the latter served as a part-time interpreter for the Holy Inquisition of Toledo).

This predominance of religious subjects in southern Europe was a consequence of the role of the Catholic church as a patron: the new religious orders founded amid the enthusiasm of the Counter-Reformation all required new churches and chapels, and new pictures to fill them. It would be wrong, however, to suggest that the church forced religious art upon an unwilling world (although it did impose strict controls on the conventions of that art: the nudes in Michelangelo's *Last Judgement* were painted over with garments as early as 1566; and Paolo Veronese was forced to retitle his *Last Supper*

'Feast at the House of Levi', because the Inquisition considered that his treatment was not serious enough). In the first place, many artists preferred on personal grounds to paint religious canvases, turning down more lucrative secular contracts in order to work for the church. Tintoretto, for example, supplied pictures for the Venetian *Scuola* of San Rocco very cheaply. Secondly, many lay patrons also demanded religious paintings: Philip II of Spain had amassed 250 in the Escorial alone by the time of his death in 1598. Thirdly, even with commissions which were apparently secular, there might be religious aspects. Thus, the magnificent panels painted by Rubens for the roof of the banqueting hall of Whitehall palace in London were intended to exalt the Stuart dynasty, but the central panel depicted the apotheosis of James VI and I, his ascent to heaven assisted by nubile handmaidens and (more appropriately) a host of attractive small boys.

The Whitehall ceiling was typical of the prevailing style of patronage in seventeenth-century Europe: the commissioned work. Rubens was persuaded to undertake the ceilings by Charles I during a diplomatic visit to England, for a fee of £3000. The Antwerp master had already completed the great series of canvases commemorating the triumphs of Marie de Medici of France for the Luxembourg palace in Paris, so he was only required to produce sketches for the Whitehall sequence before he was given the commission (which was completed in 1634). But most patrons required detailed sketches (and, in the case of sculptors and gold- or silversmiths, models too). Some artists were subjected to much closer supervision: they were required to submit their work for regular inspection and were paid their fee in instalments. Sometimes artists were required to live in the house of their master and received a regular salary like the servants (younger artists appeared in household lists together with dwarfs and butlers; more famous ones with secretaries and councillors). It was tiresome but, as one art historian of the time observed: 'To establish one's name it is vital to start with the patronage of some great man.' Most artists considered a modicum of interference in their work a cheap price to pay for their keep.

Often the patron's supervisory functions were delegated. Charles I seems to have been one of the few great princes of his day who directed in person the cultural activities of his court: negotiating successfully the purchase of the entire Gonzaga collection from Mantua in 1627–8 for £25,000; excising with his own hand a passage in Massinger's play, *A New Way to Pay Old Debts*, which criticized ship-money; commissioning, and performing in, plays and masques. Other monarchs were less determined. Although Philip IV might climb ladders to discuss the design of palace ceilings with his artists, he came to rely increasingly on Velásquez to arrange the artistic affairs of his court; in Tuscany, Bernardo Buontalenti supervised the team of decorative and reproductive artists at the court of the grand dukes of Tuscany, concentrated after 1588 in the ground floor of the great Uffizi building in Florence, newly built by Vasari. Most famous of all, Gian Lorenzo Bernini dominated the style of all other architects, artists and sculptors in Rome and therefore, to some extent, also those in the countries which looked to Rome for examples of what was considered to be 'Catholic art'. This practice of making one man the arbiter of the artistic taste of an entire court was important, for it created consistency, even uniformity, in the decorative and representational art produced in Europe. The works of art created at the courts of Rudolf II in Prague or of Urban VIII in Rome, for example, are so distinctive as to be instantly recognizable.

However, complete control could not be maintained indefinitely. Long before Bernini's death in 1680 there were many artists in Rome who were beyond his influence. Most of them had been in the service of Urban VIII and were summarily dismissed a few months after his death in 1644 as part of a vendetta against the late Pope and all his works (Urban's family was exiled in 1645 and their estates were confiscated). The dismissed artists now had to sell their work on the open market in order to make a living and, gradually, a group of dealers grew up to handle this new trade. They numbered

100 by 1674, with their sale-rooms and galleries grouped around the Piazza Navona, recently beautified by Bernini's great fountain. They attracted a new sort of middle-class client who perhaps saw paintings not only as a good investment and an aesthetic delight, but also as a cheap form of ostentation. The dealers and their clients demanded a wide range of pictures, but above all small canvases. It was thanks to them that paintings of scenes from everyday life (*bambocciate*) became a feature of Italian art for the first time.

The same development took place in the North Netherlands art. The still-lifes, tavern scenes and so on were bought even by craftsmen, shopkeepers and farmers. ''Tis an ordinary thing to find a common farmer lay out two or three thousand pounds in this commodity. Their houses are full of them,' John Evelyn noted in his diary during a visit to Holland in 1641, observing that the favourite purchases were 'landscapes and drolleries (as they call these clownish [sc. peasant] representations)'. The previous year Peter Mundy, a seasoned English traveller, had also commented on the frequency with which all in general strove 'to adorne their houses, especially the outer or street roome, with costly pieces . . . yes, many tymes blacksmithes, coblers, etc., will have some picture or other by their forge and in their stalle. Such is the generall notion, enclination and delight that these countrie natives have to painting.'[8] In the Netherlands, too, pictures were handled by dealers and sold at exhibitions, even at fairs, and artists were able to specialize to an unprecedented degree, confident that somewhere they would find a market for a large number of very similar pictures: the seascapes of van der Velde, the stoic cattle of Albert Cuyp, the ice-skaters of Hendrik Averkamp, the battle scenes of Sebastian Vranckx, the tavern cameos of David Teniers. Sometimes these specialists produced a large consignment of similar works – Adriaan van Ostade once supplied 28 'drolleries' for 40 florins – rather as an artisan might produce boots or saucepans. Several artists were indeed also artisans on the side: van der Velde traded in linen, Hobbema was a tax-collector, van Goyen sold tulips, and Jan Steen was an innkeeper.

It might have been expected that the expanding number of patrons, each with his own taste in art, would produce a wide variety of styles; but this was not always the case. All over Europe, and in all art forms, there was a transition from the sophisticated inventiveness of 'mannerism' to the vigorous monumentality of 'baroque', and the personal taste of a patron could expedite (as in the case of Urban VIII at Rome) or delay (as with Rudolf II at Prague) the change; but that was all.[9] Almost everywhere we find, in 1600, the urge to fill every available space (whether on a canvas or an *objet d'art*) with a figure; almost everywhere those figures were made either larger and more muscular than life, or (a perverse fascination of Rudolf II's artists in particular) more abnormal and freakish; and everywhere the artist tried to provide, in his work, a link between his public and the natural world in which they lived. The contorted, mystical figures of El Greco, painted in Toledo, are as much a part of 'mannerism' as the assemblies of animal or vegetable forms used by Arcimboldo in Prague to produce portraits of Rudolf II and his leading courtiers. Although these eccentricities were gradually forgotten as the simpler, monumental baroque style spread, other mannerist preoccupations survived: the idea of realism in representation (which led engravers to pour their plaster over newly dead reptiles in order to make their casts life-like); the desire to use natural forms (large Indian snail and sea shells were used by goldsmiths to make graceful bowls and ewers and were sold for £100 and more in the early seventeenth century); the convention that works of art should not be functional (which made them less permanent, for when they had ceased to be fashionable, or when their aesthetic value was unappreciated, they were given away or, in the case of gold and silver work, melted down).

Once again the role of the patron emerges as a crucial influence on the development of artistic styles. It was also vital in the youngest field of European cultural endeavour: science. During the 1640s and 1650s there was an unprecedented spate of books published on scientific subjects, especially on agriculture, mathematics and medicine. In England at least, more young men were recruited into science and medicine between 1645 and 1660 than at any other time during the century. At the same time groups of learned men began to hold formal meetings to discuss science, the most famous being the Invisible College centred around Robert Boyle the chemist and John Wallis the mathematician, which met in London in the later 1640s, moved to Oxford in the 1650s and became the Royal Society in 1661.

These developments were furthest advanced in England, where they received early support from Lord Chancellor Francis Bacon (author of two important works on scientific method: the *Novum organum* and the *Instauratio magna*, both of 1620), and where they later appealed to the millenarian eschatology of the Puritans (who believed that traditional civilization was about to end and that, through science, God would restore to Man that dominance over nature which Adam had lost, thus giving Man the means to achieve a new world). However, learned societies and scientific experimenters were to be found in most of Europe: the thermometer (1641) and the barometer (1644) were invented in Italy; the first telescope (1608) and the first accurate clock, controlled by a pendulum (1657), were made in Holland; the first reliable astronomical tables (1627) and the first experiments with the vacuum and electricity (1654) were made in the Holy Roman Empire; the crucial observations which proved that the planets move around the sun in elliptical orbits were made in Venice, Vienna, Ingolstadt, Danzig, Paris and Denmark . . . Moreover, each advance was relayed from one centre of experiment to the others. The leading scholars of the day – Justus Lipsius in the Netherlands, Erychius Puteanus in Italy, Heinrich Rantzau in Danish Holstein, Marin Mersenne in France – conducted an enormous correspondence with an impressive international collection of humanist colleagues. They even began to publish their letters, so that other friends could enjoy them: in the 1590s Lipsius began to issue his letters regularly in separate collections of one hundred, printed by Plantin in Antwerp and Wechel in Frankfurt. Knowledge was disseminated in print in many ways. Some publications were intended for scholars, such as Riccioli's *Almagestum novum* of 1651 (presenting an up-to-date survey of astronomical knowledge with full footnote references to other published work); others were aimed at a general readership, such as Galileo's *Starry Messenger* of 1610 (which not only described and reproduced his sensational observations of the moon and planets by telescope, but explained how to build a similar instrument so that the doubtful could perform the same experiments themselves).

The same eager diffusion of new knowledge occurred in the occult sciences, which also flourished at this time. The works of Dr John Dee (the English magus who chose an astrologically propitious day for the coronation of Queen Elizabeth I and was thereafter regularly consulted at his house in Mortlake by the monarch) were read from Prague to Madrid, and his services were in great demand in many countries (he worked abroad between 1583 and 1589, holding séances for aristocratic clients at Krakow, Prague and Trebon). And Dee was but one of the hundreds of astrologers who flourished in England between 1558 and 1714. Others were perhaps less famous abroad, but made a better living at home. William Lilley, the most famous English magus of the seventeenth century, had a practice between 1641 and his death in 1667 which approached two thousand cases a year; and he influenced far more people through his almanacks (which, during the 1650s, justified the Cromwellian republic and urged readers to support the new regime – not for nothing did he receive a government pension of £100 a year!) and his books (of which the most famous, *The Christian Astrologer* of 1647, explained how to cast one's own horoscope).

There was, however, a considerable overlap between religion and magic, and between natural and occult science. Few people at the time drew any distinction between them. Great astrologers like Dee or Kepler were also great mathematicians and astronomers. The interrelationship of all human knowledge was still an accepted fact, reflected in the delicate 'culture cabinets' (*Kunstschränke*) made in Germany in the decades around 1600, whose drawers and cupboards contained a vast selection of articles illustrating the whole range of human knowledge – classical mythology, humanist philosophy, chemical and alchemical knowledge, even games and toys – and taken from all known civilizations – Islamic, Jewish, Catholic and Protestant.

The intellectual community of Europe was divided neither by subject nor by nationality. French propagandists could still praise the Spaniards: Cardinal Bossuet's funeral oration for Condé, victor of Rocroi and Lens, contains one of the finest tributes to Spanish bravery to be found anywhere. Even a maverick intellectual like Jan Amos Comenius, with his advanced views on education, religious unity and scientific endeavour, could find a welcome in several countries – England, Holland and Sweden – after the collapse of the rebellion in his native Moravia in 1620. René Descartes fled from France to Holland and Sweden; Heinrich Schütz retreated from Saxony to Venice; Hugo Grotius escaped from Holland to Sweden. The freedom of movement for intellectuals in seventeenth-century Europe was one of their strongest assets. It helped to keep the elite culture of the continent unified and it assisted the 'republic of letters' to withstand the political, social and economic crises of the time. But there was one important exception: there was very little interchange of ideas or intellectuals between east and west. It was as if an Iron Curtain had come down across Europe during the sixteenth century, separating the peoples of the Russian and Turkish empires, at least, from the rest. The problem is to determine with precision its nature and its location: was Poland in front of it or behind it? And what of Hungary or Transylvania?

3. East and West: an Iron Curtain?

Of course there was a physical frontier: the steppe, or grass plains, which ran through south-east Europe from Hungary through the Ukraine to central Asia. This steppe frontier was largely depopulated except for the settlements of border raiders known as uskoks in Croatia, hajduks in Hungary, and cossacks farther east on the Christian side, and akinci and Tatars respectively, on the other side. But a geographical contrast was not only observable in the south. To the north of Poland and Muscovy lay an almost impenetrable forest belt and the uncharted Arctic Ocean. Forests were also frequent and dense in the fertile plain of 'black earth' where most Poles and Muscovites lived, and the abundance of timber dominated their lives. Wood was used to make their farm tools, their industrial machines, their houses, and even their churches. In 1600, of 447 parish churches in Mazovia, the core-area of Poland around Warsaw, 342 (76 per cent) were built of wood, and the rest were almost all of very recent construction and were situated in the prosperous royal or episcopal towns. In Muscovy, by the 1670s almost every town had a citadel but only twenty, of which the Moscow Kremlin was the most famous, had one built of brick or stone. The rest were all of wood. The pattern of human settlement also changed as the traveller moved eastwards. A landscape of hamlets and isolated farmsteads with numerous towns built of stone gave way to one of widely spaced but large villages, with few towns, built of wood. The density of population as a whole decreased dramatically as the traveller moved eastwards: from 35 per square kilometre in the West Netherlands to 20 per square kilometre in Poland, to 10 in Lithuania, and to just over 3 in Muscovy in 1600. This was a contrast which excited comment both from eastern travellers in the west and from western travellers in the east. Another was the cost and availability of foodstuffs. The accounts of travellers like Fynes Morison noted that where food was expensive, as in Italy, the Rhineland and the Alpine lands, it was also plentiful; and that where it was cheap, as in the Baltic lands, it was so scarce that meat had to be brought along on the hoof if one wished to be sure of having some to eat.

The sparseness of human population and produce east of the Elbe was connected with the climate: the growing season was short, especially in Russia. Whereas a French or Dutch farmer could count on eight or nine months in which to grow his crops, his Slav counterpart could only make use of four (around Novgorod), five (around Moscow), or six months (around Kiev). It is true that the summer months were far hotter than in the west, as the English traveller Dr Giles Fletcher noted in his description of Russia published in 1591, but the winters were so cold and lasted so long that travellers were frozen to death in their sleds and in the street, while wolves and bears made regular attacks on isolated villages. But for the abundance of furs, Fletcher opined, human life in Russia would be impossible. Average winter temperatures around Smolensk are −5°C; around Moscow they are −10°C; around Kazan they are −15°C. Such a disadvantageous climate helps to explain the extremely low productivity of agriculture, with yields of three ears of corn per grain sown, or less; but climate alone was not responsible. After all, the Scandinavian lands, with growing seasons just as short, were able to produce far more. In Russia and Poland the effects of climate were intensified by a distinctive family structure. In western Europe (including Scandinavia), the typical household comprised a mature married couple, their children and their servants; but in eastern and parts of southern Europe, the prevailing model was totally different, since an individual couple and their young children and adolescent servants simply did not have muscles and hands enough to plant, harrow and harvest enough land for their sustenance in time. Households made up of several related families were therefore the rule, with many couples married at the age of twelve or thirteen, under the control of the senior male (the *bol'shak*, or boss, in Russia; the *Wirth*, or manager, in the German Baltic communities). Perhaps three-quarters of the population of eastern Europe lived in these multiple-family households, and the women married and had their children at a younger age than those in the west. The average size of household in Poland was between seven and nine, in Russia fourteen. This form of social organization facilitated a process which was noted all over eastern Europe between 1550 and 1650: refeudalization.

In the course of the sixteenth and seventeenth centuries, one east European country after another passed legislation intended both to increase the labour services required from its peasants and to terminate their freedom to move from one estate to another. There were exceptions, of course – many serfs were freed after long service or as a reward for bravery in warfare; in 1572 Jan Przypkowski in Poland freed all his serfs in the five villages which he owned because as a Unitarian he believed serfdom was wrong – but, on the whole, serfdom was as basic to the economy of eastern Europe as slavery had been to that of the Roman Empire. Naturally serfdom did not take the same form in all places and at all times. The obligation of the peasants to cultivate their lord's domain was almost universal, it is true, but the manner of performing it differed: in Russia, sometimes seven days' service a week was required, and one of the peasant's family had to work continuously on the domain (providing his own equipment with which to do it); in Brandenburg all children of the serfs could be compelled to work as household servants of the lord for up to four years (the *Gesindezwangsdienst*); in Hungary the two systems were combined and in 1651 a court judge informed some peasant litigants that 'they were not bound to perform any special *corvée*, but they must do whatever their lord commanded'. Other judges agreed: in Hungary, at least, there was no limit to a lord's labour entitlement. By contrast, in Austria labour services were restricted after a major peasant revolt in 1595–7 to two weeks a year. In Danish Holstein, at the other extreme of the German-speaking lands, peasants were required to produce not only grain, wool, butter, cheese and horses for their lord on his estates, but even to take his ships to sea and catch herring and other fish for him to sell to merchants. The peasants who lived on a large seigneurial estate were members of a state-within-a-state. Gradually the lord acquired complete military, economic, fiscal and legal powers over his subjects (*Untertanen* in the German-speaking lands, often prefaced by adjectives such as *schlecht* – nasty, worthless – or *gemain* – vulgar). If the peasants challenged the lord's decrees or refused his demands, his courts would condemn them, and often (in Poland after 1518, for instance) the prince refused to intervene in matters involving master and serf. If the peasants tried to escape, the lord's officers were empowered to pursue, recover and punish them. The landowners of the Great European Plain were creating, as the Prussian reformer Stein noted in 1802, 'the den of a predator which lays waste everything around it and surrounds itself with the silence of the grave'.[10] In many ways, losing the freedom of personal movement was the critical step in this process, and the date at which it occurred in each major state is listed in Table 9. (Poland is omitted because freedom of movement was, in fact, never removed.)

The rural population was reduced to the status of serfs mainly in order to extend the area which the lords farmed directly. At first, new seigneurial domains were formed by bringing fresh lands under cultivation and by reclaiming areas abandoned in the later middle ages; but after about 1600 (half a century later in Germany, thanks to the devastation of the Thirty Years' War), domains expanded mostly at the expense of peasant smallholdings. This, however, created a dilemma: peasants without smallholdings could no longer perform labour services in return for their land – for they now had none. Instead they needed wages. There came a point, therefore, at which the lesser gentry in eastern Europe began to experience a fall in their incomes, for although they were legally entitled to more services from their tenants, there were fewer tenants to provide them. Only the great lords, whose estates produced a large agricultural surplus which could be sold for export, could afford to hire wage-labourers or servants on a permanent basis to make up the shortfall in labour dues. Elsewhere, the land under cultivation declined in the century following 1570, especially after 1620 when war and plagues reduced the population. In 1685, the area cultivated on the Polish estates of the archbishopric of Gniezno (most of which lay between Warsaw and Kalisz) was, on

Table 9. The 'Second Serfdom' in Eastern Europe

State	*Date at which freedom of movement was removed by courts*
Hungary	1608
Courland	1632
Ducal Prussia	1633
Mecklenburg	1645
Pomerania	1645
Muscovy	1649
Brandenburg	1653

average, 25 per cent smaller than it had been in 1620. At Gniezno itself, 96 units of land were cultivated in 1512, but only 12 in 1685.

The decline of arable cultivation in Muscovy was even more catastrophic (again through a combination of re-enserfment, war and disruption): in the province of Moscow, in the 1590s, the church of the Holy Trinity was able to till only 30 per cent of the area farmed in the 1560s; and the Kirhatz monastery was cultivating only 26 per cent. The peasants who remained, moreover, were left to carry on their work with primitive tools: it would seem that the lords expected the serfs to improve their equipment (which would be used mainly on the smallholdings), but that the impoverishment of the peasantry prevented this. Scarcely any iron was used in agriculture, either in Russia or Poland, until the eighteenth century: ploughs had wooden mould-boards and harrows had wooden teeth. (In many parts of Russia – everywhere, indeed, apart from the Dvina basin in the north and the steppe in the south – the wheeled plough was unknown until the late seventeenth century; instead the *sokha*, a two-tine fork with no mould-board, was used.) Windmills and watermills were extremely rare before 1700, the former because the high forests sheltered the sails from any wind, the latter because the sluggish rivers and endless plains of Muscovy made it almost impossible to accumulate enough head of water to turn a mill-wheel.

The only estates in eastern Europe which appear to have prospered, both relatively and absolutely, were those of the magnates along the great rivers which flowed to the Baltic. The Vistula, Niemen, Pregel, Dvina and Oder, and their tributaries, carried vast consignments of forest and agricultural produce, above all rye, to the Baltic ports where western merchants – especially the Dutch – provided salt, textiles and other goods, as well as silver coin, in exchange for the grain without which the Atlantic and Mediterranean cities of Europe would starve. The trade down the Vistula alone employed some 28,000 men. Although the primacy of Danzig as the mart where east and west met began to wane after 1630, even in the 1640s an average of 1500 ships were entering and leaving the port every year. And to some extent the decline of Danzig was offset by the rise of Archangel, Königsberg, Riga and Narva. The Baltic lands of eastern Europe, at least, were fully integrated with the growing economy of the Atlantic states. Despite their diverging modes of production – feudal capitalism in the east; bourgeois capitalism in the west – there were no barriers between the two economic systems.

The same was true of the Ottoman Empire. The political frontier made little difference to the way of life of the people along the border. There was a constant stream of peasant fugitives from Poland and Muscovy who took refuge from their lords in the Ottoman Empire, and many Jews did the same. The peasants of Turkish Hungary or Transylvania produced food in much the same way as their Habsburg neighbours, except that the taxes levied by the state appear to have been more erratic in the Ottoman part – the frontier provinces of Srem and Szeged appear to have paid under 10 per cent of their agricultural produce to the government, while the inland province of Semendire paid 25 per cent. Farther south, the peoples of the Mediterranean differed little, whether they served Islamic or Christian overlords – or both, as in the case of the Ragusans. This small Italian-speaking, staunchly Catholic Adriatic state, under Turkish protection from 1430, maintained 51 consulates in the Mediterranean in the later sixteenth century and survived as a prosperous commercial polity until an earthquake in 1667 destroyed most of the city. Other Balkan cities also divided their loyalties between Moslem and Christian: even in 1600 Istanbul was still to a large extent a Greek city, and Greek Orthodox culture was still influential. All along the political frontier there was lively trade between the Turks and the west, both by sea – most of it carried on by French, Italian and (after about 1580) by English and Dutch merchants – and by land, by Habsburg subjects using the Danube valley, by Russians using the Volga and by Poles and Russians travelling overland through Moldavia. Oriental luxury goods, either manufactured by Ottoman craftsmen or else transported by Moslem merchants from the Far East, were exchanged for western textiles, western silver, and Russian furs.

Western merchants who visited eastern Europe, whether Ottoman or Muscovite, commented not upon the economic contrasts, such as they were, but upon the political and religious differences. Europe east of the Elbe and south of the Danube was a land of absolutism: the phenomenon appeared earlier there than in the west and it lasted longer. The two empires of the east, in particular, were far larger in size than anything in the west (between 1580 and 1649

Russian colonists annexed the whole of Siberia, from the Urals to the Pacific, for Muscovy); and undoubtedly the Tsar and the Sultan were both autocratic and absolute rulers to an extent which was the envy of most western princes. They commanded a large standing army and had at their disposal an efficient bureaucracy staffed by a trained service nobility (the *pomeschiki* and the *devshirme* respectively); neither had to deal with a powerful landed aristocracy (both the boyars and the timariots were emasculated in the later sixteenth century) and neither had to face a challenge from an independent church (the Sultan was Caliph, or religious leader of Islam; the Tsar was undisputed head of the Orthodox religion in Russia).

So different was this situation that western ambassadors sent to either country tended to regard their appointment as a death sentence. When Dr Giles Fletcher returned to the comfort of his fellow's rooms in King's College, Cambridge, after an embassy to the Tsar of Russia in 1590, he sighed gratefully to a colleague that 'the poets cannot fansie Ulysses more glad to be come out of the den of Polyphemus, than he was to be rid out of the power of such a barbarous prince'.[11] He thought he was lucky to have kept his head: he had seen many who had not. And yet these despotic rulers entered into diplomatic relations with many Christian states, even small ones. The Sultan used Ragusa as an espionage centre from which to monitor movements in the whole Mediterranean; he tolerated the presence in his capital of regular ambassadors from France (after 1536), England (after 1583) and the Dutch (after 1612); and he made regular commercial 'capitulations', first with individual merchant communities resident in the chief cities of the Empire, and, after 1569, with the western states themselves, granting them general privileges.

The Tsar also intervened in the politics of his western neighbours, most spectacularly during the Thirty Years' War when, from 1628 to 1633, Sweden was allowed to import large quantities of Russian grain at cost price and free of all duties. This foreign aid played a crucial role in keeping the armies of Gustavus Adolphus in the field against the Habsburgs and their ally (Russia's arch-enemy), the king of Poland.

There was a sharp ideological clash between Russia and Poland, for political enmity was reinforced by religious rivalry. From the twelfth century onwards, the Devil was invariably depicted by Russian artists as clean-shaven and dressed like a Pole. The Russians distrusted and despised Renaissance learning and its adherents: if any western Christian strayed into an Orthodox church, the building was at once swept and purified afterwards. And yet there was, surprisingly, some contact between the western churches and the Orthodox creed (both Russian and Greek) in the seventeenth century, first through an effort to learn from the Protestants, then by an emulation of the Catholics. Both Ivan IV and Boris Godunov wished to promote in Russia the study of foreign languages. At first they tried to open schools, but church opposition proved too much; then in 1602 Boris sent thirty young Russians abroad to learn English, French and German. Not one of them ever returned (indeed, one, Nikifor Alferevich Grigoriev, ended up as an Anglican parson in Huntingdonshire until he was deposed by the Puritans in 1634). However, by then the anxiety of the Tsar to forge an alliance against the Polish-Habsburg Catholic bloc encouraged Patriarch Filaret to make contact with the Protestants at a higher level, and he ordered some Calvinist liturgical works to be translated into Church Slavonic; in this he was encouraged by the Patriarch of Istanbul, Cyril Lukaris.

Lukaris epitomized the interchange between east and west: born in Crete and educated in Venice (where he listened to Paolo Sarpi, the opponent of aggressive Tridentine Catholicism), he visited Lithuania and Egypt before becoming senior Orthodox patriarch in 1620. He became leader of a divided creed, for many of his bishops belonged, or wished to belong, to the Uniate church – that group of Lithuanian and Polish Orthodox prelates who in 1596, at the synod of Brest-Litovsk, agreed to acknowledge papal supremacy while retaining their own liturgy. It was as a counterweight to the Uniates, who enjoyed the active support of the papacy and its secular allies, that Lukaris turned to the Protestants for new ideas and new vitality. It was significant that his election took place in the Dutch embassy in Istanbul, where ambassador Cornelis Haga was an old friend of Lukaris, as was the English ambassador, Sir Thomas Roe. In 1628–9 the patriarch made contact with Gustavus Adolphus of Sweden, clearly the leading Lutheran prince, with a view to devising a common creed; and at the same time he received, through the good offices of Haga, a Calvinist secretary (Antoine Léger from Piedmont), who helped him to compose his Calvinist confession, published in Latin and Greek in 1629, of which copies were sent to Charles I of England as well as to Lutheran and Calvinist leaders. He also took steps to secure printed editions of the main Christian texts, a difficult undertaking since the Turks would not allow any printing presses in their empire: from 1632 he sent rare manuscripts to England (where Archbishop Laud placed them in the Bodleian Library) in return for multiple copies, printed in England. He also tried to arrange a similar exchange with Sweden, but with less success.

These links between Lukaris and the Protestants of the west were not popular with the patriarch's colleagues. Four times, with the assistance of the Catholic embassies at Constantinople, they had him deposed; four times, with the aid of the Protestant envoys, he was restored. But in 1638 the patriarch's enemies convinced the Sultan that Lukaris had engineered the cossacks' capture of Azov on the Black Sea, in the name of Muscovy. The patriarch was arrested and strangled; his pro-Catholic enemies were triumphant. Already, in the north, the Orthodox church of the Ukraine (which had not subscribed to the Union of 1596) was using Roman Catholic scholarship and educational techniques to arm itself better against its western rivals. In 1631 a new theological college, modelled on the Jesuit schools, was founded by Archbishop Peter Mohila in Kiev; the staff, some of them Jesuit trained, taught in Latin and used textbooks adapted from the works of western theologians such as Aquinas. In 1645 a short Orthodox catechism, based on the Latin one of Canisius, was printed at Kiev and soon became standard in all the schools of the province. Before long, the new learning spread to Muscovy: the Kiev catechism was reprinted in Moscow in 1649 and at the same time a private school for teaching Latin and Greek was established in the city. A state school followed in 1665, and an Imperial Academy in 1687, thus beginning the process of westernization which was soon to be accelerated by Peter the Great. Between 1675 and 1700, 114 Polish works were translated into Russian, compared with only 13 between 1600 and 1650.

This eastward penetration of western ideas did not take place in the Islamic world, however. A wealth of books – travelogues, chronicles and descriptions as well as translations – were produced and published in the west about the Islamic (and indeed Muscovite) lands and their government and culture. Some western printing firms, such as the Wechel Press at Frankfurt, made works on Oriental topics a regular feature of their production.[12] Some universities quickly promoted Arabic studies: a chair was founded at Leiden in 1613 and another at Oxford in 1634, a lectureship at Cambridge in 1632 and so on. But there was no corresponding movement in the Arab countries: only one Latin work was translated into a Moslem language before 1500, and only a handful before 1650.

The reason for this Islamic indifference was simple: Latin Christendom had had little to offer in the cultural field while the Moslem world was expanding and eclectic; and after about 1500, when the Renaissance had begun to improve western knowledge, the Islamic world felt that the great victories of the Ottomans betokened an intellectual as well as a military superiority. This is not to say that the leaders of Islam were totally unwilling to learn from the west: in the military field, in particular, the Ottomans continually strove to keep abreast of the latest technical innovations developed in the west by welcoming renegade Christian craftsmen (although their expertise was not passed on to native artisans).

Turkish documents and chronicles regularly included imported western terms to refer to new weapons and military techniques, and Turkish craftsmen became adept at copying them. But after about 1600, this routine mimesis was no longer enough; the west used its technological improvements (more mobile field-guns; better firearms) to make tactical and strategic reforms. To copy the new art of war required more than mere mimesis: it called for a reshaping of Ottoman military theory, perhaps of the Ottoman state itself. Not surprisingly, the Turks preferred to remain faithful to the traditional manner of making war which had won victories so many times before. As the Austrian general, de Warnéry, observed in 1770: 'The Turks have changed nothing in their tactics since the days of Suleiman the Magnificent [d. 1566].' Shortly before, the maréchal de Saxe had made much the same point. It was uncommon, he observed, for a nation to learn from its neighbours:

> . . . either through pride, idleness or stupidity. The good ideas are only accepted after infinite delays; and sometimes, even when all the world is convinced of their utility, in spite of everything the new ways are abandoned in favour of habit and tradition . . . The Turks today are in this position: it is neither valour, nor numbers, nor wealth that they lack; it is order, discipline and tactics.[13]

It was here that an Iron Curtain came down across Europe. Although the defeats inflicted on the Ottoman forces caused some ministers, like Katip Celebi (1608–57), to urge the Moslem world to learn from the west, most of the intellectual elite of Islam refused to listen. The divergence of Christian and Moslem cultures therefore proceeded at an accelerating rate, thanks to the high level of military conflict in the sixteenth century. Borrowing anything but weapons seemed to the Turks both unnecessary and disloyal; the successes of Christian traders, which were well known to the Moslem elite, failed to produce any substantial imitation of the foreigners' institutions. Instead, the introverted civilization of

Islam was left intact to face the devastating assaults of the armies and merchants of the west which began with Napoleon's invasion of Egypt in 1798.

The Christian states of north-eastern Europe proved wiser. Poland learned from her defeats by the Swedes and reformed her army along western lines; her Orthodox clergy agreed to accept the supremacy of Rome after 1596, and those that did not, adopted a revised liturgy and purified Scripture. Russia, too, westernized in the course of the seventeenth century, until her armies were able to lay low even the Swedes at Poltava (1709). By that date, Russia and Poland had definitely crossed the Iron Curtain and joined – or perhaps rejoined – the community of European states. Only the Ottoman Empire was left outside.

EXCURSUS I
The Measurement of Literacy (see page 302)

Few topics at present excite more acrimonious debate among historians than whether one can measure literacy by counting signatures on documents. Three different correlations have been deduced from the ability to sign: first, that it was no indication of any ability either to read or to write; second, that it corresponded to an ability to read only; third, that it was a proof of full literacy. It seems to the present writer that the second hypothesis is the most probable, but since the question is of some importance and there is no consensus of opinion, it is worth looking at the evidence in more detail.
1. *Are all signatures genuine?* There are two objections here. First, examples are known of a person signing by copying a *modèle* (or stamp) he carried with him. But it seems that the practice was rare, at least before 1700. Second, there are occasions on which a person who *could* sign might not have been able to: testaments signed by people near to death are obviously unlikely to give a realistic profile of literacy. It may also be that brides who could sign might make a cross if their husbands were illiterate, in order not to embarrass them. Finally, possibly all signatures to important documents – made in a strange room with someone else's pen on unfamiliar paper, and perhaps standing up – were less smooth than they might have been. But in such cases the degree of distortion is unlikely to have been so great that it led a literate person to make a mark.

2. *What should be counted as a 'signature'?* Naturally, penmanship varies from person to person, and has always done so. One might adopt the following schema: A1 – a firm signature with writing attached; A2 – a firm signature with all letters joined; A3 – a signature of well-formed letters but joined with difficulty. Such persons might be said to be fully

literate. B – poor letters and not joined; it is suggested that such people might be able to read, but no more. Categories A and B together would be called 'literate'. C1 – a mark of some sophistication; C2 – a simple cross. These people would be classed as 'illiterate'. But is that correct? Here lies the basic uncertainty of the debate.

3. Does a mark necessarily denote illiteracy? In the first place, in certain areas two languages were current – for instance Welsh and English in Wales, Breton and French in Brittany – and a person might only be able to read one of them: the one not being tested. Second, and more serious, there was a long hiatus for almost everyone between attendance at school and signing a marriage register or a property lease. Some children left school after they had learned only to read, for writing tuition cost more (because it required more skills and not all schoolteachers could give it: in France, schoolmasters seeking employment put one, two or three feathers in their hat according to whether they could teach one, two or all of the 'three Rs' – hence the expression 'A feather in your cap'). There were thus many children who had learnt to read but not to write; they could never have signed anything. There were also many who had perhaps learnt to do both by the time they were thirteen or fourteen, but then left school and thereafter read little and wrote less. Signing the marriage register might be the first time that they had held a pen for fifteen years: failure to sign on an important and isolated occasion did not mean total illiteracy, for they would not have forgotten everything.

4. Conclusion. To some extent, the various objections cancel each other out, and it may be that they all do. Certainly there is other evidence tending to support the deduction that signatures were related to reading ability. First, the volume of letters delivered by the French postal service was greatest in the areas with highest literacy scores and vice versa. More convincing still, in the nineteenth century, when literacy was examined and recorded by census enumerators, the persons who were reported as 'able to read' also signed their marriage acts; those who were reported 'illiterate' did not. In spite of the weighty objections, it seems reasonable to accept the same correlation for the seventeenth century.

For further information and some detail, see the articles of B. Bonnin, 'L'alphabétisation des classes populaires rurales de Dauphiné au XVIIe siècle', *Marseille*, LXXXVIII (1972: *supplément – Le XVIIe siècle et l'éducation*); E. Johansson, 'The history of literacy in Sweden', *Umea University Educational Reports*, XII (1977); J. Meyer, 'Alphabétisation, lecture et écriture . . . en Bretagne', *Actes du 95e congrès national des Sociétés savantes (Reims 1970): section d'histoire moderne*, I (Paris, 1970), 333–53; and W. Urban, 'Umiejetnosc pisania w Malopolsce', *Przeglad Historyczny*, LXVIII (1977), 231–57 ('Literacy in Little Poland': French summary).

EXCURSUS II
'Realism' in the Seventeenth-Century Novel

So realistic are some of the prose works of the seventeenth century that several scholars have been tempted to use them as if they were objective historical evidence. Of course they were not, as a single example will suffice to show: the description of the battle of Wittstock (1636) in book II of von Grimmelshausen's *Simplicissimus*. The narrator claims to have been an eye-witness, which is just possible since Grimmelshausen was born in 1625, and certainly the survey of slaughter and suffering is extremely convincing. An account of heads without bodies, with their brains spattered about, is contrasted with a description of bodies without heads, with their entrails spattered about, and corpses losing their own blood are juxtaposed with the living who are covered with the blood of others. About one-third of the account of the battle is taken up with a highly effective description of the fate of the horses who had been involved in the battle:

> Some lay under their dead masters, who unknightly wounds had unjustly punished for a faithful duty. Some lay upon their lords by like accidents, and in death had the honour to be born by them whom in life they had born. Some, having lost their commanding burdens, ran scattered about the field, abashed with the madness of mankind.

The image of a topsy-turvy anarchy is built up by such a wealth of perverse antitheses and penetratingly macabre analogies that one can almost smell the battle. But it is not the battle of Wittstock. The quotation above actually comes from Sir Philip Sydney's *Arcadia*, printed in English in 1590 and translated into German in 1629. Grimmelshausen simply lifted the description, more or less word for word, when he published *Simplicissimus* in 1669, preferring literary effect to autobiographical realism.

This is not to say that no literary sources at all may be used by the historian – the account of the battle of Nördlingen (1634) in the autobiographical *Vida y hechos de Estebanillo González*, for example, has considerable value – but a novel or a poem is like any other source: it must be used with care and understanding.

See H. Geulen, '"Arkadische" Simpliciana', *Euphorion: Zeitschrift für Literaturgeschichte*, LXIII (1969), 426–37 – a reference kindly communicated by Dr Jeffrey Ashcroft of St Andrews University; and A. A. Parker, *Literature and the Delinquent* (Edinburgh, 1967), *passim*. The same prudence is required in dealing with paintings which, also, may not be what they seem: see J. Berger, *Ways of Seeing* (London, 1972), and P. Burke, *Tradition and Innovation in Renaissance Italy* (2nd edn, London, 1974), 344 – where realism in seventeenth-century Japanese and European art is compared.

NOTES

Prelude

1 The level of turmoil in the 1640s and '50s was unusual but not unique. About the middle of the second millenium BC came the collapse of many of the pre-Classical civilizations of Eurasia (Shang China, the Indus valley, Minoan Crete, Mycenæan Greece, the Egyptian Middle Kingdom); in the fourth and fifth centuries AD the main Classical civilizations foundered at almost the same time (the Chin, Gupta and Roman Empires); and in the fourteenth century, even before the Black Death, the leading states of the High Middle Ages began to crumble (the Yüan in China, the Minamoto in Japan, the Ghazni in India, the feudal monarchies in Europe). There was also to be one more such general crisis after the seventeenth century: between 1810 and 1848, with 'hard times', repeated epidemics (especially cholera) and rebellions culminating in the Year of Revolutions – 1848.

Chapter I

1 P. Avrich, *Russian Rebels* (London, 1972), 55; R. Mentet de Salmonet, *Histoire des troubles de la Grande Bretagne* (Paris, 1649), ii; T. Aston, ed., *Crisis in Europe* (London, 1965), 59.
2 Cited by J. A. Eddy in G. Parker and L. M. Smith, eds.,

The General Crisis of the Seventeenth Century (London, 1978), 231.

3 Fynes Morison, *Itinerary* (ed. C. Hughes, London, 1903), 424–5.

4 Petition of the clergy of Caithness and Orkney to the Privy Council of Scotland, 1634, quoted in M. Flynn, ed., *Scottish Population History from the Seventeenth Century to the 1930s* (Cambridge, 1977), 130; J. Sym, *Life's Preservative against Self-killing* (London, 1637), 124.

5 P. Herrera Puga, *Sociedad y delincuencia en el siglo de oro* (Madrid, 1974), 17.

6 The Haarlem-Amsterdam canal was dug in 1631–2 as a result of a sailing accident on the River IJ in which the Elector Palatine Frederick V (of whom more below) narrowly escaped death and his son Henry drowned.

7 The original titles of these books were: V. Zonca, *Nuovo teatro di machine et edificii*; O. de Serres, *Le théâtre d'agriculture ou le mesnage des champs*; J. Besson, *Théâtre des instruments mathématiques et mécaniques*; S. Stevin, *Stercten-bouwingh*; G. Galilei, *Siderius nuncius*.

Chapter II

1 The Jansenist controversy is discussed in J. Stoye, *Europe Unfolding, 1648–88* (London, 1969), 227–36. Lutheran and Calvinist opinions are covered in the earlier volumes in this series by (respectively) G. R. Elton and J. H. Elliott.

2 Quoted by H. Dollinger, *Studien zur Finanzreform Maximilians I. von Bayern* (Göttingen, 1968), 11.

3 Philip IV to his confidante, Sor María de Agreda, in F. T. Valiente, *Los validos en la monarquía española del siglo XVII* (Madrid, 1963), 181.

4 J. de Salórzano Pereira (1647) quoted by J. H. Elliott, *Imperial Spain 1469–1716* (London, 1963), 157.

5 See the instructive diagram in F. Braudel, *The Medi-*

terranean, I (London, 1974), 366–7.

6 Quoted by J. Tazbir, 'La conquête de l'Amérique à la lumière de l'opinion polonaise', *Acta poloniae historica*, XVII (1968), 15.

7 R. Filmer, *The Anarchy of a Limited or Mixed Monarchy*. See also a Republican tract of 1653: 'The question never was whether we should be governed by arbitrary power, but in whose hands it should be.' Both quoted in G. L. Mosse, *The Struggle for Sovereignty in England 1603–28* (East Lansing, 1950), 174f.

8 From J. X. Evans, ed., *The Works of Sir Roger Williams* (Oxford, 1972), 33.

Chapter III

1 The converse was also true: without the Protestant-Catholic schism in the sixteenth century (and indeed without the Greek-Latin split before), the Turks would probably not have conquered as much of south-east Europe.

2 See G. R. Elton, *Reformation Europe, 1517–1559* (London, 1963), 265–6.

3 This event gave rise to an outstanding piece of imaginative journalism which should put every historian on his guard. The bridal couple were detained by winds at Dover for some days, unknown to a London printer who issued the bogus account of their triumphal entry into Heidelberg he had prepared in advance. The fraud was not discovered until after considerable sales had been made, to the amusement of wits like Sir Henry Wotton who wrote a letter about it (see British Library Additional Ms. 34,727/23–4: to E. Bacon, 29 April 1613).

4 Quoted by R. J. W. Evans, *Rudolf II and his World* (Oxford, 1973), 59.

5 See, for details, J. H. Elliott, *Europe Divided, 1559–1598* (London, 1968), 274, 285, 292–3.

6 Although Alsace was never ceded, because of the war which broke out in Germany, the clauses of the treaty concerning Italy were honoured, and the agreement was renewed on 20 October 1631.

7 See Elliott, *Europe Divided, op. cit.*, 28–9.

8 Quotations from Horsey (1590) and Fletcher (1591) in E. Bond, ed., *Russia at the Close of the Sixteenth Century* (London, 1856), 34, 45, 163, 206.

Chapter IV

1 For more detail on the terms of the Edict, see J. H. Elliott, *Europe Divided, op. cit.*, 363–4.

2 Quoted by A. Soman, 'Press, pulpit and censorship in France before Richelieu', *Proceedings of the American Philosophical Society*, CXX (1976), 462.

3 Quoted by R. Chartier, 'La noblesse française et les Etats-Généraux de 1614', *Acta poloniae historica*, XXXVI (1977), 74.

4 Quoted by G. Parker, *The Dutch Revolt* (London, 1977), 253.

5 This figure is very close to the total strength of the ruling elite of the Venetian Republic. There, too, 2500 adult males controlled affairs, of whom only 100 or so held important offices and no more than 30 were really important in each generation. For further comparisons, see P. Burke, *Venice and Amsterdam* (London, 1974).

6 O. Feltham, *A Brief Character of the Low Countries under the States* (London, 1652), 1 and 5. Sir Walter Raleigh was of the same mind: 'The Spanish king vexeth all the princes of Europe and is become, in a fewe yeares, from a poore king of Castile, the greateste monarke of this part of the worlde' (quoted by K. G. Davies, *The North Atlantic World in the Seventeenth Century*, London, 1974), 22.

7 Mateo Vázquez to Philip II, February 1591, quoted by G. Parker, *Philip II* (Boston, 1978), 181.
8 All quoted by J. A. Maravall, *Estado moderna y mentalidad social*, I (Madrid, 1972), 117–19.
9 Between 1582 and 1605, the rulers of the Venetian state extended their control over both the moral and social life of its citizens, formerly in the hands of the church, and over the church itself – taxing the clergy, punishing criminous clerks, issuing laws restraining the clerical acquisition of landed property and forbidding the introduction of new religious orders or the erection of new religious buildings without prior approval from the senate. In 1606, Pope Paul V called on the Republic to abandon these policies. When it refused, he placed all the Venetian lands under an interdict (May 1606 to April 1607), only agreeing to a reconciliation when no practical assistance was forthcoming from either France or Spain. Venetian opposition to the Papacy did not (as was once thought) signify a lack of enthusiasm for the Counter-Reformation; only that the Republic wished to control the progress of the movement in its own lands.
10 Archivo General de Simancas, *Guerra Antigua*, 808 unfol., *consulta* of 26 December 1616.

Chapter V

1 Quoted by G. Mann, *Wallenstein* (London, 1977), 111.
2 Count Solms to Frederick, 28 August 1619: quoted by A. Gindely, *Geschichte des Dreissigjährigen Krieges*, II (Prague, 1869), 164.
3 George Abbot, 12 September 1619: quoted by S. L. Adams, 'Foreign policy and the parliaments of 1621 and 1624' in K. M. Sharpe, ed., *Faction and Parliament* (Oxford, 1978), 147.
4 Students of Spanish literature should be grateful to

Calderón, who inspired two fine satirical poems and a proverb: Quevedo's *Poderoso caballero es Don Dinero* ('Mr Money is a powerful man') and Góngora's *Dineros son calidad* ('Money is quality') were both written in 1601 to celebrate the obscure Calderón's marriage to a Castilian noblewoman, bringing him two seigneurial estates; and the proverb *Andar mas honrado que Don Rodrigo en la horca* ('To be more respected than Don Rodrigo on the scaffold') refers to Calderón's dignified and courageous behaviour when, after prolonged torture, he was executed in the new Plaza Mayor of Madrid in October 1621.

5 These sums were large, and made a welcome addition to the war-chests of Emperor and League, but they should be set against the largesse bestowed by the Popes on their nephews. After 1614 Cardinal Scipione Borghese's income exceeded 350,000 florins (Pope Paul V, 1605–21, was a Borghese); between 1621 and 1623 Cardinal Ludovico Ludovisi received gifts worth five million florins and Orazio Ludovisi gifts worth 500,000 (Pope Gregory XV, 1621–3, was a Ludovisi). Likewise Philip III gave far more to his favourites than to his Habsburg cousins.

6 B. de Zúñiga, 7 April 1619: quoted by P. Brightwell, 'The Spanish system and the Twelve Years' Truce', *English Historical Review*, LXXXIX (1974), 289.

7 Carola Oman, *Elisabeth of Bohemia* (London, 1964), 265, quoting Brunswick; S. R. Gardiner, *History of England*, IV (London, 1883), 323, quoting Frederick.

8 The monetary system of many countries was disrupted between 1621 and 1623. In Germany, it was called the *Kipper- und Wipperzeit* (the 'clip and weigh period') because the debasement of all currencies with copper caused the intrinsic value of each coin to differ, although the general trend was always downwards. Thus in Würzburg, the silver thaler was worth 300 pfennigs in 1610 but 4000 in 1622, while in Munich the ducat rose in value from 735 pfennigs in 1620 to 3150 in 1622. Students were forced to stay away from schools and universities; craftsmen and farmers would only barter their wares; those

dependent on pensions or dividends starved; and silver miners at Mansfeld and Eisleben rebelled. German mints only stabilized their issues again in 1623–4, albeit at only one-eighth or one-tenth of their former values. The issue of *vellón* coin by the Spanish crown in 1598–1607 and 1617–28 achieved much the same disruption (see page 237 above).

9 Camerarius to Baron Rusdorf, 24 December 1623: quoted by F. H. Schubert, 'Die pfälzische Exilregierung im dreissigjährigen Krieg', *Zeitschrift für Geschichte des Oberrheins*, CII (1954), 672.

10 Rubens, 28 May 1627: quoted by J. R. Martin, *Corpus Rubeniarum Ludwig Burchard*, XVI (London, 1972), 19–20.

11 Wotton to Sir T. Aston, 18 December 1621: quoted by L. P. Smith, *Life and Letters of Sir Henry Wotton*, II (London, 1907), 221.

12 Marillac to Louis XIII, 15 July 1630: quoted by R. Mousnier, 'Les mouvements populaires en France' in M. Braubach, ed., *Forschungen und Studien zur Geschichte des Westfälischen Friedens* (Münster, 1965), 47. Eventually the estates were restored in Burgundy (1631) and Languedoc (1632); in Provence they were restored at first but after 1639 they gave way to an *assemblée des communautés* with reduced powers; in Périgord (from 1606), Guyenne (from 1622) and Dauphiné (from 1628) they disappeared altogether.

Chapter VI

1 Speech of Gustavus Adolphus to the Swedish Diet, 26 August 1617, quoted M. Roberts, *Sweden as a Great Power* (London, 1968), 136.

2 G. Mann, *Wallenstein* (Frankfurt, 1971), 640: letter of 10 February 1630. The Germans and the Poles never

seem to have got on well together, and this is reflected in several current expressions: the Polish name for a German, *niemiec*, also has the sense 'numbskull'; and the Germans use the phrase *polnische Wirtschaft* (Polish economy) to mean 'utter chaos'.

3 Mann, *Wallenstein*, 637–8: letters of the general dated 11 October and 10 November 1629.

4 Mann, *Wallenstein*, 756.

5 Marquis de Feuquières, *Lettres et négociations*, II (Amsterdam, 1753), 68–9: letter of 22 August 1633.

6 Quotations from J. H. Elliott, 'Self-perception and decline in seventeenth-century Spain', *Past and Present*, LXXIV (1977), 50; and J. H. Elliott and J. M. de la Peña, eds., *Memoriales y cartas del Conde-Duque de Olivares*, I (Madrid, 1978), XXXVII-LXII.

7 AGS *Guerra Antigua* 1035, unfol., *consulta* of the council of state, 27 February 1631: *voto* of Olivares. The idea of sending the princes appears in a Memorial written by the Count-Duke in the summer of 1625.

8 Quotations from AGR *Secrétairerie d'Etat et de Guerre* 195/164, king to Isabella, 9 August 1626; *ibid.*, 332/75, Oñate to Cardinal-Infante, 8 August 1634; Bibliothèque Royale, Brussels, *Ms.* 16147–48/139, Aytona to Olivares, 29 December 1633; and AGS *Guerra Antigua* 1120, unfol., paper of Olivares, February 1635.

9 Information kindly supplied from an unpublished paper by Dr J. Lindegren of Uppsala university: 'Utskrivningarnas demografiska konsekvenser [The demographic consequences of conscription] 1620–39'. Dr Lindegren's figures shed a dramatic light on one of the main reasons why Sweden could not long remain a great power.

10 Council minutes printed by M. Roberts, *Sweden as a Great Power* (London, 1968), 149–51.

Chapter VII

1 B. Porshnev, *Les soulèvements populaires en France avant la Fronde* (Paris, 1963), 53; Epernon, governor of Guyenne, to Chancellor Séguier, 26 June 1633; Richelieu quoted by O. Ranum, *Richelieu and the Councillors of Louis XIII* (Oxford, 1963), 165, 167, 176.
2 It may well have been the shift in the structure of French fiscal policy under Louis XIV, with indirect taxes increasing from 25 per cent of total revenue in the 1640s to 53 per cent around 1690, that put an end to the cycle of popular revolts in France for over a century after 1675.
3 Archivo Histórico Nacional, Madrid, *Estado libro* 961/56–59v: instructions for Don Miguel de Salamanca, November 1637.
4 J. H. Elliott, *The Revolt of the Catalans* (Cambridge, 1963), 310: *consulta* of Olivares to the king, 14 June 1635.
5 A. Leman, *Richelieu et Olivares* (Lille, 1938), 118: *consulta* of the council to Philip IV, 31 January 1640.
6 J. H. Elliott, *The Revolt of the Catalans*, 360, 375, 387, 400–1: *consultas* from Olivares on 12 March and 7 October 1639, and 14 January and 23 February 1640.
7 Elliott, *op. cit.*, 411: Dr Jacinto Valonga to the court, 24 March 1640.
8 The Madrid government, however, did regard all liaisons with the enemy as treasonable in time of war. It has often been supposed that the satirist Quevedo was imprisoned from 1639 until 1643 for his caustic attacks on Olivares; but it has recently been shown that the true reason was his secret contacts with France (see J. H. Elliott, 'Nueva luz sobre la prisión de Quevedo', *Boletín de la Real Academia de la Historia*, CLXIX [1972], 171–82).
9 T. Kendrick, *Mary of Agreda* (London, 1967), 143: letter of 30 January 1647.

10 J. H. Elliott, *The Revolt of the Catalans*, 523: letter of Duplessis Besançon, no date given.

11 For a full account of these revolts see J. Stoye, *Europe Unfolding 1648–1688* (London, 1969), 110–14.

12 The conception of Louis XIV was only able to take place in 1637 because the king was trapped in a thunderstorm while out hunting near his wife's country house, and even a night in Anne's bed seemed preferable to getting soaked.

13 D. L. M. Avenel, ed., *Lettres, instructions diplomatiques et papiers d'état du Cardinal de Richelieu*, VI (Paris, 1870), 500–1 and 881–2: Richelieu to Bouthillier, 29 August 1639 and 10 October 1641.

14 A. Chéruel, ed., *Lettres du Cardinal Mazarin*, III (Paris, 1883), 173–81: Mazarin to Servien, 14 August 1648. For the later history of the Fronde see J. Stoye, *Europe Unfolding, 1648–1688* (London, 1969), 77–106.

15 These are described in Stoye, *Europe Unfolding*, 15–40.

16 A. Chéruel, ed., *Lettres du Cardinal Mazarin*, III, 218–20: Mazarin to Servien, 23 October 1648.

17 H. Heberle, *Zeytregister 1618–72*, quoted G. Benecke, *Germany in the Thirty Years' War* (London, 1978), 20.

Chapter VIII

1 H. Boguet (1603), quoted by S. Anglo, *The Damned Art* (London, 1977), 1.

2 Quoted by R. L. Kagan, *Students and Society in Early Modern Spain* (Baltimore, 1974), 45.

3 P. V. Cayet, *Chronologie novenaire* (Paris, 1608; ed. Michaud and Poujoulat, Paris, 1838), 22.

4 Quoted by E. Rosand, 'Music in the myth of Venice', *Renaissance Quarterly*, XXX (1977), 535.

5 Burckhart Grossman and Heinrich Schütz quoted by H. Raynor, *A Social History of Music* (London, 1972), 115 and 203–4.

6 Quevedo's dedication to the manuscript of *La Hora de Todos*, written in March 1636. The work was only published, posthumously, in 1650. Alas, much of Quevedo's literary effect was achieved by a sustained and complex play on words which defies translation: see A. A. Parker, *Literature and the Delinquent* (Edinburgh, 1967), 57–8.

7 Opalinski quoted by J. Tazbir in *European Studies Review*, VIII (1977), 42; quotation from Thomasius, *Von Nachahmung der Frantzosen* ('On imitating the French'), kindly supplied by Mr André Carus of Gonville and Caius College, Cambridge.

8 E. S. de Beer, ed., *The Diary of John Evelyn*, II (Oxford, 1955), 37; R. C. Temple, ed., *The Travels of Peter Mundy*, IV (London, 1924), 71.

9 'Mannerism' is a term originally applied to certain features of painting during the century 1530–1630 which has since been used by various scholars to mean different things. Here it embraces the delight in style for style's sake; the love of marvels, whether natural or man-made; and the belief that artists were able to perceive and represent the deepest secrets of the universe. Often the conceits, disharmonies and fantastic images of mannerist art and literature were attempts to communicate profound insights. 'I conjure you all . . . to believe', wrote Sir Philip Sidney, 'that there are many mysteries contained in poetrie, which of purpose were written darkly, least by prophane wits it should be abused' (quoted by R. J. W. Evans, *Rudolf II and his World* [Oxford, 1973], 267: see all of pages 255–74). The Baroque marked a return to the perfect harmonies, fixed proportions, antique models and simpler, more massive designs which the artists and writers of the seventeenth century believed to have characterized the culture of Classical times.

10 Quoted by P. Steinman, *Bauer und Ritter in Mecklenburg* (Schwerin, 1960), 87; the whole of Stein's pungent letter on the subject is worth reading.

11 E. A. Bond, ed., *Russia at the Close of the Sixteenth Century* (London, 1856), cxxiii.

12 Western interest was not totally eclectic, however. Almost all the works translated from Arabic were by authors already known in the west – i.e. Classical writers. Very few were by Indian or Chinese scholars.

13 Quotations from V. J. Parry, in V. J. Parry and M. E. Yapp, *War, Technology and Society in the Middle East* (Oxford, 1975), 256.

Further Reading

I would gladly have confined myself to works written in English, since they are the most likely to prove useful to those who consult this book; but, not surprisingly, most of the best work on European history has been done by foreign scholars writing in their own language. This is particularly true for four of the countries where the major action narrated above took place: the Empire, the Netherlands, Poland and Spain. Only rarely, alas, do works published in those countries contain an English or French summary (those that do are marked *). Apart from a section on general reading, Chapters I, II and VIII each have an individual note of further reading, but material for Chapters III to VII is grouped by countries and covers the entire chronological period. Works mentioned in the notes are not normally included here.

General Reading

G. N. Clark, *The Seventeenth Century* (2nd edn, Oxford, 1947), is the best general introduction to the period in English, with H. Kamen, *The Iron Century* (London, 1971) and C. H. Wilson, *The Transformation of Europe 1558–1648* (London, 1976) running a close second. Further detail may be found in *The Cambridge Modern History*, IV (Cambridge, 1906), and *The New Cambridge Modern History*, IV (Cambridge, 1970). There is a useful survey of eastern affairs by J. Lisk, *The Struggle for Supremacy in the Baltic 1600–1725* (London, 1967), and the even more helpful W. H.

McNeill, *Europe's Steppe Frontier 1500–1800* (Chicago, 1964). For a reminder that Europe did not yet dominate the world, see L. S. Stavrianos, *The World since 1500: a Global History* (Englewood Cliffs, 1966). Very often, the most evocative works on the history of Europe at this time were written by contemporary travellers, of whom there were more than ever before. The English diaries and journals of Thomas Coryat, John Evelyn, Fynes Morison and Peter Mundy are all available in modern editions. See also J. Stoye, *English Travellers Abroad 1604–1667* (London, 1952), and the beautifully illustrated A. Maczak, *Zycie codzienne w podrozach po Europie w XVI i XVII wieku* (Warsaw, 1978: 'The daily life of travellers in 16th- and 17th-century Europe'), of which an English translation will appear in 1980 (published by New Left Books).

Chapter I

Many general surveys of the European economy in our period have recently appeared, of which the following are especially recommended: F. Braudel, *Capitalism and Material Life 1400–1800* (London, 1967); C. M. Cipolla, *Before the Industrial Revolution: European Society and Economy 1000–1700* (London, 1976); J. de Vries, *The Economy of Europe in an Age of Crisis 1600–1750* (Cambridge, 1976); and I. Wallerstein, *The Modern World System*, I (London, 1974) and II (London, 1979). For those who crave greater detail and more statistics, there are: E. E. Rich and C. H. Wilson, eds., *The Cambridge Economic History of Europe*, IV (Cambridge, 1967) and V (Cambridge, 1977); C. M. Cipolla, ed., *The Fontana Economic History of Europe*, II (London, 1974); and C. H. Wilson and G. Parker, eds., *An Introduction to the Sources of European Economic History, 1500–1800* (London, 1978). To select more specialized works from the enormous mass of literature in print is a fairly pointless task, but the following provided a good deal of the data used in the chapter: on climate – J. Eddy, 'The case of the missing sunspots', *Scientific American*, May 1977, 80–92, and H. H. Lamb, *Climate: Present, Past and Future*, I (London, 1972), 385–464, and II (London, 1977), 461–73; on demography – J. L. Flandrin, *Families in Former Times* (Cambridge, 1979), and F. Lebrun, *Les hommes et la mort en Anjou* (Paris, 1971); on disease – J. N. Biraben, *Les hommes et la peste en France* (2 vols., Paris, 1975), and C. M. Cipolla, *Public Health and the Medical Profession in the Renaissance* (Cambridge, 1976); on poverty – C. Lis and H. Soly, *Poverty and Capitalism in Pre-industrial Europe* (Hassocks, 1979), and B. Pullan, *Rich and Poor in Renaissance Venice* (Oxford, 1971); on tithes – M. W. Flinn, ed., *Seventh International Economic History Congress*, I (Edinburgh, 1978), papers on theme A3, and J. Goy and E. Le Roy Ladurie, *Les fluctuations du produit de la dîme* (Paris–The Hague, 1972). See also G. Parker and L. M. Smith, eds., *The General Crisis of the Seventeenth Century* (London, 1978).

Chapter II

Two excellent outline surveys are available: P. Goubert, *The Ancien Régime*, I (London, 1973) and II (Paris, 1973), and the shorter J. H. Shennan, *The Origins of the Modern European State 1450–1725* (London, 1974). There are also important and wide-ranging articles by J. Bérenger, 'Le problème du ministériat au XVIIe siècle', *Annales, E.S.C.*, XXIX (1974), 166–92; H. G. Koenigsberger, '*Dominium regale* or *dominium politicum et regale*: monarchies and parliaments in early modern Europe' (Inaugural Lecture, University of London, King's College, 1975) – see also his collected essays in *Estates and Revolutions: Essays in Early Modern European History* (Ithaca, 1971); and E. L. Petersen, 'From domain state to tax state: synthesis and interpretation', *Scan-*

dinavian Economic History Review, XXIII (1975), 116–48.

Perhaps the best way to view the work of confessional absolutism is at a local level, through studies like those of J. Ferté, *La vie religieuse dans les campagnes parisiennes, 1622–1695* (Paris, 1962), J. F. Soulet, *Traditions et réformes religieuses dans les Pyrénées centrales au XVIIe siècle: le diocèse de Tarbes de 1602 à 1716* (Pau, 1974), and B. Vogler, *Le clergé protestant rhénan au siècle de la Réforme 1555–1619* (Strasbourg, 1976). On the work of the Inquisitions, Venetian data will be presented in a forthcoming book by Dr Nicholas Davidson of the university of Leicester, and a foretaste of work to come on the Spanish Inquisition appeared in G. Henningsen, 'El "Banco de datos" del Santo Oficio. Las relaciones de causas de la Inquisición española, 1550–1700', *Boletín de la Real Academia de la Historia*, CLXXIV (1977), 547–70.

On court life, there is a marvellous collection of essays, richly illustrated, in A. G. Dickens, *The Courts of Europe. Politics, Patronage and Royalty 1400–1800* (London, 1977). On military organization, see A. Corvisier, *Armées et sociétés en Europe de 1494 à 1789* (Paris, 1976); G. Parker, 'The "Military Revolution 1560–1660" – a myth?', *Spain and the Netherlands 1559–1659* (London, 1979), 86–103; and I. A. A. Thompson, *War and Government in Habsburg Spain 1560–1620* (London, 1976).

Chapters III–VII *(reading grouped by countries)*

DENMARK

There is a desperate need for a good history of Denmark in English: it is the one major state of the seventeenth century for which little is available, although there are plenty of works in Danish. The work of E. L. Petersen stands out: *The Crisis of the Danish Nobility 1580–1660* (Odense, 1967), and 'La crise de la noblesse danoise entre 1580 et 1660', *Annales E.S.C.*, XXIII (1968), 1237–61. There are also interesting articles by W. Czaplinski, 'Polish-Danish diplomatic relations, 1598–1632' in *Poland at the XIth International Congress of Historical Sciences* (Warsaw, 1960), 179–204, and *S. Heiberg, 'De ti tondet guld: Rigsrad, kongemagt og stadsfinanser', *Historisk Tidsskrift (Dansk)*, LXXVI (1976), 25–58 ('The "Ten tons of gold": council, royal power and public finance' – 1629–43).

THE EMPIRE

Two useful handbooks also include first-rate bibliographies: B. Gebhardt, *Handbuch der deutschen Geschichte*, II (Stuttgart, 1955), and H. Aubin and W. Zorn, eds., *Handbuch der deutschen Wirtschafts- und Sozialgeschichte*, I (Stuttgart, 1971), 386–494. There are three outstanding collections of published documents: F. Stieve and others, eds., *Briefe und Akten zur Geschichte des Dreissigjährigen Krieges* (in 2 series, many volumes and even part-volumes); J. V. Polisensky, ed., *Documenta bohemica bellum tricennale illustrantia* (6 volumes of brief summaries and a few transcripts, Prague, 1971–9: the commentary and extracts are in German. Volume 1 has been translated into English as *War and Society in Europe 1618–1648*, Cambridge, 1978); and M. Braubach and K. Repgen, eds., *Acta pacis Westphalicae* (4 series are envisaged, with 45 volumes, of which 9 were published at Münster between 1962 and 1976). There are also, of course, innumerable other published documents, including memoirs and diaries. Two may be singled out: the diary of an Ulm shoemaker – G. Zillhardt, ed., *Der Dreissigjährige Krieg in zeitgenössischer Darstellung. Hans Heberles 'Zeytregister'* (Ulm, 1975); and the memoirs of the Scottish soldier Robert Monro, *Monro his expedition with the worthy Scots regiment called Mackay's* (London, 1637): vol. II, 63–7 contains a magnificent account of the battle of Breitenfeld. Those who wish to re-live the battles of the Thirty Years' War may like to purchase from the Avalon Hills Games Company a Wargame package of four Thirty Years' War battles.

For the years before the war, the roots of the quarrel within the Habsburg family are examined by H. Sturmberger, 'Die Anfänge des Bruderzwistes in Habsburg', *Mitteilungen des Oberösterreichischen Landesarchivs*, V (1957), 143–88; its later stages, and much else besides, are covered by R. J. W. Evans, *Rudolf II and his World* (Oxford, 1973). The workings of the imperial government under Matthias and his successors are illuminated by H. F. Schwarz, *The Imperial Privy Council in the Seventeenth Century* (Cambridge, Mass., 1943), the pragmatic ideology of Ferdinand by H. Sturmberger, *Kaiser Ferdinand II und das Problem des Absolutismus* (Munich, 1957). The growing and dangerous strength of Bavaria and the Palatinate are charted by, respectively: H. Dollinger, *Studien zur Finanzreform Maximilians I. von Bayern . . . 1598–1618* (Göttingen, 1968) and C. P. Clasen, *The Palatinate in European History 1555–1618* (Oxford, 1966).

The Thirty Years' War has given rise to numerous studies, almost all of them with the same title – that of the conflict. They all have their individual strengths: G. Pagès is particularly good on France, J. V. Polisensky on Bohemia, C. V. Wedgwood on Germany itself. Only the slim but popular volume of S. H. Steinberg, *The 'Thirty Years' War' and the Conflict for European Hegemony 1600–1660* (London, 1966) needs to be used with care: it is often tendentious in interpretation and sometimes unreliable in detail. There are two useful collections of articles by T. K. Rabb, ed., *The Thirty Years' War* (Lexington, 1964), and H. U. Rudolf, ed., *Der Dreissigjährige Krieg. Perspektiven und Strukturen* (Darmstadt, 1977); and a standard German account is strong on economic and social aspects: G. Franz, *Der Dreissigjährige Krieg und das deutsche Volk* (3rd edn, Stuttgart, 1960). A fascinating collection of extracts from original material has been printed in English translation by G. Benecke, *Germany in the Thirty Years' War* (London, 1978).

Bearing all this in mind, the best introductory surveys are

probably the shortest ones: H. G. Koenigsberger, *The Habsburgs and Europe 1516–1660* (Ithaca, 1971), Chapter 3, and G. Livet, *La guerre de trente ans* (Paris, 1963).

Although the Bohemian revolt has attracted a considerable amount of attention, the best short account is still H. Sturmberger, *Aufstand in Böhmen* (Munich, 1959). There are some excellent biographies of the leading personalities involved: C. Oman, *Elizabeth of Bohemia* (London, 1938); F. H. Schubert, *Ludwig Camerarius* (Kallmünz, 1955); and H. Sturmberger, *Georg Erasmus Tschernembl* (Linz, 1953). The policies pursued towards Bohemia by foreign powers have also been well covered: on Bavaria, see D. Albrecht, *Die auswärtige Politik Maximilians von Bayern 1618–1635* (Göttingen, 1962); on Britain, see S. L. Adams, 'Foreign policy and the parliaments of 1621 and 1624' in K. M. Sharpe, ed., *Faction and Parliament* (Oxford, 1978), 139–71; on the Papacy, see D. Albrecht, *Die deutsche Politik Papst Gregors XV* (Munich, 1956) and *idem*, 'Zur Finanzierung des Dreissigjährigen Krieges', *Zeitschrift für bayerischen Landesgeschichte*, XIX (1956), 534–67; on Savoy, see R. Kleinman, 'Charles Emanuel I of Savoy and the Bohemian election of 1619), *European Studies Review*, V (1975), 3–29; and on Spain, see P. Brightwell, 'Spain and the origins of the Thirty Years' War' (Cambridge University PhD, 1967; soon, it is hoped, to be published).

No other event in the war has attracted such a wealth of outstanding historical studies; for other episodes, only one or two works are worth singling out. The activities of Frederick V and his advisers after their defeat are narrated by F. Schubert, 'Die pfälzische Exilregierung im Dreissigjährigen Krieg', *Zeitschrift für Geschichte des Oberrheins*, CII (1954), 575–680. For a sidelight on the Danish war, see E. A. Beller, 'The military expedition of Sir Charles Morgan to Germany, 1627–9', *English Historical Review*, XLIII (1928), 528–39. On the struggle for the Rhineland, see H. Weber, 'Richelieu et le Rhin', *Revue historique*, CCXXXIX (1968), 265–80, and, at greater length, *idem*, *Frankreich, Kurtrier, der Rhein und das Reich 1623–35* (Bonn, 1969).

Perhaps the best approach to the history of the middle period of the war is through the excellent short study of Dieter Albrecht, *Richelieu, Gustav Adolf und das Reich* (Janus-Bücher, Munich and Vienna, 1959), but alas this book is very hard to find in British libraries. Readers may therefore prefer to make their way through the enormous but fascinating biography by Golo Mann, *Wallenstein* (London, 1976: the German edition – Frankfurt, 1971 – is preferable for those who read German because most quotations are given in the original, and their source is indicated in the notes).

On the road towards peace, see K. Bierther, *Der Regensburger Reichstag von 1640/1664* (Kallmünz, 1971); F. Dickmann, *Der Westfälische Frieden* (Stuttgart, 1965); and M. Braubach, ed., *Forschungen und Studien zur Geschichte des westfälischen Friedens* (Munster, 1965: many of the articles are in French). On the armies that fought the war, see F. Redlich, *The German Military Enterpriser and his Workforce* (Wiesbaden, 1964), and *idem*, *De Praeda Militari: Looting and Booty 1500–1815* (Wiesbaden, 1956). On the impact of armies, there is an excellent full-length study by I. Bog, *Die bäuerliche Wirtschaft im Zeitalter des Dreissigjährigen Krieges* (Coburg, 1952); and two valuable articles by G. Benecke, 'Labour relations and peasant society in north-west Germany', *History*, LVIII (1973), 350–9, and 'The problem of death and destruction in Germany during the Thirty Years' War', *European Studies Review*, II (1972), 239–53. Finally, on the role of the war in transforming the political structure of the Empire, see F. Carsten, *Princes and Parliaments in Germany* (Oxford, 1959), and G. Benecke, *Society and Politics in Germany 1500–1750* (London, 1974).

FRANCE

There is a splendid new introduction available: R. Briggs, *Early Modern France 1560–1715* (Oxford, 1977); and, in French, there is the yet more concise H. Méthivier, *Le siècle de Louis XIII* (Paris, 1965). At a more detailed level, however, coverage is less satisfactory – mainly because, since the 1940s, most of the best French historians have eschewed the study of personalities and politics in favour of regional studies which cover every non-political aspect of life. The leaders in the field are (in alphabetical order): R. Baehrel, *Une croissance: la Basse Provence rurale* (Paris, 1961); G. Cabourdin, *Terre et hommes en Lorraine, 1550–1630* (2 vols., Nancy, 1977); P. Deyon, *Amiens – capital provinciale. Etude sur la société urbaine au XVIIe siècle* (Paris, 1967); P. Goubert, *Beauvais et le Beauvaisis de 1600 à 1730* (Paris, 1960); J. Jacquart, *La crise rurale en Ile-de-France 1550–1670* (Paris, 1974); and E. Le Roy Ladurie, *Les paysans de Languedoc* (Paris, 1966: abridged English edition, Urbana, Ill., 1974). A useful synthesis of these and many other works is provided in H. Neveux, J. Jacquart and E. Le Roy Ladurie, eds., *Histoire de la France rurale*, II (Paris, 1975).

There is no satisfactory modern biography of either Henry IV or Louis XIII, and none of Richelieu or Mazarin. The only leading political figure to have received adequate treatment is Sully: D. Buisseret, *Sully* (London, 1968). His legacy is well analysed by J. M. Hayden, 'Continuity in the France of Henry IV and Louis XIII: French foreign policy 1598–1615', *Journal of Modern History*, XLV (1973), 1–23. Curiously, the childhood of Louis XIII has received a great deal of attention, following publication of the 9000 daily entries on his progress recorded by his physician, Jean Héroard: see E. W. Marwick in L. de Mause, ed., *The History of Childhood* (London, 1974), 259–301, and D. Hunt, *Parents and Children . . . in Early Modern France* (New York, 1970). The rise of Richelieu is covered, rather ponderously, by A. D. Lyublinskaya, *French Absolutism: the Crucial Phase 1620–9* (Cambridge, 1968), and several of her assumptions are questioned by D. Parker, 'The social foundation of French absolutism 1610–30', *Past and Present*, LIII (1971), 67–89. Three exemplary monographs examine the government of France under the cardinals: O. Ranum, *Richelieu and the Councillors of Louis XIII* (Oxford, 1963), R. J. Bonney, *Political Change in France under Richelieu and Mazarin*

1624–1666 (Oxford, 1978) and R. Mousnier, *La vénalité des offices sous Henri IV et Louis XIII* (2nd edn, Paris, 1971). Each book contains references to other work on their subject. Individual political events have naturally given rise to detailed studies, of which the best are: R. Mousnier, *The Assassination of Henry IV* (London, 1973), and G. Mongrédien, *La journée des dupes* (Paris, 1971). On the Fronde (most of which is covered by the next volume in this series), the standard account of A. Lloyd Moote, *The Revolt of the Judges: the Parlement of Paris and the Fronde 1643–52* (Princeton, 1971) has recently been the subject of serious criticism: R. J. Bonney, 'The French Civil War 1649–53', *European Studies Review*, VIII (1978), 71–100.

There are two quagmires in the history of seventeenth-century France, and both have claimed more than their fair share of victims: public finance and peasant revolts. On the first, only the figures in R. J. Bonney, *The King's Debts: Finance and Politics in France, 1589–1661* (Oxford, 1980) should be trusted. On the latter, there is as yet no synthesis; but the review article of J. H. M. Salmon, 'Venality of office and popular sedition in seventeenth century France. A review of a controversy', *Past and Present*, XXXVII (1967), 21–43, summarizes the literature and the interpretations up to that date. Since then, regional approaches have shed far more light on the unrest than the reports of the intendants used by Porshnev, Mousnier and others. See: Y. Bercé, *Histoire des Croquants* (2 vols., Geneva, 1974), M. Foisil, *La révolte des Nu-pieds* (Paris, 1970), and R. Pillorget, *Les mouvements insurrectionnels de Provence entre 1596 et 1715* (Paris, 1975).

Finally, two collective volumes present in English translation many of the most important articles of French historians, including R. Mousnier whose work is always reliable, solid and interesting: P. J. Coveney, ed., *France in Crisis, 1620–75* (Totowa, NJ, 1977), and R. F. Kierstead, ed., State *and Society in Seventeenth-century France* (New York, 1975). The many influential articles of J. Meuvret have been published posthumously: J. Meuvret, *Etudes d'histoire économique: receuil d'articles* (Paris, 1971).

HUNGARY

An excellent early modern history is available in E. Pamlényi, ed., *A History of Hungary* (Budapest, 1973); it was written by L. Makkai, whose *Histoire de Transylvanie* (Paris, 1946) is also most informative. On the Turkish-Austrian war fought in Hungary, see A. Randa, *Pro republica christiana: die Walachei im 'langen' Türkenkrieg* (Munich, 1964) and S. Olteanu, *Les pays roumains à l'époque de Michel le Brave* (Bucharest, 1975). The war is illustrated in *Ortelius Redivivus et continuatus, oder Ungarische und Siebenbürgische Kriegsempörungen* (Nuremberg, 1665). On the defence of Christendom at other times, see G. E. Rothenburg, *The Austrian Military Border in Croatia 1522–1747* (Urbana, Ill., 1960).

ITALY

There are no histories of the peninsula in English to which the reader can turn with confidence, and even many histories of individual states are too summary on the earlier seventeenth century to merit mention. The following are recommended: R. T. Rapp, *Industry and Economic Decline in Seventeenth-century Venice* (Harvard, 1976); B. Pullan, *Crisis and Change in the Venetian Economy* (London, 1968); F. McArdle, *Altopascio: a Study of Tuscan Rural Society* (Cambridge, 1978); E. Cochrane, *Florence in the Forgotten Centuries 1527–1800* (Chicago, 1973), Chapters 2 and 3; G. Coniglio, *Il viceregno di Napoli nel secolo XVII* (Rome, 1955); R. Villari, *La rivolta antispagnola a Napoli. Le origini 1585–1647* (Bari, 1967); and D. Mack Smith, *A History of Sicily: Medieval Sicily, 800–1713* (London, 1968).

On individual problems, the first war of Mantua is covered by A. Bombín, *La cuestión de Monferrato 1613–1618* (Madrid, 1975); the second by J. Humbert, *Les Français en Savoie sous Louis XIII* (Paris, 1960). The war of Saluzzo is the subject of a slim monograph, using only documents from Simancas, by J. L. Cano de Gardoquí, *La cuestión de Saluzzo en las comunicaciones del imperio español 1588–1601* (Valladolid, 1962: see also the review of H. Lapèyre in *Cahiers d'histoire*, VIII [1963], 341–5).

MUSCOVY

The standard histories of S. F. Platonov, *The Time of Troubles* (2nd edn, London, 1970), and G. Vernadsky, *The Tsardom of Moscow 1547–1682* (2 vols., Yale, 1969) are still reliable. On agriculture there are two excellent studies by R. Goehrke, *Die Wustüngen in der Moskauer Rus* (Wiesbaden, 1968), and R. E. F. Smith, *Peasant Farming in Muscovy* (Cambridge, 1977). Peasant revolts are ably covered by P. Avrich, *Russian Rebels 1600–1800* (London, 1972), 10–47; the conquest of Siberia by G. V. Lantzeff and R. A. Pierce, *Eastward to Empire* (London, 1973).

THE NORTH NETHERLANDS

The classic general survey remains P. Geyl, *The Netherlands in the Seventeenth Century*, I (London, 1961), but see also the illustrated outline studies of K. H. D. Haley, *The Dutch in the Seventeenth Century* (London, 1972), and C. H. Wilson, *The Dutch Republic and the Civilization of the Seventeenth Century* (London, 1968); and P. Zumthor, *Daily Life in Rembrandt's Holland* (London, 1962). The bibliographies in Haley and Wilson make it unnecessary to cite any further works here, except for some important new studies of rural society: J. de Vries, *The Dutch Rural Economy . . . 1500–1700* (Yale, 1974); *J. A. Faber, *Drie eeuwen Friesland: economische en sociale ontwikkelingen* (2 vols., A.A.G. Bijdragen XVII, 1972); and *A. M. van der Woude, *Het Noorderkwartier* (3 vols., A.A.G. Bijdragen XVI, 1972).

THE SOUTH NETHERLANDS

Ever since the Dutch revolt created two states in the Netherlands, attention has been focused on the North to the detriment of the South. There is no general study of the 'state of the Archdukes' and modern research has tended to concentrate on the connexion between Spain and the South Netherlands. The reader may consult (in alphabetical order): J. A. Alcalá-Zamora, *España, los Países-Bajos y la mar del Norte* (Madrid, 1975); C. H. Carter, *The Secret Diplomacy of the Habsburgs 1598–1625* (New York, 1964); J. I. Israel, 'A conflict of empires: Spain and the Netherlands 1618–48', *Past and Present*, LXXVI (1977), 34–74; *idem*, 'Spain and the Dutch Sephardim 1609–60', *Studia Rosenthaliana*, XII (1978), 1–61; G. Parker, *The Army of Flanders and the Spanish Road 1567–1659* (Cambridge, 1972); *idem*, *The Dutch Revolt* (London, 1977); and *idem*, *Spain and the Netherlands 1559–1659* (London, 1979). Finally, on the peace of Münster and the final stages of the war in the Low Countries, there is A. Waddington, *La République des Provinces Unies, la France et les Pays-Bas espagnols de 1630 à 1650* (2 vols., Paris, 1895–7), and J. J. Poelhekke, *De vrede van Munster* (The Hague, 1948).

For the Netherlands overseas, the reader will naturally turn to C. R. Boxer, *The Dutch Seaborne Empire* (London, 1965), and *idem*, *The Dutch in Brazil 1624–1654* (Oxford, 1957).

OTTOMAN EMPIRE

Two useful new books have appeared which present a general history of this vast empire: M. A. Cook, ed., *A History of the Ottoman Empire to 1730* (Cambridge, 1976), and S. J. Shaw, *History of the Ottoman Empire and Modern Turkey*, I (Cambridge, 1976). Unfortunately, the riches of the central government's archive for the Ottoman period are still in the process of being discovered and studied, and therefore many important matters are still not understood; it will be a long time before they are. (For the Balkan principalities, see HUNGARY above.)

POLAND

There are several excellent general works on which the reader can rely: A. Gieysztor, ed., *History of Poland* (Warsaw, 1968), 169–271; A. Attman, *The Russian and Polish Markets in International Trade 1500–1650* (Gothenburg, 1973); W. Kula, *An Economic Theory of Feudalism: towards a Model of the Polish Economy 1500–1800* (London, 1976); and J. Tazbir, *A State without Stakes: Polish Religious Toleration in the Sixteenth and Seventeenth Centuries* (New York, 1973). There are books and articles of excellent quality in Polish, many of them with a summary in French or English. Those by M. Bogucka, A. Maczak, H. Samsonowicz, J. Topolski and J. Tazbir are particularly recommended. Several of the articles have been printed in English or French translations in *Acta poloniae historica*, which appears annually.

PORTUGAL

There is no satisfactory history either of Portugal in the seventeenth century, or of the revolt of 1640; but much may be gleaned from F. Mauro, *Portugal et l'Atlantique . . . 1570–1670* (Paris, 1960), and C. R. Boxer, *Salvador de Sá and the Struggle for Brazil and Angola 1602–86* (London, 1952).

SPAIN

Four general studies of Habsburg Spain are available in English, and each has something different to say: M. Defourneaux, *Daily Life in Spain in the Golden Age* (London,

1970); A. Domínguez Ortiz, *The Golden Age of Spain 1516–1659* (London, 1971); J. H. Elliott, *Imperial Spain 1469–1716* (London, 1963); and J. Lynch, *Spain under the Habsburgs*, II (London, 1969). Each of these works has a bibliography, and so it is only necessary to cite more recent publications. Most of these concern rural history: J. Casey, *The Kingdom of Valencia in the Seventeenth Century* (Cambridge, 1979); E. Fernández Pinedo, *Crecimiento económico y transformaciones sociales del País Vasco 1100–1850* (Madrid, 1974); and M. R. Weisser, *Peasants of the Montes* (Chicago, 1977). Other studies are expected from J. P. Le Flem and G. Anes (on Segovia) and by P. Ponsot (on Andalusia). On the internal government of Castile, see J. H. Elliott, 'The statecraft of Olivares' in J. H. Elliott and H. G. Koenigsberger, eds., *The Diversity of History* (London, 1970), 119–47; J. H. Elliott and J. F. de la Peña, *Memoriales y cartas del Conde Duque de Olivares*, I (Madrid, 1978); C. J. Jago, 'The influence of debt on the relations between crown and aristocracy in seventeenth-century Castile', *Economic History Review*, XXVI (1973), 218–36; and P. L. Williams, 'Philip III and the restoration of Spanish government 1598–1603', *English Historical Review*, LXXXVIII (1973), 751–69.

SWEDEN

Our understanding of Swedish history during the period is dominated by the work of Michael Roberts, whose books provide a clear, entertaining and authoritative account of all important matters. See his four works: *The Early Vasas . . . 1523–1611* (Cambridge, 1968); *Gustavus Adolphus . . . 1611–32* (2 vols., London, 1953–8); *Essays in Swedish History* (London, 1967); and *Sweden as a Great Power 1611–97* (London, 1968). There is also, of course, a wealth of material by Swedish writers, of which a selection is presented in English translation in M. Roberts, *Sweden's Age of Greatness* (London, 1973). Most recent articles in the *Historisk*

Tidsskrift (Svensk) have English summaries – see, by way of example, the important article of R. Nordlund, 'Kontribution eller Satisfaktion. Pommern och de Svenska krigsfinanser na 1633', *Historisk Tidsskrift Svensk* (1974), 321–402 ('Contributions or satisfaction: Pomerania and Sweden's war finances in 1633').

THE SWISS CANTONS

The best account of the Valtelline question is Chapter 2 of *The Cambridge Modern History*, IV (Cambridge, 1906). Readers desiring more information may find it in P. Marrades, *El camino del imperio: notas para el estudio de la cuestión de la Valtelina* (Madrid, 1943); A. Rotondò, 'Esuli italiani in Valtellina nel '500', *Rivista storica italiana*, LXXXVIII (1976), 756–91; and R. Pithon, 'Les débuts difficiles du ministère de Richelieu et la crise le la Valteline, 1621–7', *Revue d'histoire diplomatique*, LXXIV (1960), 298–322. Some developments elsewhere in Switzerland are noted in the early chapters of H. Wahlen and E. Jaggi, *Der schweizerische Bauernkrieg, 1653* (Bern, 1952).

Chapter VIII

There have been three important, albeit somewhat impressionistic, recent studies of popular culture during this period: Y. Bercé, *Fête et révolte. Des mentalités populaires du XVIe au XVIIIe siècles* (Paris, 1976); P. Burke, *Popular Culture in Early Modern Europe* (London, 1978); and R. Muchembled, *Culture populaire et culture des élites dans la France moderne* (Paris, 1977). There are also many new works on individual aspects of popular culture. On witchcraft, see the collection of recent essays in S. Anglo, ed., *The Damned Art* (London, 1977), and a spirited attack on many other scholars in the field by A. Soman, 'The *Parlement de Paris* and the great witch hunt, 1565–1640', *The Sixteenth-century Journal*, IX, 2 (1978), 31–44; but these works, like all the rest, ignore the different experience of eastern Europe. See *B. Baranowski, *Procesy czarownic w Polsce w XVII i XVIII wieku* (Lódz, 1952: 'Sorcery trials in Poland in the 17th and 18th centuries'). On newspapers, see F. Dahl, *Dutch Corantos 1618–1650* (The Hague, 1946). On chapbooks see G. Bollême, *La Bibliothèque bleue* (Paris, 1971) and *idem*, *La Bible bleue: anthologie d'une littérature 'populaire'* (Paris, 1976). On broadsheets and 'comic strips' see: W. A. Coupe, *The German Illustrated Broadsheets in the Seventeenth Century* (2 vols., Baden-Baden, 1966–7), and D. Kunzle, *The Early Comic Strip* (Berkeley, 1973). On games, see L. C. Stone, *English Sports and Recreations* (Washington, 1960), and K. V. Thomas, 'Work and leisure in pre-industrial society', *Past and Present*, XXIX (1964), 50–66.

There has been a spate of works on literacy and education recently, and some of it contradicts the rest. There is, however, much to be learnt on all forms of education from R. L. Kagan, *Students and Society in Early Modern Spain* (Baltimore, 1974). For literacy, see pages 334–6 above; for schools see also F. de Dainville, 'Effectifs des collèges et scolarité', *Population*, X (1955), 455–88; *idem*, 'Collèges et fréquentation scolaire au XVIIe siècle', *Population*, XII (1957), 467–94; and R. Chartier, D. Julia and M. M. Compère, *Education en France du XVIe au XVIIe siècle* (Paris, 1976). On German universities, see J. H. Overfield, 'Nobles and paupers at German universities', *Societas*, IV (1974), 175–210.

There are, of course, innumerable monographs on all aspects of the intellectual life of Europe – even the dreams of some intellectuals have been analysed: P. Burke, 'L'histoire sociale des rêves', *Annales E.S.C.*, XXVIII (1973), 329–42. I have selected just one recent work in each field discussed in the text, and from its bibliography the interested reader can explore further: C. Webster, *The Great Instauration: Science, Medicine and Reform 1626–60* (London, 1975); J. L. Price,

Culture and Society in the Dutch Republic during the Seventeenth Century (London, 1974); F. Yates, *The Rosicrucian Enlightenment* (London, 1972); R. M. Isherwood, *Music in Service of the King* (Ithaca, 1973); and the synthesis on patronage, A. G. Dickens, ed., *The Courts of Europe* (page 354 above).

Finally, on the divergence between east and west, see B. Porshnev, 'Les rapports de l'Europe occidentale et de l'Europe orientale à l'époque de la guerre de trente ans', *Rapports du XIe congrès des sciences historiques*, IV (Stockholm, 1960), 136–63, and L. R. Lewitter, 'Poland, the Ukraine and Russia in the seventeenth century', *Slavonic and East European Review*, XXVII (1948–9), 157–71 and 414–29. On the fascinating case history of Cyril Lukaris, see H. R. Trevor-Roper, 'The church of England and the Greek church in the time of Charles I' in D. Baker, ed., *Studies in Church History XV: Religious Motivation* (Oxford, 1978), 213–40.

Index